Oxfordshire Archaeological Unit Report 2
(CBA Research Report 32)

Iron Age and Roman riverside settlements at Farmoor, Oxfordshire

By George Lambrick and Mark Robinson

with sections by Janet Sanders, Warwick Rodwell, Trevor Saxby, Andrew Sherratt, Sian Rees, G T Brown, Susan Denford, Martin Jones, Bob Wilson, Don Bramwell, and John Martin.

1979 Published by the Oxfordshire Archaeological U
and the Council for British Archaeology

© Oxfordshire Archaeological Unit 1979

ISBN 0 900312 57 2
ISSN 0141 - 7819
Designed by Allan Cooper FSIA and Henry Cleere

Cover design by George Lambrick and Mark Robinson

Published by
The Oxfordshire Archaeological Unit
46 Hythe Bridge Street
Oxford
and
The Council for British Archaeology
112 Kennington Road
London SE11 6RE

Lambrick, George
Iron Age and Roman riverside settlements
at Farmoor, Oxfordshire. - (Council for
British Archaeology. Reseach reports; no.32 ISSN
0589-9036). - (Oxfordshire Archaeological Unit
Reports; no.2 ISSN 0141-7819).
1. Farmoor site, Eng.
I. Title II. Robinson, Mark
936.2'5'76   GN780.22.G7

ISBN 0-900312-57-2

Printed by Silverdale Press, Silverdale Road, Hayes,
Middlesex.

Contents

PART I : INTRODUCTION

Summary

Extensive excavations coupled with intensive biological analysis of all types have provided important new evidence for the changing settlement patterns and land use of Iron Age and Roman settlements on the first gravel terrace and floodplain of the Thames Valley.

The original settlement of the early Iron Age was represented only by a group of storage or rubbish pits on the relatively dry ground of the gravel terrace. Daub suggested the existence of a building and slag and other evidence indicated small-scale ironworking, but there was little indication of the overall character of the settlement. A subsequent gap in the occupation of the site was evident from marked changes both in the fabric and style of the pottery and in the settlement pattern itself, indicating different land use and farming practice.

In the middle Iron Age three farmsteads comprising small ditched enclosures for circular houses and subsidiary yards or stock pens were constructed on the open floodplain, while other small enclosures, probably for stock, were made on the edge of the gravel terrace. One of these incorporated a fenced yard with an unusual semicircular post-built structure, perhaps a workshop. One of the floodplain enclosures had been stripped of turf (possibly used to build a round house) and was later crossed by raised gravel paths. The floodplain farmsteads were situated in wet open grassland, subject to flooding from the river and used principally for pasture. The economy was entirely pastoral, and because of the flooding the settlement must have been seasonal, maximizing the value of the rich grassland in the spring and summer. The absence of some common perennial plants liking disturbed ground shows that each farmstead was used for no more than about five years. After the middle Iron Age the rate of alluvial deposition on the floodplain greatly increased.

The settlement pattern underwent a further change in the 2nd century AD. During the Roman period the floodplain remained unenclosed, but was abandoned as an area of habitation while the gravel terrace was enclosed for the first time with small fields or paddocks and a droveway crossing the terrace and turning along its edge. This laid-out field system and the probable existence of thorn hedges, indicated by botanical remains, suggests a much more permanent settlement than that of the Iron Age. Roman occupation of the site probably dates from the late 3rd centruy and by the late 4th century gardens with box hedges were established. The economy was still largely pastoral, and it is likely that some paddocks were used for intensive stock management, while the floodplain was almost certainly used for hay as well as for grazing. Corn was probably brought in, and evidence for the de-husking and milling of spelt wheat was recovered from a corndrier and various pits.

In the medieval period the area formerly enclosed by the Roman field system was converted to open arable land. The floodplain remained grassland as the meadow for the nearby village of Cumnor. The site was no longer occupied, but was probably farmed from a hamlet or farm near the edge of the new reservoir.

Acknowledgements

Firstly, our thanks go to the Thames Water Authority (Thames Conservancy Division) who allowed the excavation to take place, and provided funds for extra machine work.

Throughout the excavation on the site itself the cooperation of the engineers, Binnie and Partners, and the contractors, Shephard, Hill Ltd, was invaluable and their ever-increasing assistance and watchfulness greatly contributed to the amount of information which was retrieved; particular thanks go to Messrs C Strouts and M Hyatt of Binnie's and to Mr D Ogden of Shephard, Hill. Shephard, Hill also kindly financed an exhibition of the results of the excavation.

During the main season of excavation in 1974 the Farmoor Village Hall Committee kindly allowed us to stay in the Hall, and after the completion of the work provided much help in mounting the exhibition for the village.

For assistance during the excavation itself we are especially grateful to Mike Hall, the archaeological officer of the Thames Water Authority, who not only did most of the initial salvage observation, but also undertook all the original negotiations, made all the necessary arrangements with the Engineers and Contractors, and continued this task throughout the main excavation, thereby relieving us of much of the administrative work. Almost all the work on site was done by the Oxford University Archaeological Society, as whose Summer Excavation the project began, and our thanks go to all those concerned: Roger Ainslie, Ernest Black, Mark Blackburn, Jenny Cockett (now Robinson), Richard Davies, Mark Horton, Norbert Krapf, Martin Linskill, Tamar MacIver, Pipkin Mays, Gordon Murray, Anne Redston, Trevor Saxby, Thérèse Saint Paul, Chris Tyler-Smith, and Piers Wildman. Lesley Garrud acted as finds assistant and we are particularly grateful to Jerome Bertram and Nicholas Palmer who supervised Areas I and II and also helped with much of the later salvage work. We would also like to thank Jonathan Christie, Phillip Page, Callum Rollo, and Richard Thomas who as Unit volunteers or trainees worked on the final excavation in January 1976.

In the preparation of the report on the archaeological side we are most grateful to Miss R Askew, Miss W Lee, Miss P Roberts, and Mrs R Spey for their small-find drawings, to Miss S Rees for her drawing of Roman scythes, and to Mrs J Sanders for drawing the Roman pottery. We would like to thank Mr G T Brown and Miss S Rees for their reports on the scythe, Dr W Rodwell and Mrs J Sanders for their reports on the samian and coarse Roman pottery, Mr A Sherratt for his report on the flints, and Mr T Saxby for his coin report. Mr H Cleere kindly provided comments on the slag. Thanks are also due to Mr R L Otlet for providing the Carbon 14 dates. We are grateful to Mr W A Baker for permission to reproduce Pl I, to Mr G T Brown for Pls VIII and IX, and to Mr R Wilkins, Institute of Archaeology, Oxford University, for preparing the other plates, some of them from difficult original site photographs. We had many useful discussions with colleagues and in particular we would like to thank David Miles, Michael Parrington, and Dee De Roche. Tom Hassall and Nicholas Palmer read the text and made many useful comments towards its improvement. We are grateful to the Thames Water Authority (Thames Conservancy Division) for allowing us to use their maps to show the extent of flooding in Fig 1; and to Binnie and Partners for the geological contours shown in Fig 2.

Most of the biological work on the invertebrates and plants was undertaken in the Hope Department of Entomology, Oxford, and we are extremely grateful to Professor G C Varley for the provision of working facilities and the use of the collections there, without which this part of the project could not have been carried out. We would like to thank Professor G W Dimbleby for the use of the seed collection at the Institute of Archaeology, London, and his pollen analysis, Dr R B Angus for his help with identification of the glacial *Helophorus*, Miss J Sheldon for her help with wood identification, Mr R N L B Hubbard for work on cereal pollen, Mr P Powell for identifying the glacial faunal remains, and Mr C O'Toole who identified the ants. We are pleased to include the reports of Mr D Bramwell on the bird bones, Mrs S Denford on the mites, Mr J Martin on the geology, Mr M Jones on carbonized seeds, and Mr R Wilson on mammal bones for which Mrs R Spey prepared the illustrations. Mr J Greig, Mr H Kenward, and Dr M R Speight provided useful information on their unpublished work and we are grateful to Mr D Williams for the use of the seed collection at the Environmental Archaeology Laboratory, York. We are very grateful to Mr C S Elton for discussing the results and for allowing us use of the Wytham Survey, and to Lt-Col D Williams for discussions of flooding and for providing Thames Conservancy flood records. We would like to thank Miss C Cottingham for her assistance in the final stages of the biological work. Mr P Armitage kindly read and commented on the bone report and thanks are due to G J Baker, J B Tutt, and J Cay for their helpful correspondence on the ages of the horses in F 37. We are most grateful to Dr K D Thomas for reading all the biological sections and providing many helpful comments.

We are particularly grateful to Mrs Annie Lipson who typed the whole report and to Professor Barry Cunliffe for reading and commenting on the complete text.

The work was financed by the Department of the Environment and we are grateful to Mr B K Davison and Mr A Fleming of the Inspectorate of Ancient Monuments for their interest. The publication of the report has also been made possible by a large grant from the Department of the Environment. Finally we would like to acknowledge the support of the Oxfordshire Archaeological Committee, and in particular we owe much to Tom Hassall who has given us constant encouragement and support in our work.

GHL,MAR
January 1978

Presentation of results

Numbering systems used

The site was divided into three 'areas', I and II being the original areas of controlled excavation, III being the rest, mostly excavated under salvage conditions. The feature/layer numbers ran in three sequences beginning at 1 in Area I, 501 in Area II, and 1001 in Area III. Layers within a feature were given suffix numbers: thus L528/3 was the third layer in F528 in Area II. All drawn sections were given letters in the order in which they appear in the notebooks; the sequence for each Area began A-Z and continued with A^1-Z^1, A^{11}-Z^{11} etc. It will be made clear from the context to which Area a particular letter applies. On the plans the published sections are marked with the letters at their left-hand end as viewed. In the finds section and biological part of the report contexts are given as the Area number, the context number, and, where appropriate, the small find (SF) number.

Divisions in the report

The report has been divided into four parts:
Part I   Introduction
Part II   The Archaeological Evidence
Part III   The Biological Evidence
Part IV   Conclusions and Discussion
The middle two sections are each separated into basic data and interpretation. In the Archaeological Evidence the description of the features is arranged by Area since that was how they were excavated, though a chronological element is included in that Area II (mostly Iron Age) comes before Area I (mostly Roman) and the Iron Age of Area III is dealt with before the Roman. Interpretations have, as far as possible, been avoided in this section. The Archaeological Interpretation itself deals only with individual features or complexes, not the whole landscape or economy, which are left for the Conclusions, but the Area divisions have largely been dropped so that the site as a whole is covered in roughly chronological order. The finds reports and a summary of the radiocarbon dating have also been included in Part II, as has any discussion exclusively concerned with specialized aspects of these topics.

In the Biological Evidence the same formula has been followed, though in two subsections, Plants and Invertebrates, and Vertebrates. In each the basic data is presented, with separate sections of interpretation. Again discussion of aspects exclusively concerned with the biology has been included at this stage.

The Conclusions which begin Part IV of the report bring together all the evidence from Parts II and III to present a complete overall picture of the settlements, their economies, and their environments. In the following Discussion the implications of the work at Farmoor are considered, both in detail and in terms of the general conclusions.

There are two objectives in making these divisions: firstly, to present the basic data objectively so that our interpretations and conclusions may be tested; and secondly (on the assumption that many people will not want to read the report from cover to cover) to make it easy to extract different types and levels of information. The Discussion has also been kept separate to ensure that the account of the results is as straightforward as possible, free from our particular opinions of their importance.

These divisions have inevitably led to some repetition and, even worse, to the recurrence of particular topics in different parts of the report. We have tried to overcome these deficiencies by cross-referencing and by providing a detailed table of contents, and an index to features and layers (Appendix VIII), which should make it fairly easy to follow up particular points of interest. We hope that any remaining difficulty in this respect will be outweighed by the report being generally easier to use.

Unpublished material

All the finds, the site notebooks, supplementary data on finds, etc, the original site drawings, and a set of photographs are to be deposited with Oxfordshire County Council Department of Museum Services, Woodstock, Oxfordshire. The plant and invertebrate biological remains are for the moment held by the Oxfordshire Archaeological Unit. Microfiche copies of all the original written or drawn data have been deposited with the National Monuments Record, Fortress House, 23 Savile Row, London W1.

General Description

Local geology and topography

by Mark Robinson

The site at Farmoor lies partly on the present floodplain and partly on the first gravel terrace of the Thames about 10 km (6 miles) upstream from Oxford (Fig 1). It is situated on the east bank of the river where it flows northwards before making a great loop around Wytham Hill to Oxford. The floodplain at Farmoor is an area of 1½ sq km (0.6 sq miles) enclosed by the present course of the river and a large late Devensian buried river channel. Before the construction of the two-stage reservoir (1962-5 and 1974-6) the floodplain was inundated whenever the river was in flood (see p 6 and Figs 1 and 2).

The gravel terrace here is confined to an area at the south-west corner of this expanse of floodplain and forms a strip of land running 1½ km southwards by the river. The ground here has normally been above the level of flooding and it forms a fairly small, rather better drained plateau. Round the southeast edge of the gravel and the rest of the floodplain is Oxford Clay.

Elsewhere in the region under consideration (Fig 1) the present floodplain of the Thames and its tributaries can be over 2½ km (1½ miles) wide. It is covered with a calcareous alluvium, which overlaps or cuts off the limestone gravel terraces which tend to be present on either side (Sandford 1924, 148). The alluvium is still liable to flooding. The youngest and lowest of the gravel terraces is the first terrace which rises to about 3 m above the present river level (Sandford 1924, 157) but there are islands of first terrace gravels in the alluvium which are much lower (Gilbert 1954, 166). Above the first terrace are three more principal gravel terraces. The gravels can be very extensive, especially in the Stanton Harcourt area.

Rising above these riverine deposits on both sides of the Thames is the Oxford Clay. To the east of the site at Farmoor this runs in a broad valley across to Oxford, but to the north-east, south-east, and south it forms the steep lower slopes of Wytham and Cumnor Hills, part of the Oxford Heights.

These hills form the north-east end and scarp of a long east-west Jurassic ridge, consisting of mixed sand and narrow clay strata capped by the limestone of a coral reef. The interface of these beds with the Oxford Clay forms an almost continuous springline from which very many small streams begin.

The top of the Corallian ridge is a plateau which slopes away almost imperceptibly to the south. Rising above it are Cumnor Hurst and Boars Hill, formed of Kimmeridge Clay and Lower Greensand with glacial drift on top. Wytham Hill is somewhat lower than these, which, combined with the slope of the strata, means that it consists only of the Corallian beds with a small patch of glacial drift (Fig 1).

The locality thus provides a wide range of soils. On the floodplain are the poorly drained alluvial clay loams and clays of the Thames series which are neutral to alkaline (Jarvis 1973, 181-2). A variety of soils is to be found on the first gravel terrace: the Sutton series, well drained neutral sandy loam; the Badsey series, a calcareous and sometimes more clayey equivalent; and the Carswell series, neutral to calcareous imperfectly drained clay or clay loam. The soil on the gravel terrace of the Farmoor site probably corresponds to the Badsey series. On the higher terraces is only the Sutton series, a non-calcareous soil over calcareous gravel (Jarvis 1973, 117, 179-81).

The clays and clay loams of the Oxford Clay range from calcareous to acidic. They are all rather poorly drained (Jarvis 1973, 172-3, 175). The lower Corallian and lower Greensand both have soils derived from sand with thin clay bands. The Corallian sands and grits were originally calcareous but in some places have been leached to a considerable depth (Jarvis 1973, 24). A similar range of soils has developed on them, loamy sands and sandy loams which are well drained and acidic to neutral (Jarvis 1973, 175-7). The most naturally fertile soils in the region are the calcareous well drained loams on the Upper Corallian, the Sherbourne and Marcham series (Jarvis 1973, 177-8).

The soils on Wytham Hill tend to be more basic than those on the hills to the south, and unlike elsewhere, those on the glacial drift are not acidic. The only acidic soils are those on some gentle slopes of colluvial calcareous grit and a few nearby level areas of grit (Osmaston 1959, 16-22).

Church, writing before extensive mechanization of Oxfordshire's agriculture (1922, 23), states that the alluvium and the clays were mostly devoted to grass. The soils of the valley gravels, Corallian series and lower Greensand were predominantly arable. Some woodland is present on the higher ground at Wytham, Bagley, Boars Hill, and Tubney.

It would be dangerous to speculate what the landscape was like during the Iron Age and Roman period on the basis of soil types, especially as, for example, the difficult soils of the Oxford Clay which were extensively cultivated during the Middle Ages are now largely modern pasture and coppices. However, it would be reasonable to assume that before arable agriculture spread on to the clays it would be widespread on the lighter soils and that the alluvium particularly is most unlikely to have been ploughed. Clearance must have begun quite early in this area on the gravels because there are extensive Neolithic and Bronze Age sites around Stanton Harcourt (Benson and Miles 1974, 46-50).

Modern flooding at Farmoor
by Mark Robinson

The Upper Thames is well known for its extensive winter floods and at one time there was much marshy land on the Thames floodplain (Emery 1974, 81) with, for example, a layer of peat on it near Eynsham (Clarke 1954, 55). Major river improvements and the construction of flood embankments since the disastrous floods of the nineteenth century (Emery 1974, 155-6) have reduced the area liable to flooding and the frequency of all but the most serious floods. Similarly, recent drainage operations have enabled some of the floodplain to be used for arable agriculture.

3

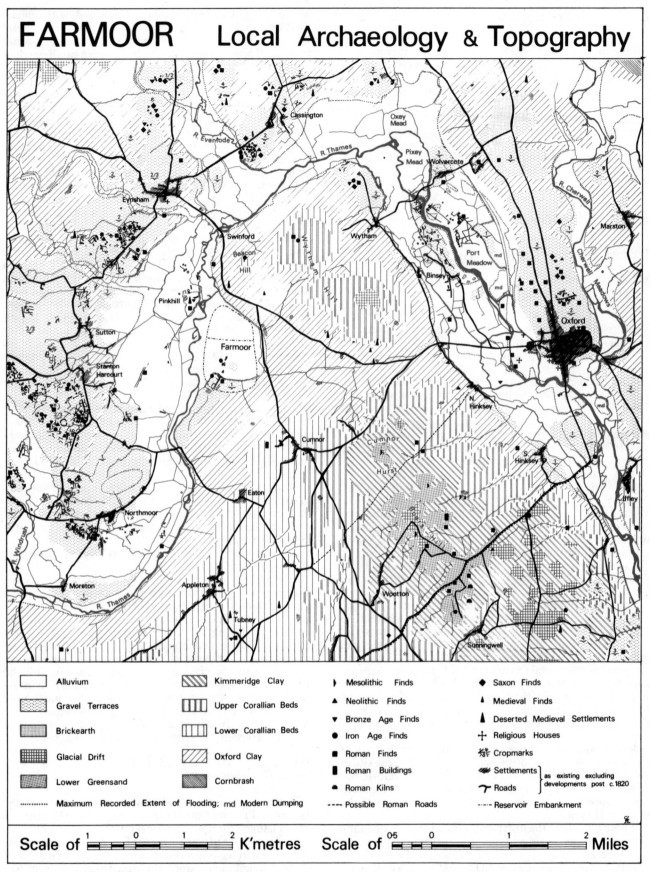

FARMOOR Local Archaeology & Topography

Legend:

- ☐ Alluvium
- ▨ Kimmeridge Clay
- ▸ Mesolithic Finds
- ◆ Saxon Finds
- ▦ Gravel Terraces
- ▥ Upper Corallian Beds
- ▲ Neolithic Finds
- ◣ Medieval Finds
- ▦ Brickearth
- ▥ Lower Corallian Beds
- ▼ Bronze Age Finds
- ▲ Deserted Medieval Settlements
- ▦ Glacial Drift
- ▨ Oxford Clay
- ● Iron Age Finds
- ✚ Religious Houses
- ▦ Lower Greensand
- ▨ Cornbrash
- ■ Roman Finds
- ⁂ Cropmarks
- ▮ Roman Buildings
- ⚒ Settlements } as existing excluding developments post c.1820
- ⚲ Roman Kilns
- ⊤ Roads
- ·········· Maximum Recorded Extent of Flooding; md Modern Dumping
- ----- Possible Roman Roads
- ----- Reservoir Embankment

Scale of ▦▦▦ K'metres

Scale of ▦▦▦ Miles

Fig 1

4

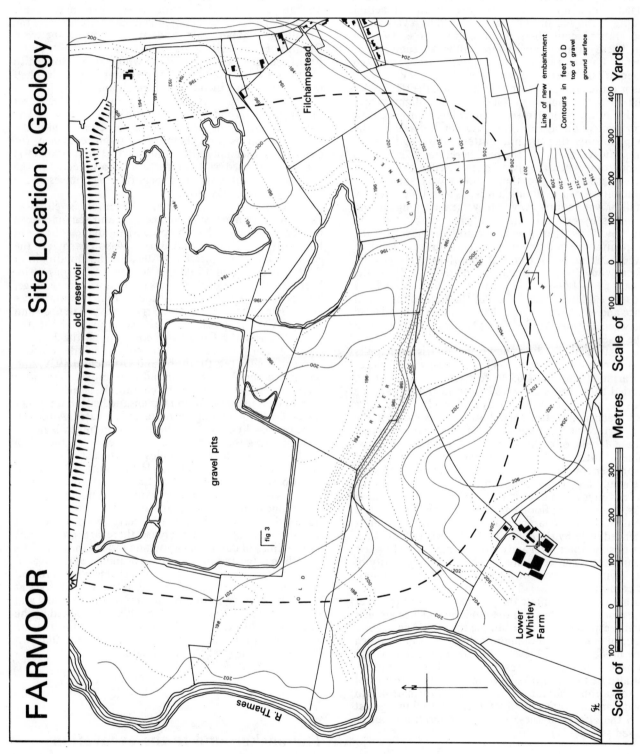

FARMOOR

Site Location & Geology

old reservoir

gravel pits

fig 3

Filchampstead

R. Thames

Lower
Whitley
Farm

N

Line of new embankment

Contours in feet O D
top of gravel
ground surface

Scale of 100 0 100 200 300 400 Yards

Metres Scale of

Fig 2

5

The Thames Conservancy Division of the Thames Water Authority has kept records of flood levels since 1894 at weirs, and levels along the river have been interpolated from these at 1000 feet intervals. This information, combined with the detailed contour survey of the site (Fig 2), means that it is possible to estimate the number of years in which various parts of it would have flooded. (It is not possible to give details of actual flooding of the site since it was protected by a very small flood embankment about 0.5m high to the east of the river. These estimates are as if this embankment were not present). The relevant levels are those which were taken at a point 6000 feet upstream of Pinkhill Lock.

As is quite common along the Thames, the floodplain at the site rises about 0.6 m (2 feet) to form a slight levée at the edge of the river. However, these levées provide little or no protection against flooding for the rest of the floodplain since they are intermittent, allowing the river to find ways through them. Therefore it has been assumed that when the river level exceeded the ground level of parts of the site, they would have flooded.

Inundation of the floodplain is also partly caused by the minor watercourses which traverse it backing up, and sometimes by excessive rainfall being unable to drain away. The three Iron Age enclosure complexes on the floodplain were all under a modern ground level of between 200 and 201 feet OD (Newlyn). This ground surface would have suffered flood in 79 to 81 of the 81 years from 1894 to 1975. In 27 to 60 of these years floods would have extended on to the edge of the gravel terrace and over Area I which had a modern ground level of between 202 and 203 feet OD. (This was also the height of the levée).

The extent of flooding shown in Fig 1 is principally that of the flood of March 1947, when the water level at the Farmoor site was 203.46 feet OD. This has been exceeded three times since 1894 and in these years the floods would have extended over Area II. They have never reached 204 feet OD, however, so most of the gravel terrace at Farmoor would have remained dry.

These details, of course, are for the modern canalized Thames. Water levels are maintained artificially high in the summer for navigation and in an uncontrolled state there would only be water flowing in a small portion of its bed. In winter normal flooding is controlled by the flood banks, but once the flood embankments are topped, in a serious flood, the character which the river takes on is influenced little by the controls. The effects of locks and weirs raising water level and dredging improving flow are insignificant when compared with the total quantity of water trying to travel downstream (Lt-Col D Williams, pers comm).

Attempting to estimate the past behaviour of the river at Farmoor on the basis of the modern evidence alone is difficult, especially as for example the Iron Age ground surface of one of the floodplain enclosures was very much below modern ground level. The level of the river could also have been lower, however, and such considerations must also be taken into account in the light of results of the excavation. The value of the modern information is to provide an accurate record of recent flooding against which the effects of these other considerations can be assessed (see p 111).

The archaeology of the area

by George Lambrick

Although several sites are known in the loop of the Thames where Farmoor is situated (Fig 1), there is

virtually no detailed information. Mesolithic material has been found on Cumnor Hurst and Boars Hill; cropmarks have been recorded north of Wytham village, and Iron Age and Roman finds have been made on Wytham Hill and the neighbouring Beacon Hill; Roman material has also been found near Swinford (just north of the Farmoor floodplain) and on the Corallian plateau just west of Cumnor, where there may be the remains of a building. A possible Roman road crosses the Corallian plateau east and west running between Cumnor Hurst and Boars Hill (Lambrick 1969, 88-9). From the late Saxon period the whole area belonged to Abingdon Abbey, and for a time Cumnor was the chief manor of an area including the neighbouring parishes of Wytham and Seacourt and making up the northern part of Hormer Hundred (Gelling 1976, 720-22). The medieval settlement pattern seems to be reflected in the surviving farms and hamlets, though evidence for deserted settlements (Beresford and Hurst 1962, 97) suggests late medieval contraction, also reflected in the enclosure of arable and the appearance of coppices on the formerly arable clay slopes.

In a slightly wider context Farmoor is close to extensive cropmark sites on the first and second gravel terraces around Northmoor, Standlake, Stanton Harcourt, Cassington, and Binsey. Also nearby are the earthwork and pasture-mark sites on the floodplain at Port Meadow and Pinkhill (Benson and Miles 1974, Maps 21-8). Most of these sites cover a wide date range, but certainly include Iron Age and Roman material. Sites are known to cover most of the river gravels (Benson and Miles 1974, *passim*), but less is known about the claylands and the Corallian beds, though the Frilford area *c* 9 km (5½ miles) to the south includes various important sites (eg Bradford and Goodchild 1939) and recently others have been found on the Corallian ridge further west (D Miles, pers comm). It is also on the Corallian, Kimmeridge, and Greensand beds that most of the Oxford Roman pottery industry is located. Although most of the kiln sites are on the corresponding hills east of Oxford along the Dorchester-Alchester road, there is a smaller site only 6 km (3½ miles) south-east of Farmoor on the southern slopes of Boars Hill (Young 1977, 10-12), again beside a probable road (Lambrick 1969, 86-7).

The river could have provided a major line of communication, but it seems likely that the Corallian ridge to the west would also have been important (Lambrick 1969, 79). Otherwise there are no obvious natural lines of communication and indeed the end of the Corallian ridge and the numerous branches of the river to the east tend positively to interrupt them. Westward and northward river crossings existed in the Middle Ages at Bablock Hythe (*c* 2 km downstream from Farmoor) and Swinford (*c* 2 km upstream), the latter overlooked by the steep slopes of Beacon Hill; eastwards the main crossing was at North Hinksey. The origins of the latter two crossings are at least Saxon in date.

The background to the excavation

The excavation began as a limited project intended only to investigate two areas of cropmarks visible on the air photograph (Pl I; Fig 3): firstly, a large pit which, because of the low-lying nature of the site, could be expected to produce good biological remains (F17 in Area I);

6

secondly, what appeared to be a small Iron Age enclosure (F503 etc in Area II). As time went on, and as other features were discovered, more and more was done (largely by salvage digging), and in particular the biological work was very considerably extended as it became apparent that very many features would produce valuable evidence of the past environment and economy. None of the most interesting results could have been predicted beforehand because the known surface evidence was limited to the one photograph of rather poor cropmarks; as a result, except in a few chance cases, it was impossible to pre-empt the often damaging work of the contractors which initially exposed features. The project thus developed largely as a response, rather than a preconceived plan, to make the most of an unusual opportunity to investigate an ancient landscape not well revealed by cropmarks, but capable of much elucidation from the more useful biological evidence.

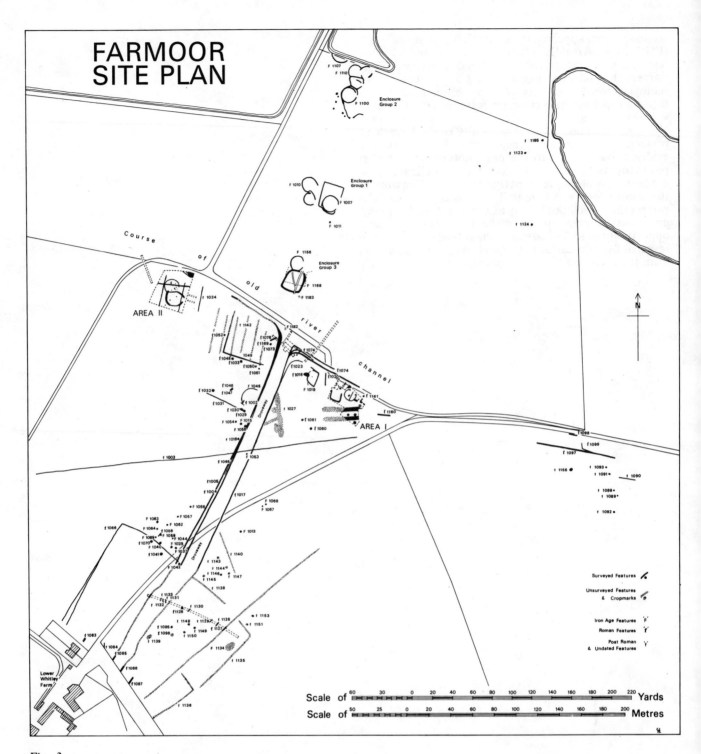

FARMOOR
SITE PLAN

Enclosure Group 2

Enclosure Group 1

Enclosure Group 3

AREA II

AREA I

Course of old river channel

Lower Whitley Farm

Surveyed Features

Unsurveyed Features & Cropmarks

Iron Age Features 'f'
Roman Features 'f'
Post Roman & Undated Features 'f'

Scale of Yards
60 30 0 20 40 60 80 100 120 140 160 180 200 220

Scale of Metres
50 25 0 20 40 60 80 100 120 140 160 180 200

Fig 3

PART II: ARCHAEOLOGICAL EVIDENCE

The excavation
by George Lambrick

Area II (Plan Fig 4, Sections Fig 5 and Pl II)

Methods

The topsoil was removed by a scraper working without a bulldozer. This exposed a layer of light yellowish-brown clayey loam (L501) covering the whole area, cut only by a 19th century field drain (F504), and varying in thickness from 0.2 m at the south to *c* 0.4 m to the north. A small trial trench, dug to see if the expected archaeological features were beneath, encountered the top of Ditch 503. The cleanness of L501 and its uniformity suggested that it represented a build-up of ploughsoil and possibly material thrown out of the nearby field ditch. It was therefore removed by a JCB digger using a bucket without teeth working down to the top of the underlying features or the top of natural gravel. The extent of the area uncovered was dictated by the discovery of features. A machine trench was also dug down to natural gravel across the ditch and bank which formed the nearby field boundary to examine their relationship to L501 (Fig 3). Towards the end of the main excavation, two trial trenches were dug by hand down to natural gravel east of the main area to establish the extent of occupation in that direction.

After thorough cleaning by hand the whole area was planned before excavation began. During excavation sections were normally left to be drawn and many were then removed. Time did not permit total excavation of some of the larger features. The whole area was planned again when excavation was complete.

The main enclosure

The most obvious feature revealed by the removal of L501 was the enclosure which had shown up on the air photograph (Pl I). The feature was more irregular than the air photograph had suggested and it seemed likely that several phases of development were involved. It was therefore divided up into what appeared to be its five component parts (ie F503, F505, F528 and F529, F530, F531) to avoid, if possible, confusion of separate phases. Cuttings were made across the main parts of the enclosure ditch and were then expanded to leave a few baulks as standing sections. The relationships between the various parts of the ditch were recorded by cutting longitudinal sections down the middle of the ditch. This was done between F505 and F528, F529 and F530, and between F530 and F531, but was not done between F503 and F505 since the division between them was not immediately apparent. Sections were also cut along F530 and the northern end of F528. The longitudinal sections followed the curving line of the feature to represent the true profiles of the ditch and its layers.

The north-west corner of the enclosure provided the largest sequence of recuttings of the ditch. The earliest ditch was filled with L528/6, a light grey, slightly clayey, silty gravel, about 0.50 m thick (Section D). Where it was not destroyed its profile was U-shaped. Its position suggested that it respected F560 by terminating or turning eastwards without impingeing on F560 or the area enclosed by F560 and F505. South of Section K it was entirely destroyed by later recuts, and it was also cut to the north by a recut filled with orange-brown gravelly loam and clay (L528/7; Section N). Much of this had in turn been destroyed by later recuts. It was deeper than L528/6 at 0.65 m and at 1.50 m was probably also wider. Its profile was U-shaped. It projected about 1.00 m into the area enclosed by F560, cutting the fill of one of its post-holes. None of the rest of the enclosure could be shown stratigraphically to be contemporary with either L528/6 or L528/7. At the south end of the west side of the enclosure, for example, a layer of solid yellowish-grey clay with very little gravel (L529/4) was confined to a narrow slot cut about 0.70 m into the gravel, butt-ending at the southern end of F529 (Section L). Similarly on the other side of the enclosure the lowest layer of F505, a slightly gravelly yellowish-grey sticky clay (L505/3) was entirely confined within F505 by the shallow butt ends in the bottom at either end (Section D). There was no apparent change in the profile of F505 between this layer and its successors (Section I).

The next series of layers still did not continue between the constituent parts of the enclosure, but their partial similarity suggested that they were connected. Mostly they consisted of wet grey silty gravel, sometimes with a considerable clay content. Starting from the north side of the enclosure, L503/3 was fairly clayey and existed only at the east end of the ditch owing to subsequent disturbance to the west. It filled the bottom of the ditch to a depth of about 0.10 m and also spread up the sides, which showed no change of profile between this layer and its successor (Section A). In F528, L528/5 was similar and filled the recut which had destroyed the southern end of L528/6 and L528/7 (Sections D, J, and K). This part of the ditch was flatter-bottomed and deeper than F503 with steeper sides so that L528/5 was confined more to the bottom of the ditch. It continued in F529 (as L529/3) becoming more clayey, so that it was almost indistinguishable from L529/4, except that it contained more gravel and instead of terminating in a butt end it simply tailed off above L529/4. It did not continue into F530, though there was no clear division between the two (Section L). In F531 a layer of silty clayey gravel reappeared (L531/2), changing from the loamy gravel at the bottom of F530, through yellow silty and clayey gravel to grey silty gravel at the east end of the feature (Section G). The relationships between these gradual changes along the ditch were not at all clear and certainly no definite recuts were identifiable. The profile of F531 was less regular than other parts of the enclosure ditch, with a slot, more than filled by L531/2, at the bottom. Its depth was comparable to that of F503 (approximately 0.60 m below the surface of the gravel). No pottery was found in these layers, but L528/5 and L531/2 each produced a loom weight.

Above these layers of clayey and silty gravel was a layer of orange-brown, slightly gravelly clayey loam which could be traced through F503, F505, and F528 and F 529. This was the only layer which was almost continuous through the enclosure but even so varied in its depth, profile, and (in the case of F530) composition. This layer was everywhere visible at the top of the ditch, and except at the north-west corner of the enclosure (L528/6 and L528/7), it defined the maximum width of the ditch. In F503 it was identified both east (L503/2) and west (L503/5) of Section B, though later recuts had destroyed the central portion. Its profile was visible in Section A, and the traces of it surviving on each side of F503

9

FARMOOR
Area II

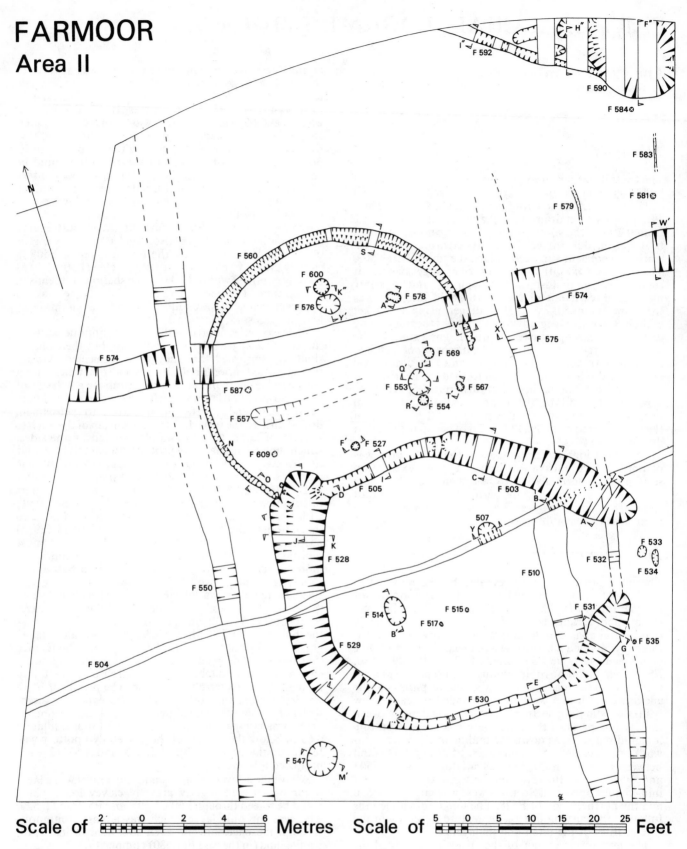

Scale of █▄█▄█ 0 2 4 6 Metres   Scale of █▄█ 0 5 10 15 20 25 Feet

Fig 4

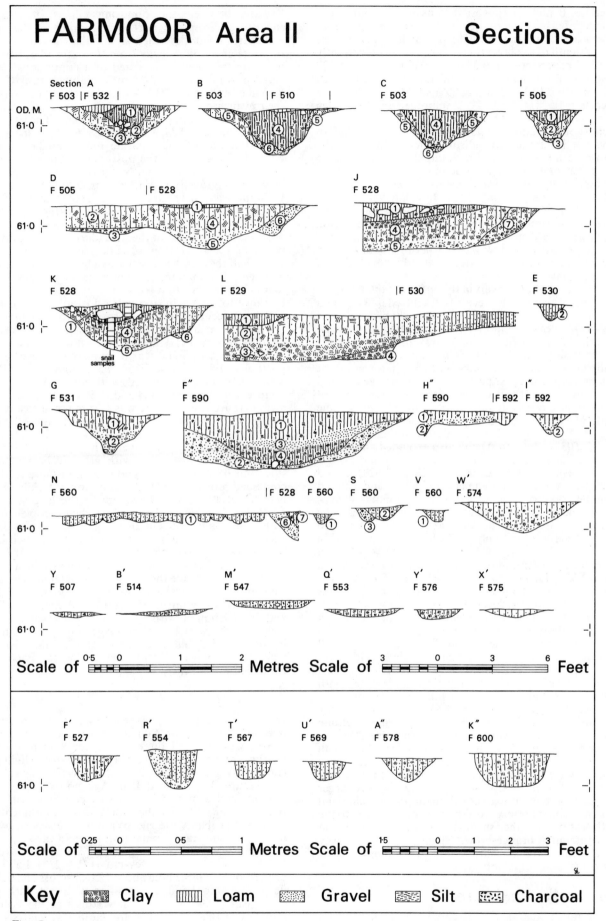

Scale of 0·5 0 1 2 Metres   Scale of 3 0 3 6 Feet

Scale of 0·25 0 0·5 1 Metres   Scale of 1·5 0 1 2 3 Feet

Key ▨ Clay ▥ Loam ▧ Gravel ▤ Silt ▦ Charcoal

Fig 5

(Sections B and C) suggest that its profile and depth remained fairly constant, being a flattish U-shape about 0.50 m to 0.60 m deep. In F505 the ditch was narrower, but the depth of the layer (here L505/2) was only slightly less (0.45 m at Section I; 0.35 m at the junction with F528 at Section D). It had also cut through the original butt ends of F505. In F528 and F529 again the profile of the layer (here L528/4 and L529/2) smoothed out the sudden changes of depth exhibited by the general shape of the ditch, though changes in its width were considerable. In F530 the layer merged indistinguishably into gravelly brown loam (L530/1). A longitudinal section cut along the length of F530 gave no definite indication of post settings, though there was some unevenness. At its east end L530/1 merged into L531/1, again without any marked change except some unevenness in profile. L531/1 was similar to the orange-brown clayey loam elsewhere. The distinction between these layers and the grey clayey gravel below was sharper in colour than in texture and was probably largely caused by oxidation of the upper layer.

The final group of layers in the enclosure ditch appear to represent two further recuttings, centred on F503 and F528 and F529. In F503 a large bath-shaped hole was dug in the western end of the ditch cutting through all previous layers down to natural gravel. Its lowest layer was grey silty gravel (L503/6) up to 0.15 m thick and confined between two shallow butt ends in the gravel at each end of the deepest part of the recut. Above this and extending beyond the deep part of the recut was a layer of almost black clayey loam. Apart from a considerable depth of this in the main part of the recut (L503/4; Sections B and C) it extended almost to the east end of F503 (L503/1; Section A) and also extended about 3.50 m along F505 (L505/1; Section I). In F528 and F529 a similar layer existed (L528/1, L528/2, L529/3, and L529/1). It was not contiguous with L505/1 and differed from the F503 recut in being shallower (about 0.30 m as against 0.60 m) and containing many large stones. The stones were large pieces of Corallian limestone (up to 0.40 or 0.50 m across) randomly and patchily scattered within the layer (Pl III). The layer stretched from about 0.80 m inside the northern end of F528 to 1.80 m from the south end of F529. Two base sherds, one from L529/1 and the other from L503/4, joined. Much pottery and parts of six loom weights were recovered from these layers.

Within the area surrounded by the complex ditch described above there were few archaeological features. Many small irregular holes were investigated, nearly all of which contained reddish-brown clay, and were presumed to be periglacial. The only two possible stakeholes (F515 and F517) were not definite, both containing the same reddish clay fill. Between the ends of the enclosure ditch (F503 and F531) were two equally dubious holes (F533 and F534). The only definite features within the enclosure were two very small shallow pits or scoops, neither more than 0.10 m deep: F507, half destroyed by the modern land drain F504, contained grey slightly gravelly clayey loam, and produced no finds (Section Y), while F514 (Section B) was slightly larger with dark blotchy orange-brown loam fill with charcoal flecks and some pottery. Just outside the enclosure to the southwest was another small shallow pit (F547; Section M) containing orange-brown slightly gravelly clayey loam with charcoal, burnt stone, two loom weight fragments, and some pottery.

The smaller enclosure

To the north was an almost circular enclosure (Pl II) formed by F560 with F505 compromising in its slight S-shape between the opposing curves of the two enclosures. From the north-west corner of the larger enclosure F560 described a circular arc to a point opposite and 4.50 m away from the east end of F505. At its south-west end it consisted of a continuous row of small postholes about 0.25 m in diameter sunk 0.10 to 0.15 m into the gravel (Pl IV; Section N). At its south end the row turned inwards, ending in two separate postholes with the same fill of gravelly brown loam. The postholes and the end of F528/6 clearly seemed to respect each other but one of the separate holes had been cut by F528/7. To the north the postholes became little more than an uneven shallow gully, the fill (L560/1) changing to yellower gravelly clay (Sections O and N). North of F574 this was partly removed by a later recut (Section S) which would have obscured any postholes. At the southeast end the brown gravelly loam and possible postholes reappeared in the irregularity of the gully just south of F574 (Section V). The recut, which covered about half the length of F560, was a broader, much flatter profiled gully containing slightly clayey gravelly brown loam (L560/2; Section S). In the middle of the eastern entrance to the enclosure was a posthole (F567) which had been recut on its southern side, the original hole being filled with slightly clayey dirty loamy gravel, the recut with brown clay and sand (Section T). Within the area enclosed by F560 was a semicircle of five further postholes (F527, F554, F569, F578, and F600). These were fairly regularly spaced, with about 3 m between them, except between F554 and F569 (2.00 m). All fell on a circular arc whose centre was 1.65 m north-east of that for the surrounding gully F560. The size and fill of the postholes varied (Sections F, R, U, A, and K): F527 contained brown loamy gravel with some clay; F554 had a hole for the post filled with gravelly brown loam, surrounded by dirty clayey gravel packing material; F569 contained brown mixed loam, clay, and gravel; F578 had been recut like F567; F600, much the largest of the postholes, contained dirty yellow clayey gravel mixed with some loam. Diligent cleaning of the interior of the enclosure revealed no more postholes, though two small very dubious stakeholes were discovered (F587 and F609). Both were filled with loose, brown-stained gravel and were well outside the arc of the main semicircle. They were probably natural features. Just inside the semicircle were two shallow pits (F553 and F576) similar to F507 and F514, though with no charcoal but some stones which in F553 were burnt. Iron Age pottery was found in F560 and F553 but not in any of the other features apparently connected with the enclosure. F560 also contained a few scraps of slag.

The sump

In the north-east corner of the area was a large somewhat irregular hole, about 4.00 m across and 1.00 m deep (F590) with a small ditch traced for 8.00 m running northwest from it. The lowest layer of F590 was light grey clayey silty gravel (L590/2), 0.45 m deep at the sides of the feature. It produced Iron Age pottery, two loom weights, and a twisted bronze wire coil finger ring (see p 55 and Fig 29). To the east L590/2 continued into what was probably the end of a ditch, suggested by the fact that it constantly remained damp in the section as though it was still collecting water. The lowest layer of Ditch 592 was brown clayey gravel (L592/2). F590 had been recut by a large hole about 1.20 m across and 0.30 m deep, dug into L590/2 and filled with wet dark grey clayey silt (L590/4) with a few stones at the bottom. Samples of this were taken for biological analysis (see p 113). Above L590/4 was a layer of fairly clean yellow gravel, 0.17 m thick and concentrated on the south side of the feature. A layer of brown clayey loam covered the whole feature and spread into F592 (L592/1). Iron Age pottery was also recovered from this layer. Beside F590 were two undatable small stakeholes (F584 and F581), both containing gravelly brown loam. Two undated shallow plough marks containing brown loam (F583 and F579) were also recorded in this area.

Roman and later features

In the Roman period an east-west ditch (F574) was dug across the area bisecting the smaller enclosure. It was cut 0.30 m into the gravel with a flattish profile, and was filled with light brown loamy clay and gravel (L574/1; Section W). About 6.00 m inside the western edge of the area its line deviated slightly.

Parallel to this ditch 1.50 m to the south F557 was an undated shallow scoop filled with brown gravelly loam. Its eastern end survived only as a stain. At right-angles to it were two shallow ditches or furrows and a gully (F550 to the west, F510 and F575 to the east, and F532 east of the latter). All these had very flat profiles and were filled with light brown clayey loam indistinguishable from L501. They were quite distinct at the southern edge of the site but disappeared north of F574. F510 and F532 cut the ends of the main enclosure ditches (F503 and F531) and also the Roman ditch (F574).

Other trenches

Of the three other trenches opened in Area II (Fig 3) the two trial trenches to the east produced no features while the trench across the field boundary's ditch and bank revealed a sequence of undated ditches. An original small ditch had been recut at least four times, each cut usually being deeper and further north than the last. The spoil from some of them had clearly been used to form a bank. The layers of upcast could not be traced far, however, and the very homogeneous light brown slightly gravelly clayey loam of the bank was practically indistinguishable from L501.

Area I (Plan Fig 6 and Sections Fig 7)

Methods

Initially the topsoil was removed from the area by a scraper but this was stopped when the stones of F2 appeared and the work was then continued by hand. This area was extended 3 m to find the north part of F5, using a JCB digger working with a toothless bucket, and it was extended further by hand to the east to include F43 and to the west to include the whole of F18. Two narrow trenches were also dug north of this intending to define the extent of occupation. The methods of excavation and recording were the same as for Area II and again time did not permit the total excavation of all the features.

The Iron Age enclosure

The only definite Iron Age feature in the area was F18, a three-sided sub-rectangular enclosure measuring 9.00 m by 11.00 m, formed by a ditch approximately 1.00 m wide

by 0.70 m deep with a slot in the bottom of it (Sections Q, O, P, N, R). Its lowest layer was slightly silty greyish gravel similar to the natural gravel (L18/6), and clearly identified only at Section Q; it is possible that it was missed in Section O. Elsewhere it was not distinguishable from L18/5, a layer of grey silty gravel, filling the bottom of the ditch and spreading up its sides. The top of the ditch contained yellow to brown clay (L18/2) overlain by a patchy layer of dirty gravel (L18/7) and dark brown loamy clay (L18/1; Sections Q, O, P, N, R). A few sherds of Roman pottery were found in the top layer (L18/1), but the other layers produced only Iron Age material.

2nd century features

Near the north-east end of F18 was a small rectangular pit (F74) about 1.20 m by 0.80 m, dug 0.45 m into the gravel with vertical sides and a flat bottom, filled with brown loamy gravel. This was cut by a circular posthole (F58) about 0.18 m deep filled with black sandy loam, in turn cut by F16, a shallow scoop (about 0.10 m deep) containing dark brown loam. All three features produced 2nd century Roman pottery. East of these were three undated postholes, F15, F59, and F60. F15 was 0.16 m deep and contained brown gravelly loam with charcoal and part of the butchered carcass of a sheep (see p 132). F59 and F60 were 0.24 m deep and contained dark brown gravelly loam with some daub and flecks of charcoal, and both were cut by F4.

The penannular slot and associated features

Apart from F18 the other main structural feature in the area was a penannular slot about 10.5 m in diameter (F5), with various associated postholes (F69, F51, and F83) and another slot (F7) crossing it diametrically (Pl V). The penannular slot ended with inturned postholes (F83 and F51) leaving a 6.00 m wide opening to the north-east which was bisected by the north end of F7. F5 varied in width and depth. Several longitudinal sections showed no definite evidence of post settings, except the irregularities and general narrowness (c 0.30 m) of the slot. Opposite the south end of F7 it became noticeably deeper (Sections C, H, and D), though it was not the case that the eastern half of the feature was generally deeper than the western half (Sections B, C, and E). Immediately west of this deepening, the slot had not survived the scrapers. Its fill was generally fairly uniform brown slightly gravelly clay (L5/2), but on the west side this was overlain by brown loam (L5/1; Sections B and C). In places there was a layer of dirty gravel (L5/3) in the bottom (Section H), but this could have been stained natural gravel. Only a very few Romano-British sherds of uncertain date were recovered. F5 was cut by three later features, F3, F4, and F24; F4 contained 2nd century pottery, but this might have been residual; F24 was undatable; F3 was post c 375. F3 had almost destroyed the slot where it met the inturned posthole on the west (F83). Although its internal edge just survived, the link between F5 and F83 was not entirely secure. F83 was fairly shallow (0.25 m deep) but much wider (0.60 m) than F5. Its fill was uniform brown gravelly loam very similar to L5/1, but with stones, some of which could have acted as packing. Its function as a posthole was suggested more by its position, however, than by its shape or contents. Late 4th century pottery was recovered from it. The other inturned posthole (F51) was much deeper (0.60 m) but

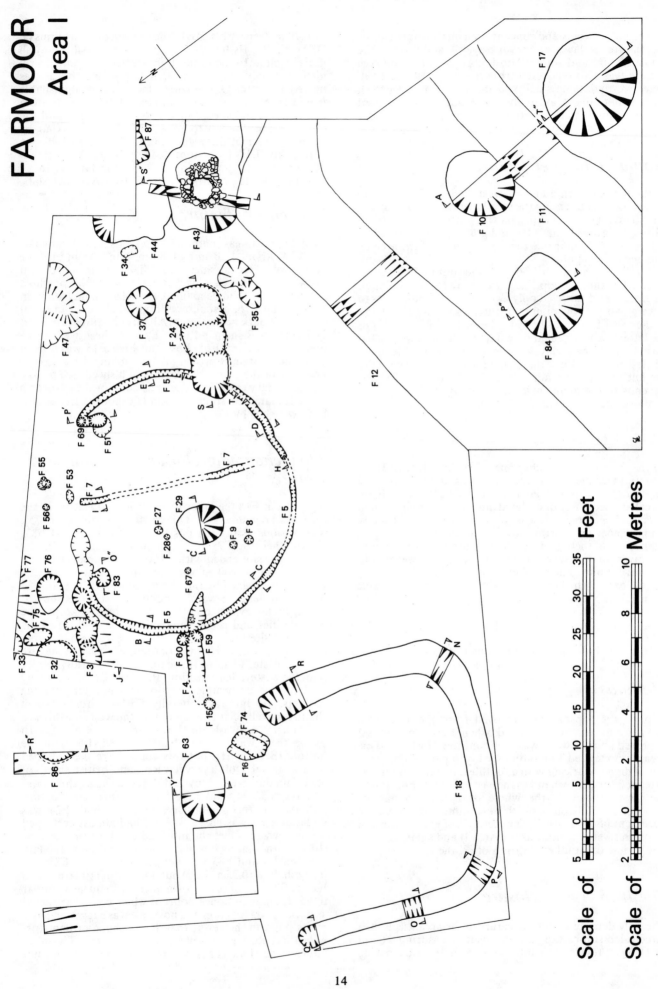

FARMOOR
Area I

Scale of Feet
5 0 5 10 15 20 25 30 35

Scale of Metres
2 0 2 4 6 8 10

Fig 6

14

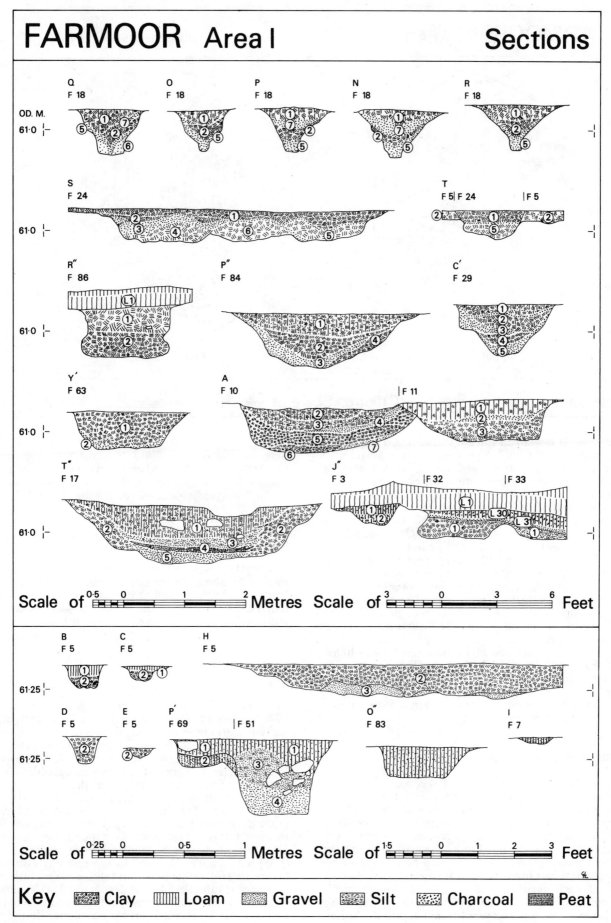

FARMOOR Area I

Sections

Fig 7

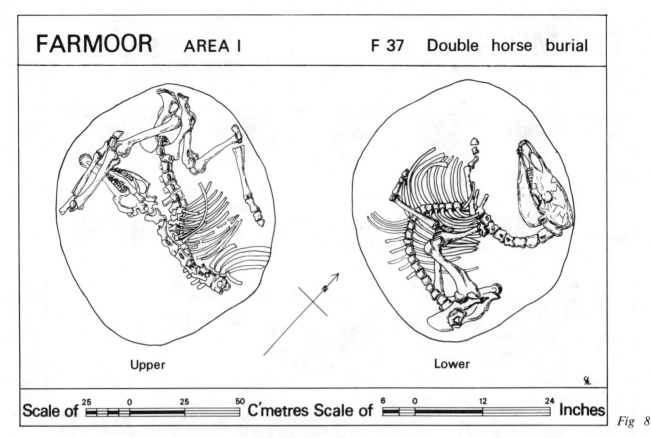

FARMOOR   AREA I   F 37   Double horse burial

Upper   Lower

Scale of 25 0 25 50 C'metres Scale of 6 0 12 24 Inches

Fig 8

not wider. It contained three layers (Section P): L51/4, grey silty gravel; L51/3, light brown clayey gravel with probable packing stones; and L51/1, brown gravelly loam with more packing stones. L51/1 was indistinguishable from the top fill of F69, a shallow possible posthole at the inturning corner of F5, which contained pottery datable to post *c* 250. The lower layer of F69, dark brown gravelly loam (L69/2), dipped down and was cut by F51. F7, the partition slot, was extremely shallow, no more than 0.05 m deep (Section I) and more often was only a definite but unexcavatable stain. At the northern end it clearly ended on a line between the ends of F5, but to the south it had been lost to the scrapers and its relationship to F5 was not clear though F5 became deeper opposite its end. The fill of F7 where it existed was brown gravelly loam.

Beyond the north end of F7 were three small holes, F53, F56, and F55, which had no established connection with the penannular slot. Each contained brown gravelly loam, F55 consisting of three holes. All may have been post- or stakeholes but this is not certain. F55 produced a few sherds of Roman pottery.

The horse and sheep burials

East of the penannular slot, F37 was one of the most curious features of the whole excavation. It was a small bowl-shaped pit 1.25 m in diameter and about 0.35 m deep, filled with solid, slightly gravelly brown clay which surrounded the skeletons of two horses, one lying on top of the other (Pl VI and Fig 8). Beneath them at the bottom of the pit were several sheep bones. The entire forequarters had been removed from each horse, but the rest of each skeleton was articulated though partly disjointed (see p 130 for the detailed description). No dating evidence was recovered from beneath the horses, though the top of the feature contained some

Oxfordshire colour-coated ware dated post *c* 250. There were no stratigraphic links to assist with the dating. Further east was an undated sheep skeleton in a very shallow (*c* 0.10 m) scoop in the gravel (F34), whose fill was indistinguishable from the topsoil (see p 132).

Gully 4

Cutting the west side of the penannular slot was a shallow gully (F4), about 0.15 m deep, filled with black gravelly loam with charcoal and at its east end some stone and much daub. The only datable pottery was 2nd century, but it was very abraded and may have been residual.

Pits

The eastern side of F5 was cut by a group of three pits, F24 (Section T). These were very similar to each other, fairly uniform in size and depth (Section S) with rather undercut sides and similar layers of brown clay and gravel. The lowest layers of clay (L24/4, L24/6) were sealed by a layer of gravel (L24/3) whose profile (Section S) suggested that the eastern pit cut the central one. The brown clay fill of the western pit (L24/5) overlay this layer. The tops of all three pits were covered by a layer of gritty dark brown clay (L24/1). Virtually no finds were recovered. Pits similar to this were found elsewhere in the area. Immediately to the south were two shallow scoops (F35) with similar fills, and to the east F87 also had a brown clay fill, rather undercut sides, and very little trace of domestic rubbish. F44 was deeper (0.80 m), again with undercut sides, containing grey silty gravel at the bottom with grey sticky clay and brown clay above. In the west half of the penannular structure Pit 29, apart from its

16

lowest layer of grey silty gravel (L29/5), contained alternating layers of brown clay and gravel (L29/4, L29/3, L29/2, L29/1; Section C[1]). Its south side was also rather undercut. F86 (the only feature found in the trial trenches in the north-west corner of the area) contained dark grey clay (L86/2) up to the level of the undercutting, with brown clay (L86/1) above (Section R). East of this were smaller, shallower pits with sticky grey fills and undercut sides (F32, F75 and F76; Section J).

Other pits were different. Pit 33 had no undercut sides and a gravelly fill with grey clay and silt (Section J), while F77 was a wide scoop rather than a pit and contained brown gravelly clay. South-west of these, F63 contained damp grey clay (Section Y[1]). In the southern corner of the area another large bowl-shaped pit (F84; Section P[11]) contained sticky grey clay (L84/4) confined to the southern part of the pit, overlain by layers of grey silty gravel (L84/3), sticky dark grey clay (L84/2), and gravelly loamy brown clay (L84/1). All the pits mentioned so far were characterized by a lack of much pottery or other domestic refuse, though F84 contained Oxfordshire colour-coated pottery of post c 250.

Pits 10 and 17 in the south-eastern corner of the area were the only ones with much domestic rubbish. F10 was bowl-shaped (Section A) and its lowest layers were grey silty gravel on its southern side (L10/7), partly overlaid by wet, dark grey silty clay (L10/6). Both these were covered by a thick layer of sticky dark grey-brown clay (L10/5), overlain on the south side by a layer of gravel (L10/4). The top two layers were brown gravelly loamy clay (L10/2, L10/3; Section A). A coin of Licinius I (AD 316) was found in the top of the pit, and L10/2 contained a set of hobnails. The pottery was consistent with being late 3rd to mid 4th century.

Pit 17's original fill was gravelly brown clay (L17/2) present on the sides of the pit but not the bottom, the profile of the pit on the north side suggesting that this layer had been cut through, though conceivably it could have been a lining (Section T[11]). This hole contained grey silty gravel (L17/5), covered by well preserved organic material consisting largely of cereal rubbish (L17/4; see p 110 for details of this material). This was covered by grey-brown clayey gravel (L17/3) and black clayey loam (L17/1), which contained a substantial amount of pottery datable to the late 4th century, and various small finds including three coins, the latest of which was a coin of Valens (364-375).

The well

Nearby there was also a stone-lined well (F43). Its internal diameter was 0.80 m, its depth 1.60 m (for plan and section see Fig 19, Section S). It was built in a construction trench which was back-filled largely with mixed layers of brown gravelly clay (L43/1 and L43/4) and thin layers of grey gravel (L43/2) and black clayey loam containing daub, charcoal, and other burnt material (L43/3). Immediately next to the stone lining was a layer of softer, darker brown clayey loam (L43/5). The fill of the well itself consisted of waterlogged layers of dark grey or black silt (L43/8 to L43/10) covered by drier dark grey-black silty loam containing numerous stones (L43/7). The top layer was brown clayey loam (L43/6). Late 4th century pottery was recovered as well as two child's shoes, a whetstone, and the tenon from a structural timber (see p 59). A biological analysis was made of the lowest layer in the well (see p 118).

Other late 4th century features

In the area immediately north-east of the penannular structure (F5) were further late 4th century features. A fairly extensive gravel layer (L31 and L57) covered F32, F33, F75, F76, and F77, and was itself covered by a fairly thick occupation layer of dark brown loam with charcoal flecks which contained a coin of Valens (AD 367-375) (L30; Section J). F3 was a series of three small pits which appeared to define the southern limit of L31, L30 and L57 and associated irregularities, and also cut F5, the penannular slot. The bottoms of the pits were filled with grey or black loam mixed with clay and gravel. The two eastern pits also contained much stone. Above them was a layer of black gritty loam and some stones (L3/1) which covered the whole of the feature (Section J). It produced late 4th century pottery and seven coins with another five in the topsoil immediately above. Of the eight legible coins all but one were 364-375, the eighth (from the topsoil) being of Constantine I (330-331) (see p 54). Further east, on the northern edge of the area was a wide, shallow, irregular pit or depression (F47) containing yellow clay (L47/2) overlain by a fairly thin (0.05 m) layer of black loam which contained charcoal and other traces of burning. These produced late 4th century pottery, a post-337 coin, and a fragment of quernstone with three other pieces in the topsoil above.

A layer of loam and stones covered many of the features in the west half of the penannular structure (L2/1) including F29 and five nearby postholes (F8, F9, F27, F28, and F67), all of them filled with gravelly brown loam and about 0.08 m deep except F67 (0.13 m). The brown loam (L2/1) which surrounded the fairly sparse random scatter of stones (F2) contained a coin of Theodosius I (388-392), the latest from the site (see p 55). Other finds included a shale spindle whorl and a bronze spoon handle. The stone scatter extended into the tops of several features in the northern part of the area including F5, F3, F83, and L30.

Post-Roman features

The two parallel east-west ditches (F11 and F12) in the south-east corner of the area contained layers of brown clay and gravel (Section A). F12 contained three pieces of white china as well as some abraded Roman sherds, while F11 contained one sherd of medieval pottery.

Area III: Iron Age (Site plan Fig 3)

Methods

Except for Areas I and II, the area at the north end of the Roman droveway, and the group of Iron Age enclosures immediately north of this, work was limited entirely to salvage digging. In every case features were discovered during or after stripping by scrapers when often much had been lost from the top of them. Often features were discernible only as ruts where the machines had sunk into soft fill; others were covered by up to half a metre of redeposited gravel and were found by digging long shovel slots down to genuine natural gravel or were detected by the differential drying of the redeposited material after rain. A few features were largely dug out by the contractors as unwanted soft spots, but others, including one of the groups of Iron Age enclosures, were first

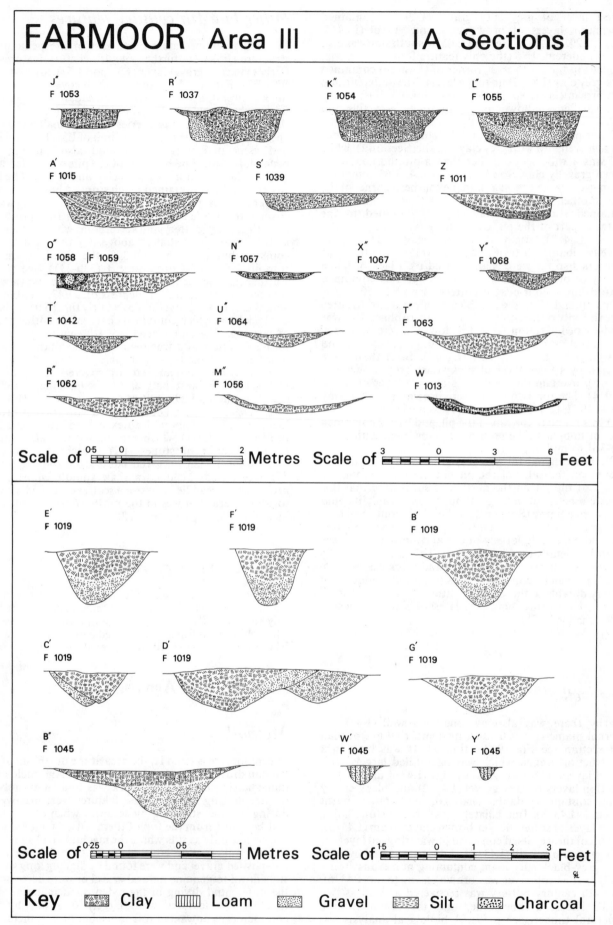

Fig 9

pointed out by the scraper drivers. Salvage observation varied, being most thorough where most features were found. The contrast between the relatively blank areas and those with many features may therefore be somewhat exaggerated, and although in general it is almost certainly genuine, it is difficult to estimate accurately how much was missed. The bulk of the salvage work was carried out in the two months after the end of the main excavation by two or three people working full time. For the rest of the time less effort could be spent and during the main excavation this work was deliberately restricted to one of the groups of Iron Age enclosures (group 1) and one of the Roman corndriers (F1002), to ensure that the main areas were not neglected. Before the main excavation and after the two months of full-time salvage excavation, work consisted of regular visits while stripping took place and occasional bouts of digging as features appeared (such as with Iron Age enclosure group 2). Sometimes time did not allow excavation of features which were discovered in this way and only their position was recorded. Apart from these the recording of features was fairly full.

Almost all features were plotted on the main site plan by triangulating with a level. Angles between sightings and known base lines were measured using the level's base plate (graduated to ten minutes), while distances were established using its tacheometric scale. The accuracy of this method was reckoned to be within 2%, so that positions were normally fixed to within 3 or 4 m on the ground. No formal checks were made but the results were entirely consistent when in one or two cases features were surveyed twice on different occasions, when they appeared at different stages in the contractors' work without immediately being recognised. Pits and most of the long linear ditches were not planned in more detail than this except where they came within the area of larger scale plans of more complicated features, or where they were of intrinsic interest (eg F1060). The vast majority of pits had sections dug and drawn and dating evidence was recovered from virtually all these. Where sections were not dug, dating evidence was seldom recovered. The more interesting features such as the enclosures, wells, and corndriers were recorded in more detail and in most cases to a standard not far below that of the main areas.

Early Iron Age pits

The majority of the Iron Age pits in Area III were not physically associated with enclosures, most being concentrated in the southern part of the site near the old road to Lower Whitley Farm, on a slight rise in the surface of the gravel terrace (compare Figs 2 and 3). The pottery from these pits suggests that they belonged to the early Iron Age (see p 37).

The group consisted of (from the north) F1054, 1015, 1055, 1053, 1056, 1057, 1068, 1067, 1063, 1062, 1064, 1013, 1059, 1044, 1040, 1039, 1037, 1042 (Site plan Fig 3). Almost all were probably fairly shallow (estimated to have been dug c 0.6 m into the natural gravel). In many cases only the bottom few centimetres had survived the scrapers but it was clear from these as well as the better preserved ones that in general they were fairly flat-bottomed or only slightly rounded. Where sides of the pits survived they were often fairly steep (Sections J[11], R[1], K[11], L[11], A[1], Fig 9). Their fill was commonly greenish-grey to brown clayey loam often with some gravel and almost always with charcoal flecks. Some contained daub (notably F1037) as well as pottery and bone. F1055 was exceptional in producing little domestic refuse, but

containing a lump of iron forging slag (identified by Mr H Cleere). It was filled with layers of dirty gravel and clay with a brown clay layer at the top. A thin layer of dirty gravel at the bottom of F1054 covered the more or less articulated skeleton of a dog (see p129). This was overlain by the usual type of pit fill. The most distinctive pit was F1013 (Section W) of which only the bottom survived. It contained three layers: black burnt clay and charcoal with red burnt patches which was only 0.03 to 0.10 m thick but covered the whole of the bottom of the pit (L1013/3); patchy pinkish-red to white burnt clay with grey ash and charcoal only about 0.02 m thick (L1013/2); and black loam containing a great deal of ash and charcoal as well as pottery and burnt bone and a few burnt stones (L1013/1). It was estimated that the bottom of the feature was about 0.60 m below the top of natural gravel. It was sampled for charred plant remains (see p 103).

F1134

Also in the southern part of the site, but not dated as being contemporary with either the pits or the later enclosures, was a very large pond-like feature (F1134) which was about 11.00 m wide and 1.00 m deep. It was filled with compact dark grey-brown loamy clay with some gravel. The only dating evidence recovered was one reasonably large Iron Age rim sherd which seemed unlikely to have been residual though this is not definite. The position of the feature was plotted from the air photograph.

The remaining Iron Age features in Area III were parts of five enclosures or groups of enclosures, and pits apparently associated with them, dating from the middle Iron Age.

Enclosure 1019

On the gravel terrace south of the old river bed just north-west of F18 in Area I was a roughly parallelogram shaped enclosure (F1019) with an opening to the north-west (see Plan Fig 10; Sections Fig 9). North of the opening, the enclosure gully had been recut twice on the inside and considerably shortened (by 3.00 m). The main gully contained grey silty clayey gravel overlain by a greyish orange-brown gravelly clay, the characteristic fill of most of the enclosure gullies, probably being one accumulation with oxidation near the top. The main gully recut an earlier one on the same line filled with light grey clayey gravel. The earliest cut ended where it would have met the projected line of the west side of the enclosure. The opposite end of the gully had been destroyed by a large Roman pit (F1018). A very small slot (F1022) only about 0.10 m wide ran half-way across the entrance of the enclosure. Another tiny slot (F1021) was traced 1.50 m south from the south-west corner of the enclosure.

Gully 1045

The simplest, least well preserved, and least well dated of the enclosures, F1045, was situated south-west of F1019. This was a tiny (0.30 m wide) gully which survived as a rough semicircle, open to the south-east (see Plan Fig 10; Sections Fig 9). At its south-east end the gully had largely been scraped away and was only patchy, but at the other end it deepened into a wider (1.00 m) and deeper (0.45 m) gully which ended beneath a Roman corndrier (F1002;

19

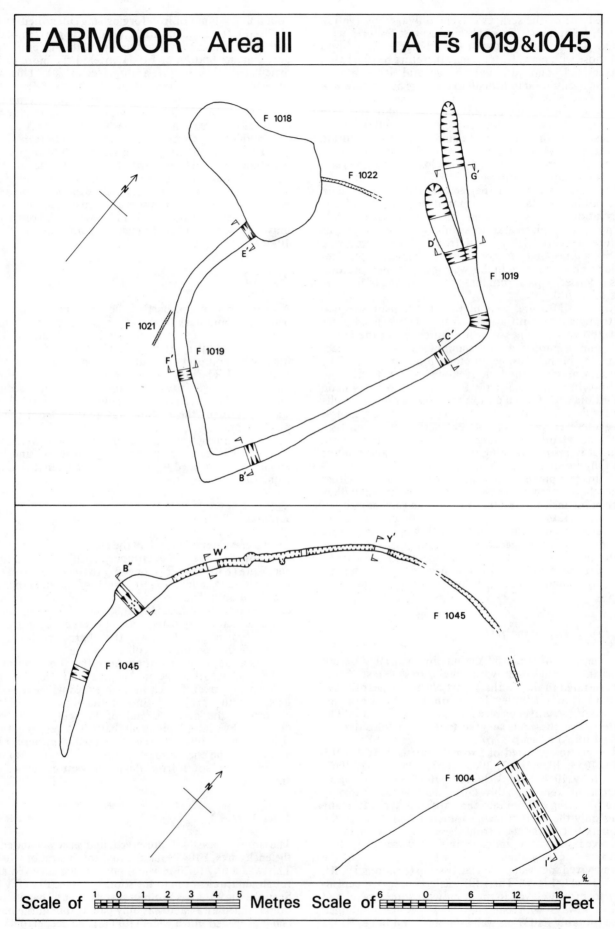

F 1018

F 1022

G'

D'

F 1019

C'

F 1021

F'

F 1019

E'

B'

W'

Y'

B"

F 1045

F 1045

F 1004

I'

Scale of 1 0 1 2 3 4 5 Metres Scale of 6 0 6 12 18 Feet

Fig 10

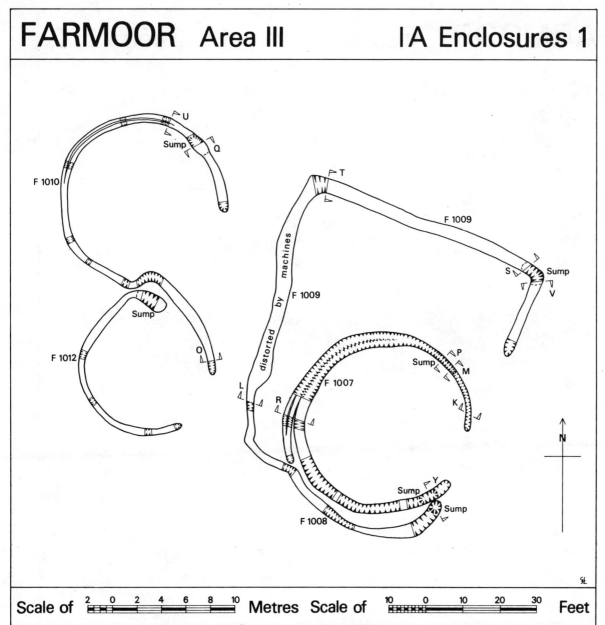

Fig 11

Scale of 2 0 2 4 6 8 10 Metres Scale of 10 0 10 20 30 Feet

Section B¹¹). The narrow part of the gully had an irregular flat bottom with slightly undercut sides and followed rather an irregular course. Its fill was dark brown gravelly loam (Sections W¹, Y¹). At the deeper south-west end it contained silty clayey gravel overlain by brown clay (Section B¹¹). The relationship of this part of the feature to the small gully was not clear. There was no trace of any contemporary features inside or near this gully.

Enclosure group 1

To the north on the other side of the old river bed in the alluvial floodplain of the river were three groups of enclosures. The middle one was a rectangular complex composed of four parts: a circular gully (F1007) about 13.75 m in diameter with a south-east opening; a gully enclosing a sub-rectangular area mostly north of this (F1008 and F1009); and two further gullies (F1010 and F1012) making up two roughly circular enclosures to the west, again with openings to the south-east (see Plan Fig

11; Sections Fig 12). All these gullies were partly waterlogged. F1007 had been recut at least twice on its western side where a spur ran off on the line of F1008. The inner ditch was wide and shallow with an uneven profile suggesting recuts or clearings (Section R). Elsewhere the profile was fairly consistently U-shaped. In two places there were deepenings or 'sumps', one near its south-east end (Section Y), the other about 5.00 m from its north-east end (Sections M, P). The former contained dark brown slightly clayey loam with charcoal mixed with thin bands of silted orange sand, the latter wet sticky grey gravelly clay and silt with a band of matted vegetation in it, and a few lumps of reddish-brown clayey loam, probably lumps of old topsoil or turf. Elsewhere the fill was mostly the usual gravelly clay mixture, sometimes with charcoal, especially on its southern side. To the south there was a deepening at the end of F1008 filled with material similar to that in the end of F1007 (Section Y). Opposite the end of the recuts of F1007, but not joining them, F1008 turned west into F1009, almost immediately turning northwards to form the west side of the rectangular enclosure. The profile of the gully varied

21

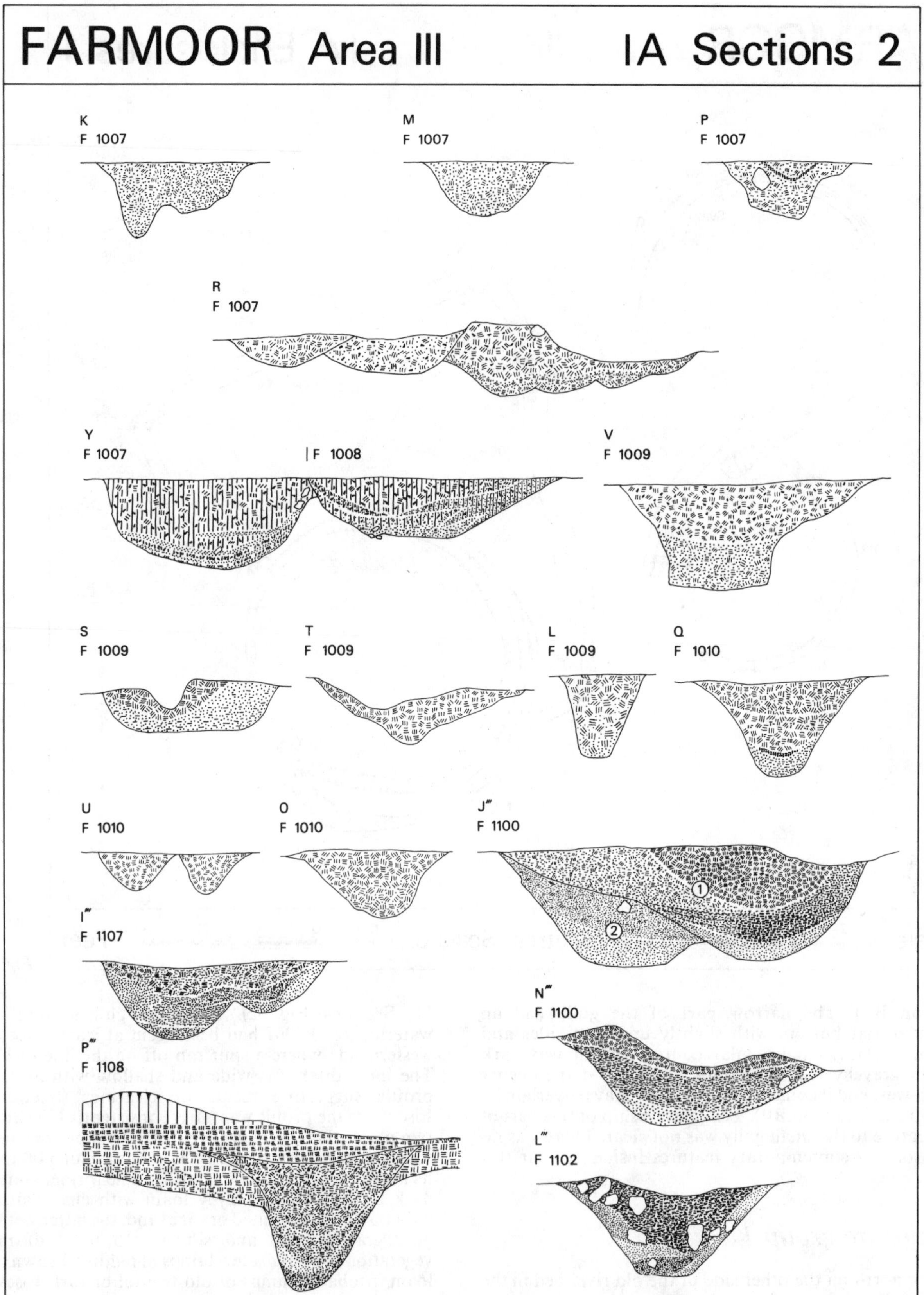

FARMOOR Area III
IA Sections 2
K
F 1007
M
F 1007
P
F 1007
R
F 1007
Y
F 1007
F 1008
V
F 1009
S
F 1009
T
F 1009
L
F 1009
Q
F 1010
U
F 1010
O
F 1010
J‴
F 1100
1
2
I‴
F 1107
N‴
F 1100
P‴
F 1108
L‴
F 1102
Scale of 0·25 0 0·5 1 Metres
Scale of 1·5 0 1 2 3 Feet
Key
Clay
Loam
Gravel
Silt
Charcoal
Peat

Fig 12

from the rounded shape of F1008 to a steep-sided slot at Section L, and a flat, irregular V-shape at Section T where the fill was simply brown clay. At the north-east corner of F1009 was another deepening containing wet dark grey gravelly silt overlain by sticky grey-brown clay and charcoal flecks (Section V). From this corner the gully turned south again on a tangent to F1007 ending 7.00 m from the north-east end of F1007 to leave an entrance.

The two gullies to the west (F1010 and F1012), like F1007 and F1008 and 1009, were very close to each other but did not join, though together they clearly made a unit with the rest. The northern one was crook-shaped with evidence of recutting on its north-west side (Section U). The deepening on its north-east side contained dirty silted gravel overlain by dark grey organic clay with a mat of preserved vegetation at the bottom (Section Q). The gully continued 5.00 m south-east from this deepening, leaving a 7.00 m wide gap between its end and the bend of the crook. The shaft of the crook formed the eastern part of the other circular enclosure. The northern end of F1012 terminated in a large deepening in the angle of the crook of F1010, filled with wet, dark blue-grey organic clayey silt. Its eastern end curled round to leave a gap 4.50 m wide between it and the south-east end of F1010.

Samples for biological analysis were taken from the deepenings in F1007, F1009, and F1010 at Sections P, V, and Q (see p 111 ff).

Enclosure group 2

60 m to the north of this complex was a further group of enclosures again situated on the alluvial floodplain (see Plan Fig 13; Sections Fig 12). In plan it seemed not so neatly self-contained. Its various gullies were not separate from each other, nor did they have so many obvious deepenings. The penannular gully in this case (F1100) had cut earlier gullies (F1100/2, F1101, and F1117) which were probably continuous. F1101 was fairly deep (0.60 m), containing layers of reddish-brown sand and dark grey organic clayey silt. These continued in F1100/2 (Section J[111]) and were also found in F1117. There was no clear division between F1117, F1113, F1103, and F1102. F1102 also contained layers of dirty sand and dark grey clayey silt. At its butt-end to the south, opposite the entrance of F1100, it contained a large number of small stones (Section L[111]). There was no corresponding gully opposite this to make an enclosure, though the recutting of F1100 might have destroyed one.

To the north a polygonal enclosure with an entrance to the south-east was formed by F1103, F1117, and F1111. All these were fairly shallow and filled with the usual gravelly clay. At the north end of F1113 the gully was deeper, containing alternate layers of dirty gravel and sticky dark grey organic silt. Inside this irregular enclosure were traces of a small curving gully (F1104) most of which had been scraped away. It contained gravelly grey clay.

To the north again was another enclosure formed by F1110, another shallow gully describing a semicircle starting at the corner formed by the junction of F1111 and F1113. This enclosure had a 4.50 m wide entrance to the east where it met the arc of a circular enclosure to the east, formed by the dubious F1112 projecting northwards from F1111, F1108, and F1109. The enclosure formed by these thus had two equal entrances 3.50 m wide either side of F1109 to the east and south, and another entrance to the subcircular enclosure to the west. Most of F1108

survived only as a narrow gully, but at its eastern end it disappeared under an unexcavated datum point, providing an opportunity to observe the full width of the top of the ditch and its relationship to the layers between the topsoil and the gravel (Section P[111]). It had been cut through the orange-yellow slightly sandy/gritty clay which overlay the gravel and had filled up with black silty gravel, sand, and sticky grey silty clay with some gravel and a few charcoal flecks. It became browner and less gravelly towards the top. Overlying both the ditch and the orange sandy clay was a layer of slate blue clay beneath the dark grey-brown clayey loam topsoil. Soil analysis elsewhere showed that the orange-yellow clay overlying the gravel and the blue clay sealing F1108 were probably alluvial (see p 141). F1109 was filled to a depth of 0.30 m with layers of clean gravel with occasional bands of dark grey silt. The remaining 0.30 m was dark grey organic clayey silt.

South of F1100 the deep part of F1101 gave way to a very narrow shallow sinuous gully (F1115) filled with grey silty clay, running into a round pit (F1122) with a similar fill. 2.00 m east of this, Pit 1105 was filled with dirty brown silted sand, dark grey silt, and brown clay. Another small gully (F1114) with identical fill ran north-eastwards from this, turning eastwards and ending 8.00 m away. Fairly thorough searching revealed no continuation of the gully in any direction.

The only feature in the complex where there was clearly a recut was F1100, the penannular gully cut inside the area between F1102, F1117, and F1101. Its fill was dirty brown silted sand or gravel, covered by black silty clay with some charcoal and by grey silty gravel at the top (Sections J[111], N[111]). Samples of the black silty clay were taken for biological analysis (see p 111 ff). An eastern entrance 3.00 m wide was left between the butt-ends of the ditch, in which rested the lower jaw and the upper part of the skull of two horses (see p 129). In front of this entrance the butt-end of F1102 had been filled with stones (Section L[111]). The fill of the butt-ends consisted mostly of black sandy silt, and pottery from the feature was concentrated in these layers.

Pits 1106, 1116, 1118-21

West of this complex of enclosures was a group of six pits (F1121, F1120, F1119, F1118, F1116, and F1106). Except for F1121 which was approximately 2.50 m in diameter they were all small. Only F1106 was excavated. Its fill was silty gravel and grey clay with a little pottery of a type associated with the enclosures.

Enclosure 1107

North-west of the enclosures was the southern part of another enclosure (F1107), its northern half having been destroyed by a gravel pit. The surviving arc was roughly circular and terminated in a butt-end on its eastern side. The fill was black gravelly loam with much charcoal, which gradually changed along the gully to the usual mixed layers of clay and gravel. On the western side the gully had been recut, a smaller gully describing a tighter arc on the inside (Section I[111]). The fills were too similar to tell which was later. There was no direct link with the rest of the enclosure complex, but the little pottery that was recovered from F1107 fell within the general type associated with the enclosures.

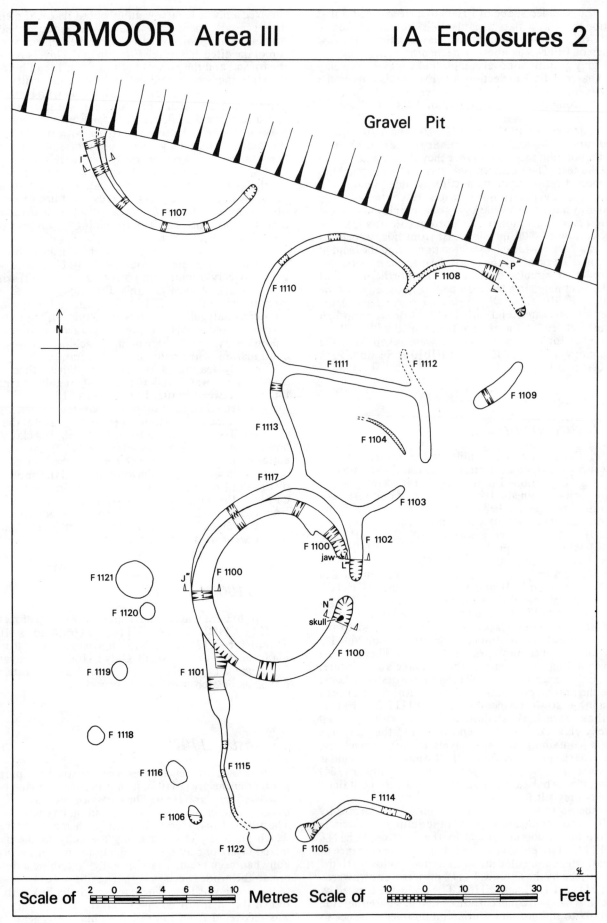

Gravel Pit

F 1107

N

F 1110

F 1108

P'''

F 1111

F 1112

F 1109

F 1113

F 1104

F 1117

F 1103

F 1102

F 1100
jaw
L'''

F 1121

F 1100

F 1120

J''

N'''
skull

F 1119

F 1101

F 1100

F 1118

F 1116

F 1115

F 1106

F 1122

F 1105

F 1114

Scale of 2 0 2 4 6 8 10 Metres Scale of 10 0 10 20 30 Feet

Fig 13

Enclosure group 3

The third set of enclosures on the floodplain was found in January 1976 just north of the old river bed in the last piece of undisturbed ground to be dug out for the reservoir. It consisted of a penannular gully with a larger ditch to the south forming a roughly rectangular enclosure (see Plan Fig 14; Sections Fig 15). The penannular gully was noticed after the bulldozing of overburden and was removed after rapid recording, but a break in the work enabled a three-week excavation to take place on the undisturbed area, incorporating the southern side of the penannular gully and about threequarters of the larger one. Everything was sealed by a thick layer of alluvium covered by thick trample from one of the contractors' haul roads. These were removed to within a few centimetres of the archaeological levels by an O & K excavator with a 2.00 m toothless ditching bucket. A north-south baulk left to provide a section from the topsoil down had been too heavily disturbed to be of any use, but such a section was provided by the trench running south from the main area (Section U[111]). The preserved Iron Age stratigraphy was exposed by the removal by hand of the remaining alluvium, narrow baulks being left as sections (eg Sections S[111] and T[111]). The main enclosure ditch was excavated only in sections, and some of it was observed only when the rest of the area was stripped by the contractors. The methods used in the final stripping precluded any further detailed recording.

The earliest features were two parallel gullies running north-west to south-east 3.00 m apart (F1157 and F1174). They had U-shaped profiles cut 0.10 - 0.20 m into the gravel and were filled with silty gravel and clay. Iron Age pottery was recovered from these but it was not closely datable. Only about 14.00 m had survived being stripped with the overburden. Both gullies were cut by later enclosure features (F1156, F1159, and F1168).

Only some of the bottom of the penannular gully (F1156) had survived the bulldozing. Its entrance was 4.50 m wide on the east side, and its diameter was about 12.00 m. The gully was the usual type with a concentration of domestic rubbish and pottery in the butt-ends either side of the entrance. No evidence of recutting was noticed, nor was there any obvious sump. Virtually no stratigraphy survived inside this enclosure except on its southern side, but the overburden from it had been rolled up like a carpet by the bulldozer blade with the layers more or less distinguishable. These included a layer of small lumps of soft limestone mixed with silty grey clay and a few sherds of Iron Age pottery. At the southern edge of the enclosure where some stratigraphy survived, the natural yellow silty clay soil (L1184) appeared to have been cut through and replaced by grey silty clay (L1172). This was visible only in Section X[111], having been disturbed either side and to the north. Nowhere, however, was the original ground surface found.

The rectangular enclosure was 17.00 m by 14.00 m and had an entrance 2.50 m wide facing north-east, near the entrance to the circular enclosure. Its ditch (F1159, F1168, and F1179), at 1.50 to 2.00 m wide and 0.80 m deep, was larger than those of the other floodplain enclosures; it mostly had a U-shaped profile with fairly steep sides, and was filled with black organic silt with sand or gravel lenses overlain by finer black organic silt. The top of the ditch was filled with the grey gravelly silt covering the rest of the enclosure, which was everywhere overlain by alluvium (Sections Q[111], X[111], S[111], T[111]). There was no sign of recuts in the fill of the ditch, but the shape of its butt-ends and perhaps its inner edge at the north-west corner suggested possible recuts. Outside the main area of excavation such variations would not have been observed.

The layer of gravelly grey silt (L1172) covered the whole of the enclosure and also spread outside it. It overlay the natural gravel with the undisturbed remains of natural soil surviving only in patches. The surface of the gravel was generally lower in the middle of the enclosure than at its edges (Sections S[111], T[111]) and it was pitted with small hollows in the south-west corner of the excavated area. The layer produced a little pottery, one piece of daub or loom weight, and a few residual worked flints (see p 61).

Crossing the enclosure were two gravel banks (F1170 and F1171) about 1.50 m wide and 0.20 - 0.30 m high. They tended to overlie the patchy remains of the natural silty soil, often where calcium carbonate pans occurred. In one place the western bank partly overlay the grey silty layer (L1172). Each bank had been heightened by the addition of more gravel (Sections S[111], T[111]). This partly overlay the grey silt which had accumulated on the sides of the original banks but which subsequently accumulated on the enlarged ones. The gravel of both banks was very hard-packed and each had a hard smooth surface; they were both the same absolute height (c 60.35 m OD) and were both dead level. The relationship between the two banks was not clear as F1171 petered out before they met. At its northern end there was no clear stratigraphic relationship between F1171 and the enclosure ditch (F1179), though it certainly did not cross it or reappear north of it. The eastern bank (F1170) went through the entrance of the enclosure at its north end, but overlay its silted up ditch to the south (Pl VII; Section U[111]). Both ends of the 22.00 m excavated length had already been removed with the overburden. Possible continuations of both banks (F1182 and F1183) were observed south of the main enclosure, both only in section during the removal of overburden. F1182, 40 m from the excavated portion and on the other side of the old river bed, was not surveyed accurately and had been seen, only in section, almost by chance during earlier salvage work (see Site plan Fig 3).

No dating evidence was recovered from the gravel banks, but the enclosure ditch and L1172 produced pottery similar to that from the other enclosures. The main enclosure ditch and L1172 were sampled for biological analysis (see p 111).

The whole area was covered by up to 0.60 m of alluvial clay (L1164) (Pl VII; Section U[111]) containing aquatic snails (see p 109). It was similar to the top layers in the old river channel (Fig 40) and was the same type of deposit as the clay overlying F1108, though it was thicker because of its proximity to the old river channel where the level of the underlying gravel was lower. (See p 141 for details of the pre- and post-Iron Age alluvial deposits).

Area III: Roman (Site plan Fig 3)

The droveway

The most prominent Roman feature in Area III was a droveway marked by two parallel ditches which ran from the edge of the site at Lower Whitley Farm, north-eastwards to the edge of the gravel terrace (see Site plan Fig 3; Sections J, M[1], I[1], Fig 18). Near the farm the ditches (here F1085 and F1086) were approximately 2.00 m wide

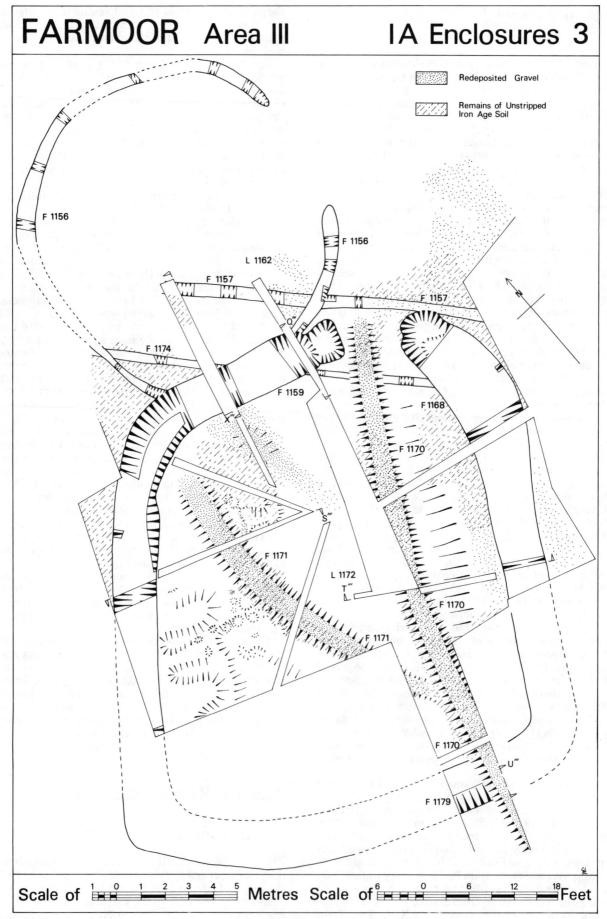

Redeposited Gravel

Remains of Unstripped Iron Age Soil

F 1156

F 1156

L 1162

F 1157

F 1157

F 1174

F 1159

F 1168

F 1170

S'''

F 1171

L 1172

T'''

F 1170

F 1171

F 1170

U'''

F 1179

Scale of   1 0 1 2 3 4 5   Metres   Scale of   6 0 6 12 18   Feet

Fig 14

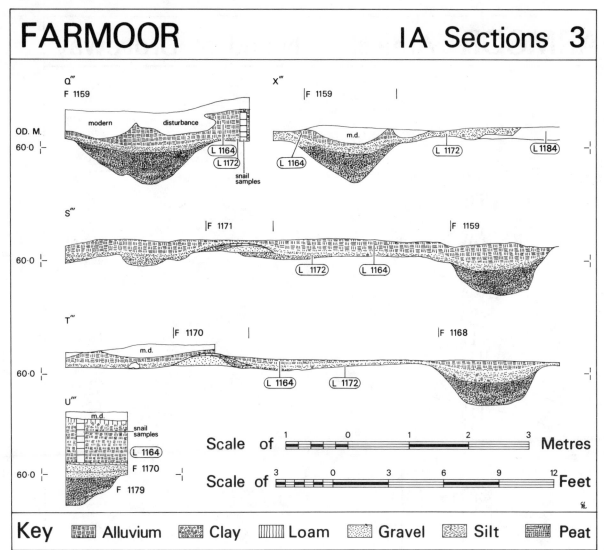

Q'''
F 1159

OD. M.
60·0

modern   disturbance

L 1164
L 1172

snail
samples

X'''
F 1159

m.d.

L 1164   L 1172   L 1184

S'''
F 1171   F 1159

60·0

L 1172   L 1164

T'''
F 1170   F 1168

m.d.

60·0

L 1164   L 1172

U'''
m.d.

snail
samples

L 1164

60·0

F 1170

F 1179

Scale of   1   0   1   2   3   Metres

Scale of   3   0   3   6   9   12 Feet

Key   Alluvium   Clay   Loam   Gravel   Silt   Peat

Fig 15

and flat-bottomed, filled with slightly gravelly sticky brown clay with some Roman pottery. In a machine-dug trial trench about 100 m to the north-east, only the western one was observed though both were clearly visible on the air photograph (Pl I). Just north of the trial trench the line of the droveway bent before straightening out to the north where both ditches were clearly traceable to the edge of the gravel terrace. The western ditch was recut producing two slightly diverging ditches (F1004 and F1005). The two western ditches also had a smaller gully (F1065) between them, which was traced for 24.00 m south of F1003. Where they were sectioned, such as approximately 5.00 m north of F1003 (Sections J, M¹), all the ditches contained dark brown gravelly loam. F1005 was dated post-250 by Oxfordshire colour-coated pottery. A section across the western ditch near F1045 (see Plan Fig 10) showed four recuttings, all containing grey or brown gravelly clay except one of the two latest which contained charcoally layers (Section I¹). North of this the eastern ditch (F1024) produced calcite-gritted pottery of post *c* 350 and the western one (F1025) post250 pottery. On the east side of the northern end of the droveway a small gully (F1023) ran parallel to F1024 and like it turned eastwards, apparently to run parallel to the edge of the gravel terrace. It was dug only about 0.30 m into the gravel, was 0.40 m wide, with a U-shaped profile, and contained yellow-grey gravelly clay.

The northern end of the droveway

At the northern end of the droveway there was greater stratification, and the presence of the old river bed caused the stripping of topsoil to be restricted, allowing a more thorough investigation to take place (see Plan Fig 16; Sections Fig 17). A trench 25.00 m long was dug by hand across the droveway, and another was dug by machine north-eastwards roughly along the line of it. In addition a small area 6.50 m by 3.00 m in the middle of the droveway was taken down to the top of a peat layer (L1072) by machine, and then continued by hand. To the east three small shovel trenches were dug to pick up the line of the eastern group of ditches (F1074). These all turned eastwards almost at right-angles to the line of the droveway. Of the three cuts of the ditch the outer two (F1074/3 and F1074/1) curved round cutting the corner more than the inner ditch (F1074/2) which turned at a sharp angle well inside the others. The western ditches did not turn within the area of the controlled excavation, and a small trench in the north of the area was too small to establish whether they continued that far. One possible ditch (F1076) and the edge of another (F1077) were found at the northern end of the machine trench, but again too little was seen for any definite interpretation. Subsequent salvage observation showed that the eastern ditches ran eastwards along the edge of the gravel terrace, passing

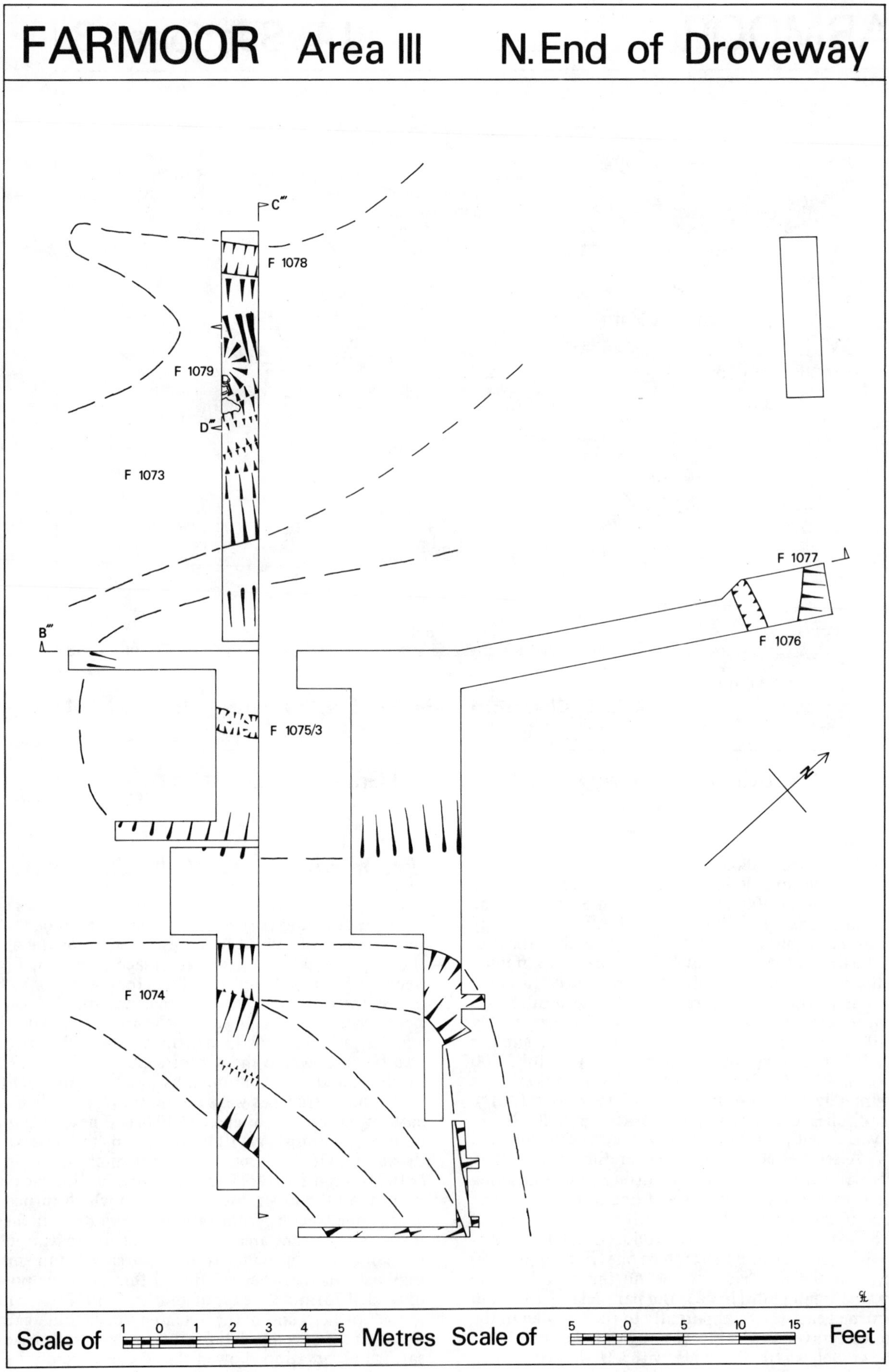

FARMOOR Area III   N. End of Droveway

C'''
F 1078
F 1079
D'''
F 1073
B'''
F 1077
F 1076
F 1075/3
F 1074

Scale of 1 0 1 2 3 4 5 Metres Scale of 5 0 5 10 15 Feet

Fig 16

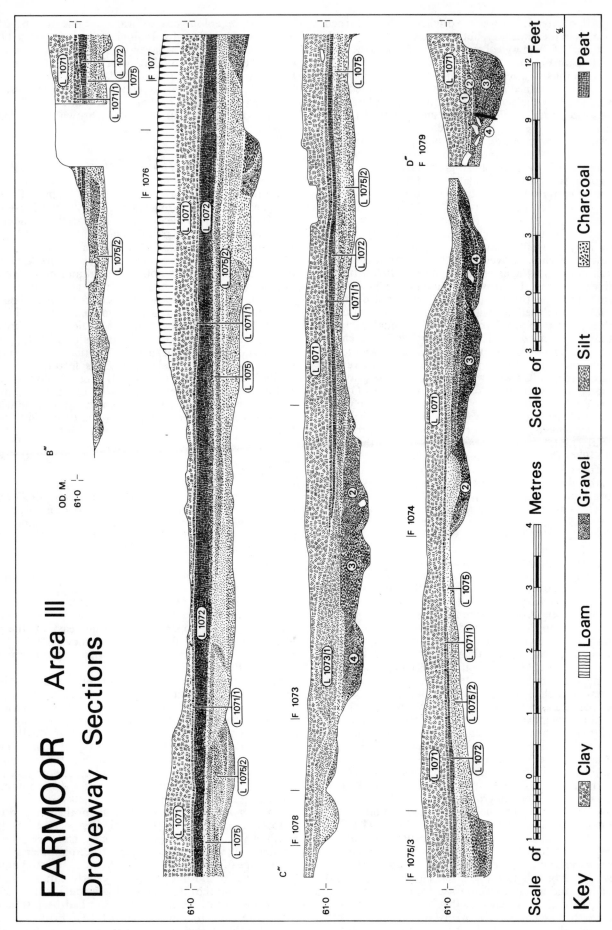

FARMOOR   Area III
Droveway Sections

Key   Clay   Loam   Gravel   Silt   Charcoal   Peat

Scale of   Metres   Scale of   Feet

Fig 17

just north of Area I. The western ditches probably turned westwards in the same way, but were not easily followed, though part of them was observed about 50 m to the west (see Site plan Fig 3).

Between the two ditches in the main area of excavation was a layer of churned up gravel (L1075/2) confined to a wide band along the centre of the droveway. It began to shelve away under the old river bed, and extended almost to the end of the machine trench (Section B[111]). It consisted of many lenses, layers, and pockets of dirty clayey or silty gravel, varying in colour from pale yellow or pinkish-buff to dirty bluish-grey. These were more obvious in section than in plan, but did not form any particular pattern. In the centre of the droveway, cutting this layer, were two small pits (F1075/3) filled with dark greenish-grey gravelly silt (Section C[111]). These were covered by a layer of light grey slightly silty gravel overlain by grey silty gravel, cut by one of the western droveway ditches. Covering this was an extensive, though fairly thin, layer of white gravel (L1075). It was confined between the droveway ditches except for the innermost cut on the east (F1074/2), which it overlay. The layer produced a small bronze bracelet, but no datable pottery except two pieces of residual samian. This layer was observed during salvage work stretching about 35 m west of the main area of excavation and some distance over the old river bed. The main droveway ditches were all filled with wet, dark grey sticky gravelly silt, sometimes with peat, loam, or sand lenses. Of the eastern ditches, F1074/2 was shallow, about 1.70 m wide, and was overlain by the layer of white gravel (L1075) which also covered it where it turned east. This ditch was cut by the middle one (F1074/3) which also cut the outer one (F1074/4). F1074/4 was deeper than F1074/2 and wider (over 2.00 m) and contained a lens of organic peaty silt in the usual gravelly black silt. These ditches were cut or overlain to the east by a possible further recut (F1074/5) containing greenish-brown loamy gravel.

The western ditches were similar, the earliest being the middle one (F1073/3) which was cut to the east by F1073/2. This was about 2.00 m wide with an irregular profile on its eastern side, possibly suggesting recuts invisible in the fill. Above it was a shallow (0.25 m) scoop filled with brown peaty gravel (F1073/5). West of F1073/3, also cutting it, the other main recut (F1073/4) was 1.80 m wide. About 1.20 m further west was another ditch (F1078) approaching the droveway at a slight angle from about 6.00 m to the south-west. It was fairly narrow (0.80 m) and was filled with grey silty gravel. Cutting the western ditches was a pit (F1079) approximately 1.40 m wide and 0.75 m deep. Its fill was almost indistinguishable from that of the ditches, being wet, dark blue-black gravelly silt overlain by dark grey clayey silt and brown gravelly clay. On its eastern side were two wooden stakes behind which rested a layer of dirty brown gravel and a number of stones (Section D[111]). The pit produced a shoe, but the only dating evidence was one piece of samian which was probably residual. All the western droveway ditches were covered by a thick (0.40 m) layer of heavy brown gravelly clay (L1073/1). It was similar to the grey-brown clay of L1071 above, but whereas that was above the layer of peat (L1072), L1073/1 ended beneath it. A large scythe blade of the Great Chesterford type was found at the interface between these layers. (See Figs 32 and 33 and p 61.) The layer of dark brown peat (L1072) was fairly thin (0.10 m) in section, and was largely confined to the area between the droveway ditches. Towards the river bed, however, it became thicker (to c 0.25 m) as the layers beneath gradually sloped away. Pottery from it included

Oxfordshire colour-coated ware datable to post-250. Samples were taken for biological analysis (see p 119). Above the peat was a layer of alluvial slate blue clay (L1071/1) similar to that overlying F1108 on the floodplain (see p 23). It was overlain by a thick (0.30 m) layer of yellow-brown to grey clay with rusty brown staining (L1071), also probably largely alluvial. This was covered by up to 0.30 m of dark brown clayey loam topsoil.

The eastern section of the droveway

The droveway did not reappear to the north of the old river bed but a section of what might have been droveway was found 300 m to the east, running parallel to the river bed on the edge of the gravel terrace (see Site plan Fig 3). It consisted of two parallel ditches spaced like the other droveway ditches approximately 12.50 m apart. F1097, the southern one, was not excavated and produced no datable pottery though a length of about 70 m was exposed. F1098 to the north produced one undatable Roman body sherd and part of a wooden bowl (see Fig 30 No 16). Both ditches contained sticky grey-brown gravelly clay. Between them a small gully (F1099) joined F1097 at its east end but turned north further west. Its fill was dark brown gravelly clay. This feature and two similar undatable gullies (F1131 and F1132) in the section of droveway near Lower Whitley Farm (370 m to the west) were the only features which occurred between the droveway ditches which were not definitely pre-Roman (as F1053) or post-medieval (F1003).

Other ditches

A number of ditches, mostly undatable in any direct way, had, however, been dug at right-angles to the main part of the droveway without crossing it. West of the northern end of the droveway, near the old river bed, F1049 was shallow with only the bottom 0.05 m surviving. Its east end had not survived, but it ran roughly westwards from the droveway for about 50 m before turning northwards, parallel to it, where it was traceable on the ground largely as a stain for about 18 m, and on the air photograph as a crop mark for another 20 m or so (Pl I). At the end near the droveway it appeared no further east on the air photograph than it did on the ground. Its fill where excavatable was gravelly light brown clay producing no finds (Section E[11], Fig 18).

40 m to the south was a very similar shallow ditch (F1031) which was traced for 45 m but did not turn before it was lost, having been scraped away. At its east end, 8.00 m short of the droveway, it disappeared into two pits (F1029 and F1030). There was no clear distinction between the fill of the ditch and the top of the two pits. F1030 was dated by pottery and a coin to the late 3rd or early 4th century. The fill in the bottom of both pits was fairly wet grey or dark grey gravelly silt. F1030 contained a few largish stones (approximately 0.30 m long).

Another 150 m to the south-west another small ditch (F1066) ran 65 m to the north-west before turning south-west at right-angles, where it had been recut possibly more than once, and was traced another 105 m to the edge of the site near Lower Whitley Farm. Roman pottery was found but it was not clearly datable. At its south-east end the ditch was cut by the outer cut (F1005) of the western droveway ditches, but had been scraped away short of the inner cut (F1004). From the air photograph it does not appear to have crossed the

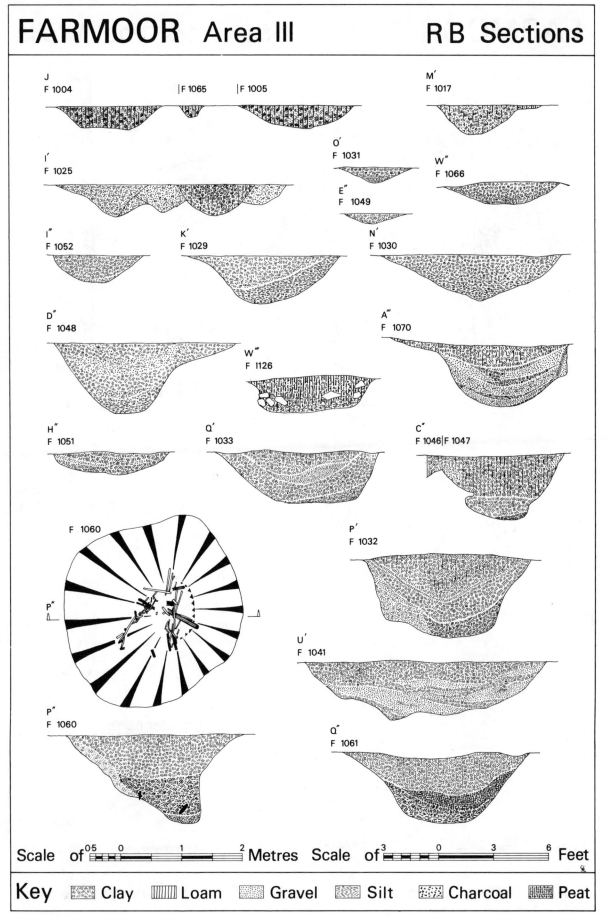

FARMOOR Area III   R B Sections

Scale of [0.5 0 1 2] Metres   Scale of [3 0 3 6] Feet

Key [ ] Clay [||||] Loam [ ] Gravel [ ] Silt [ ] Charcoal [ ] Peat

Fig 18

31

FARMOOR   Corn-driers and Wells

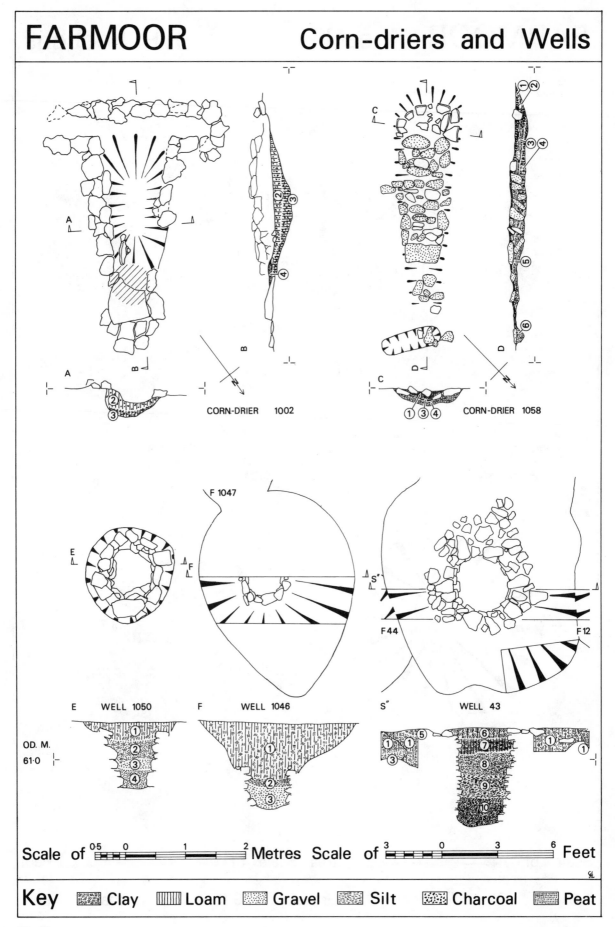

CORN-DRIER 1002

CORN-DRIER 1058

F 1047

E   WELL 1050

F   WELL 1046

S"   WELL 43

F 44   F 12

OD. M.
61·0

Scale of ⊢━━━ 0·5   0   1   2 ⊣ Metres Scale of ⊢━━━ 3   0   3   6 ⊣ Feet

Key ▨ Clay ▥ Loam ▨ Gravel ▨ Silt ▨ Charcoal ▨ Peat

Fig 19

droveway. Crop marks showed a possible corresponding ditch on the opposite side of the droveway (F1135) also turning south-west to enclose a similar rectangular area, but this was not observed on the ground.

Miscellaneous ditches

A number of other possibly or definitely Roman ditches were found. Two were revealed by the drain round the site near Lower Whitley Farm. F1083 was 3.50 m wide, dug to 1.40 m below the top of the natural gravel and filled with rather gravelly brown clayey loam which at the bottom, below water level, was dark grey. No secure dating evidence was recovered. F1087, 10.00 m south-east of the droveway, was about 2.50 m wide and flat-bottomed and contained wet brown-grey clay. Another ditch running north-east/south-west (F1127) just south-east of F1087 was recorded almost entirely from the air photograph; a small section of ditch, which was probably this one, was recorded in the trial trench and produced a few sherds of Roman pottery. The only other ditch which could be shown probably to be Roman was F1020, a short length just east of the northern end of the droveway. It began in the area between the Iron Age enclosures F1019 and F18 and was traced about 10.00 m almost to the eastern branch of the droveway. It was about 1.50 m wide and 0.50 m deep, contained dark grey silty clay with some gravel lenses, and produced a little Roman pottery and one of the very few pieces of Roman roof tile from the site.

Pits

The Roman pits were variable but were mostly larger, deeper (often dug to well below water level), and more bowl-shaped than the Iron Age pits. Commonly the fill of these pits was a mixture of layers of solid brown gravelly clay and layers of grey silty or clayey gravel (Sections Fig 18). These included F1033, F1048, F1032, F1070, F1041, and also F1030 and F1029 already described. F1033 and F1048 were part of a line of features (the others being F1050 and F1051) parallel and close to Ditch 1049. F1033 was dated late 3rd or early 4th century. None of the other pits close to ditches (F1048, F1032, F1070, and F1041) produced any dating evidence, though F1030 at the end of Ditch 1031 was also late 3rd or early 4th century.

Of the remaining pits, F1052 near the western arm of F1049 was smaller (1.20 m) and shallower (0.50 m) than most, filled with brown clay overlying grey silty gravel. F1051 near the eastern end of F1049 was similar in size but filled with dark brown gravelly clay. F1047, 32 m south-west of F1051, was larger (2.00 m wide and 1.00 m deep) with the characteristic slightly gravelly solid brown clay, but with undercut sides beneath this and a fill of wet, black organic clayey loam at the bottom (Section C¹¹). It was dated to post-350 by the pottery. F1061, 35 m south-west of Area I, also contained waterlogged organic material. It was 3.00 m wide and 1.00 m deep, with wet black silty clay about 0.25 m thick at the bottom covered by black organic peat 0.25 m thick, and gravelly brown clay (Section Q¹¹).

12 m to the south-east was a third pit dug to below water level and containing preserved organic material (F1060) (see Plan and Section P¹¹, Fig 18). It was 1.40 m deep and 3.00 m wide at the top but in section narrowed considerably to a small hole in the bottom where several stakes and pieces of wattle had been preserved. Some of the stakes were vertical and had wattle strands woven round them, but others were leaning at considerable angles and there were also many loose fragments. Above the wattle was the stump of a bush about 0.75 m in diameter (see p 81). It was upside down and had had its roots and several shoots up to 0.10 m thick chopped off. The fill round this and the wattle was waterlogged dark greenish-grey clayey silt. The ground-water flowed into the pit extremely rapidly so that a 3 inch bore sludge pump could only just cope with the flow. The top of the water level at the time of excavation was about 0.65 m below the surface of the gravel, covering the wattle and the tree stump. Samples for biological analysis were taken from the waterlogged material (see p 120f). Above the silty clay was a thick (0.60 m) layer of brown to grey somewhat gravelly silt, with gravelly slip on the north side.

Stone-lined pits

Three pits, F1169 (west of the north end of the droveway), F1126, and F1096 (both in the southern part of the site), appeared to have rough stone linings at the bottom and all were dug to below water level. They had flat bottoms and their fills were soft, wet, dark brown loam or grey silt (Section W¹¹). F1126 and F1096 were both dated post-250, and F1169, while producing no datable pottery, contained biological remains remarkably similar to those in F17 which was dated post-350 (see p 121).

Wells

Two definite stone-lined wells (F1050 and F1046) were in the area between F1049 and F1031 (see Plan and Sections E, F, Fig 19). F1050 was part of the row of features close to the small ditch F1049. It was smaller and shallower than the well in Area I (F43) with only a small construction pit (L1050/5), hardly larger than the outside diameter of the stone lining, and containing dark brown gravelly clay. The stones were local Corallian ragstone and were not consistent in size, apparently having simply been piled up in a circle inside the construction trench, splaying out somewhat towards the top. The bottom was about 0.25 m below water level at the time of excavation (August). The well contained four layers: wet darkish grey clayey gravel (L1050/4); clean yellowish gravel (L1050/3); sticky brown clay and gravel (L1050/2); and solid brown slightly gravelly clay (L1050/1). The pottery (from L1050/2) was not closely datable but was 3rd or 4th century.

The other well (F1046) was 30.00 m south-west of F1050. It was slightly deeper but less well preserved, having been robbed almost to water level (about 0.50 m above the bottom of the well in this case). It was at the bottom of a large robbing pit (2.60 m wide) filled with brown gravelly-clayey loam which produced no finds (L1046/1), and had been constructed in the same way as F1050. The bottom layer of the well was wet yellow gravel 0.40 m thick (L1046/3), above which was a layer of wet dark grey organic silt (L1046/2). Pottery was recovered only from this layer but was not closely datable. The robbing pit (F1046/1) overlapped another pit (F1047) dated to post-350, but it was impossible to tell which, if either, was later than the other (Section F, Fig 19).

Corndriers

15 m south-east of F1046 cutting the south end of F1045 was a stone-built T-shaped corndrier (F1002; see Plan and Sections Fig 19). Only up to two courses of stonework (Corallian limestone) had survived the scrapers and the end of one of the arms of the T had been destroyed. The stonework was roughly mortared with a pale yellow sandy-loamy friable mortar which in places survived where stones had been lost. The drier was about 3.00 m wide and 4.00 m long, orientated with the leg of the T pointing north-east. Its 'arms' were about 0.30 m wide internally while the 'leg' tapered from 1.00 m to 0.60 m. At the base of the T was a large flat stone where the fire for the drier had been concentrated. A hollow had been scooped out in the middle of the drier to a depth of 0.50 m below the lowest course of stones. It was filled with black loam with much charcoal, carbonized grain, and chaff (L1002/3; Sections A and B), and most of it was kept for analysis of the carbonized remains (see p 103f). This layer stopped at the edge of the large stone at the base of the T. Overlying both the stone and L1002/3 at this point was a patch of half-fired clay, still in a plastic state. From the edge of this to the further edge of the central hollow, overlying L1002/3, was a layer of dark brown loam and charcoal (L1002/3; Sections A and B). Embedded in it was a fairly large, flat, pitched stone just inside the south-east side of the drier. The top layer was virtually topsoil (L1002/1). Pottery datable to post-350 was recovered from L1002/1 and L1002/2, but it cannot be regarded as very securely stratified within the corndrier.

Another possible corndrier (F1058; see Plan and Sections Fig 19) was 140 m south-west of F1002 near ditch F1066, and cutting an Iron Age pit (F1059). It was 1.00 m wide and 3.20 m long, orientated south-west to north-east. It consisted of a long shallow (0.25 m) hollow filled with layers of brown clayey loam with charcoal flecks (L1058/5), dark brown sandy loam with charcoal (L1058/4), and dark brown to black clay (L1058/3; Section D). Lumps of gravel concretion and some limestone were laid or pitched in these layers to give a rough cobbled surface. At the south-west end was a roughly semicircular hearth made of a few flat pieces of limestone providing a fairly even, slightly concave surface part of which consisted of the end of the clayey layer (L1058/3; Section C). At the other end the surface of concretions ended with one large, flat pillow-shaped lump above the end of the deeper part of the hollow. Other lumps of concretion, possibly dislodged, and a small slot about 1.00 m long at right-angles to the main structure, were further to the north-east. The slot contained dirty grey-brown gravel (L1058/6; Section D). It was not clearly connected with the main structure. All the stones and concretions had been heated pink or a dark purplish-pink. The hearth at the south-west end was filled with slightly gravelly black loam and charcoal with a few stones (L1058/2) and the whole feature was overlain by a layer of black loam and charcoal (L1058/1; Sections C and D). These two layers contained carbonized grain and were almost entirely saved for analysis. Unfortunately, however, the sacks containing the samples were not immediately removed and (inevitably) were unwittingly destroyed by the scrapers next morning. No useful dating evidence was recovered, though a few sherds showed it to be Roman.

An area of burning about half way between Areas I and II may have been another corndrier, but only a trace of it had survived the removal of topsoil.

Area III: Post-Roman and undated features (Site plan Fig 3)

Ridge and furrow

No Saxon or medieval structures were found on the site and the only probably medieval features were a number of furrows running roughly north-south on the same alignment as those in Area II (see p 13). They were clearly visible on the air photograph in the area north of ditch F1049, but most had disappeared with the stripped topsoil. One surviving west of the main group (F1034) contained grey-brown rather gravelly-clayey loam. The spacing of this furrow and those excavated in Area II was double the spacing of the furrows further east. A few sherds of medieval pottery and one or two glazed tiles were found unstratified, but no other features were found.

Post-medieval features

A number of features excavated or observed on the air photograph could be shown to be post-medieval. Ditches 11 and 12 in Area I continued westwards only for about 20.00 m. West of them, near the droveway, an area of amorphous undated features (F1027) included a 19th or 20th century pit containing much china. Apart from these a number of archaeologically undated ditches appear on Rocque's map of Berkshire (1761) and the Cumnor Enclosure map (1814): F1003 ran east-west across the main part of the site; F1140 ran north-south just south of where the modern farm track crossed the Roman droveway; and F1136, the southernmost feature on the site, ran south-west to north-east turning at right-angles to the north-west 45 m from the edge of the site. In addition to these there was a ditch running along the south-eastern side of the modern farm track turning southwards (F1084) near Lower Whitley Farm, presumably to run along the field boundary which preceded the present road to the farm. Only F1003 and F1084 were observed in section. F1003 was about 2.50 m wide and was shallow with a flat bottom, filled with dark brown gravelly loam, indistinguishable from the fill of the Roman droveway ditches. It produced no modern pottery, only a few abraded Roman sherds. F1084 was about 1.10 m deep, about 2.00 m wide with a U-shaped profile.

Undated features

Many features were completely undatable either by analogy, finds, or historical record. Most were pits which were observed and surveyed but not excavated. In the southern part of the site were F1143, F1144, F1145, F1146, F1147, F1148, F1149, F1150, F1151, F1139, and F1153, which contained stone and could have been a well. Beside the western droveway ditch just north of F1003, Pit 1016 was 1.20 m deep, 1.70 m wide, U-shaped with steep sides, and contained layers of grey silty gravel, greenish-grey clay, and brown gravelly clay, but no finds. In the easternmost part of the area observed, just south of the possible continuation of the droveway, were six pits (F1088, F1089, F1091, F1092, F1093, and F1155) and a short length of a small gully running east-west (F1090). Roughly 250 m north of this in the alluvial floodplain were three widely spaced isolated pits (F1123, F1124,

F1185). In the middle of the site on the eastern side of the droveway was a large complex of pits (F1027). A machine trench was kindly dug through this by Mr Howse, the farmer. One pit was modern, but the rest merely formed a series of shallow undated scoops dug about 0.50 m into the gravel, and filled with wet, sticky dark grey-brown clay. The group included two areas of burning, one at its northern end and the other on its south-west side.

A number of undatable gullies and ditches were also found. These included F1128, F1129, F1130, F1131, and F1132 in the machine trial trench south-east of the droveway. All were small, U-shaped, and contained brown clayey loam.

Finds: The Iron Age pottery
by George Lambrick

1275 sherds of Iron Age pottery, weighing 354 oz, were found at Farmoor, but these made up very few reasonable groups, since most Iron Age features produced very little material. The pottery was considered in terms of its fabric, form, decoration, finish, and firing.

Fabric

Despite the smallness of the sample, a statistical analysis of the fabrics was undertaken, largely as an experiment to see whether it could add anything to the meagre information supplied by the forms. The fabrics were divided according to the types of predominant inclusion: *A* representing sand and mineral grit; *B* shell; *AB* a mixture of sand, calcareous grit, and shell; *C* flint; *D* ochreous red inclusions, probably clay pellets; *E* vegetable matter; and *F* calcareous grit. Fabrics *A, B, AB*, and *F* were subdivided according to the fineness of the inclusions; thus *B1* is a very fine shelly ware, while *B3* is a very coarse, rough fabric. Only one purely flint-tempered sherd was found, and both the *C* and *D* fabrics otherwise represent variations of the other main fabrics where flint or ochreous inclusions occur; *C* and *D* have thus mostly been used as prefixes to the main fabric types. A more detailed description of each fabric is given in Table 1.

The division of the fabrics was based on three assumptions. The first was that the types of tempering used were not mutually exclusive, though there is a clear general distinction between sandy and shelly fabrics. Fabric *AB* tends to include sherds which do not clearly belong to *A* or *B* but nevertheless was probably a fabric in its own right. The second assumption was that fineness or coarseness was only controlled by selecting or producing fine tempering for fine pottery: the coarse pottery conversely did not contain only coarse tempering. Thirdly it was assumed that the quantity of tempering was not carefully controlled: this was not established with any certainty, but no obvious variations were detected. All three assumptions were based on the idea that relatively primitive hand-made Iron Age pottery was unlikely to have required or used very carefully sorted material. Although the classification of the pottery was based on these assumptions, the system was sufficiently flexible for them to be modified or discarded on the basis of objective observation as the analysis progressed. The classification is more elaborate than that used for Ashville (De Roche in Parrington 1978, 41) where a twofold division between shell and calcareous grit (Fabric 1), and quartz and sand (Fabric 2) was used. Although these correspond roughly with Farmoor Fabrics *B, F, ?AB;*

and *A*, the correlation is not close, and it is particularly blurred in the fairly abundant wares with mixed tempering.

The quantities of each fabric present in a feature were measured both by sherd count and by weight. The actual analysis of the results was based only on the main fabric types (*A* + *F, B*, and *AB*) since the samples were statistically too small for a more complicated analysis using the more precise divisions. *F* was only classified separately from *A* at a later stage; little of it was recovered however, and it seems reasonable to have treated it as though it were a coarse version of *A*. Particularly distinctive fabrics, on the other hand, were separated out, as in the case of *A1, AB1*, and *DB*, and in addition the *D* fabrics were considered both separately and together with their predominant fabric types. An attempt was also made at a division between coarse and fine wares.

Having measured the pottery both by weight and sherd number, it seemed worthwhile to compare the percentages of the fabrics in each feature given by the two methods.

The results are set out in Fig 20: all the percentages are given by individual features or phases within features rather than by whole complexes or groups of feature. This was originally done so that individual pits in

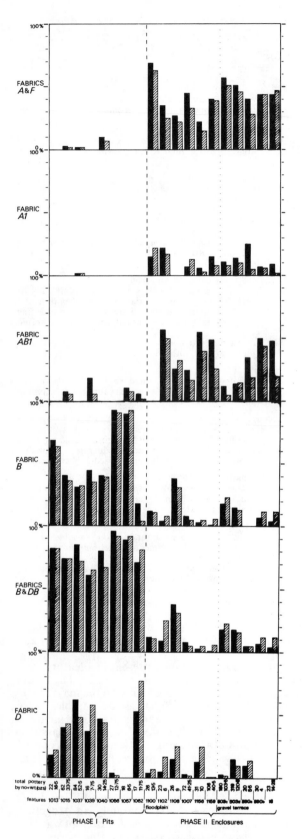

Fig 20   Proportions of Iron Age pottery fabrics

limited period of occupation (see p 000) would justify combining for each complex the results from individual features, even where they were shown stratigraphically not to be contemporary. Nevertheless the results are revealing, since they show quite marked variations between contemporary features, and also help to show which fabrics are chronologically most diagnostic.

The broader comparison between fine and coarse fabrics was attempted on the basis of groups of features to show the basic trends.

The results of the fabric analysis given in Fig 20 reveal a clear change from mostly shell-tempered pottery in the group of pits on the gravel terrace (Phase I) to more sandy wares in the enclosures on both the terrace and the floodplain (Phase II). This break was apparent in the proportions of the shelly (B), sandy (A), and ochreous (D) fabrics. The ochreous shelly wares (DB) were particularly characteristic of the pit group; the fine black sandy ware ($A1$) was almost equally distinctive for the enclosure group. $AB1$, the fine shelly or gritty equivalent of $A1$, was also characteristic of the enclosure group, but AB as a whole seemed totally undiagnostic. $AB2$ may thus not have been a distinct fabric, or alternatively may have been an all-purpose ware, produced throughout the Iron Age period on the site, for which little effort was made to control the fabric: there was certainly a fairly wide, undifferentiated variation in the tempering of AB.

Within the two broad groups there were no distinct changes, but two minor variations are worth observing: firstly, the exceptional figures for fabrics B and D in Pits 1056 and 1057; secondly, the higher proportion of $AB1$ in the floodplain enclosures. These may reflect chronological differences, but it should be noted that such fabric changes are not apparent from a comparison of individual features.

All the raw materials for the pottery were readily available on or near the site. The shell tempering was usually from the fossil oyster (*Gryphea*) common in the gravel, but in its fine form may also have been provided by snails or mussels; the sand present in the gravel was already naturally graded in very fine to very coarse layers; sand mixed with some shell, also already graded, could also have come from the gravel or from exposed Corallian beds further away on Cumnor or Wytham Hills; other calcareous grit and flints occur with the sand in the gravel; clay pellets could easily have been made. Clay for the body of the pots was also available from various sources: the natural soil covering the gravel was basically clay; the old river channel contained clay layers; the Oxford clay surfaces in a reasonably weathered form at the bottom of the nearby hills; and further up the hills Kimmeridge clay would have been available. The alluvial clay deposits in the old river channel were of interest since they contained almost enough sand, shell, and other calcareous grit to be ready-tempered, and an experimental firing of this with no extra inclusions produced a very passable version of $AB1$. The material actually used was post-Iron Age, but there seems little reason to doubt that similar deposits would have been available in the Iron Age.

No obviously imported pottery was found, the most uncharacteristic sherd being the solitary flint-tempered example which had no other diagnostic features. Since flint was present in the gravel this could have been produced on the site, but if so it is difficult to explain why more such sherds were not found, and superficially the flint inclusions did not look like flint from the gravel.

The sorting of the inclusions used was variable, but in most cases the tempering was probably already graded, and for the AB fabrics may already have been mixed as well. On the whole manual sorting, grading, and mixing

particular could be tested to see whether they all fell within one group. In the case of the floodplain enclosures, however, the biological evidence for a very

36

could thus have been avoided for the sandy wares, requiring only the extraction of the odd over-large grit or pebble, or the occasional addition of clay pellets or flint. Shell for the *B* fabrics, on the other hand, would have had to be sorted out from the gravel and probably crushed. Not surprisingly there was a very wide overall gradation in the shelly fabrics with no clear divisions in the range from fine to coarse; but at the same time the fine shell tempering was usually of a fairly consistent grade in any one sherd.

The comparison between fine and coarse wares in the major groups is very problematic, partly because of the large differences between measuring by weight and sherd number, and partly because the division is itself subjective since some fabrics such as *B2* or *A3* could be assigned to either group. It is thus impossible to quantify the trend, though subjectively it seemed that the pottery from the enclosure phase, dominated by the sandy fabrics, was generally finer than the more shelly pottery of the pits of Phase I.

The comparison of measuring by weight and by sherd number made no difference to the basic results of the analysis, but one revealing aspect concerned the consistency in the degree of variation between the figures. The variations in the *D* fabrics, for example, were much more erratic than those of the *B* fabrics. Since the *D* classification covered all the basic fabric types whereas the *B* fabrics formed possibly one of the more homogeneous basic groups, it seems reasonable to suggest that the degree of consistency in the variations may reflect the 'purity' or 'genuineness' of the fabrics.

Form

There was an insufficient number of sherds of recognizable form for any statistical analysis to be possible. Forms were therefore considered simply in terms of their presence or absence from the main phases or features. The forms were not classified on an internal system as the fabrics were, but were correlated with the Ashville form series (De Roche in Parrington 1978, 41). Only the illustrated sherds (which represent the bulk of the pottery of recognizable form) have been classified.

The pottery from the Phase I pits included expanded rims (Nos 1, 4, and 17; Ashville form A0), shouldered vessels (Nos 8, 18, 20, etc; form B1), angular jars (Nos 3, 25, 29, etc; form C1), and barrel jars (Nos 16 and 19; form B3). Globular bowls (form D0) were absent as were bead and everted rims. In Phase II angular and shouldered vessels were absent, as were expanded (as opposed to thickened) rims. Barrel jars (Nos 46, 47, 51, 76, 81, 86, 106, etc), globular bowl rims (Nos 39, 43, 44, 55, 95, 108, etc) and bulbous jars (Nos 94 and 97; form D0) were the chief forms present. Bead and everted rims were common and thickened rims (Nos 101, 102; form A0) were also present. Apart from the barrel jar forms no distinct types were present in both groups. Only one lug handle was found (not illustrated, F1169).

Decoration

The decoration of pottery from the pits was confined to occasional finger impressions on rims (Nos 1 and 17) and shoulders (Nos 18, 24, and 38). Except for No 36 these did not occur in the enclosure features where the only decoration was impressed lines in fine fabrics (Nos 56, 59, 50, 51, 82/83, and 88). These, however, did not occur in

the floodplain enclosures. Decoration in general was very sparse, nearly all the examples being illustrated.

Finish

The coarse fabrics were seldom finished with any care, normally only being wiped or partly smoothed. The fairly coarse sandy fabric *A3* was sometimes carefully smoothed and even burnished to give a surface texture like *A1*. The fine fabrics usually had smoothed surfaces, especially on the exterior, which in the case of *A1* was usually burnished or slightly polished. This applied also to the fine shelly fabrics *B1* of the angular bowls from the pits. Hematite coating was entirely absent.

Potting techniques

The preparation of the clay has already been partly discussed under 'Fabric'. The pottery itself was entirely hand-made, but on the whole too little had survived of any one pot to tell how well made it was. Colours were variable: the coarse shelly wares of the pit group often fell within reddish hues, and this was less obvious among the enclosure features where greys and browns became more common. There was no sign of very careful control of firing conditions and colour, however, except for the fine sandy black ware, *A1*, where there is evidence for a fairly well controlled use of reducing conditions, producing pottery of a fairly uniform dark grey to black colour (eg No 97). Even so, mistakes apparently occurred, such as with No 60 where part of the pot had been oxidized to a bright orange colour.

Discussion

Dating: comparisons with other material

The two main groups of pottery from the pit and enclosure phases clearly date from two separate periods. The very marked separation between them in terms of fabric, form, and decoration is sufficient to suggest a decisive break in the occupation of the site. The most important evidence for this is that of the fabrics and without it the difference would have been less clear, or in the case of some pits almost totally lacking. For dating these phases, comparisons with other material is necessary, and the results of this must then be compared with the direct evidence of the few radiocarbon dates available (see p 38).

On ceramic grounds the pits may be placed in the early Iron Age dating from around 550 to 300 BC. The pottery is fairly similar to the published material from the early pits at Ashville (De Roche in Parrington 1978, 47) and Mount Farm (Myres 1937, 28-34, figs 6, 7, and 8) and to a lesser extent with other groups such as some of the pottery from Stanton Harcourt, though there the fine ware angular jars were absent (Hamlin 1966, 20). Harding argues for what might be termed a 'pre-angular' phase of pottery (Harding 1972, 73-85), but supporting evidence for this was lacking at Ashville, where the first reasonably good stratified sequence of pottery in the area was recovered. Possibly the Ashville sequence begins at the period of overlap between Harding's pre-angular and angular forms, but the same sort of mixture of the two is also apparent for other sites, notably with the published material from Mount Farm (Myres 1937, 28-34 and figs 6, 7, and 8) — which is one of the sites on which Harding bases his argument (Harding 1972, 85) — and now Farmoor. At Farmoor the different fabric proportions in Pits 1056 and 1057 combined with the solitary expanded rim with finger tipping (No 1) may seem to support Harding's idea, but the evidence is exceedingly flimsy and in any case relies on parallels such as from Mount Farm where sherds similar to this were found in association with angular forms (eg Pit λ Nos 5, 6, and 16). If the chronological difference between the pre-angular and angular forms is thus not reliable, no closer date than the broad range already given can be established from the ceramic evidence alone.

The very clear break between the Phase I and Phase II pottery is consistent with the evidence from Ashville (De Roche in Parrington 1978, Table IV) and elsewhere (Harding 1972, 97-98). Harding also distinguishes between the introduction of 'smooth dark ware', which he places in the early 3rd century, and the appearance of curvilinear decoration from the late 3rd century (Harding 1972, 97 and 103). This distinction may be reflected at Farmoor in the different siting of enclosures on the floodplain and the gravel terrace, and by slight differences in the proportions of fabric *ABI* (Fig 20), but this is not supported by any stratigraphic sequence, nor by any clearer change in the fabrics, and the radiocarbon dates suggest the opposite. As a group the Phase II material compares best in both form and fabric to the pottery from Cassington, which Harding uses as the basis for defining the types current in the 'post-angular' phase (Harding 1972, 97-102), but absolute dating remains extremely difficult on the basis of the pottery alone: Harding's sequence relies on typology and comparison with pottery and metalwork from other regions, while the Ashville sequence is not at all clearly dated by some very problematic radiocarbon dates (Parrington 1978, 39). Furthermore Harding's division of the middle Iron Age between the initial introduction of 'smooth dark ware' and the later appearance of curvilinear decoration is a difficult distinction to use: the paucity of decoration in the groups where it occurred at Ashville and Farmoor suggests that its mere absence is not a sufficient criterion for suggesting an earlier date. As Harding points out, the globular bowls on which this decoration most commonly occurs are not exclusively associated with it and may date from the beginning of the phase, making the distinction even less useful (Harding 1972, 105). Once again dating based only on the pottery is thus tenuous and covers a wide period, from the beginning of the 3rd century or earlier to the end of the 2nd or even into the 1st, though it must stop short of the widespread use of Belgic forms.

Dating: the radiocarbon dates

Clearly the accurate dating of Iron Age pottery on purely stylistic grounds remains very difficult in the Oxford area, despite the work on typology and the excavation of a site with a stratified sequence of groups. The broad outline of three basic periods, the old A, B, and C, remains fixed, but within these the subdivisions are still fairly fluid, and the whole sequence needs to be tied to an absolute time scale. The Ashville radiocarbon results were unfortunately inconsistent, and are difficult to use

with any confidence, and it is therefore important that the Farmoor dates should be carefully assessed.

Unfortunately there are again problems with the radiocarbon dating (see Appendix VI). Two of the samples submitted were by no means ideal. There was insufficient bone from most of the Phase I pits to produce reliable dates, and in retrospect it may in particular have been a mistake to choose the antler from Pit 1053, both because a single bone may be less reliable than a group (especially perhaps antler because of the possible effects of its short growing life), and because this pit did not produce a good group of pottery (only eleven sherds, though these were consistent with the early pottery). The sample from F1007, as Mr Otlet points out, was small and the charcoal used could have come from the centre of an old tree. A general short-coming of the samples is that the number of samples submitted was too small to provide internal cross-checks as well as a reasonable spread over different features and periods.

The two samples which did not show particular problems (from F1159 and F528) are the two which provide dates most in agreement with the currently accepted stylistic dating for pottery in the region. They suggest that the Area II complex was earlier than at least group 3 of the floodplain enclosures; the ceramic evidence to the contrary (see above) is only very flimsy and on these grounds may reasonably be dismissed. The date around the end of the 3rd century BC is reasonable for the appearance of curvilinear decoration.

The samples from F1007 and F1053, if the dating and the pottery associations were to be relied upon, would clearly create serious problems for the currently accepted chronology of Iron Age pottery, actually reversing the present sequence. The dates cannot be dismissed out of hand, but the problems connected with them must be recognized, and it must be remembered that at least the basic chronology of Iron Age pottery styles has been confirmed by the stratigraphic sequence at Ashville (De Roche in Parrington 1978, 40).

The results are therefore partly inconclusive, and it must be hoped that a more extensive and reliable series of interconnected samples can be dated from a site in the area which produces a better range of large pottery groups.

The fabric analysis

Chronology and dating
The clear distinction in the fabric types between Phase I and Phase II reflects a common change apparent also at other sites in the area. The contrast has been noted before, for example at City Farm and Cassington (Harding in Case *et al* 1964/5, 80; Harding 1972, 98), but until recently no attempt had been made to quantify the changes. Both the two-tier classification at Ashville (De Roche in Parrington 1978, 41 and Table IV) and the rather more elaborate classification at Farmoor show that the change is very marked indeed. The clarity of this division is useful because it establishes the possibility of broadly dating groups on the basis of fabric when insufficient information is forthcoming from other attributes.

Pottery production
The analysis has also highlighted various considerations concerning the manufacture and distribution of the

pottery. The ubiquitous, heterogeneous *AB2* fabric, for example, seems likely to have been made very locally, perhaps not by specialist craftsmen. This possibility might also be suggested by its not noticeably being used in any distinctive (or perhaps fashionable?) form, but often for the apparently equally ubiquitous barrel jar. By contrast the quality of the homogeneous fine wares, particularly the burnished *A1* and *B1* fabrics, suggests, together with their associated forms, a more specialized and perhaps not so local type of production. The persistence of *AB2* and of barrel jars may thus not be any indication of cultural continuity, but merely of what remained locally most convenient and useful, quite separate from any cultural influence. It should be remembered also that while *AB2* and barrel jars provide the aptest illustration of the point, other forms and fabrics would obviously not be excluded from this type of local manufacture.

Thus while it was emphasized that all the materials for the pottery were available on the site, it is most unlikely that all the pottery was made there, if indeed any of it was. It is extremely difficult to define more closely the localization of production until more analysis is done elsewhere on a detailed level. Already the contrasting abundance of flint-tempered material at Appleford (De Roche in Hinchliffe forthcoming) in contrast to its paucity at Ashville and Farmoor is indicative, but much more information is required from other sites before any conclusions can be drawn.

Outside contacts

Connected with this is the problem of trying to define areas of local contact and trade. This is possibly even more difficult to solve since the distribution of fine wares may reflect the economic status of settlements, just as the coarse wares may reflect the extent of local geological strata. In the case of Phase I at Farmoor, for example, the absence of hematite-coated wares which were found at Frilford (and in small quantities at Ashville) may reflect the particular status of the Frilford site rather than the absence of contacts over the Corallian scarp. Similarly the strong superficial similarity between the Cassington City Farm material and that from Farmoor Phase II cannot be used to demonstrate a link between the two sites, especially in the absence of more detailed analyses; however pleasing it might be to demonstrate a connection between Farmoor and Cassington via a river crossing at Swinford (see p 6 and Fig 1) it is not possible at present, and, in view of the extent of the gravels and their likely influence on the coarse wares, it may never be.

Analysis technique

The use of different units of measurement in the analysis was an interesting exercise even though it did not produce very useful results. The variation between the two methods was not at all consistent even for particular fabrics. The most serious distortions were among small samples and the lighter fabrics, but were by no means confined to them: compare for example the figures shown in Fig 20 for fabrics *B* and *B + DB* in F1037 and F1015 (containing 84 and 62 sherds respectively). Nevertheless all the variations fell well inside both the differences between the two main phases, and even those between contemporary features (eg F1156 and F1159). The two methods were thus equally valid in this case, and neither seemed more accurate. The Farmoor material was not ideal for the comparison, however, and the methods could only be assessed properly on a well stratified site occupied for long periods.

The value of one form of analysis over another for Iron Age pottery is thus doubtful, but the basic quantification of fabric types does remain a valuable source of information, even, or indeed particularly, where such small groups are recovered. It would have been impossible to demonstrate convincingly that the pottery from the Phase I pits made up one group on the basis of form and decoration alone, and it is clearly better to try to quantify the differences in fabric type, and show which fabrics seem diagnostic, than it is to state baldly without substantiation that such differences exist. Finally there is perhaps an inherent objective value in using information from every sherd excavated rather than a few selected for their particular characteristics.

Catalogue of illustrated sherds

The illustrated sherds have been arranged in the following manner: 1-33 Phase I pits (Fig 21); 34-109 Phase II enclosures and associated features (Figs 21, 22, 23). For the phasing see p 65 - 72. The sherds are given in order of fabric (see Table 1) within each feature, and the features are arranged, for want of any better order, by decreasing proportions of fabrics *DB+B*. To each description is appended first the fabric code, and second, where possible, the Ashville form code (De Roche in Parrington 1978, 41). The quoted parallels relate chiefly to form and are based on published drawings; the fabrics may not be the same, though where they were clearly different possible parallels have mostly been omitted.

> D = Diameter
> I = Interior
> E = Exterior
> Bk = Break

Pottery from the Phase I pits
(Fig 21; 1-33)

F1056

1 Angle and D uncertain. E hard slightly lumpy surface roughly smoothed, few protruding inclusions; dark pinkish-grey. I as E, yellowish buff. Bk hard with coarse fossil shell inclusions and a few coarse mineral grits; pinkish-red. *B3*; A1 (cf Myres 1937, 31 and fig 7 λ 5)

F1053

2 D *c* 90 mm. E/I hardish and smooth (I slightly burnished) much very fine shell visible; dark brown. Bk hard with fine shell; dark brown-black. *B1*; M (cf Harding 1972, 156 and pl 50 P, Q)

3 D uncertain (? *c* 220 mm). Fabric and colour as 2, though slightly thicker, burnished and slightly less shell. *B1*; C2 (cf Harding 1972, 156 and pl 51)

4 D uncertain (? *c* 100 mm). E/I hardish and smooth with medium to fine shell visible; E brownish-buff; I black. Bk hard with medium to fine shell; black. *B2*; A3 (cf Hamlin 1966, 18 and fig 7, No 35)

5 D uncertain (? *c* 110 mm). E softish and lumpy with much fine and some coarse shell visible on bottom. Bottom brownish-red, side blackened red. I as E but with less shell visible, orangish-red. Bk softish with fine shell ochreous inclusions; black. *DB3*; M

F1057

6 D uncertain. E/I hardish and smoothed but lumpy with some medium shell visible, dark brownish-grey. Bk hardish with medium shell, dark grey. *B2*; M

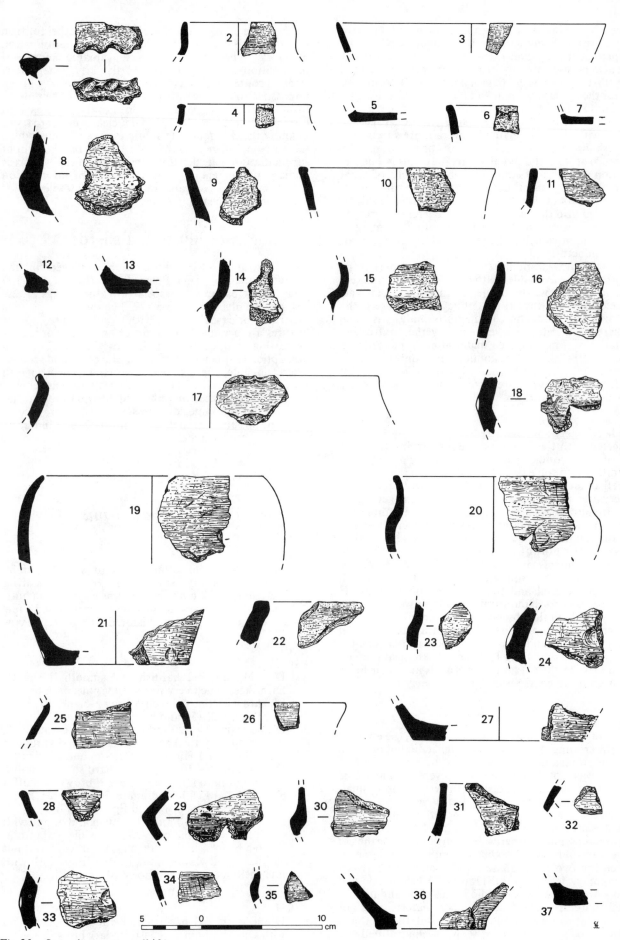

Fig 21   Iron Age pottery (1/3)

F1037

7 D c 110 mm. E/I softish, bottom lumpy, side smoothed, much medium shell visible; E bottom dark brownish-grey, side brownish-red; I black. Bk softish with some medium shell, black. *B2*; M

8 D uncertain. E hardish and rough with fine to coarse shell and some grit protruding; dark grey. I hardish, rough and lumpy with few visible inclusions; lightish grey coating. Bk hardish and coarser with much fine to coarse shell and some grit; dark grey-black. *A B2*; B1

9 Angle and D uncertain. E/I hardish, lumpy and smeared, medium shell, very few quartzitic grits and ochreous inclusions; reddish grey-brown. Bk hardish with medium shell, ochreous inclusions, very little grit; dark brownish-grey. *DB2;* C0

10 D c 16 mm. E softish and uneven with a few small vertical striations and with some medium shell and pitted ochreous inclusions; pinkish-grey/brown. I as E but more lumpy and without striations; black. Bk hardish with medium shell and ochreous inclusions; dark grey. *DB2*; C0 (cf Harding 1972, 157 and pl 152 B)

11 D uncertain. E/I hardish and smooth (E slightly burnished, I more uneven) some medium shell and ochreous inclusions visible; dark greyish-brown with red tinge internally. Bk hard with some medium shell and ochreous inclusions; dark grey. *DB2*; M

12 D uncertain. E softish and uneven with medium shell and some ochreous inclusions visible; pinkish-light buff. I missing. Bk softish and friable with much fine to coarse shell and some ochreous inclusions; dark grey. *DB3*; M

13 D c 140 mm. E/I hardish and smoothed (though E bottom worn and pitted) some medium shell and grit visible; dark reddish-brown/grey. Bk hard with medium to very coarse fossil shell (one piece 15 mm long), some mineral grit and ochreous inclusions; dark grey/brown. *DAB2*; M

14 Angle and D uncertain. E/I hardish roughly smoothed tending to flake, medium shell and small ochreous inclusions visible; E black; I buff-light grey. Bk friable, slightly sandy and very coarse with much medium to coarse shell, a few mineral grits and some ochreous inclusions; dark grey-brownish buff. *DAB2*; B1

15 Angle and D uncertain. E hardish, worn and slightly rough with small grits and some fine to medium shell; dark grey-buff with dark buff-red patches where most abraded. I as E but pitted with ochreous inclusions; dark pinkish buff-grey. Bk hardish with medium shell, some grit (including small pebble 7 mm long) and ochreous inclusions; dark grey. *DAB2*: B1/C0

F1040

16 D uncertain. E/I softish and uneven slightly smeared or smoothed, medium and some coarse fossil shell, very little mineral grit and ochreous inclusions; buff to dark grey. Bk hardish with medium to coarse fossil shell and very little grit and ochreous inclusions. *B3* (or *DAB2*); B3 (or B2) (cf Hamlin 1966, 20 and fig 7, No 65)

17 Angle and D uncertain (? c 280 mm). E/I hard and fairly rough with a few grass and seed impressions and smearing marks, fine to coarse shell with very little grit; buff to dark grey/black. Bk hard with fine to coarse fossil shell; black. *B3*; A2

18 Angle and D uncertain. E/I hardish slightly smoothed and uneven with fine to coarse fossil shell; E pinkish-buff to dark grey; I light grey coating. Bk hardish much medium to coarse fossil shell; orangish-pink. *B3*; B1

F1013

19 D 180 mm. E/I hardish smoothish but uneven and with scratches and striations, medium shell; E black, slightly sooted with pinkish-buff patch; I grey-buff to pinkish-orange. Bk hardish with some medium shell; black. *B2*; B3 (cf Fowler 1960, 34 and Fig 15, No 3)

20 D 160 mm. E/I hardish uneven but smeared and with few striations, some medium shell and grit; orangish-buff to red-buff. Bk hard with medium to coarse fossil shell and many angular grey grits; mostly red-buff but with dark grey core in one place. *A B2*; B0 (cf Avery *et al* 1967, 281, 283 and fig 29, No 133; 275, 280 and fig 27, No 111)

21 D c 120 mm. E hardish moderately smooth but uneven with small scratches, coarse shell; brown-buff to dark brown. I as E but rougher and with very small pitted ochreous inclusions; grey to dark pinkish-grey. Bk hard but friable with coarse shell and some grit; dark grey. *DAB2*; M

F1015

22 D uncertain. Softish with medium shell throughout, surfaces smooth but uneven; buff to grey-brown throughout. *B2*; M

23 Angle and D uncertain. E/I softish fairly smooth but uneven with fine to medium shell; E orangish-buff to black; I black. Bk softish with fine to medium shell; black. *B2*; B1

24 Angle and D uncertain. E softish moderately smooth but uneven and with protruding medium shell and grit; buff to reddish orange-buff. I softish and lumpy with some shell and ochreous inclusions; pinkish-buff. Bk softish with medium shell and grit and some ochreous inclusions; reddish orange-buff. *DAB2*; B1

F1039

25 Angle and D uncertain. E/I hard smooth (E burnished) with fine shell and ochreous inclusions, some scratches; dark brown. Bk hard fine texture with fine shell and minute ochreous inclusions; dark grey core with orange to dark brown edges. *DB1*; C2

26 D c 140 mm. E/I hard smooth slightly burnished (but abraded) with fine shell and ochreous inclusions; dark brown. Bk hard with fine shell and ochreous inclusions; dark grey. *DB1*; C2

27 D 140 mm. E/I hard rather rough especially on worn, pitted bottom, medium to coarse fossil shell grit and ochreous inclusions; reddish buff-brown. Bk hard, coarse shell and some ochreous inclusions and grit; dark grey. *DAB2*; M

28 D uncertain. E/I hardish fairly smooth but uneven with fine to medium shell; E buff to light brown; I light grey. Bk hard with fine to medium shell; dark grey. *B2*; M

F1042

29 D c 180 mm. E hard smooth slightly burnished with medium shell and finely pitted with ochreous inclusions; black. I as E but not burnished with less shell but more ochreous inclusions; pinkish-grey to dark grey. Bk hard with medium shell and ochreous inclusions; dark grey. *DB2*; C2 (cf Harding 1972, 156 and pl 50 R)

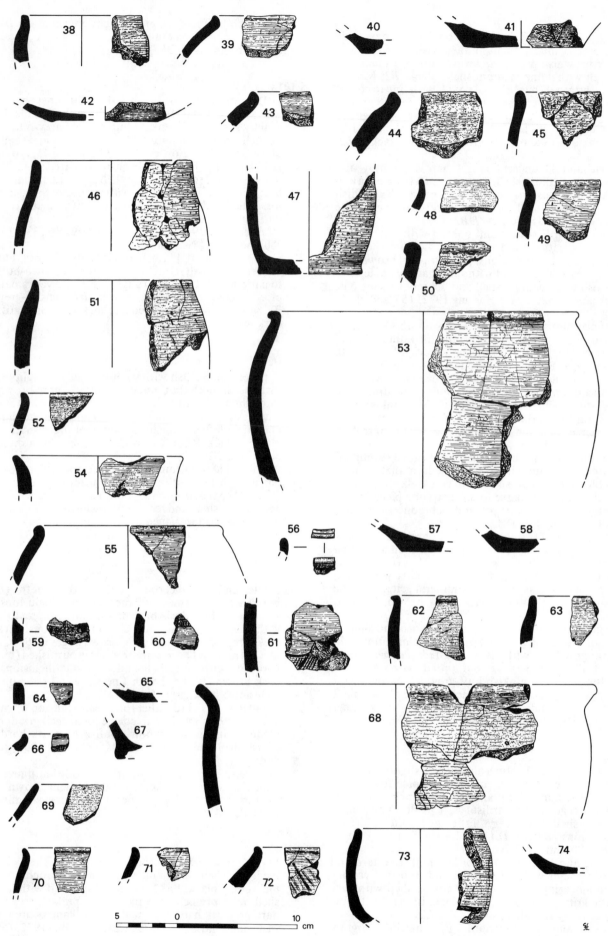

Fig 22   Iron Age pottery (1/3)

F1043

30 Angle uncertain, D *c* 170 mm. E/I hard, very smooth slightly burnished (though I and edge of shoulder abraded) fine sandy; black. Bk hard fine sandy; dark brown/grey. *A1*; C2 (cf Bradford 1942, 47 and fig 10, No 16; Head and Piggot 1944, fig 3, No 30)

31 Angle and D uncertain. E/I hardish and smooth but very uneven with much fine to medium shell and some pitted ochreous inclusions; fairly dark grey to brown. Bk hardish with much medium shell and some ochreous inclusions; dark grey. *DB2*; M

F1059

32 Angle and D uncertain. E/I hard smooth fine sandy; E orangish-brown; I black. Bk hardish fine sandy; black. *A2*; C2

33 Angle and D uncertain. E/I hard and smooth but rather uneven and with striations and small grass and seed impressions, fine sandy; red-buff to dark grey-brown. Bk hard fine sandy with very few grits; reddish-brown to dark brown. *A2*; B1

Pottery from Phase II enclosures and associated features

(Figs 21, 22, 23; 34-109)

F1011

34 D uncertain (? *c* 170 mm). E/I hard, slightly lumpy and smeared, some fine shell and very little grit; dark grey to black. Bk hard, some fine shell; mid-grey. *B1* (or *AB1*); M

35 Angle and D uncertain. As 34 but with more shell and smoother, slightly burnished surfaces. *B1* (or *AB1*); M

36 D 90 mm. E hardish, lumpy, uneven but smeared, medium to coarse shell; buff/pink to dark pinkish-grey. I as E but smoother; dark brownish-grey. Bk coarser and friable with coarse fossil shell; orangish-brown to dark brown/grey. *B3*; M (cf Richardson and Young 1951, 140 and fig 5, No 21)

37 D uncertain (? *c* 90 mm). E softish and lumpy, sandy, some medium shell, ochreous inclusions and grit; pinkish-buff to reddish-brown. I as E but inclusions not visible; sooty black. Bk softish and sandy with some medium shell and grit; darkish grey. *DAB2*; M

F1108

38 D 100 mm. E/I softish smoothed but uneven and slightly pitted, fine sandy with some fine shell; dark buff to dark brown with much soot blackening. Bk softish fine sandy with some shell; very dark grey. *AB1*; B2 (or B3) (cf Williams 1951, 20 and fig 10, No 30)

Main Enclosure Area II Phase c

(L531/1, L529/2, L529/3, L528/4)

39 D uncertain (? *c* 180 mm). E hard, smooth slightly burnished but worn, fine sandy; black. I hardish uneven and worn, fairly fine sandy; very dark grey. Bk hardish fine sandy; black. *A1*; D0

40 D uncertain. E hard, smooth slightly burnished (but bottom worn) fine sandy; side very dark grey, bottom grey-brown. I as E bottom. Bk hardish, fine sandy; mid-grey. *A1* (or *A2*); M

41 D *c* 100 mm. E hardish smooth but worn, fairly fine sandy with minute quartzitic grits on bottom; side black, bottom dark yellowish-brown to black. I hard, very smooth, very fine sandy; black. Bk hardish fine sandy; black. *A1*; M

42 D 90 mm. E/I hard, very smooth (I slightly burnished) slightly abraded, very fine sandy; dark grey to black. Bk hard fine sandy; dark grey to black. *A1*; M (cf Harding 1972, 165 and pl 65 A to D; Myres 1937, 34 and fig 8, Pl VIII, 38; Collins 1947, 18 and fig 9, No 6)

43 D uncertain. E hard, smooth slightly burnished, fine sandy; black. I hardish, much abraded, medium sandy; mid-grey. Bk hardish medium sandy; mid-grey core, orangish-red and beneath I surface. *A1* (or *A3*); D0

44 D uncertain. E/I hardish rough, very abraded though once smoothed, medium to coarse sandy; fairly dark grey. Bk softish medium to coarse sandy; reddish brown to mid-grey with band of red beneath E surface. *A3*; D0 (cf Myres 1937, 35 and fig 9, AI 14)

45 D uncertain (? *c* 200 mm). E/I softish, uneven, very abraded and pitted fairly fine sandy; mid-grey. *A3* (or *A2*); B0

46 D 130 mm. E/I hardish smooth but slightly lumpy, much medium shell; mid-grey to black. Bk hardish with much medium shell; black. *B2*; B0/B3 (cf Leeds 1931, 401 and fig 21, LT2; Case *et al* 1964/5, 78 and fig 32, No 6)

47 D 85 mm. E/I hardish smoothed but uneven or lumpy, very much medium to coarse fossil shell; E buff to dark grey-brown; I mid-grey with reddish-brown blotches. Bk hardish with much medium to coarse shell; reddish-brown to dark grey. *B3*; B2 (cf Hamlin 1966, 20 and fig 7, No 57)

48 D uncertain. E soft and dusty, smooth but worn, fine sandy with very little fine shell; pinkish-red but mid-grey where worn. I as E but more abraded; mid-grey. Bk soft fine sandy with little shell; mid-grey. *A2* (or *AB1*); M

49 D uncertain (? *c* 120 mm). E hardish, smooth, fairly fine sandy with some fine shell; light brown to dark grey. I hardish, slightly rough medium sandy with some fine shell; buff to black. Bk hardish, fine to medium sandy with fine shell; brown to dark grey. *AB1*; ? D0 (cf Harding 1972, 165 and pl 64, R)

50 D uncertain. E hardish, slightly rough medium sandy with some fine to coarse shell and fine grit; darkish pink-buff. I hardish, much abraded and pitted medium sandy with some shell; brownish-grey. Bk hardish medium sandy with some shell; mid-grey. *AB2*; M

51 D *c* 130 mm. E/I very soft, dusty, fairly smooth but uneven and pitted, fairly fine sandy with fine to medium shell; E buff-orange; I yellowish-buff to light grey. Bk soft, fine sandy with some fine to medium shell and very few grits; mid-grey. *AB2*; B3 (cf Hamlin 1966, 20 and fig 7, No 65)

52 D uncertain. E hardish, fairly smooth but worn medium sandy; black. I softish, fairly smooth but worn, medium sandy; orange-brown to grey-brown. Bk softish medium sandy with a few small flint grits; dark grey. *CA3*; M

53 D 255 mm. E hard, smooth medium to fine sandy with very few protruding flint grits, surface fire-crazed; light brown-buff to black. I hard rough rather pitted, medium to coarse sand with quartzitic grits and a few pieces of flint; orange-light brown buff. Bk hardish, coarse sandy with some grit and flint; black. *CA3*; B0/G (cf Avery *et al* 1967, 260, 274 and fig 21, No 43; Fowler 1960, 34 and fig 14, No 1)

Main Enclosure Area II Phase d

(L503/4, L503/6, L528/1, L528/2, L529/1, L529/2, L505/1)

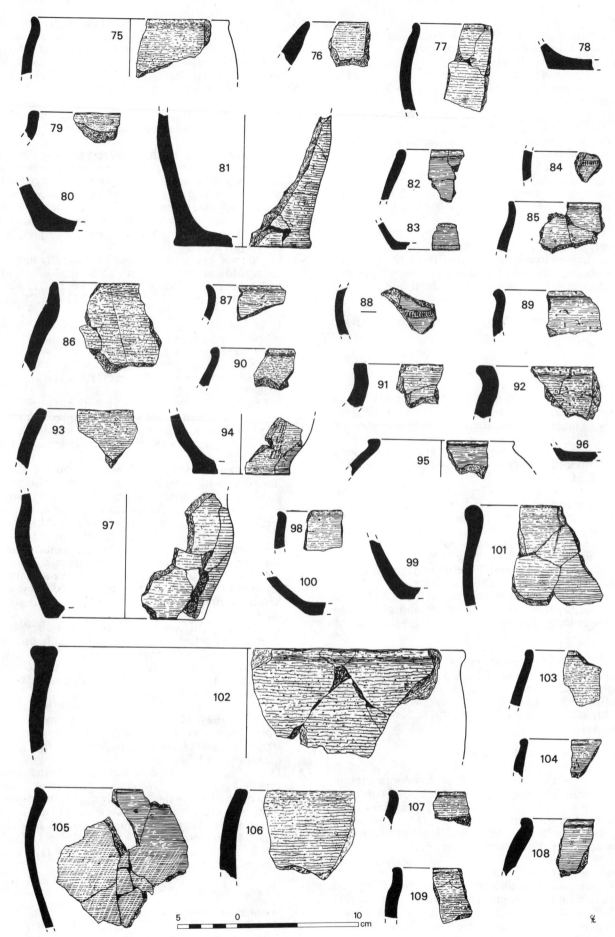

Fig 23   Iron Age pottery (1/3)

54 D uncertain (? *c* 160 mm). E/I hard, smooth slightly burnished but worn, fine sandy; black. Bk hardish, fine sandy; black. *A1*; M

55 D 160 mm. E hard, smooth burnished but worn on rim, fine sandy; black. I hardish, rough very abraded medium to fine sandy; mid to dark grey. Bk hardish medium to fine sandy; dark grey with orange-brown beneath E. *A1*; D0 (cf Harding 1972, 164 and pl 64 M)

56 D uncertain. E/I hard, smoothish but worn, fine sandy; dark grey. Bk hardish, fine sandy; black. Decorated with impressed lines on top of rim and on external face either side of small oval punch marks. *A1*; D0 (cf Bradford 1942, 58 and fig 13, No 46)

57 D uncertain. E/I hard, smooth, but slightly pitted and abraded, slightly burnished fine sandy, one flint visible; black. Bk hard fine sandy, one flint visible; black. *A1* (or *CA1*); M

58 D uncertain. E hardish, roughish medium to fine sandy with small quartzitic grits much abraded; dark grey-brown with reddish-buff patch on bottom. I hard smooth fine sandy; black. Bk hardish fine sandy; black. *A1*; M

59 D uncertain. E/I hardish, smooth but abraded, once burnished on E, fine sandy; grey brown to black. Bk softish fine sandy; grey-brown. Decorated with curved impressed lines either side of crescent-shaped punch marks. *A1*; D0 (cf Bradford and Goodchild 1939, 22 and fig 7, No 78)

60 D uncertain. E/I hard, smooth slightly burnished, fine sandy; black, but orange-buff patch on E. Bk hard, fine sandy; black. Similar type of decoration to 59. *A1*; D0

61 E/I hard, smooth, slightly worn, fine sandy; dark grey to black. Bk hard, fine sandy; dark grey to black. *A1*; M (cf Harding 1972, 167 and pl 68 B and G)

62 D uncertain. E/I hardish smooth but uneven and worn fine sandy; E orange-buff to grey-brown; I orange-pink. Bk softish fine sandy; light grey core. *A2*; ?G (cf Bradford and Goodchild 1939, 20 and fig 6, No 40)

63 D uncertain. E/I hardish, smooth fine sandy; light grey-buff to mid-grey. Bk hardish fine sandy; light grey/buff to mid-grey. *A2*; B3/B2

64 D uncertain. E/I hard, smooth (E slightly burnished, I worn), medium to fine sandy; mid-grey. Bk softish medium sandy; mid-grey core thin orange band beneath surface. *A2*; M

65 D uncertain (? *c* 90 mm). E/I hard, smooth (though I much worn) fine sandy; reddish grey-brown. Bk hardish, fine sandy; mid-grey core, orange-red to red-grey band beneath E/I. *A2*; M

66 D uncertain. E/I hard, smooth, slightly burnished fine sandy; dark grey to red-grey. Bk hardish fine sandy; mid-grey core with thin red bands beneath E/I. *A2* (or *A1*); D0

67 D uncertain. E/I hard, fairly smooth though uneven fine sandy; E red to buff; I mid-brownish grey; Bk hardish, fine sandy; brownish-grey. *A2*; M

68 D 330 mm. E softish, very abraded, coarse sandy; orange-buff or brown to darkish grey. I hard, smooth, somewhat worn but with burnishing, fine to medium sandy with one or two flints; black. Bk softish, coarse sandy with one or two flints; dark grey to black. *A3* (or *CA3*); B0/H (cf Rowley 1973, 38-9 and fig 7, No 12; *Berkshire Archaeol J* 1960, 57 and fig 1, No 1)

69 D uncertain. E/I softish, dusty medium sandy; orange-brown to mid-grey. Bk soft, dusty medium sandy; mid-grey. *A3*; B3

70 D uncertain. E hardish, smooth with worn patch, fairly fine sandy; brownish-grey. I soft, dusty and worn, medium to coarse sandy; brown-grey. *A3*; M

71 As 70, but one large flint fragment and one small pebble visible. *A3*; M

72 D uncertain. E/I hardish, medium sandy with very distinct smearing/grass impressions on E, worn and pitted; black with red patch on E. Bk softish, coarse sandy; darkish brown-grey. *A3*; B2

73 D *c* 105 mm. E/I hard, fairly smooth though uneven, fine to coarse sandy with many small quartzitic grits and very little shell; dark grey to black. Bk hard, fine to coarse sandy with quartzitic and other grit and very little shell; dark grey. *F1*; B2/J

74 D uncertain. E/I hardish, slightly rough with many medium grits; pinkish-red to brownish-buff. Bk hardish with many medium grits and a little coarse fossil shell; black or brownish buff-orange. *F1*; M

75 D *c* 165 mm. E/I hard, smooth (though slight scratches on E and pitted I), much fine to medium shell; orange-brown on rim to mid-grey brown elsewhere. Bk hard with medium shell; darkish grey-brown. *B2*; D0/B2 (cf Harding 1972, 164 and pl 63 R)

76 D uncertain. E/I hard, smooth (though I abraded) slightly uneven, fine to medium shell; dark grey to black. Bk hardish with fine to coarse shell and a little fine grit; brownish-grey red. *B3* (or *A B2*); B3

77 D uncertain. As 76 but Bk less red. *B3*; ?B2 (cf Harding 1972, 164 and pl 64 C)

78 D uncertain. As 76 and 77, but E/I softer; E mid-reddish grey-brown. Bk softer; light grey-brown. *B3*; M

79 D uncertain. E/I hardish, smooth though E much abraded, fine to medium sandy with some fine shell; black. Bk hardish, fine sandy with some fine shell; dark grey with red beneath E. *A B1*; M

80 D uncertain. E/I soft, rather dusty, roughish medium sandy with fine grit and some coarse fossil shell; E pinkish-red; I pale pinkish-grey. Bk soft medium sandy, with some large grit and coarse fossil shell; lightish grey. *A B2*; M

81 D 115 mm. E/I hardish, slightly rough, uneven and rather lumpy medium sandy with medium to coarse grit and shell; mid to dark grey-brown. Bk hardish, medium sandy with grit and shell; mid to dark grey. *A B2*; B0 (cf Harding in Case *et al* 1964, 85 and fig 34, No 31)

82/ D and complete profile uncertain. E/I hard, very
83 smooth burnished, fine sandy; black. Bk hardish medium to coarse sandy with some ochreous inclusions; deep pinkish-red. *DA1*; D0

84 Angle and D uncertain. E/I hard, fairly smooth though slightly pitted. I fine sandy with ochreous inclusions; E dark grey-brown; I mid red-brown to grey. Bk hardish fine sandy with small grit and some ochreous inclusions; mid red-brown. Decorated with impressed curving lines either side of small vertical strokes. *DA2*; D0

85 D uncertain. E/I hard, smooth (but I much pitted) fine, sandy with a little medium shell and grit and a very few ochreous inclusions; dark slightly reddish-brown to black. Bk hard sandy with medium shell and grit and ochreous inclusions; black. *DAB1*; B2

86 D uncertain. E/I softish, rough and uneven, slightly dusty coarse sandy with grit and fine to coarse shell and very small ochreous inclusions; mid-grey with yellow-brown patch on E. Bk softish coarse sandy with shell grit and some ochreous inclusions; mid-grey. *DAB2*; B3

F560

87 D uncertain. E/I hardish, slightly rough medium

sandy; E black; I yellow-grey. Bk hardish medium sandy; darkish grey. *A3*; M

F514

88 D uncertain. E/I hard, very smooth burnished, fine sandy; black. Bk hardish medium sandy; dark grey. Curvilinear impressed decoration with crescent-shaped punch marks. *A1*; D0 (cf Bradford and Goodchild 1939, 22 and fig 7, No 78)

F1100

89 D uncertain (? *c* 160 mm). E/I hard, smooth slightly burnished with fine to medium shell protruding; mid-brown to dark grey. Bk hard with medium shell; dark grey. *B2*; ? D0 (cf Harding 1972, 163 and pl 63 A)

F1107

90 D uncertain. E/I hardish, smoothish medium sandy; uniform dark grey. Bk hardish, medium sandy; buff to mid-grey. *A3* (or *A2*); D0 (cf Harding 1972, 164 and pl 64 E)

F1102

91 D uncertain. E/I hardish smoothed but uneven and lumpy with protruding medium shell; E light grey coating on pinkish-red; I darkish grey. Bk hardish with medium to coarse shell; purplish-grey to mid-grey. *B3*; B2

F1104

92 As 91 but with slightly coarser shell; E light buff; I red brown-grey. Bk dark grey. *B3*; B2 (cf Harding in Case *et al* 1964, 83 and fig 33, Nos 4, 5 and 6)

F1105

93 D uncertain. E/I softish, rough slightly dusty medium to coarse sand and some shell; brown-buff to dark grey-brown. Bk softish medium to coarse sandy with coarse fossil shell; darkish grey-brown. *AB2*; B3

F1106

94 D 80 mm. E/I hard, smooth (though some marked striations E) fine sandy; black. Bk hard fine sandy; darkish grey. *A1*; M (cf Richardson and Young 1951, 141 and fig 6, No 32; Myres 1930, 379-80, 383 and fig 5, No 16)

F1007

95 D 120 mm. E/I hard, smooth burnished fine sandy with very little fine shell; dark brown to black. Bk hard fine sandy with very little fine shell; dark grey to black. *A1* (or ?*B1*); D0/G

96 D uncertain. E/I hardish, smooth fine sandy; black. Bk hardish fine sandy; black. *A1*; M

97 D *c* 130 mm. E/I hard, smoothish though slightly pitted, fine sandy; E sooted black; I greyish brown. Bk hard fine sandy; dark grey to black. *A1*; B2 (cf Bradford and Goodchild 1939, 20 and fig 6, No 39; Harding 1972, 164 and pl 63 R; Myres 1937, 36 and fig 4 A I 13)

98 D uncertain. E/I softish, smooth but worn and dusty fine sandy; mid-brownish grey. Bk softish fine sandy; dark grey. *A2*; M

F1012

99 D uncertain. E/I softish, slightly rough uneven and pitted, fine sandy with some ochreous inclusions; E light buff to dark grey; I light buff. Bk softish, fine sandy with ochreous inclusions; black. *DA2*; M

100 D uncertain. E/I hard, smooth slightly burnished,

fine sandy with fine shell visible; E dark grey-brown; I black. Bk hardish, fine sand and shell; dark grey to black. *AB1*; M

F1009

101 D uncertain (? *c* 260 mm). E/I hard, smooth fine sandy; E yellowish-buff; I black. Bk hard, fine sandy; black. *A2*; M (cf Collins 1953, 30, 47 and fig 17, No 5)

102 D 360 mm. Two very indistinct grooves round top of rim. E/I hardish, rough uneven and slightly lumpy, fairly sandy with some fine to medium shell and many small protruding ochreous inclusions; dark grey. Bk softish, fine sand and shell with ochreous inclusions; black. *DAB1*; ?A3 (cf Hamlin 1966, 16, 18 and fig 6, Nos 8 and 32)

F590

103 Angle and D uncertain. E/I softish, roughish medium sandy with fine to medium shell; E reddish-brown; I brownish-yellow. Bk softish, medium sandy and shell; mid-brown. *AB1*; B0 (cf Harding in Case *et al* 1964, 83 and fig 33, No 10)

104 D uncertain. E/I hard, smoothish but uneven fine sandy; black. Bk hardish fine sandy with some ochreous inclusions; brick-red. *DA1*; M

105 D uncertain. E/I very hard, smooth with burnishing marks, fine sandy with one or two quartzitic grits and a few flint flakes on I; E black with pink-red patch; I black. Bk hard medium sandy with a few flint flakes. Black. *CA1*; B2 (cf Avery *et al* 1967, 260, 271 and fig 21, No 26; Case *et al* 1964, 78 and fig 32, Nos 2 and 7)

F18

106 D uncertain (? *c* 250 mm). E/I very soft, smooth but very dusty medium sandy with a little medium to coarse shell; E patchy, orange-red, light grey, grey-brown; I dark grey-brown. Bk soft, medium sandy with very little medium to coarse shell. *A3* (or *AB2*); B3 (cf Harding 1972, 162 and pl 62 H)

107 D uncertain. E/I hardish, smoothish; E sooty medium to coarse sandy with a little grit; black. Bk softish coarse sandy with one burnt flint flake; black. *AB1*; D0

F1045

108 D uncertain. E hard, very smooth burnished, fine sandy; black. I hard, slightly rough fine sandy; darkish grey. Bk hard, fine sandy; dark grey. *A1*; D0 (cf De Roche in Parrington 1978, 65 and fig 52, No 350)

109 D uncertain. E/I hardish, worn uneven fine sandy; dark grey. Bk hardish, fine sandy; pinkish grey-brown. *A2*; B2

Finds: The Roman pottery

by Janet Sanders with a section by Warwick Rodwell

Methods and results

The Roman pottery from Farmoor was recovered mostly from a series of individual features having little or no stratigraphical relationship to one another, very few containing coins. Only three groups — F3, F10, F17 — were of any size and that not large, and therefore dating evidence which has had to be gleaned from the pottery is necessarily precarious as it is based on a very few shreds from any one feature. All but four of the fragments of samian ware — from F1073, F1074, F1075, F1079 — are obviously residual and in only one of these four cases is there any evidence that it is actually indicative of date.

Most of the pottery, both fine and coarse, is probably the product of the Oxfordshire pottery industry, as one might expect from the proximity of the site to the kilns (see Fig 1). This is certainly so for the fine wares; the grey wares in the area were produced not only in the main group of kiln sites but also at a number of small ones and are unlikely to have been transported very far (Young 1977, 207-8). Importations in the early part of the Roman period are limited to the samian, a mica-dusted beaker from F1060, and a few sherds of burnished black ware which is also found in the later period. Of the late Roman colour-coated wares only four examples were not made by the Oxfordshire kilns: two fragments of Nene Valley ware from F43 and F1061 and two pieces of 'Rhenish' colour-coat from F1030 and F1096. A comparatively large amount of shell-gritted ware was imported in the late Roman period. This is a type widespread over southern central England after *c* AD 350 (Sanders 1973), made in centres probably in the Northamptonshire area. About 30% of the coarse ware in the two larger, late 4th century deposits, F3 and F17, was shell-gritted ware. There is also a coarser variety of shell-gritted pottery — Nos 82, 83 and 26 — which appears to be distributed locally in the Oxfordshire area (Brodribb *et al* 1973, 69) and to have come into circulation before the other (Brodribb *et al* 1971, 302-8, second half of 3rd century).

In setting out the report below I have followed the formula established by C J Young in his reports dealing with similar pottery from sites in the area. The sherds are therefore described in the following way: shape; texture of fabric and visible inclusions; colour (E = exterior surface, I = interior surface, Bk = core); other observations and place of manufacture and C J Young's type numbers for Oxfordshire products (Young 1977) where applicable. The pottery is listed by feature with approximate dates where possible. Reasonably well dated features are given first, in chronological order (1 - 99); the rest are given largely according to feature number (100 - 123).

Features containing Oxfordshire colour-coated sherds dated post AD 250—Illustrated: F30, F57, F1025, F1072. Not illustrated: F37, F69, F84, F1005.

Features containing shell-gritted ware dated post *c* AD 350 — Illustrated: F43, F47, F1002, F1047. Not illustrated: F1018, F1024, F83.

The samian

by Warwick Rodwell

Only the numbered sherds are illustrated (Fig 24).

F2/1 (residual)
1   Form 37 decorated. fragment, abraded. Central Gaulish, showing part of a figure of Apollo (Oswald 1936-7, type 83), which was used by various potters during the 2nd century. This sherd is probably first half of the 2nd century. Form 33, Antonine; burnt.

F10/2 (residual)
Form 33, Central Gaulish; Hadrianic or Antonine.

F11/1 (residual)
Chip, probably Central Gaulish.

F17/1 (residual)
Form 37, blurred ovolo fragment. Central Gaulish, Antonine.

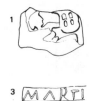
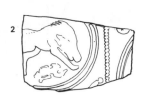

Fig 24   Samian pottery (1 and 2: 1/2; 3: 1/1)

Form 31 (2 pieces). Central Gaulish, Antonine.
Form 45 mortarium, partly worn. Central Gaulish, Antonine.

F1002/2 (residual)
Rim fragment, probably Form 18. South Gaulish, late 1st century.

F1033 (residual)
Form 31. East Gaulish, Antonine. (Very slight trace of stamp.)
Form 31R. East Gaulish, Antonine.

F1047 (residual)
Form 79 or Tg. Central Gaulish, later Antonine.

F1047/1 (residual)
Form 18. South Gaulish, Flavian.

F1071 (residual)
Form 33. Central Gaulish, Antonine.

F1073
2   Form 37, decorated fragment. Central Gaulish, showing decoration divided into panels and roundels, with bead-rows between and astragali in the field. One roundel contains a boar to the right (Oswald 1936-7, type 1638) and a pygmy (Oswald 1936-7, type 696A) placed sideways. The style of the decoration is in keeping with the work of Cinnamus or one of his associates and is datable to the second half of the 2nd century.

F1074 (not residual)
3   Form 33, part base, stamped MARTI(NV). This is the work of Martinus III of Lezoux; die 6a; *c* AD 155-190. (Information kindly supplied by Mr B R Hartley.)

F1075
Form 33. Central Gaulish, mid or later 2nd century. Base with unusual moulding at wall-angle; apparently a variant of Form 18/31 (but probably not Form 15/31). East Gaulish (?), first half of 2nd century. Two unidentifiable fragments. Central Gaulish.

F1079/3
Fragment of dish, probably Form 15/17 or 18. South Gaulish, Flavian.

F1095 (residual)
Form 18/31R or 31R. Central Gaulish, Antonine.

F1096 (residual)
Form 31 (2 pieces). Central Gaulish, Antonine (and probably late). One has several distinct scorings on the outer surface which are truncated by the break. They are certainly ancient and quite possibly part of a graffito.

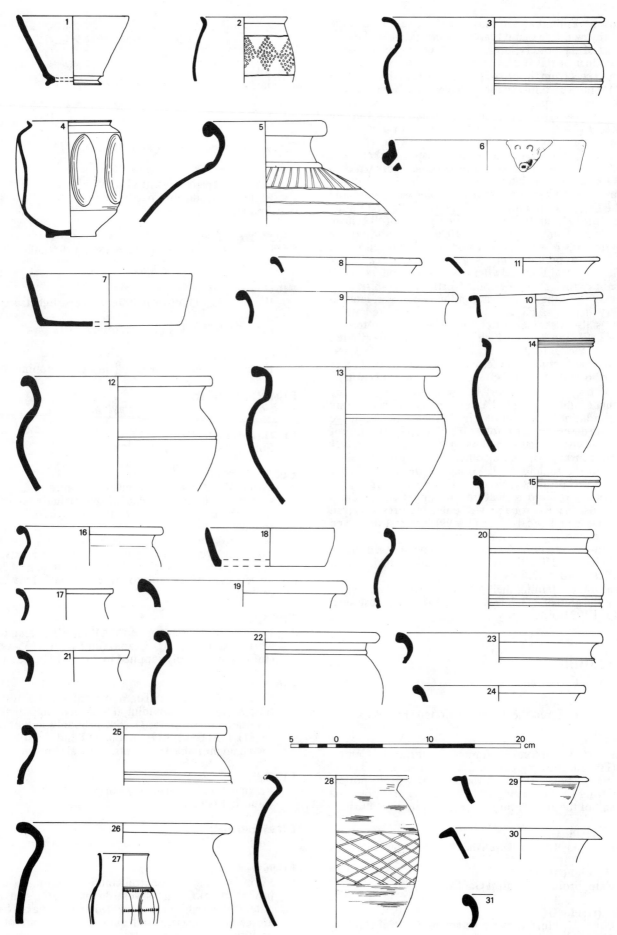

Fig 25   Roman coarse pottery (1/4)

48

The coarse pottery
(Figs 25, 26, 27, 28)

F16 (see p 13). 2nd century
1 Cup in close imitation of Dr33. Hard, crumbly, few small white inclusions. E, I, red-orange. Bk lighter orange. No traces of slip or burnish.
2 Poppyhead beaker decorated with barbotine dots. Hard, smooth, few small quartzitic inclusions. E, I, Bk, light grey (cf Frere 1962, 176, late 2nd century; Frere 1972, Nos 426-8, 604, 1047-9, all 2nd century; Woods 1972, Nos 163-4, Antonine).
3 Jar with two neck and two girth grooves. Very hard, sandy micaceous, small grey inclusions. E, I, buff-grey. Bk, buff and grey laminated (cf Harris and Young 1974, No 14).

Not illustrated: fragment of the internal bead and rolled-over flange of a mortarium. E, I, Bk, white. Pink translucent grits: product of the Oxfordshire kilns (cf Young 1977, M2 c AD 100-170).

F1060 (see p 32). Probably 2nd century
4 Folded beaker; hard, smooth, very small grey inclusions. E, I, Bk, light red-orange. Interior of the folds have the golden metallic sheen of mica dusting (cf Frere 1972, No 836, AD 155-160; for form Nos 787, 789, AD 155-60).

F1074/4 (see p 29). Both jar and samian indicate a late 2nd century date but are the only sherds from the deposit.
5 Narrow-mouthed jar, with neck cordon and a zone of lightly burnished decoration above thin burnished bands extending down the body further than was reconstructable for the drawing. Hard, sandy, few quartzitic inclusions. E, dark grey; I, Bk, mid-grey. The form is generally considered to be 2nd century (cf Brodribb et al 1971, 196, c AD 140; but for an example in a 4th century context see Brodribb et al 1973, 619, from the fishpond deposit, AD 330 onwards).

F10 (see p 17). This feature contained no shell-gritted ware at all, whereas in F3 and F17, both late 4th century with coins of a late date, c 30% of the coarse pottery was shell-gritted ware. This and the coin of AD 316 indicates a date of AD 316-c 350 for the final filling of the feature.
6 Walled mortarium with appliqué spout in the form of a lion head. E, I, Bk, red. Red colour-coated surfaces; product of the Oxfordshire kilns. Spout has a hole pierced through the wall of the pot, an unusual feature (Young 1977, C97.8). (L10/1)
7 Dish. Hard sandy, micaceous, small black and quartzitic inclusions. E, I, mid-grey. Bk, red and grey laminated. (L10/1)
8 Jar. Fabric as for 7. (L10/1)
9 Jar. Hard, sandy, micaceous, small black inclusions. E, I, mid-grey, Bk, lighter grey. (L10/1)
10 Bowl. Hard, sandy, small dark grey inclusions. E, I, Bk, mid-grey. Waster with slightly sagging rim. (L10/1)
11 Dish. Very hard, micaceous, well-tempered. E, I, dark grey. Bk buff-orange. (L10/1)
12 Jar with girth groove. Hard, sandy, micaceous, few small white inclusions and one or two small stones. E, I, mid-grey. Bk lighter grey (cf Brodribb et al 1973, 538, fishpond deposit, AD 330 onwards). (L10/1)
13 Jar with shallow shoulder groove. Fabric as for 12 (cf Brodribb et al 1973, 598, fishpond deposit AD 330 onwards). (L10/1)
14 Jar with grooved, squared rim. Hard, sandy, many small red and black inclusions and some larger bits of grog. E, I, Bk, white, rim discoloured dark grey (cf Young 1977, 113-6 BW2). (L10/1)
15 Jar with groove on everted squared rim. Hard, sandy, micaceous, small black inclusions. E, I, dark grey, Bk, light grey (cf Brodribb et al 1973, 686-8, fishpond deposit, AD 330 onwards). (L10/2)
16 Jar with slight angular groove at the base of the neck. Hard, sandy, micaceous, small black inclusions. E, I, Bk, mid-grey. (L10/2)
17 Jar. Hard, smooth, few small black inclusions. E, I, Bk, mid-grey. (L10/2)
18 Dish. Hard, sandy; E, I, Bk, black. Burnished on the exterior. (L10/2)
19 Jar. Hard very gritty, much quarzitic and small black and red inclusions. E, I, buff-pink, Bk buff. (L10/2)
20 Jar with neck cordon and 2 shallow girth grooves. Hard, sandy, slightly micaceous. E, I, Bk, mid-grey. Residual 2nd century type. (L10/3)
21 Jar. Fabric as for 20. (L10/3)
22 Jar with neck cordon. Hard, sandy, micaceous. E, I, dark grey. Bk light grey. Residual 2nd century type. (L10/5)
24 Jar. Soft, occasional lumps of grey grog. E, I, Bk, light grey. (L10/5)
25 Jar with two girth grooves. Fabric as for 24. (L10/5)

F1030 (see p 29). Late 3rd/early 4th century; coin 270-73
26 Jar. Hard, crumbly, large shell inclusions. E, I, light orange with grey patches, Bk, light orange. Badly made compared with other shell-gritted sherds from the site. See below L43/10 (cf Brodribb et al 1977, 302-8, second half of 3rd century; Brodribb et al 1973, 666-8, 4th century).
27 Beaker with folded decoration and lines of rouletting. Very hard, fine. E, I, mid-grey. Bk, grey and red laminated. Surfaces covered in a very hard shiny black 'Rhenish' slip. (cf Frere 1972, 1132, AD 310-15; Brodribb et al 1971, 267, c AD 160-250; Gillam 1968, No 46, AD 220-60).

F1033 (see p 32). Late 3rd/early 4th century
28 Jar, everted rim, burnished on the exterior above and below a matt zone with burnished lattice decoration. Hard, sandy, small white inclusions. E, I, Bk, black (cf Gillam 1968, No 145).
29 Flanged bowl, burnished on and below the flange. Fabric as for 28.
30 Flanged bowl. Hard, sandy. E, I, Bk, light grey.
31 Jar. Hard, sandy, micaceous. E, I, dark grey. Bk light grey.

F3 (see p 17). Post AD 375; coins 364-75
32 Mortarium. Hard, sandy, small black inclusions. Translucent pink and grey grits. E, I, white; Bk, pink (Young 1977, M22, AD 240 onwards).
33 Mortarium with spout and groove on the flange. Fabric as for 32. Grits are larger than normal (Young 1977, M22, AD 240 onwards).
34 Bowl with moulded rim. Hard, sandy, small red inclusions. E, I, cream Bk, pink (Young 1977, P 24, AD 240 onwards).
35 Bowl in imitation of Dr 31R. Hard, sandy. E, I, Bk, red orange. Red colour-coated surfaces. Oxfordshire kiln product (Young 1977, C45, AD270 onwards).
36 Small undecorated bowl. Fabric as for 35 (cf Brodribb et al 1973, No 778; Young 1977, C113, AD 340 onwards).
37 Bowl in imitation of Dr38. Fabric as for 35 but Bk grey (Young 1977, C51, AD 240 onwards).
38 Jar. Hard, small shell inclusions. E, I, pink and grey patchy. Bk, grey.
39 Jar. Fabric as for 38.

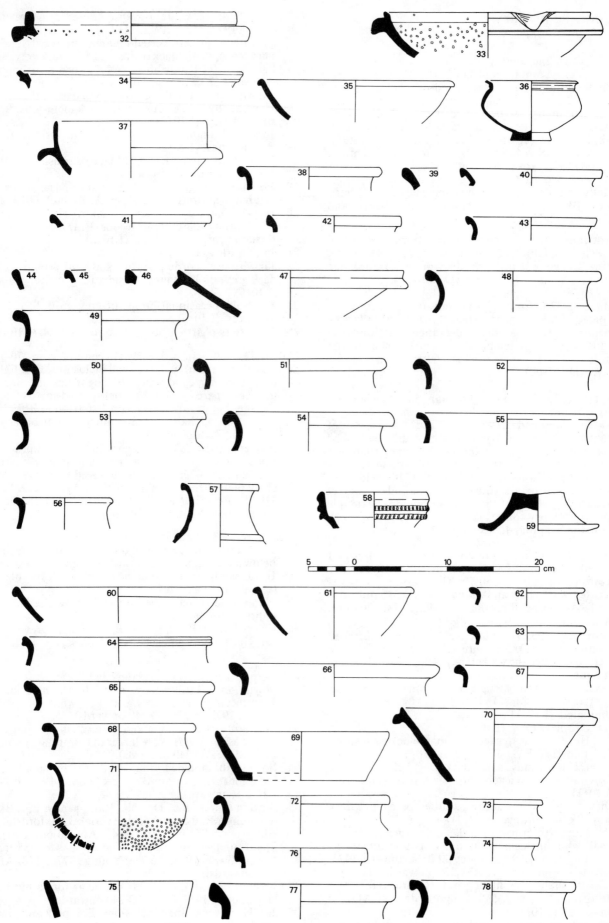

Fig 26   Roman coarse pottery (1/4)

40 Jar. Hard, small shell inclusions. E, I, pink. Bk, grey.
41 Jar. Fabric as for 40.
42 Jar. Hard, small shell inclusions. E, I, Bk, dark grey/black.
43 Jar. Fabric as for 42.
44 Jar. Fabric as for 42
45 Jar. Fabric as for 42.
46 Jar. Hard, small shell inclusions. E, I, light orange. Bk, grey.
47 Flanged bowl. Hard, sandy, micaceous, small black inclusions. E, I, mid-grey. Bk, light grey.
48 Jar. Fabric as for 47.
49 Jar. Fabric as for 47.
50 Jar. Hard, sandy, micaceous, small black inclusions. E, I, mid-grey. Bk, red and grey laminated.
51 Jar. Fabric as for 50.
52 Jar. Fabric as for 50.
53 Jar. Hard, sandy, micaceous. E, I, Bk, mid-grey.
54 Jar. Hard, sandy, small black inclusions. E, I, Bk, light grey.
55 Jar. Hard, sandy, large quartzitic and black inclusions. E, I, Bk, very light grey.
56 Jar. Hard, sandy, micaceous, small black inclusions. E, I, Bk, buff-grey.
57 Narrow-mouthed jar with neck cordon. Fabric as for 47. Probably residual.
58 Narrow-mouthed jar decorated with stabs on a moulded rim. Hard, sandy, micaceous. E, I, mid-grey, Bk, light grey (cf Brodribb et al 1968, 125-6; 1971, 345; 1973, 606-9; Young 1977, R9, who considers the type 4th century only).
59 Lid. Very hard, sandy, many small red and quartzitic inclusions. E, I, mid-grey. Bk, red. Waster (cf Brodribb et al 1971, 179-82, 287-9).

F17 (see p 17). Post AD 375; coins 270-375
60 Bowl in imitation of Dr31R. Hard, micaceous. E, I, red-pink. Bk, grey. Red colour-coated surfaces: product of the Oxfordshire kilns (Young 1977, C45 AD 270 onwards). (L17/1)
61 Bowl in imitation of Dr31R. Fabric as for 60. (L17/3)
62 Jar. Hard, micaceous, small black inclusions. E, I, Bk, mid-grey. (L17/1)
63 Jar. Fabric as for 62. (L17/1.)
64 Jar with grooved rim. Hard, sandy with small black inclusions. E, I, mid-grey-buff, with darkened patches; Bk, grey. (L17/1)
65 Jar. Fabric as for 63. (L17/1)
66 Jar. Hard, sandy, micaceous. E, I, mid-grey; Bk, light grey. (L17/1)
67 Jar. Fabric as for 66. (L17/1)
68 Jar. Fabric as for 66. (L17/1)
69 Dish. Fabric as for 66. (L17/1)
70 Flanged bowl. Fabric as for 66. (L17/1)
71 Colander, in fragments. Hard, sandy, small white inclusions. E, I, dark grey. Bk, red and grey laminated. (L17/1)
72 Jar. Very hard, sandy and micaceous with some large quartz stones. E, I, grey. Bk, red-orange. (L17/1)
73 Small jar. Hard, sandy, small red inclusions. E, I, Bk, white, discoloured grey on parts of the exterior and rim (Young 1977, 113-6, BW2). (L17/1)
74 Jar. Fabric as for 73. (L17/1)
75 Dish. Hard, sandy, small white inclusions. E, rough red-orange as though burnt. I, black and burnished. Bk, black. (L17/1)
76 Jar. Hard, small shell inclusions. E, I, Bk, black. (L17/1)
77 Jar. Fabric as for 76. (L17/1)

78 Jar. Hard, small shell inclusions. E, I, Bk, light orange. (L17/1)
79 Jar. Fabric as for 78. (L17/1)
80 Jar. Hard, small shell inclusions. E, I, patchy pink and grey. Bk, dark grey. (L17/1)
81 Jar. Fabric as for 80. (L17/1)
82 Jar. Hard, shell inclusions. E, I, pink and grey, patchy. Bk, grey. Not as well made as the rest of the shell-gritted sherds listed above. (L17/1)
83 Jar. Fabric as for 82. (L17/1)
84 Flanged bowl. Very hard, gritty. E, I, orange. Bk, grey. Traces of white slip (?) on the surfaces. (L17/1)
85 Rim of a storage vessel. Hard, large white inclusions. E, I, pink-orange. Bk, thick dark grey. (L17/1)
86 Storage vessel. Fabric as for 85. (L17/3)

F43 (see p 17). Post c AD 350
87 Bowl in imitation of Dr31R. Hard, small black inclusions. E, I, Bk, red. Red colour-coated surfaces. Oxfordshire kiln product (Young 1977, C45, AD 270 onwards). (L43/10)
88 Jar. Hard, sandy, micaceous. E, I, mid-grey. Bk, light grey. (L43/10)
89 Jar with two girth grooves. Very hard, sandy, micaceous, small quartzitic inclusions. E, I, mid-grey. Bk, orange-red (cf Brodribb et al 1973, 589 and 600, fishpond deposit, AD 330 onwards). (L43/6)
90 Flanged dish. Hard, smooth, small black inclusions. E, I, Bk, mid-grey. (L43/8)
91 Flanged dish. Hard, fine, small black inclusions. E, I, mid-grey. Bk, lighter grey. Exterior very thoroughly burnished and well fired to an almost metallic sheen. (L43/9)
92 Jar. Hard, sandy, small red and black inclusions. E, I, Bk, white (cf Young 1977, W33). (L43/8)
93 Jar. Hard, small shell inclusions. E, I, pink and grey patchy. Bk, dark grey. (L43/8)
94 Jar. Hard, shell inclusions. E, I, pink. Bk, grey. Fabric not as good as 93. (L43/10)

Not illustrated: several fragments of bases and body sherds of red colour-coated Oxfordshire vessels, base and small fragment of the rim of a shell-gritted jar (see 93 above), 3 very small fragments of a folded beaker in very hard, very fine grey fabric with a brown colour-coat, probably a product of the Nene Valley kilns.

F47 (see p 17). Post c AD 350
95 Beaker. Hard, sandy, small red inclusions. E, I, buff-grey. Bk, red and grey laminated.

Not illustrated: body sherds of flange and body of an imitation Dr38 in Oxfordshire red colour-coated fabric (Young 1977, C51), body sherds of shell-gritted ware.

F1002 (see p 34). Post c AD 350
96 Flanged bowl with burnished exterior and arcaded decoration. Hard, sandy, small white inclusions. E, I, Bk, black. (L1002/1)
97 Bowl with vertical rim and flanged carination. Hard, sandy, small red inclusions. E, I, Bk, off-white. (L1002/2)

Not illustrated: body sherd of shell-gritted ware.

F1047 (see p 32). Post c AD 350
98 Flanged bowl with stabbed decoration on the upper surfaces of the flange. Hard, small shell inclusions. E, I, Bk, light orange.

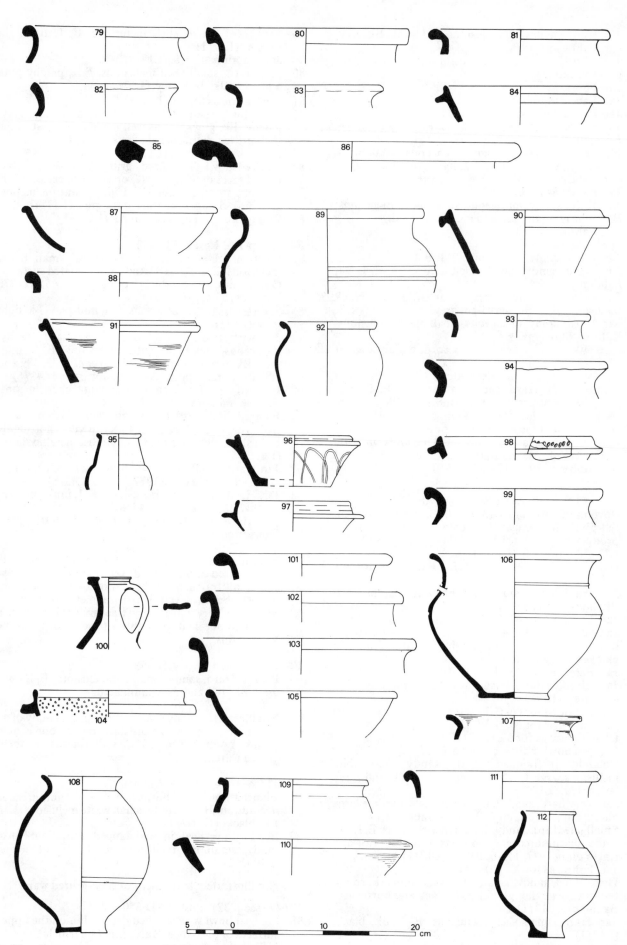

Fig 27   Roman coarse pottery (1/4)

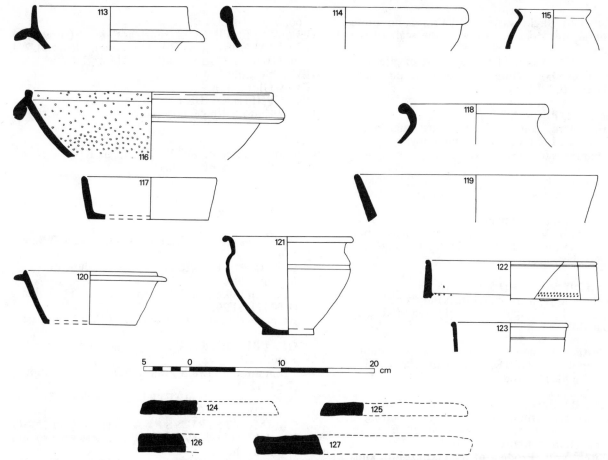

Fig 28   Roman coarse pottery and ceramic discs (1/4)

99 Jar. Hard, small shell inclusions. E, I, light orange. Bk, grey.

F30 (see p 17). Post *c* AD 375; coin 367-75

100 Rim and neck of a strap-handled flagon. Hard, sandy, few small red inclusions. E, upper I, light orange. Lower I, Bk, light grey.

101 Jar. Hard, sandy micaceous, small quartzitic inclusions. E, I, mid-grey. Bk, light grey.

102 Jar. Fabric as for 101.

103 Jar. Fabric as for 101.

104 Mortarium. Hard, sandy, small red inclusions. E, I, Bk, light orange. Translucent pink grits. Oxfordshire kiln product (Young 1977, WC7, AD 240 onwards).

105 Bowl in imitation of Dr31R. E, I, red-orange. Bk, grey. Red colour-coated surfaces. Oxfordshire kiln product (Young 1977, C45, AD 270 onwards).

F4 (see p 16). 2nd century pottery, but perhaps residual

106 Jar with everted rim, small neck cordon and girth groove. Hard, sandy, small black inclusions. E, I, Bk, buff-grey (cf Brodribb *et al* 1971, 200 and 207. Mid 2nd century or earlier).

107 Jar. Very hard, sandy, small black and red inclusions. E, I, black. Bk, white. Burnished on the exterior and on the cavetto rim part of the interior.

F57 (see p 17). Post *c* AD 250

108 Jar, very badly burnt. Hard. Indications on the interior that originally the fabric was light grey (cf Frere 1972, No 1073, AD 175-275).

109 Jar. Hard, sandy. E, I, red. Bk, grey. Red colour-coated surfaces. Oxfordshire kiln product (Young 1977, C18).

110 Bowl. Hard, sandy, small white inclusions. E. I, Bk, black. All surfaces highly burnished (cf Brodribb *et al* 1968, 32-6, 2nd century; and for form, Frere 1972, Nos 724-9, 955-9, all 2nd century). Probably residual.

111 Jar with hooked rim. Hard, sandy, small black inclusions. E, I, Bk, light grey.

Not illustrated: in Oxfordshire red colour-coated ware, fragment of a bowl with crescent-shaped stamps and fragment of an imitation Dr31R.

F1050 (see p 32)

112 Beaker with slight girth groove. Hard, sandy small black inclusions. E, I, mid-grey. Bk, light grey. This shape is current in the 3rd and 4th centuries.

Not illustrated: one fragment burnished, black with small white inclusions, straight-sided dish.

F1025 (see p 27). Post *c* AD 250

113 Bowl in imitation of Dr38. Hard, sandy. E, I, Bk, orange-red. Red colour-coated surfaces. Oxfordshire kiln product (Young 1977, C51, AD 240 onwards).

114 Bowl, large imitation Dr31R. Fabric as for 113 (cf Brodribb *et al* 1971, 364-6, post AD 350; Young 1977, C46, AD 340 onwards).

F1046 (see p 32)

115 Beaker. Hard, micaceous, many small black and grey inclusions. E, I, mid-grey. Bk, light grey.

F1071 (see p 29). Post *c* AD 240

116 Mortarium. Hard, sandy. E, I, Bk, off-white. Translucent pink and grey grits (Young 1977, M21,

53

AD 240-300). Slight waster, as the rim is not quite horizontal; this does not show at the scale of the drawing.
117 Dish. Soft, micaceous, few inclusions of grits like those of an Oxfordshire mortarium, ie pink and translucent. E, I, Bk, pink.

F1072 (see p 29). Post *c* AD 250
118 Jar. Very hard, sandy and micaceous, small black inclusions. E, I, dark grey. Bk, mid-grey.
119 Dish. Fabric as for 118.

Not illustrated: fragment of red colour-coated Oxfordshire mortarium.

F1095 (see p 29). Late Roman
120 Flanged dish. Very hard and gritty, many small quarzitic inclusions. E, I, patchy light orange and grey. Bk, dark grey.

F1096 (see p 29). Post *c* AD 250
121 Jar with slight girth groove. Hard, sandy, small black inclusions. E, I, light grey. Bk, red and grey laminated.

Not illustrated: fragments of Oxfordshire red colour-coated imitation Dr31R, two body sherds of a 'Rhenish' folded beaker.

F1126 (see p 32). Post *c* AD 250
122 Wall-sided mortarium with a band of rouletting at the lower edge of the wall. Hard, sandy. E, I, Bk, red-pink. Red colour-coated surfaces. Few pink translucent grits. Product of the Oxfordshire kilns (Young 1977, C97, AD 240 onwards).
123 Bowl. Fabric as for 122. (Young 1977, C55 or C81, AD 240 onwards).

Ceramic discs
124 Segments of roughly circular, hand-made ceramic
to discs, possibly lids for storage vessels. Soft small
127 white inclusions and some small stones; E, I, buff-grey. Bk, dark grey; except 126, harder, crumbly, E, I, brown-red. Bk, brick-red. From L1060/2, L17/1, L43/5, and L1075 respectively.

Finds: The coins
by Trevor Saxby

The site produced a total of 28 coins, of which all but two came from Area I. Owing to an uncommonly harsh soil and, in some cases, the heavy pressure of earth-moving vehicles, the condition of the coins was poor. With the exception of three radiates, the coins form a uniform 4th century spread. Abbreviations as follows:

RIC *Roman Imperial Coinage* by Mattingly, Sydenham *et al*
H-K *Late Roman Bronze Coinage, Vol I* by Carson, Hill, and Kent
C-K *ibid Vol II*
D Diameter

Summary

Area I
Barbarous radiate of TETRICUS I (two)
AE follis of LICINIUS I   RIC VII TRIER 120
AE follis of CONSTANTINE I (two)   RIC VII TRIER

266, 523 (H-K 52)
AE3 of VALENTINIAN I (four) as C-K 279 (three), 284
AE3 of VALENS (six) as C-K 303 (three), 306 (two), 294
AE of GRATIAN (two)   as C-K 314 or 318 (two)
AE3 of 'Securitas' type
AE3 of 'Gloria' type
AE4 of THEODOSIUS I   C-K 166
Illegible, but all 4th century (six)

Area III
Barbarous radiate of TETRICUS I   as RIC V2 (2) 87
AE3 of VALENS   C-K 1030

Classification

1 Barbarous radiate of TETRICUS I, AD 270-3 Barely legible
Obv (IMP) TET(RICVS AVG) rad, cuir, bust r
Rev illegible
From an unknown Southern mint   D 17 mm
(I L17/1 SF26)

2 Barbarous radiate of TETRICUS I, AD 270-3 Barely legible
Obv IMP TET(RICVS AVG) rad, cuir, bust r
Rev illegible
From an unknown Southern mint   D 16 mm
(I L1 SF5)

3 Barbarous radiate of TETRICUS I, AD 270-3   RIC V2 (2) 87
Obv IMP C TETRICVS PF AVG rad, dr, cuir, bust r
Rev LAETITIA AVGG Laetitia stg l, with wreath and anchor
From an unknown Southern mint   D 20 mm
(III L1031/1 SF1009)

4 AE Follis of LICINIUS I, AD 316   RIC VII TRIER 120
Obv IMP LICINIVS PF AVG laur, dr, cuir, bust r
Rev GENIO - POP ROM Genius stg l, with patera and cornucopiae
$\frac{T|F}{ATR}$ of Trier   D 20 mm
(I L10/1 SF12)

5 AE follis of CONSTANTINE I, AD 320   RIC VII TRIER 266
Obv CONSTAN-TINVS AVG helm, cuir bust r
Rev VIRTVS - EXERCIT standard VOT XX, captive stg either side
$\frac{|}{STR}$ of Trier   D 20 mm
(I L17/1 SF16)

6 AE Follis of CONSTANTINE I, AD 330-1   RIC VII TRIER 523, H-K 52
Obv CONSTAN-TINOPOLIS laur helm bust l, imp cloak, rev spear
Rev Victory stg l on prow with spear and shield
$\frac{|}{TRS}$ of Trier   D 18 mm
(I L1 SF29)

7 AE3 of VALENTINIAN I, AD 364-75   as C-K 279, 281, 284, 286 or 287
Obv DN VALENTINI-ANVS PF AVG diad, dr, cuir bust r
Rev GLORIA RO-MANORVM Emperor facing, with captive and labarum
$\frac{OF|II}{\cdots\cdots}$ exergue illegible, style Lyons   D 16 mm
(I L3/1 SF40)

8 AE3 of VALENTINIAN I, AD 364-75   as 7 above
Obv DN VALENTINI-ANVS PF AVG diad, dr, cuir bust r

54

Rev GLORIA RO-MANORVM as above
$\dfrac{\text{OF}|\text{I}}{\dots\dots}$ exergue illegible, style Lyons   D 16 mm
(I L3/1 SF32)

9   AE3 of VALENTINIAN I, AD 364-75   as 7 above
Obv DN VALENTINI-ANVS PF AVG diad, dr, cuir
    bust r
Rev GLORIA RO-MANORVM as above
$\dfrac{\text{OF}|\text{II}}{\dots\dots}$ exergue illegible, style Lyons   D 16 mm
(I u/s SF19)

10   AE3 of VALENTINIAN I, AD 364-75   as 7 above
Obv DN VALENTINI-ANVS PF AVG diad, dr, cuir
    bust r
Rev GLORIA RO-MANORVM as above
Mint illegible   with D 14 mm, possibly an
    imitation
(I L3/1 SF45)

11   AE3 of VALENS, AD 364-75   C-K 1030
Obv DN VALEN-S PF AVG diad, dr, cuir bust r
Rev SECVRITAS - REIPVBLICAE Victory adv 1
    with wreath and palm
$\dfrac{\perp}{\text{SMAQP}}$ of Aquileia   D 18 mm
(III u/s SF1006)

12   AE3 of VALENS, AD 367-75   as C-K 303, 305, 306,
    309 or 312
Obv DN VALEN-S PF AVG as 11 above
Rev SECVRITAS - REIPVBLICAE as above
$\dfrac{\text{OF}|}{\text{LVG}\dots}$ of Lyons   D 18 mm
(I L1 SF44)

13   AE3 of VALENS, AD 367-75   as 12 above
Obv DN VALEN-S PF AVG as above
Rev SECVRITAS - REIPVBLICAE as above
$\dfrac{\text{OF}|}{\dots\dots}$ exergue illegible, probably Lyons   D 18 mm
(I L30 SF43)

14   AE3 of VALENS, AD 367-75   as 12 above
Obv DN VALEN-S PF AVG as above
Rev SECVRITAS - REIPVBLICAE as above
Mint-mark illegible   D 18 mm
(I L17/1 SF27)

15   AE3 of VALENS, AD 367-75   as 12 above
Obv DN VALEN-S PF AVG as above
Rev SECVRITAS - REIPVBLICAE as above
$\dfrac{\text{OF}|\text{I}}{\dots\dots}$ exergue illegible, style Lyons   D 17 mm
(I L1 SF36)

16   AE3 of VALENS, AD 367-75   as C-K 291 or 294
Obv DN VALEN-S PF AVG as 12 above
Rev SECVRITAS - REIPVBLICAE as above
$\dfrac{\text{OF}|\text{I}}{\text{LVG}..}$ of Lyons   D 17 mm
(I L1 SF18)

17   AE3 of VALENS, AD 367-75   as 12 above
Obv DN VALEN-S PF AVG as above
Rev SECVRITAS - REIPVBLICAE as above
$\dfrac{\text{OF}|\text{I}}{\dots\dots}$ exergue illegible, probably Lyons   D 16 mm
(I L3/1 SF42)

18   AE3 of GRATIAN, AD 367-75   as C-K 314 or 318
Obv DN GRATI-ANVS PF AVG diad, dr, cuir, bust r
Rev GLORIA RO-MANORVM as above
$\dfrac{\perp}{..\text{G}..}$ of Lyons   D 17 mm
(I L1 SF4)

19   AE3 of GRATIAN, AD 367-75   C-K 304
Obv DN GRATI-ANVS PF AVG as 18 above
Rev SECVRITAS - REIPVBLICAE as above
$\dfrac{\text{OF}|\text{I}}{\text{LVGPA}}$ of Lyons   D 16 mm
(I L3/1 SF41)

20   AE3 of 'Secvritas' type, badly mutilated, AD 367-75
Obv Illegible
Rev SECVRITAS - REIPVBLICAE as above
Mint-mark illegible   D 16 mm
(I L1 SF35)

21   AE3 of 'Gloria' type, badly mutilated, AD 364-75
Obv Illegible
Rev GLORIA RO-MANORVM as above
Mint-mark illegible   D 16 mm
(I L1 SF37)

22   AE4 of THEODOSIUS I, AD 388-92   C-K 166
Obv DN THEODOSIVS PF AVG diad, dr, cuir bust r
Rev VICTOR-IA AVGGG Victory advancing 1 with
    wreath and palm
$\dfrac{\perp}{\text{TR}}$ of Trier   D 13 mm
(I L2/1 SF8)

23   AE3, illegible, but obverse is diademed. 4th century.
D 16 mm.
(I L3/3 SF56)

24   AE3, illegible, but obverse is diademed. 4th century.
D 16 mm.
(I L3/3 SF54)

25   AE, badly mutilated, but with obverse paluda-
mentum. 4th century.
(I L1 SF30)

26   AE4, totally illegible. Late 4th century.
(I L3/1 SF46)

27   AE4, totally illegible. Late 4th century.
(I L47/1 SF48)

28   AE, crushed and held together by corrosion.
Probably 4th century.
(I L1 SF38)

Finds: The other finds

*by George Lambrick with sections by Andrew Sherratt
Sian Rees, and G T Brown*

Iron Age small finds

(Fig 29)

Objects of bronze

1   Coiled finger (or ?toe) ring of twisted bronze wire,
worn smooth on exterior. D 18 mm (II L590/2
SF507; mid IA) cf Wheeler 1943, 265 and fig 86,
10-17.

2   Small chain consisting of four circular links. L 15
mm; D each link 4 mm (III L1167 SF1030; mid IA).

Objects of bone

(identification by Bob Wilson)

3   Highly polished sheep tibia with worn indentations
consisting on each side of a broad one at the proximal
end and a pair of small ones near the distal end. Each
side matches the one opposite, but these two opposing
pairs are slightly offset from each other. Overall
L 180 mm; distance between identations 55 mm in
each case. Possibly used in weaving or leather working
(III F1168 SF1029; mid IA) cf Parrington 1978, 81
and fig 61; Wheeler 1943, 306, Nos 4 and 5 pl 35A.

Not illustrated: fragment of polished bone, probably
part of another example from the same context (III
F1168 SF1029; mid IA).

Objects of fired clay

4   Triangular clay loomweight with three suspension

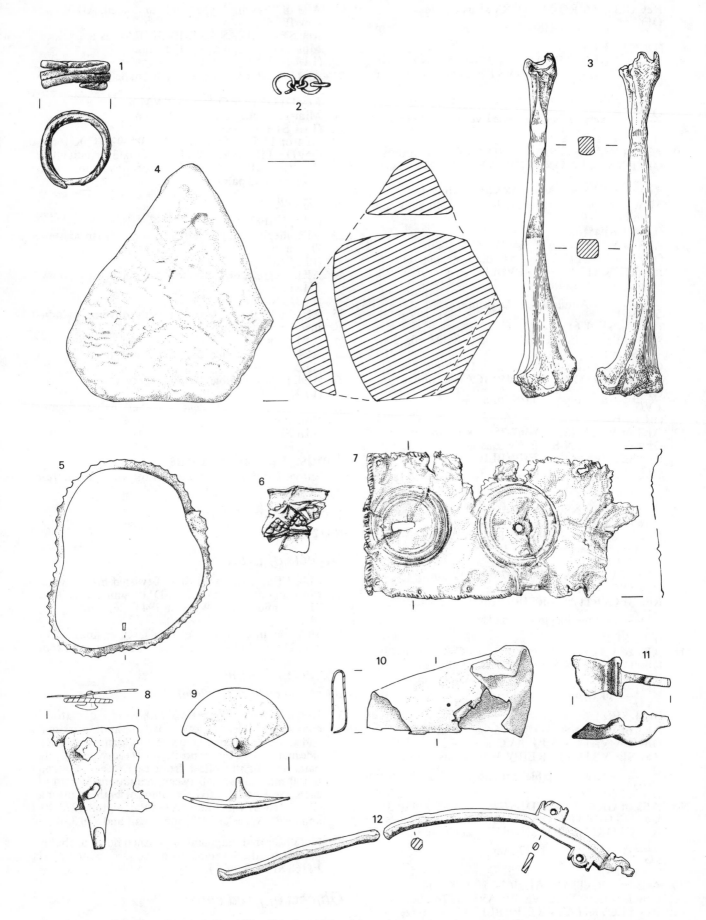

Fig 29   Small finds: Iron Age (1 and 2: 1/1; 3 and 4: 1/2) and Roman (1/1; except 6, 7 and 12: 1/2)

holes. Approximately equilateral, L of side *c* 140 mm; Th *c* 50-60 mm (III L590/2 SF510; mid IA).

Not illustrated: fifteen other loomweights or fragments of loomweight. Almost all of these were of a fairly distinctive fabric, usually moderately hard, quite well fired clay with little tempering. All the fragments identified had uneven but quite definite smoothed faces, often with the remains of the characteristic suspension holes pierced at an angle to the side faces. These holes were clearly weak points since in most cases at least one corner had broken off from this point. In some cases corners had no hole pierced through them, although by having three holes the weight would have remained usable until all the corners had broken off. In all the cases (8) where the angles between two sides were measurable they approximated to 60°. The weights varied in thickness from 50-60 mm to 70-80 mm; their length of side from *c* 120 mm to over 180 mm. Table 2 gives their contexts.

Table 2: Loomweight provenances

Area	Feature/Layer	Date	No
II	main enclosure phase c	(mid IA)	2
	main enclosure phase d	(mid IA)	6
	514	(mid IA)	2
	590/2	(mid IA)	2
III	1015	(early IA)	1
	1157	(mid IA)	1
	1168	(mid IA)	1
	1033	(RB)	1
Total			16

Roman small finds
(Figs 29, 30)

Objects of bronze

5 Small bracelet with toothed outer edge. D *c* 50 mm; W 2 mm; Th 1 mm. Made from a strip cut off a bronze sheet, the ends being bent round, overlapped and rivetted with a small ? iron rivet (III L1075 SF1010; late 4th century).

6 Sheet with repoussé decoration, much crumpled, ends and ? bottom edge broken off. L 35 mm; W *c* 40 mm; Th 0.2 mm. Unbroken edge folded over, with plain band (W 7 mm) below; then a band of decoration (W 17 mm) and another plain strip (W 11 mm). The bottom edge is broken along an embossed line. The decoration consists of a simple intertwined line turning back on itself in an indented loop, with 'scales' in the triangles formed between this and a double horizontal line marking the bottom of the decorated band. Dr M Henig suggests that this might be a stylized representation of vine branches and grapes, and the object part of a bronze cup or mug (III L1002/1 SF1003; ? late 4th century).

7 Decorative plate from a wooden box consisting of gilded sheet with repoussé decoration. One end broken off. L 50 mm with at least 20 mm missing; W 78 mm; Th *c* 0.1 mm. The decoration consists of cables round the edge, with three roundels along the centre of the plate (D 44 mm) formed by one broad embossed ring flanked by narrower ones on each side. The roundels have holes at their centres probably for the attachment of bosses (though the elongated one might possibly be a rather jagged key hole). There are several pin holes round the edge of the sheet with slightly larger ones at the two surviving corners (III/I u/s SF1028); cf Bushe-Foxe 1947, 142 and pls XLVII and XLVIII, Nos 176a and b.

8 Bronze hook riveted to bronze strip(s). Hook beaten out of a rod. L 34 mm; Plate L at least 50 mm; W 20 mm; Th *c* 0.1 mm. Pierced in several places with different sized holes. One separate piece of similar strip not joining the rest is probably from the other side of the hook. Probably a belt fitting. (III u/s SF1001)

9 Circular, slightly convex undecorated stud. D *c* 33 mm (II u/s SF501)

10 Tapering folded bronze sheet. L 45 mm; W 25 mm tapering to 10 mm. Probably wrapped round the end of a wooden object or round the joint of two pieces of wood, since there is an opening, possibly genuine, in the wider, enclosed end. (II u/s SF512)

11 Part of a spoon from the junction of the handle and the bowl (I L10/3 SF63; late 3rd to early 4th centuries).

Not illustrated: spoon handle (lost on site but sketched) (I L2/1 SF2; late 4th century). Curved piece of round wire; L 73 mm; D *c* 1 mm (I L17/1 SF60; late 4th century). Twisted square-sectioned wire; L 26 mm (as above SF58). Narrow, thin, plain strip; L 47 mm; W 2.5 mm; Th *c* 0.2 mm; very slight traces of gliding on one edge (as above SF15 and 17).

Object of lead

12 Small 'steelyard' broken with the end of the arm missing. L originally at least 235 mm. Arm octagonal in section (Th 5 mm). Suspension end beaten flat and cut out (L 62 mm; W 8 mm; Th 2.5 mm) with a groove scored along the centre of each side. The suspension and weight lugs are placed in the normal positions (the suspension lug at the junction of the arm and the flat section; one weight lug forming the end, the other on the bottom edge between these two). Each lug is decorated with 'ears'. The horizontal distances between the weight lugs and the suspension lug are 45 mm and 23 mm respectively. The proportion of these measurements (*c* 1.9 : 1) is similar to the ratio of the same dimensions on the Appleford steelyard for which the horizontal measurements (from the drawing) give a ratio of 2.1:1 (the figures given in the text are from direct measurements which distort the equation by not allowing for the steelyard being in balance). This example is unusual in being so small and made of lead, and it is doubtful whether it was intended for actual use. No graduations are visible on the arm (though these might not have been preserved) and the steelyard could only have been used, if at all, for very small quantities (III L1002/1 SF1002; ?late 4th century); cf Brown 1973, 195-7 and fig 6.

Objects of iron

13 (Fig 32) Large scythe blade. Surviving L 1.40 m. For detailed description, discussion, and metallurgical analysis see p 61-5. (III L1075 SF1021)

14 Roofing nail. L 50 mm. Square section and with a long flat head in the form of a bar. (I L3/1 SF47; late 4th century)

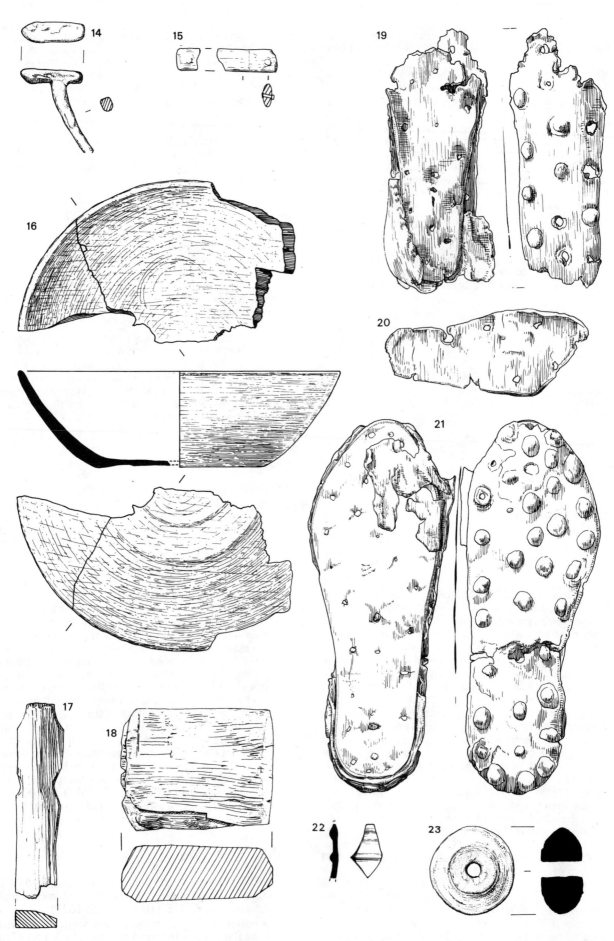

Fig 30   Small finds: Roman (1/2; except 14, 15 and 17: 1/1)

Not illustrated: set of hobnails found *in situ.* (I L10/2 SF62; late 3rd to early 4th centuries)

Objects of bone

15 Small fitting once bound with bronze attached by a small pin. Both ends broken. L surviving 16 mm; W 6 mm; Th 2 mm. Another fragment of this, also heavily stained and coated with bronze corrosion, was also found. (I L17/1 SF24; late 4th century)

Not illustrated: fragment of pin/needle with both ends broken; L 28 mm; D up to 35 mm (I L17/1 SF59; late 4th century). Pin with round head; L 38 mm; D up to 3.5 mm (III u/s SF1029).

Objects of wood
(identification by Mark Robinson)

16 Part of a small willow wood bowl. D 180 mm; Ht 50 mm (drawn before conservation). Very simple in form with a rounded rim and no pronounced footring, though with a slightly concave base. On the inside is a small hollow possibly made during use. (III F1098 SF 1027)
17 Part of a small notched stick of ring-porous hardwood with both ends missing. L 61 mm; W 11 mm; Th 5 mm. Cut from a fairly small branch or possibly a stake, with one side corresponding to the rings of the wood, the other three being cut flat. The two pairs of notches cut into the sides of the stick (22 mm apart) suggest that it was probably a tally stick. (III L1060/2 SF1012; ? late 2nd century)
18 Piece of squared-off oak with one end chamfered on both sides, the other end broken. L 85 mm; W 50 mm; Th 25 to 30 mm. Apparently cut or finished off with a chisel rather than a saw, giving uneven though fairly smooth surfaces to the larger faces and the chamfered end. The smoother sides may have been planed flat. Near the break on one of the faces is a vertical chisel cut (L 23 mm). This may be a tenon broken off the end of a structural timber. This is suggested by its general size and proportions and to some extent by the way in which it was worked: in particular the vertical chisel cut suggests the squaring off of a shoulder; the difference between the chiselled faces and the planed sides also suggests that there were shoulders preventing the main faces being planed; the chamfered end is also common on tenons being designed to make it easier to fit the mortice. There is no hole for a dowel. (I L43/10 SF72; late 4th century)

Objects of leather

19 Bottom of a small ? left foot shoe. L 145 mm; W 50 mm. Comprising a hobnailed sole, a thick insole, fragments of upper lasting margin, and most of the heel-stiffener. There are traces of thonging on the insole. Possibly from the same shoe (not illustrated) were two fragments of upper (one ? side piece, one ? heel or toe with a central seam, and part of the lasting margin) and one fragment possibly of a L43/10 SF66; late 4th century)

20 Part of the bottom of a small child's right-foot shoe. L 110 mm; W 45 mm. Probably a lamina or the insole, with nail holes but no evidence for thonging (as above).
21 Bottom part of a fairly small left-foot shoe. L 198 mm; W 70 mm. Comprising a hobnailed sole and stout insole with surviving lasting margins for heel stiffener and most of the uppers. Small fragments of the toe uppers survive with possible, but very dubious, stamped decoration along the centre. (III F1079 SF1026; ?late 4th century)

Not illustrated: several fragments of shoe sole (with large nail holes) and insole, possibly all from one shoe, but not from either of the others in the same layer. (I L43/10 SF73; late 4th century)

Objects of glass

22 Small fragment of glass vessel decorated with two ribs. (I L3/3 SF53; late 4th century)

Not illustrated: piece of large flat bead; D 30 mm; Th 7 mm; one side convex, the other flat (I L2/1 SF10; late 4th century). Minute turquoise bead with no hole; D 2 mm (III L1071 SF1017; late 4th century). Blue glass bead; D 10 mm; Th 6 mm; D of hole 3 mm (III u/s SF1007). Fragment of glass vesel with rib (I L43/10 SF68; late 4th century). A few fragments of plain glass from various 4th century contexts.

Object of shale

23 Lathe-turned shale spindle whorl. D 46 mm; Th 20 mm; D of hole 8 mm (I L1 SF1; ? late 4th century); cf Brodribb *et al* 1973, 44 and fig 22, Nos 9 and 10.

Iron Age and Roman whetstones and quernstones (Fig 31)
(identifications by John Martin)

24 Whetstone. Worn on all unbroken surfaces. Medium-grained feldspatic sandstone not typical of Mesozoic rocks of the Oxford area. (III L1030/1 SF1020; Roman, late 3rd/4th century)
25 Whetstone. Worn on top and one side. Thin section showed it to be non-fossiliferous fine-grained calcareous sandstone thickly laminated. 95% quartz; 5% feldspar; detrital zircon. Calcareous cement replaced by chalcedony in places. Probably middle/upper Jurassic of fairly local origin. (I L16/1 SF14; Roman, 2nd century)
26 Whetstone. Worn on one side only. Similar rock type to 25. (III L1050/2 SF1014; Roman, 3rd to 4th century)
27 Flat quernstone. Similar to fragment (SF32) not illustrated, which a thin section showed to be fossiliferous medium-grained calcareous sandstone with angular to sub-rounded quartz grains and bivalve fragments in coarsely recrystallized calcite/siderite cement/matrix. Probably local: similar lithologies seen in lower greensand although not identical to the typical 'Faringdon Greensand'. (II L528/1 SF515; mid Iron Age)
28 Flat quernstone. Possibly similar rock type to 27 but finer grained. (III F1007 SF1018; mid Iron Age)

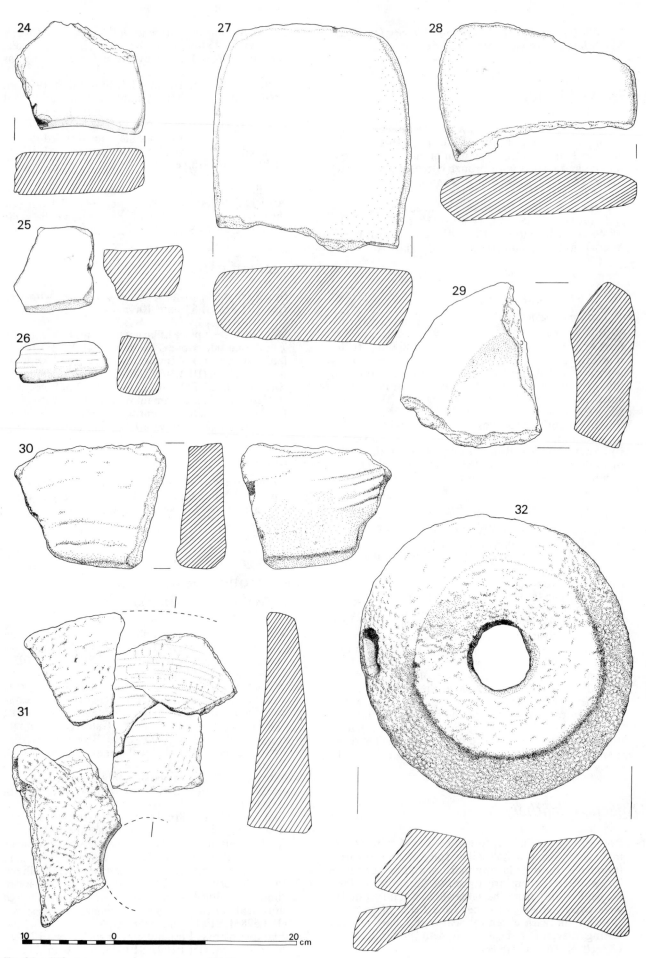

24

27

28

25

26

29

30

32

31

10   0   20 cm

Fig 31   Whetstones and quernstones (1/4)

29 Fragment of rotary quernstone. Pebbly arkosic sandstone not typical of Mesozoic rocks of the Oxford area. (III u/s SF1005)

30 Fragment of rotary quernstone, possibly reused since there are rather indistinct grooves on both sides apparently following opposing arcs. Similar to fragment (SF71) not illustrated, which a thin section showed to be arkosic grit fairly well cemented and non-calcareous. Closely resembles millstone grit (carboniferous) of Yorkshire. (III F1074/1 SF1010; late Roman)

31 Fragments of rotary quernstone. Thin sections showed it to be medium-grained pink arkosic sandstone. 35% quartz; 35% feldspar; 30% rock fragments. Sphene opaque oxides; fine grained sericitic matrix in places; well cemented and non calcareous. Not typical of any mesozoic rock-type of the Oxford area. (I L1 SF33-34; late Roman)

32 Upper rotary quernstone with socket for handle. Fine/medium-grained non-calcareous grey-green subarkose with some ?glauconite and small fragments of phosphatic material. Probably not local. (III u/s)

Not illustrated: whetstone fragments similar to 25 and 26 but not obviously laminated (III F1013 SF1004; early Iron Age). Two fragments of quernstone, similar rock type to 30, 40 mm and 90 mm thick respectively (I L17/1 SF71, see 30; late 4th century; I L3/4 SF55; Roman late 4th century. Fragment of quernstone, see 27 (I L1 SF32; late Roman).

The flints

by Andrew Sherratt

With one exception (No 8) all the pieces were of poor-quality flint from small nodules and many show areas of cortex. Some have heavy white patination whereas others are largely unpatinated. All are residual, probably late neolithic, of which No 6 is most distinctive.

1 Flake with minor retouching or edge-damage at distal end; white patina (II L529|3).
2 Thick flake, 47 x 25 mm, with abraded edge; white patina (II L531|1).
3 Small flake from prismatic core; white patina (II L529|3).
4 Blade fragment from double-ended prismatic core; white patina (III F1040).
5 Thick irregular blade; deep white patina and fire cracking (III F1172).
6 Small triangular keeled core in grey flint, 30 x 30 x 25 mm; incipient white patina (III F1157).
7 Core of brown flint, worked down to large irregular inclusion of triangular section, 60 x 40 x 30mm; no patina (III L1172).
8 Stout flake of good-quality flint, snapped and irregularly retouched on two edges as small scraper, 35 x 70 mm; no patina (I L3|1).
9 Small discoid scraper on broken end of blade, 20 x 25 mm; no patina, large area of cortex (III F1173).
10 Discoid scraper on stout flake, 40x35mm; Th 10mm; no patina, large areas of cortex (III F1176).
11 Two blades (one broken) of brown flint, with edges damaged but no retouching; no patina (III L1172).
12 Irregular blade unretouched, 40 x 20 mm; no patina (III F1175).
13 Three small unretouched flakes; no patina (II L528|1).
14 Small flake, no patina (II F503).

The Roman scythe blade (Figs 32, 33)

Description and discussion

by Sian Rees

This scythe is an example of the extraordinarily long scythes known to have been used in the Roman period in Northern Europe. At least seventeen of these scythes have been discovered in Britain; all of those which had a datable context belong to a late stage in the Roman period, probably to the 4th century.

Description (Fig 32)
The scythe from Farmoor is now *c* 1.40 m long, but is broken near the point of the blade. The short separate fragment, *c* 80 mm long, was perhaps not quite contiguous with the main section. The scythe consists of a long, fairly straight blade, which has a cutting edge chord of 1.25 m and a maximum width of 55 mm, and which is separated by a pronounced heel from the curving elbow piece and straight tang. The blade has a thickened back edge which gradually enlarges from 5 mm near the broken point of the blade to 13 mm at the elbow, whence it tapers into the tang. The blade, though corroded at the cutting edge, can be seen to widen gradually from 33 mm at the broken end to 55 mm at the heel. A groove on the upper surface of the blade, up to 3 mm wide and 2 mm deep, runs from the broken end of the blade where it is 8 mm from the back edge, to the top where it is 16 mm from the back edge. A slighter groove is present on the under surface of the blade just behind the back rib; this groove, in places partly obscured by the beading of the back rib, also runs around the blade from the broken end to the top of the tang. In cross section, the under surface of the blade forms a convex curve. The upper surface is flatter and rises sharply at the groove to form the thickened back rib. The elbow is a consistent 45 mm wide. The thickened back edge and the grooves on the upper and under surfaces continue directly from the blade along the elbow to the top of the tang. The inner edge of the elbow is blunt, 8 mm thick, and it describes an arc of *c* 5/12ths of a circle, so that the tang is set at *c* 30° to the main direction of the blade. The tang is 250 mm long, with a maximum width of 45 mm where it joins the elbow. It is rectangular in section, 6 mm thick, with straight sides which taper to a blunt point, 22mm of which is turned upward.

The blade has been mended at a point of 360 mm from the broken end by a piece of iron 162 mm long, 27 mm wide, and 2 mm thick which has been attached to the upper surface of the blade over a break. The piece of metal is wrapped around the back rib and appears to have been beaten out on to the under surface. It is attached by four rivets, 57, 45, and 31 mm apart (measuring from tang to tip). The condition of the scythe is fair. The parts of the scythe which incorporate most metal — ie the back rib, elbow, and tang — are inevitably the best preserved. The blade edge is corroded and damaged in many places, and at a point 580 mm from the heel, the blade is bent and very broken.

Comparison with other Romano-British scythes (Fig 33; Table 3).
The discovery of scythes on Romano-British sites is by no means uncommon; over 30 sites have from Romano-British contexts produced over 50 scythes. These are, however, usually incomplete, if indeed more than a small fragment survives. It is often very difficult to classify fragments but sufficient numbers of almost complete scythes survive to reveal that a surprising variety of types of scythes were used in Britain in the Roman period. The

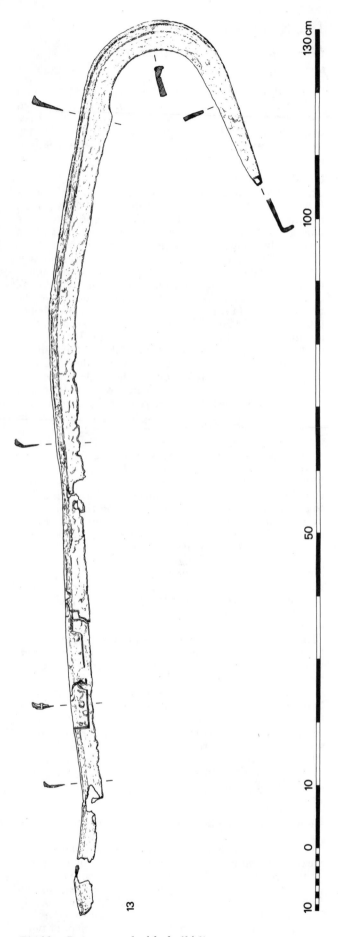

Fig 32 Roman scythe blade (1/6)

scythe from Farmoor is a member of a class of scythes which are quite distinct because of their remarkably large size. There are at least seventeen scythes in this group - twelve from a hoard from Great Chesterford, Essex (Neville 1856, 1-13), one from a hoard from Abington Piggotts, Cambridgeshire (Applebaum in Finberg 1972, 76), one isolated find from Hardwick, Oxfordshire, two from the Roman villa site at Barnsley Park, Gloucestershire (Webster 1967, 77), and the one from Farmoor. All the members of the group are very similar in shape, and their similarity should be made clear in Fig 33 and the table, which compare the large scythes with the smaller but broader scythes from Newstead; the Newstead scythes are, of course, earlier than most if not all of the larger scythes. The size of the complete examples varies from 1.47 mm to over 1.615 m. The Farmoor scythe is broken, but to judge from the width of the blade at the break, it is likely to have originally been 70-150 mm longer; this would bring it to within this size range. The four scythes from Newstead (Curle 1911, 284, plLXII and figs 3-6) are the next largest group of scythes to have survived entire from the Romano-British period, and only one of these is over 1.00 m. The large scythes all have similarly narrow blades — 37 to 55 mm maximum widths — with distinctive downward pointing ends. The blades seem to vary slightly in their degree of curvature, though this is often difficult to see because of the damaged condition of many of them. The blades are all set at very similar acute angles to the tangs which, all roughly similar in shape, terminate in an upturned point. Some scythes, eg those from Farmoor and Abington Piggotts have a distinct heel separating the tang from the blade: others, eg Great Chesterford, No 48 1093 J, have blades which merge directly with the elbow. None has the rivet or rivet hole which is present at the top of the tang on all four of the scythes from Newstead. The blades also vary somewhat in the presence or absence of grooves or ribs on the upper surface. The Farmoor scythe has a groove on the upper surface, and some of the Great Chesterford scythes have an additional rib, while others, such as the Hardwick scythe, have no features additional to the back rib. Repairs using riveted iron pieces are quite common: several of the scythes from Great Chesterford and those from Farmoor and Hardwick are mended in this way.

Method of use
There is no direct evidence for the method of attachment of the blade to the snead, nor for the use to which these large scythes were put. In 1967, the Museum of English Rural Life in Reading examined two of the Great Chesterford scythes; metallurgical analysis of one scythe was carried out by the Iron and Steel Institute (Brown, forthcoming), and a reconstruction was made with which experiments were performed to test the practicability of the scythes in use (Anstee 1967, 365-9). The reconstructed scythe of mild steel weighed 5lb 8oz, the estimated weight of the original after allowing for loss of weight by corrosion. Various types of snead were used in the experiments, all shoe-shaped at the lower end to facilitate clamping on the lower tang by means of two iron rings, each tightened by a small wedge under the tang. The upturned tang tip acted as an end stop. The experiments showed that a straight snead was fairly effective but Anstee comments that the minor difficulties experienced with it were probably of the kind that later caused the emergence of the curved snead. Although the scythe was heavy, the experiments showed that the elbow acted as a counter weight, the scythe working best when slightly tail-heavy. Apparently, the elbow tended to collect the cut crop and to deposit it in a swathe well out of the operator's way. The scythes were

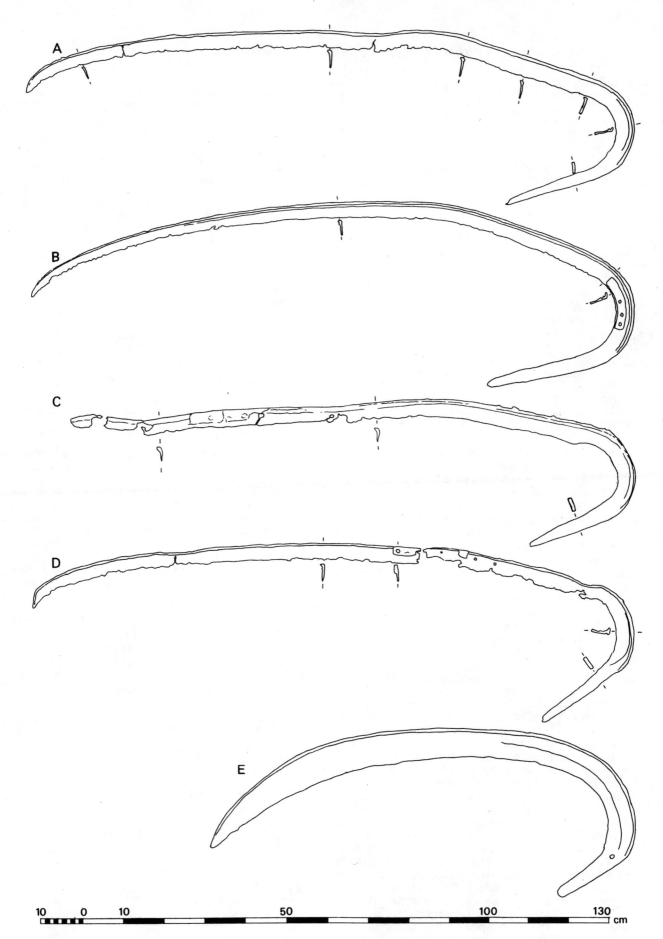

*Fig 33 Comparative scythe blades (1/9) A Abington Piggotts; B Great Chesterford 48 1093J; C Farmoor; D Hardwick;
E Newstead*

63

Table 3: Comparative dimensions of Romano-British scythes

Provenance	Present Location	Overall L (cms)	Chord of Blade (cms)	Max W Blade (cms)	L Tang (cms)	Max W Tang (cms)
Abington Piggotts	University Museum of Archaeology & Ethnology Cambridge	151.7	134	4.5	27.5	3.5
Great Chesterford 48 1093 A	University Museum of Archaeology & Ethnology,	(149.5)	(130)	4.7	30	3.9
B	Cambridge	(144.5)	(133)	4.7	26	3.3
C	,,	(151)	(138)	5.5	30	4.0
D	,,	(161.5)	(152)	4.8	23	3.3
E	,,	(141.5)	(130)	4.5	28	3.9
F	,,	(146)	(135)	4.7	25	3.8
G	,,	(123.5)	(108)	3.7	19	3.2
H	,,	147	140	5.1	24	3.8
I	,,	(148)	(138)	-	27	-
J	,,	158.7	139	4.5	28	4.1
K	,,	(130.5)	(120)	4.8	29	3.9
L	,,	(90)	-	3.8	-	-
Farmoor	Oxfordshire County Museum	(140.2)	(125)	5.5	25	4.5
Hardwick	Oxfordshire County Museum	(154)	(140)	4.2	21.5	3.5
Barnsley Park	Bristol Museum	154	127	5.0	25	4.5
	,,	200	188	5.6	16.8	2.8
Newstead FRA288	National Museum of Antiquities of Scotland, Edinburgh	119	85	8.5	16	4.5
FRA289	,,	83.5	73.5	7.6	17	3.5
FRA290	,,	97	83.5	8.0	17	3.5
FRA291	,,	97	85.3	7.4	15	3.5

Measurements in brackets affected by incompleteness of example.

used in the experiments to cut a thick crop of tall grass, and crops of a modern winter wheat and barley, both cut when nearly ripe. An experienced mower used the tool with little bother, using either a full swing with a wide cut, the mower walking forward, or short chopping strokes, the mower moving sideways. Inevitably the scythe worked best on flat ground which had no tussocks or stones.

It is difficult to know for what purpose the scythes were used. Agronomists of the Roman period are of little help in attributing function to the scythe. White (1967, 98-9) considers that the *falx* mentioned in Varro's account of hay harvesting (Varro I xlix 1) must be the *falx faenaria*, or scythe. Pliny mentions two types of scythes in connection with mowing of hay meadows: a one-handled short Italian type suitable for cutting brambles as well as hay, and a longer type used on the large estates in Gaul (Pliny XVIII lxvii 261). White states, 'The single-headed reap hook or sickle [*falx messoria*] was the only implement used [for harvesting], the scythe being the implement for mowing hay or grass', and certainly none of the classical agronomists refer to the scythe as being used for harvesting cereal crops (White 1970, 182). The experiments at Reading showed that the scythes were quite practical for cutting hay or wheat and barley, but Anstee suggests that the long scythes developed from cutting the relatively widely spaced stalks of cereal crops, whereas the Newstead scythes would be better suited to the hay harvest being shorter and wider. White, on the other hand, suggests that if hay were being cut on a large scale on estates such as at Great Chesterford, very large implements would have effected a considerable saving in labour. He suggests that time would have been at a premium, particularly in Britain where the hay harvest was presumably cut at a time when summer storms could damage or ruin a crop. White points to other factors which would influence the development of the scythe as a hay mowing tool: firstly the increased demand for fodder created by improvements in animal husbandry; secondly the change in farm management leading to the

development of larger open fields and properly managed meadows; and thirdly a probable shortage of seasonal labour for harvesting operations. These long scythes are found also in the Rhineland and France, the probable home of other labour-saving agricultural inventions such as the *vallus* harvesting machine. The long scythes seem to have gone out of use after the 4th century.

The discovery of the Farmoor scythe makes a useful contribution to the discussion of the use of these implements: both its location at the side of the droveway where it reached the floodplain, and the general biological evidence for a grassland environment strongly suggest that it was used for mowing hay. This is the most direct type of evidence that is likely to emerge for their use, and so far Farmoor is the only case where the context of the find has provided any useful information in this respect: all the other examples from reasonably well stratified deposits have been associated with hoards of ironwork or (at Barnsley Park) with iron-working itself.

Acknowledgements
I am most grateful to Miss M D Craster of the University Museum of Archaeology and Ethnology, Cambridge, for allowing me to study the Great Chesterford scythes and metallurgical report, and the Abington Piggotts scythe, and to Mr J Rhodes of the Oxfordshire County Department of Museum Services, Woodstock, for allowing me to study the example from Hardwick. I profited greatly from discussions with Mr A Jewell of the Museum of English Rural Life, Reading.

Metallurgical examination
by G T Brown

Sample
One small piece, from a position near the point, was examined metallurgically. It measured 50.80 mm x 31.75

mm overall and was extremely corroded. After removal of the corrosion product, the sample was only c 0.795 mm thick. This precluded meaningful cross-sectioning; the blade segment was mounted and the flat face ground until solid metal was exposed. This was then polished and etched as appropriate.

Metallography

In the unetched condition a number of elongated 'slag' stringers were apparent. Corrosion had proceeded along the slag/metal interface and so the size of the original particles was in some doubt.

After etching, the structure was shown to range from ferrite to areas predominantly of pearlite. Pls VIII and IX show typical structures. The finer-grained ferrite (Pl VIII) had a peculiar structure, rather like cored etching. This is not unusual in Roman iron and is frequently associated with a significant level of phosphorus.

In general the structure was relatively coarse-grained and showed no signs of residual cold work or transformation part way through the alpha-gamma region.

As is normal in this type of iron, high- and low-carbon regions existed side by side (Pl IX). The cutting edge appeared to have more high-carbon regions than the backing strip. Carbon content estimates suggest levels as high as 0.5% in places.

In general, slag and high-carbon regions were elongated along the blade length.

Discussion

The sample was typical of Roman iron, ie extremely heterogeneous with respect to carbon content, and the presence and elongation of slag inclusions. This type of structure results from the Roman iron-making process which was one of reduction in the solid state (Brown 1965), the metal never having been molten. Clearly, the blade had been produced by hot forging from a bloom. The finishing temperature was relatively high (above 850°C?) since grain size was coarse and the structure was fully recrystallized.

Although the cutting edge appeared to be higher in carbon it must not be assumed that this was deliberate. Had an attempt been made to select and weld on a separate cutting edge there would have been evidence of this. Such evidence was lacking from the present sample.

Conclusions

The sample was entirely consistent with Roman iron examined from other sources (Angus *et al* 1962, 956-68) and with a scythe examined from elsewhere (Brown forthcoming). The blade had been hot-forged to the finished shape. Its metallurgical structure was heterogeneous in character.

Archaeological interpretation

by George Lambrick

Phase I: Early Iron Age

Pits

The earliest occupation on the site was represented by the early Iron Age pits on the gravel terrace (see p19; Figs 34 and 9). No structure was found, but the daub from Pit 1037 suggests that there may have been a building in the area.

The lack of positive structural evidence is equally explicable as having been missed, lost to the scrapers, or never having penetrated below the topsoil anyway. Most of the pits contained enough domestic rubbish to suggest that the site was inhabited, while the lump of forging slag, and the layers of burning in F1013 suggest that ironworking was carried out. Smithing or iron roasting pits of this sort have been found in association with domestic pits of much the same date at Abingdon (Ashville), Cassington, and City Farm, Hanborough (Parrington 1978, 38; *Oxoniensia* 1937, 201; Case *et al* 1964, 94-5). The Farmoor example seems to be the same sort of feature, although no slag was recovered from it.

The possible functions of the other pits are debatable. Their flat bottoms and steep sides may indicate that originally they were for storage, but it is nevertheless plausible that they were made for rubbish disposal: after all, that is what they were used for eventually and if there was no arable land the use of rubbish as fertilizer would be less likely, so that some other means of disposal would be sought. The complete absence of carbonized grain in the Farmoor smithing pit (see p 103) may indicate that there was no arable since by contrast the Ashville examples both contained reasonable quantities of cereal remains. The pits cannot have been dug as sources of water or gravel because of their small size and shallowness. Elsewhere such features have been interpreted as storage pits (Parrington 1978, 31; Riley 1946, 38: Williams 1951, 12), but the small size of some of those in the City Farm West Settlement led Sutermeister to consider other functions including rubbish disposal (Case *et al* 1964, 49). In practice, the evidence is at present insufficient to arrive at any firm conclusions about their functions (see also Discussion, p 137).

The distribution of the Farmoor pits resembles more closely the City Farm East Settlement (Case *et al* 1964, Pits E/1, N/1-5, 42 and fig 2) than Ashville, Mount Farm, or Beard Mill (Parrington 1978, fig 30; Myres 1937, fig 3; Williams 1951, figs 4 and 7). Possibly, as suggested for the City Farm pits, they were outliers with a more concentrated area of occupation nearby, but there was no indication of this and they could be explained in terms of a fairly fluid settlement (Harding 1972, 19). The lack of evidence for the location of any habitable structure and the uncertainty of the pits' function, however, make such considerations highly speculative.

Phase II: Middle Iron Age

General chronology

A clear change between the first and second phases of occupation is apparent from the types of pottery used (see Fig 20) and from the types and location of features excavated (see Fig 34). The difference suggests an abandonment and reoccupation of the site, and perhaps reflects a more fundamental change of economic and social structure. The same sort of break seems to some extent apparent at Mount Farm (Myres 1937) and Ashville. At Ashville the change in pottery styles is less clear, but on such an intensively occupied site the break may well be obscured by the presence of residual material (De Roche in Parrington 1978, 71). Within the second main phase of occupation the Farmoor pottery reveals no very clear chronological development, but possibly the floodplain enclosures were later than the Area II complex according to the carbon 14 dating (see p 143).

FARMOOR

Main Phases

Floodplain

Old River Channel

Gravel Terrace

Early Iron Age

Middle Iron Age

Roman

Medieval

Scale of 100 0 100 200 Metres   Scale of 50 0 100 200 300 Yards

Fig 34

The enclosures and associated features in Area II

(Figs 4, 5)

Of the Iron Age features on the gravel terrace in Area II the main enclosure probably consisted of four phases (see Fig 35). It was made up of so many different parts, so varied in form, however, that it is difficult to arrive at any entirely convincing interpretation.

The circular enclosure to the north belonged to the first phase (a) since the earliest part of the main enclosure (F528/6) and the end of the palisade of the circular enclosure (F560) clearly respected each other. It is likely that the slightly sinuous length of the ditch to the east (F505) also belonged to this phase, and the position of its original butt-ends suggests two entrances to the northern enclosure, a wide one to the east and a narrower one to the south between F528/6 and F505. This entrance was also marked by the inward return of the palisade (F560). A side entrance in a similar position was found at Twywell, Northamptonshire (Jackson 1975, fig 14). The extent of F528/6 southwards is unknown, but cannot have been further than the end of F529.

Both F505 and F528/6 were thus short and probably acted simply as sumps for the drainage or collection of surface water, as is consistent with their fills. It is unlikely that the larger 'enclosure' at this stage incorporated more

66

than these two ditches: F530 could conceivably have held a palisade in this phase, and the digging of F503 and F531 might have destroyed earlier features; but there is no evidence for this, and in any case it seems inherently unlikely that the enclosures would thus be made of alternating lengths of palisade and ditch. Nevertheless the fact that the south side of the circular enclosure was different from the rest, and that its line seemed to compromise between the opposing arcs of the enclosures, suggests that there must at least have been a well defined area to the south which could not be intruded upon by the smaller enclosure, even though the purpose of such an area is obscure.

The existence of a house cannot be excluded: it is unlikely to have been post-built as postholes survived elsewhere, but any other method of construction is feasible, and the absence of domestic refuse need not rule this out since a south-east facing door would be some way from the ends of the ditches. As with the floodplain enclosures (see below, p 69) other interpretations are possible and the existence of a fence or bank which left no trace must be considered.

The circular enclosure is rather clearer : the palisade (F560) presumably continued round to the south-east entrance, in which the central post (F567) may have supported gates. There was no evidence for a post on the south-west side, but a posthole might have been destroyed when F503 was dug. Within the enclosure, probably dating from this phase, was the semicircle of postholes. It is conceivable that the structure was no more than a fence or a windbreak; but if it was contemporary with the palisade it could have served no purpose as a fence except as something like a continuous drying rack (and there is no good parallel for such a structure), while as a windbreak it would be unnecessary and was the wrong way round to be effective against the prevailing winds. Another possibility is that the posts were free-standing. In this form they could have served various functions: anything from totem poles in a sacred enclosure to hayrick supports or tethering posts (cf Richmond 1968, 20 and fig 13) in a simple yard; but there is no supporting evidence for such interpretations.

In the past such post-built structures have tentatively been considered as semicircular buildings, examples having been found at Stanton Harcourt (Williams 1951, 10-12 and fig 6), Ivinghoe Beacon (Cotton and Frere 1968, 195-6 and fig 7) and Weakley (Jackson 1976, 76 and fig 3). Two semicircular gullies interpreted as wall foundation trenches were excavated at Gun Hill, Essex (Drury and Rodwell 1973, 53-4, 96-7, fig 6), where hearths and pits and a large posthole on the diameter of one structure suggested its use as a workshop. The Gun Hill excavators cite Rainsborough as another instance, though the report carefully avoids saying that the gully was to support vertical timbers (Avery *et al* 1967, 223 and fig 5). A possibly more convincing example indicated by a slot was found at Wakerley, Northamptonshire (this was kindly pointed out to me by Dr W Rodwell; *Britannia* 1974, fig 12, facing 434). The Farmoor example, however, if it is not to be explained merely as a group of posts, may be more convincing as a building than any of these.

Various reconstructions are possible. The arc of postholes may represent a permanent wall with the diametrical side semi-permanent, comprising movable screens, as suggested at Gun Hill (Drury and Rodwell 1973, 97); this would suggest a covered working space in the building with an easily accessible open yard in front surrounded by the palisade. Alternatively, the diametrical side could have been permanent if it were

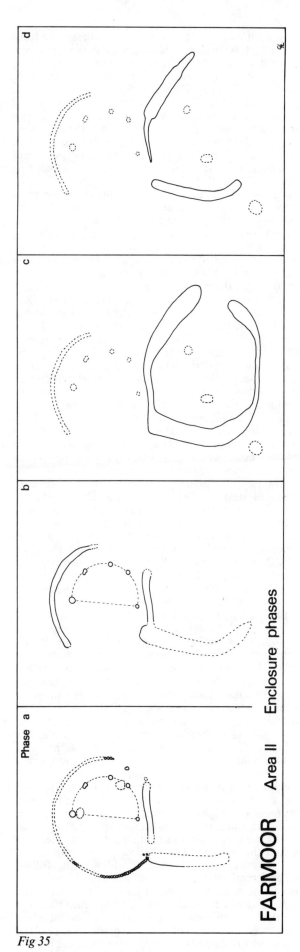

FARMOOR   Area II   Enclosure phases

Fig 35

built on a sill beam or of turf which would leave no trace in the ground. A third possibility is that all the walls were permanent. In any of the reconstructions it seems likely that there was a permanent doorway through the narrower gap between Postholes 554 and 569, opposite the entrance to the enclosure (though if so, Pit 553 could not have been contemporary). Structurally any of these reconstructions would work, each requiring a long diametrical tie beam and beams tying the posts of the semicircle together. As Drury and Rodwell point out there would be no difficulty in roofing such a building (Drury and Rodwell 1973, 97).

On the whole, the first reconstruction seems the most reasonable, fitting most closely the excavated evidence as well as conforming most logically to the layout of the rest of the enclosure. The exact purpose of the supposed building, however, is not clear. No hearths or other sign of domestic or industrial activity were found. The two pits (F553 and F576) provide no help: they were associated with the rest of the building only on the basis of their position just inside its walls, and their size and contents throw no light either on their own function or that of the building. This absence of positive evidence, however, need not exclude the interpretation of such a building as a workshop since there are plenty of domestic and agricultural activities which could not be expected to leave any trace. Only activities such as metal-working or pottery-making can reasonably be excluded as possibilities. The length of life of the building is uncertain: all that can be said is that it survived long enough to require the replacement of one post. Easy access to the rest of the enclosure, avoiding having to go round the side of the building, would have been provided by the side entrance between F505 and F528/6.

By the second phase (b) of the main enclosure (represented only by Ditch 528/7 and Ditch 505) the smaller enclosure may already have fallen into disuse since the fill of one of the palisade postholes was cut by the new ditch, which also blocked the side entrance, encroaching upon the enclosed area. Possibly the gully (F560/2-3) which replaced the palisade to the north also belonged to this phase. Its purpose is unclear, though if the semicircular building still stood it could have been to carry surface water away from it (perhaps having been made just for one storm). The function and extent of the main 'enclosure' remain uncertain: its ditch may have been continuous between F528 and F505, but it still consisted only of these two elements.

Phase (c) of the large enclosure was the only one in which it was probably complete: the pre-existing sections were largely cleared out and extensions were made to form the ultimate horseshoe shape (F503, F530, F531). The ditches also mostly reached their maximum size. The layers of grey gravelly silt and gravelly clay loam above probably represent one gradual accumulation, possibly with some deliberate backfilling. The fill of the narrow gully (F530) on the south side appeared to be contemporary, but it was not clear whether the feature was a gully or a robbed palisade: its shallowness, narrowness, and slight unevenness might have been left by a palisade, but there were no definite post settings, and in view of the variability of the other sides it is at least as likely that this was simply a shallow gully between two larger, sump-like sections of ditch. This would follow more consistently the function of the earlier phases, and moreover the existence of filled-up earlier ditches may partly have affected how the new ones were dug: the large hole at the west end would have had to be cleared out if the water were to soak easily into the gravel, whereas the new sections would not need to be so deep, though quite

large sumps seem to have been provided in F503 and F531.

The purpose of the enclosure is again obscure: enough domestic refuse was found (including loomweights) to suggest that people lived nearby, but there was no evidence for any building. The three small pits, F507, F514, and F547, might each have belonged to any phase and they provide no further clarification. Perhaps there was a building which left no trace, but this cannot be asserted with any conviction, as it can for the floodplain penannular enclosures (see p 69), because of the curious nature of the ditch itself. The other usual possibilities of storage or animal penning must also be considered.

The final phase (d) consisted of the large deepening in F503, creating two small butt-ends in the bottom, and the shallower recutting of F528 and F529. The recut in F503 seems to have been another sump with a shallow gully running back most of the way along F505. Its fill was contemporary with that of the recut in F528 and F529. There was again plenty of material to suggest domestic occupation, but no sign of any building, nor any indication of what purpose the enclosure served (if indeed the ditches still marked the position of an enclosure). The persistent redigging of the same two sides of the enclosure remains inexplicable.

The dumping of stones in the top of F528 and F529 cannot have long postdated their silting up since the ground must still have been soft enough to require consolidation, and indeed so soft that the stones half buried themselves in the fill of the recut.

Possibly contemporary with the enclosures was the large hole in the north-east corner of Area II. It was clearly a large sump, with an overflow channel (F592) to the east. Possibly it served both to drain surface water and to collect ground water, thereby also acting as a waterhole. The recut had been dug down to gravel, possibly to ensure a reasonably rapid supply. The biological evidence shows that it could have been part of a functioning system of ditches, perhaps linked to a stream or ditch in the old river bed, but this is not conclusive and some of the aquatic remains could have been brought in by flooding. There was no clear evidence for flooding or short-term occupation as with the floodplain enclosures (see p 125), but these cannot be ruled out.

Other enclosures on the gravel terrace
(Figs 6, 7, 9, 10)

The most likely, but not the only possible, function of F18 in Area I is that it was an animal pen. Its three ditched sides were probably permanent with the fourth side left open to facilitate driving the animals in. This could then be closed with hurdles when the operation was completed. The ditch itself may have been sufficiently steep-sided to be animal-proof, and the slot at the bottom may have been to ensure that this was not seriously affected by silting, or may have been created by repeated cleaning out for the same purpose. There would have been a danger of driving animals into the ditch, but this could be overcome by the provision of a fence or light-weight barrier on the inside. An internal bank (arguably suggested by the silting at Section P and Q) made of spoil from the ditch, or perhaps turf stripped from the interior, would restrict the area of an already small enclosure.

Sometimes small enclosures are thought suitable for sheep, but it is quite reasonable for them to have been used equally well for pigs, or for a small number of cattle or horses, perhaps for individual animals.

Dating evidence was lacking in any quantity, though the pottery conformed to the general middle Iron Age material. The Roman sherds in the top of the ditch sugest that it remained visible as an earthwork for some time.

To the west F1019 seems to have marked another tiny, relatively undatable enclosure, again perhaps used for animals. The lack of domestic refuse and its curious shape at least show that it was not the site of a house. The gullies were clearly for drainage and consisted of three phases, the later ones diminishing the size of the enclosure. Once again it could only have functioned as an enclosure if there were fences, and the small slots (F1021 and F1022) may be an indication of these.

The third of the enclosure features on the gravel terrace (F1045) was the most fragmentary and the oddest, apparently consisting of a waterworn gully ending in a man-made sump. Much may have been lost to the scrapers, but it gave the impression of being a storm water gully rather than a more permanent feature.

Enclosure group 1 (Figs 11, 12)

It is clear from the neat layout of the middle group of floodplain enclosures that they formed one unit (presumably a small farmstead), though its overall plan was not its original form: Section R, through the west side of F1007 and F1008, showed that the penannular gully had already been cleared a few times before being recut and realigned to make the spur aligned on F1008 which formed the new southern side of the enlarged penannular enclosure. Since this new gully (F1008) continued into F1009 to define the rectangular area to the north, this compound clearly must have been an addition to the original enclosure. From their layout it is likely that F1010 and F1012 were also additions.

The penannular gully formed the standard type of enclosure for a round house. Such enclosures have a diameter of about 13.00 m, a south-east or east entrance (facing away from the cold north-east and the prevailing winds and rain of the south-west), and a concentration of domestic rubbish in the ends of the ditch, presumably just outside the door. Even though no structural remains survive, such evidence is now usually regarded as sufficient to demonstrate the existence of a round house (Parrington 1978, 34; Jones 1974, 194-6; Jackson 1975, 50; Williams and Mynard 1974, 8 and 16). The lack of structural evidence makes any reconstruction possible, since postholes, stakeholes or wall slots could have been removed by the scrapers, while a turf construction would in any case probably leave no trace in the subsoil. The last possibility is perhaps the most likely in view of the evidence from the enclosures to the south (see p 70). It is, at any rate, certain that the surrounding gully was not a wall trench (see below).

The possible functions of the other enclosures are debatable. At Ashville there appeared to be buildings in one annexe (Parrington 1978, 35), but there is no evidence whether they existed at Farmoor. Possibly they were stock pens or yards for work or storage (see also below, p 71); they might even have included a vegetable garden — there is no positive botanical evidence for this, but since vegetables are eaten before they set seed little could be expected and in any case wild plants which could be used as vegetables were present. Although the purpose of the enclosures is unclear, they nevertheless were almost certainly connected with the control of animals. The biological results provide ample evidence of animal husbandry but it is not clear whether the animals were to be kept in or out, or exactly how it was achieved.

The gullies themselves were undoubtedly open because of the accumulation of rubbish in them, particularly either side of the entrance of the penannular enclosures (Jones 1974, 196; Williams and Mynard 1974, 18; Jackson 1975, 52). It was also clear that they were for drainage, each gully being separate and incorporating deepenings, which must have been sumps, usually placed so as to avoid water accumulating near the entrances. The biological evidence independently confirms both these conclusions, also showing that the ditches must have had puddles of water (at least) in them almost all the year round to support the aquatic fauna and flora (see p 110). This evidence for a high water table also shows that the gullies can only have been any use in draining surface run-off, and even so were probably not very effective, since the water would not easily soak into the partly waterlogged subsoil. This would have been relieved to some extent by the provision of the sumps, for which possible parallels can be found on other gravel sites such as Langford Downs (Williams 1946, 50, fig 16, and fig 15 No 16) and Ardleigh, Essex (Erith and Holbert 1970, fig 4; fig 12, Sections 2-3 and 4-5).

Even allowing for the loss of overburden the gullies would have been small and are unlikely to have been animal-proof, even if the spoil from them was made into a bank. The control of animals must therefore have been achieved by other means, for example with hurdles or a fence, as suggested at Ardleigh (Erith and Holbert 1970, 12 and fig 4). From the biological evidence it is clear that hedges were certainly not used, but it is possible that turf walls were.

There are no exact parallels for the layout of the farmstead, though the house circle with rectangular annexes at Ardleigh is fairly similar, making up a compact, neatly laid out complex formed by drainage gullies, possibly including sumps (Erith and Holbert 1970, figs 4 and 12). Circular annexes are more common, with examples at Ashville, Mucking, Hod Hill, and elsewhere (Parrington 1978, fig 3; Jones 1974, figs 3 and 4; Richmond 1968, fig 2). Such comparisons should be treated with caution, however, since these sites are in other ways very different from the Farmoor enclosures, especially in two respects.

Firstly the Farmoor enclosures were subject to flooding. This might have been expected from their position on the floodplain, and from the records of flooding held by the Thames Conservancy dating from before the development of the most recent river controls (see p 6); the layers of alluvium sealing F1108 and most of the southern enclosure complex provided further evidence, but the proof that flooding was contemporary with the occupation of the farmsteads came from the biological remains in the ditches of all three complexes (see p 109).

Secondly it can be shown that they were probably occupied for no more than about five years each: the evidence for this is entirely botanical, and relies on the absence of particularly common perennial plants of disturbed ground, such as elder and perennial nettle which, on the basis of the other evidence, would certainly have flourished in that environment (see p 114).

These two considerations substantially affect the interpretation of the farmstead. The house was presumably occupied seasonally to avoid the flooding, especially as the problem could have been avoided by siting the farmstead on the higher ground only about 200 m to the south. It is also clear that the enclosures cannot be interpreted as long-term settlements just because their plans seem fairly elaborate and carefully designed or because the gullies were recut. The clearing out of the ditches may simply have been an annual chore when the occupants returned after the winter's flooding, or a more frequent need if the ditches also tended to be filled with mud because of animals moving about. The short life of the enclosures also makes normal dating evidence useless in considering what other features were contemporary.

Much of this interpretation applies equally to the other floodplain enclosures, and need not be repeated. More attention will be given to the differences exhibited by the other enclosures and the additional information provided by them.

Enclosure group 2 (Figs 12, 13)

In the case of the northern complex the gullies were linked together, and rather than having several sumps apparently had one large one (F1101) to cope with the greater intake. A possible subsidiary one at the junction of F1110, F1111, and F1113, may have been intended merely to avoid blockages caused by the confluence of the three ditches. Gully 1115 and Pit 1112 at its end were presumably an overflow channel with its own sump. Gully 1114 and Pit 1105 were also for drainage, possibly leaving an entrance between the two sumps to an apparently incomplete enclosure to the north, though it is by no means certain that such an enclosure existed.

The functions of the enclosures are again debatable: it would be reasonable for some to be animal pens, but the reasons for their exact configuration are not clear. Again there were no hedges, but the actual narrowness of the ditches is illustrated where F1108 was protected by the datum point (Fig 12, Section P111) which emphasizes the need for a fence or some other barrier. The penannular ditch (F1100) was clearly another house enclosure, but in this case it postdated some of the other ditches. The butt-end of F1102 had been filled with stone to provide a firm footing at the entrance, and the fills of F1117 and Sump 1101 were cut by F1100 suggesting that the drainage system had fallen into disuse. There may have been a break in occupation, but it cannot have been very long as the fill of F1102 must still have been soft for the stones to have been embedded in it. Biological evidence for short-term occupation was recovered from F1100, so that either the whole complex must have been made, modified, and abandoned within around five years, or else it must have reverted to undisturbed grassland before F1100 was dug, and the site reoccupied with the construction of the penannular enclosure (again for no more than about five years). Either interpretation is plausible and it is impossible to determine which is correct.

The presence of the horse jaw and skull either side of the entrance to the round house enclosure is of some interest. Possibly they were coincidental rubbish deposits, but in view of the known reverence for horses in the Iron Age (Ross 1967, 321; Harding 1974, 70) it is possible that they may have had a 'ritual' purpose; after all this need mean no more than that they were put there for luck just as horseshoes are nailed to stable doors today. At Heath Farm, Milton Common, in Oxfordshire, a horse's mandible was found in a similar position, but while it is marked on the plan, its presence is not discussed in the text and there is nothing to show that it was not fortuitous (Rowley 1973, fig 3).

Pits

The pits west of the enclosures were probably contemporary, though only one was excavated and very little dating evidence was recovered. Their functions are unclear: as usual storage and rubbish disposal are possible, but in view of the high water table storage is unlikely and it is more plausible that they were originally to provide a water supply.

Enclosure 1107

To the north, just enough of F1107 survived to show, on the basis of its diameter, the position of its entrance and the rubbish in the ditch end, that it was a house enclosure. It is unknown whether it was part of another complex lost in the gravel pit or an isolated house enclosure, as presumably F1007 had originally been (see p 69).

Enclosure group 3 (Figs 14, 15)

In the southernmost enclosure group insufficient of the two parallel ditches (F1157 and F1174) survived for any interpretation to be possible except that they appeared to be unlike any other Iron Age gullies on the floodplain, and may be the remnants of an earlier type of enclosure.

The usual evidence for the penannular house enclosure was supplemented in this case with two important though indirect pieces of evidence for the house's construction. Firstly, the layer of small stones bulldozed from its interior may have been a cobbled floor: although the evidence was not *in situ*, it is difficult to think of any other explanation for the layer, and the interpretation is supported by a parallel at Port Meadow Site 7 where surviving cobbling was excavated (*Oxoniensia* 1946-7, 163). Floors are not uncommon on upland sites (Wheeler 1943, 94 and fig 17; Hogg 1960, figs 5 and 6; Whitley 1943, 105-7, fig 2 and pl 21; Jobey 1959, 235, fig 5) and there are instances on other lowland sites (Jackson 1975, 54 and fig 17).

Secondly, there is good evidence for the turf being stripped from the area, and it seems reasonable that it was used to build a round house, though again any direct evidence would already have been destroyed by the bulldozer. The stripping of the natural topsoil was indicated by where it had been cut away in Section X111 (L1184), and by its almost complete absence from the rest of the area excavated, where L1172, consisting mostly of finer alluvial silt with some general rubbish and dung (see p 111 and 141), had replaced it. The surviving natural soil in Section X111 may have been left as a platform for the house or its walls, but insufficient survived to be able to tell.

Provided the right tools were available (ie good spades) the use of turf would almost certainly have been the quickest and easiest way to build a round house. It is evident from the botanical evidence that wood was not readily available on the site itself (see p 112) and it has been established by experiment that a large number of trees are required to provide enough wood for an entirely timber-built round house (P J Reynolds, pers comm). Three people working on the site took only two hours to build a clay lump site hut out of the alluvial overburden, including cutting the blocks. Alternating freezing and thawing and the absence of vegetation to bind the blocks led to rapid erosion of the walls; but given more care, time, and experience, and better materials (ie turf rather than pure clay) it seemed evident that a sound structure could be constructed with considerable ease and speed. With the walls built of turf it would then have been relatively easy to use timber and thatch or hides for the roof, and timber for the door.

There is no positive evidence for a turf building, but certainly enough turf was stripped to build the house. Supposing its walls to have averaged 1.00 m thick by 1.50 m high, its diameter 9.00 m and its doorway 1.00 m wide, 41 cubic metres of turf would have been required. If it were 0.10 m thick this would cover 410 square metres. The area of the supposed round house would be only 78 square metres so that a much larger area would have had to be stripped. The internal area of the enclosure to the south was about 240 square metres, and the natural topsoil had been stripped from the whole of the excavated area leaving only sandy lenses and areas where tufa had formed. There is no reason to suppose that the unexcavated portions had been treated differently. The areas just outside the enclosure had also been stripped and salvage work established that this area extended some way (perhaps about 15.00 m) to the east, though probably not to the west. It is thus clear that enough turf for at least one round house was probably removed.

If the turf was not used for a house, some other explanation for its stripping and for its disposal is required. It could have been used for walls or banks round the enclosures (possibly instead of the fences suggested earlier, or as a support for them). The absence of evidence for large banks, however, cannot be explained by their having been destroyed already, as could have happened with the house enclosure. If the turf were stripped for some other reason, to avoid the creation of a quagmire for example, it seems unlikely that the material would not have been put to some constructive use, and the construction of a round house is a likely possibility.

There are few other examples of turf houses perhaps because the evidence is so elusive; there are possible ones from Danebury, using stakes, but these are doubtful (Cunliffe 1976, 205 and figs 5, 6). The employment of the most readily available building material is apparent, however, in the use of earth and chalk (or just chalk) for the walls of round houses at Hod Hill and Maiden Castle (Richmond 1968, 19; Wheeler 1943, 94-6 and fig 18) and the use of other local materials elsewhere (Whitley 1943, 105-7, fig 2 and pl 21; Hogg 1960, 34-35 and fig 14; Cunliffe 1974, 184 and fig 12:4). It is hardly surprising that stone-built structures should seem very much more common considering how easily turf examples could be destroyed, and the comparison is probably more one of survival than of actual usage.

The rectangular enclosure was probably contemporary with the penannular ditch: there was no clear distinction between their fills and near the house enclosure Ditch 1159 contained a reasonable amount of domestic rubbish including loomweights.

The ditch was larger than that of the other floodplain enclosures, but even so it is unlikely that it would have been animal-proof by itself, and as suggested above, a bank, turf wall, or fence would have been necessary. No convincing evidence for any of these was found, and the absence of any structural remains cannot be explained by lack of stratigraphy or any indication of deliberate levelling, though the outside edge of the enclosure ditch was not very carefully or extensively examined. The thin spreads of gravel either side of the ditch may have been dug out of it and could have been the remains of completely flattened banks. The erosion of earthworks by flooding has been suggested for the Bronze Age barrows at Grendon, Northamptonshire (McCormick 1975, 12-14), but this is unlikely to have removed substantial banks composed largely of clay, and the ample evidence for the deposition of fine alluvium at Farmoor suggests that flood waters would have had

insufficient erosive force. On the other hand, if the banks were largely made of loose gravel with virtually no turf covering, or with only a turf core, they could have been eroded, especially if this were coupled with destructive trampling by animals. This is not unreasonable in comparison with the external gravel banks excavated on Port Meadow Site 5 (Atkinson 1942, 33 and fig 5), but the evidence here is still not very convincing.

There might have been an external fence since postholes may possibly have been missed, but this is doubtful and it is certainly not true of the inside where the only possible barrier of this sort would be free-standing hurdles.

During the life of the enclosure the ditch was probably recut, though this was suggested only by the shape of its ends (and possibly the north-west corner), not by its fill. The deviation of its internal edge at the north-west corner was opposite the end of one gravel bank (F1171) but this relationship does not indicate an old opening, as there was no evidence of the bank being cut by the ditch or of it continuing on the other side, and in fact both banks probably postdated the enclosure (see below).

The surviving stratigraphy shows that this enclosure could not have been used either for buildings or (since the soil had been removed) as a garden. The apparent cleanness of the area before the gravel banks were put down does not rule out its use for animals: pure manure, unlike domestic refuse, could have disappeared entirely. As the topsoil seems to have been removed, the mud could only have been brought in by flooding and on the animals themselves, neither of which would cause a substantial build-up in the short term. The relatively undisturbed state of the gravel does not preclude the enclosure having been used for animals, though this depends on the type of animals, the agricultural activities involved, and the dampness of the ground. If, for example, it was used only occasionally, such as for calving, little disturbance might be caused, especially as drainage would have been fairly quick into the exposed gravel and the ditch.

Some other functions can more or less be ruled out. Food storage is out of the question: the space is excessive for the supplies presumably of one family for only part of the year, and in any case there was no structural evidence for it. The storage of timber or hay are further possibilities. Timber would have been needed for fuel, probably for parts of the house, and possibly for fencing. As wood was not readily available on the site (see p 112) it would have been brought from elsewhere and presumably stored. Hay might be collected and stored during the summer before being removed elsewhere for use in the winter. Although the biological evidence indicates grazed grassland and the presence of animals in the immediate vicinity, the existence of more distant hay meadows is perfectly possible. However, the biological evidence also shows that long-term storage of both these commodities certainly did not occur, although temporary storage remains possible (see p 126). It also shows that activities such as threshing, which would certainly have left obvious traces, did not occur (cf the Roman samples, p 127).

These arguments apply equally to the other floodplain enclosures, but for them the lack of stratification makes it difficult to narrow down the possibilities as far. Even in this case the function of the enclosure cannot be defined exactly, and in fact a variety of functions may have been fulfilled.

The gravel banks (F1170 and F1171) probably postdated the enclosure. F1170 overlay the fill of its ditch on the south side, and the fact that it passed through the

71

enclosure entrance may be coincidental. There is no proof that the western bank was also later than the ditch, but its likely continuation south of the enclosure makes this probable. The fact that it seemed to respect the north-west corner of the ditch may also be coincidental. Possibly it was earlier than the east bank, however, since it petered out where they met, as though gravel had been removed from it to build F1170. The generally lower level of the gravel towards the centre of the enclosure could be attributed to the building or heightening of the banks: the ditch had already silted up and therefore could not have been the source of the gravel. The silt and rubbish layer (L1172) also at least partly postdated the silting up of the ditch, and was clearly in the process of accumulating before, during, and after the building and heightening of the gravel banks.

The banks were almost certainly raised pathways above the surrounding mire (L1172). Judging by their size, and hard, smooth, level surface, they were only for people on foot, not animals. Furthermore, it is most unlikely that they would have survived in such good condition if animals had been confined in the same area, and clearly some care had been taken in keeping them clear of the accumulating mud. Originally the paths seem not to have been necessary; the areas of subsoil beneath them had probably not served that purpose, but possibly had been left because the material was too sandy to be taken with the turf and had then been protected by the paths themselves from being dug out with the material for their heightening. The need for the paths may have arisen only when the ditch silted up and no longer provided drainage and a place for rubbish and alluvium to accumulate: certainly little material of this sort predated them.

There are no close archaeological parallels to support the interpretation of these banks as paths (though cf Bulleid 1968, 33-4), but there is a good modern example on the other side of Oxford where just such a gravel causeway crosses the Cherwell floodplain from the first gravel terrace to the old Marston foot ferry.

The appearance of the paths after the silting up of the ditch may indicate the disappearance of the enclosure: this would be consistent with the ditch having been allowed to silt up, and the accumulation of mud (L1172) might well have resulted from the freer movement of cattle over the area as well as from the lack of drainage. Furthermore if Path 1170 did continue to the south as F1182 it must have been intended to provide access between the floodplain and the gravel terrace across the old river bed (which was probably still fairly marshy) rather than being concerned specifically with the enclosure.

Before the post-Iron Age alluviation the position of the supposed crossing point of the old river bed may have been the narrowest point between two areas of marginally higher ground (Fig 2). The layout of the three main groups of enclosures in a straight line may not be coincidental if there were some sort of track leading across the floodplain from this point. Such a track might well provide the only chronological continuity between the enclosures which could individually be of widely differing dates as well as being very short-lived.

Phase III: Roman

General chronology

The third separate major phase of occupation was confined entirely to the gravel terrace (Fig 34), and appears to have lasted from the 2nd century AD to the late 4th century. Unfortunately, however, dating evidence was unsatisfactory, for while certain features were quite closely dated, most were hardly datable at all, and in the absence of good stratigraphy it is impossible to reconstruct a watertight chronology for the settlement's development. In many cases it was clear that features were broadly of the same date, but it was very seldom possible to show whether they were exactly contemporary.

2nd century features: the droveway and other features

The datable 2nd century features on the site consisted of the first phase of the eastern droveway ditch (F1074/4), three small inexplicable features in Area I (F74, F58, and F16), possibly Pit 1060, and just possibly F4 in Area I, in which case the penannular slot (F5) and its associated features would also have to be assigned to this early period.

Although hardly any stratified 2nd century pottery was recovered, it is likely that the droveway had been laid out by the 2nd century, though the small gullies on the same line (F1065 and F1023) might be earlier (Fig 3). Its position seems significant in relation to the Iron Age floodplain enclosures: it meets the old river bed near the suggested crossing point of one of the Iron Age paths (F1182), and it is quite possible that the same route was used in the intervening period even though the site was not settled and there was no formal ditched trackway. If there was still a stream there, it is possible that a ford was made if one did not already exist.

There is no indication of the destination or extent of the droveway south of the site, but to the north its purpose must have been to provide access to the floodplain as well as to the fields either side of the track. It clearly ran eastwards, and possibly also westwards, along the edge of the gravel terrace dividing it off from the floodplain. The ditches to the east (F1097 and F1098) were probably a continuation of the droveway, being the right distance apart and again following the edge of the gravel terrace. Apart from this section only one ditch seemed to mark the edge of the droveway where it ran next to the old river bed, but this need not preclude the existence of the droveway there: if there was a stream in the old river bed it would have served as well, and otherwise that side may have been left open to the floodplain. There are quite good examples of trackways heading for the edges of gravel terraces in the region, such as at Kelmscott, Northmoor, Radley, Appleford, and Long Wittenham (Benson and Miles 1974, Maps 3, 22, 32, 34, 35), but there are few clear instances of such tracks turning along the edges of gravel terraces. Just south-west of Lower Whitley Farm there appears from some air photographs to be another length of trackway running along the edge of the gravel terrace, which might possibly be another part of the Farmoor complex, being only about 500 m away; there are also possible local examples just north-east of Standlake (Benson and Miles 1974, Map 21, and cf Fig 1) and at Meadow Farm, Aston.

The areas delineated by the small ditches running off from the droveway might have been enclosed at much the same time as the laying out of the track itself, though lack of dating evidence from the ditches makes this uncertain. One or two features apparently respecting Ditch 1049 were 3rd or 4th century, but the ditches could well have been in existence some time before these features were made.

Of the other possible 2nd century features Pit 1060 was probably a wattle-lined well. The lining had collapsed or had been destroyed by the sides slipping in and perhaps partly by the tree stump being thrown into it. The stump itself is of interest in illustrating the practice in the Roman period of coppicing, a form of woodland management which became common in the area in much later periods. The rather scanty biological evidence for the presence of stock (see p 122), and the absence of any evidence for occupation nearby suggests that the well was probably used principally for watering animals. The only dating evidence for the pit, the folded beaker from the top of the fill, had been too complete (before being crushed by the machines) to have been residual. It has good 2nd century parallels, but nevertheless could be somewhat later (see p 49).

In Area I (Fig 6) the three small 2nd century features, each cut by the next (F74, F58, and F16), were impossible to interpret coherently. The same applies to F4, which again contained only 2nd century pottery, though in this case its abraded condition suggested that it might be residual. The problem is particularly awkward because F4 cut the penannular slot (F5) and therefore its date affects that of the penannular structure. From other evidence (see below) it seems marginally more likely that F5 was later than 2nd century, but this is not certain and remains open to argument.

3rd and 4th century features: the field system

Very few features could securely be dated to the late 3rd and early 4th centuries, and though in the following consideration some features have been grouped together, it must be emphasized that the groupings are exceedingly tenuous, being based on scanty and very superficial evidence.

There is a slight indication that in the enclosed fields or paddocks beside the droveway, pits and other features belonging to this period may have been dug close to the edges of the fields (Fig 3). Pits 1048, 1033, 1051, 1052, and Well 1050 were all positioned close to Ditch 1049, though only F1033 was clearly dated late 3rd or early 4th century. On the southern side of the same area F1032 may fall within the same category, while of the two pits (presumably sumps) at the end of Ditch 1031, F1030 was of the same date. The only other Roman pits close to a field boundary, F1070 and F1041, were again not closely datable. No features certainly of this date were found in the middle of any field.

The extent and exact configuration of the fields is uncertain: only in the case of the northernmost were all four sides found (enclosing an area of about 0.20 hectares or 0.50 acres). The gaps between Ditches 1049 and 1031 and the droveway seemed genuine and probably represent gateways. All the lengths of Roman ditch found on the site were fairly close to the droveway or its projected line, suggesting that these small enclosed areas only lined the track rather than making up a more extensive grid. This is not certain because of the relatively sparse coverage of observation outside this area, but it is to some extent supported by the apparent absence of small fields east of the northern part of the droveway where observation was quite thorough. The interpretation is also reasonable when compared to other sites where extensive cropmarks reveal a similar pattern, such as at Appleford and at Northfield Farm, Long Wittenham (Benson and Miles 1974, Maps 34, 35). On the other hand many small lengths of unexplained gully, at least some of them Roman, were

found at Farmoor showing that much evidence may have been lost which would have revealed a more complicated pattern.

The purpose of the fields is also uncertain. All the biological evidence from both early and late features indicates a largely grassland environment and there is no positive evidence for any arable land on the site. It is most likely therefore that some of the fields at least were paddocks enclosing pasture land for animals, which is supported by the presence of pits and wells. The pits were clearly neither for storage nor rubbish: many were dug to below water level, most were bowl-shaped and contained very little domestic rubbish, suggesting that they were not closely associated with human habitation (Fig 18). Some such as F1070 and F1041 seemed to have been backfilled deliberately with a mixture of loamy clay and gravel, while others, dug below water level, such as F1048, F1033, F1032, contained silted layers at the bottom. Possibly some were small gravel pits, but the smaller ones with silting were probably waterholes. In the case of F1032 the original silting had partly been cleared out, presumably to improve the supply. Well 1050 again contained virtually no domestic rubbish and its rough construction suggests that it was intended only to be a slightly more permanent waterhole.

While the presence of the waterholes and wells clearly suggests that the fields were not arable and that some were used for livestock, it does not exclude the use of some (perhaps any smaller ones) as yards for general work or as gardens.

The penannular slot in Area I (Figs 6, 7)

In Area I once again there are problems of dating. Only Pit 10 clearly belonged to the late 3rd or early 4th centuries, and otherwise dating was based merely on whether features were cut or overlain by late 4th century material. The penannular slot is particularly problematic: of the postholes at either end, F83 produced late 4th century material and F69 pottery later than c AD 250. On the other hand F5 was cut by F4 containing only 2nd century pottery. The material from F83 could have been intrusive since there was much late disturbance in that area. The presence of stones in the northern parts of the slot, however, suggested that it had not entirely filled up by the late 4th century when the layer associated with the stones (L2) was deposited. It seems impossible that such a small slot could have remained partly open for over one hundred years, so that the abraded 2nd century pottery in F4 indeed seems likely to have been residual. The backfill of F5 must predate the late 4th century occupation in the area by some margin, however, since neither F4 nor F24 which cut it contained late pottery. It is thus safest, if it is to be dated at all, to assign it to the early 4th century.

The function of the penannular slot is debatable. The slot itself probably supported upright timbers and one possible interpretation is that it was a round house: its size would be about right; the partition, perhaps built on a sill beam or very shallow posts, would be unusual though not unreasonable, a possible parallel being found in the stone houses at Tre'r Ceiri (Hogg 1960, 34-5 and fig 14); there would also be no difficulty in roofing such a structure, especially if the partition provided extra support. Alternatively the house might have had turf walls supported externally by small posts placed in the slot, with the inturned entrance posts marking and supporting the ends of the turf wall. There is no clearly associated domestic refuse, though this could have been lost amidst the later material or might be represented by Pit 10.

The major objection to these interpretations is the size and orientation of the entrances: two 3.00 m wide doors facing the coldest quarter (north-east) seem most unlikely for a house, and can hardly be regarded as mere doorways when they took up almost the whole of one side, each large enough for a cart. If the structure were to be interpreted as a house it would be necessary to suggest some sort of porch on the north side, for which there is no good evidence.

A more convincing interpretation is that it was a small stockade for animals. Provided the tops of the posts were tied together and possibly braced, the wall would have been sufficiently rigid to be left free-standing, especially if the entrances had tie beams across them. There is no reason why the structure should not still have been roofed to make a shed, but there would be no structural need for this. The posts either side of the entrance, perhaps braced by the tie beams, would have held gates. The eastern post seems to have required replacement, and the hole for the new post may have been made deeper to take additional strain, perhaps because it was no longer tied into the old structure. The partition would enable animals to be divided into separate groups. Such a structure if used for animals was clearly not a simple enclosure of the kind suggested for the Iron Age examples: it was small but also elaborately constructed. A possible use is that it was for protecting particularly valuable animals (perhaps one in each half) such as prize bulls or stallions. A stockade or shed thus constructed would provide adequate protection not only against the weather but also wild animals and even thieves or rustlers.

No exact parallels for this structure have been found. Probable buildings with wall foundation trenches have been found in Roman contexts at, for example, Tallington, Lincolnshire (Peacock 1962, 111 and fig 3), and in Glamorganshire (*JRS* 1969, 200 and fig 26). In plan the closest parallel is from Deanshanger, Northampton-shire (*Britannia* 1973, 293, fig 8), but the gully there seems too large for posts, and in none of these examples was the orientation of the structure the same as at Farmoor.

The animal burials F37 and F34 (Fig 8)

For the double horse burial (F37) dating evidence consisted only of Oxfordshire colour-coated pottery from above the skeletons. The interpretation of the burial is more fully discussed on p 130. There are considerable problems with any simple domestic explanation for the burials, but nor can they very convincingly be interpreted in other ways. For example, any explanation in terms of ritual is doubtful: the removal of the front limbs might be taken as ritualistic in the light of horse forequarters found in Iron Age pits and interpreted as indicating ritual activities (B W Cunliffe, pers comm), but it could also be part of normal butchery techniques (see p 131). The removal of the hide could have ritual overtones (Piggot 1962), but again would be perfectly reasonable as an ordinary domestic process.

On the whole the burial seems most convincingly explained as rubbish disposal, and as such it gives only indirect evidence of the reason for the horses' slaughter. The problem is only worsened by the fact that there seem to be no close parallels: although horse burials in either ritual or rubbish contexts are known, those with potential ritual overtones are mostly Iron Age (eg Harding 1967, 85) and there are virtually no Roman examples (Green 1976, 49-50), other than a double burial on the Berkshire Downs (Peake *et al* 1935, 103). Furthermore none of the examples, Iron Age or Roman, seems to exhibit the

peculiarities which must be regarded as crucial to the interpretation of this case.

The sheep burial (F34) was not clearly connected with the horses and could have been modern (see p 132).

Other probable 3rd and 4th century features in Area I (Figs 6, 7)

A number of pits, again undated, except that they were cut or sealed by late 4th century material, seemed to form another tenuous group (F24, F29, F32, F44, F75, F76, F86). They all had steep, usually undercut sides and mixed clay and gravel fills. The undercutting was probably caused by water; furthermore it occurred in each case at roughly the same depth and corresponded to the level of organic preservation in F17 and F43 (Fig 7) and probably represents the height of the watertable. Because they were cut to below water level and contained no domestic rubbish, they cannot have been used as storage or rubbish pits. The smaller ones, such as F24, seem unlikely to have been waterholes, but possibly they were cess or slurry pits. There is some evidence for Roman manure pits outside Britain (Pliny XVIII, viii, 47) and Applebaum suggests their use for his typical villa (Applebaum 1966, 105), but this explanation is by no means certain and there may be others as convincing. The deeper pits in this group such as F86 and F29, may alternatively have been waterholes, and this could also apply to Pits 10, 63, and 85. Silt had accumulated in the bottoms of Pits 10 and 84 before they were backfilled (presumably deliberately) with clay and gravel. The domestic rubbish in F10 was largely confined to the top layer overlying most of the other backfill. It was reasonably well dated to the early to mid 4th century, but whether this date can be applied also to the other pits is unclear.

The fields, droveway, and associated features in the ?late 4th century (Figs 3, 16, 17, 18)

The presence of shell-tempered pottery of post *c* AD 350 provided useful dating evidence for the late period, though in general more pottery and coins, at least in Area I, made dating easier. The droveway continued in use until this period; its ditches had been recut at least three times and near the old river bed the gravel had been churned up in the centre of the track, presumably by the constant poaching of the surface by animals in wet weather (L 1075/2). These layers did not appear to have much topsoil mixed with the gravel, and it seems possible that originally the soil was removed to avoid too much mud accumulating. The mud could not have been avoided entirely, though, and it evidently became necessary to lay down a new gravel surface (L1075). Conceivably the holes previously dug in the middle of the droveway (F1075/3) had been to provide some sort of drainage. The continuation of the new gravel layer to the east and west indicates that the droveway continued along the edge of the gravel terrace in both directions.

The western droveway ditches at least ceased to function before the site was entirely abandoned: Pit 1079 was dug through the silted up ditch, probably as a waterhole with stakes and wattle as a lining; Layer 1073/1 appeared to be some sort of embankment made on top of this, though its north-south extent is not known; and the large damaged scythe blade had been discarded, perhaps after being used to mow hay in the meadows, on the edge of this layer. The final abandonment was represented by the accumulation of peat (L1072), and then thick layers of alluvial clay.

The use, and indeed existence, of the fields at this period is uncertain. There is some indication that pits and wells etc were no longer confined to the edges of the fields, as suggested by the position of Pit 1047, possibly a water-hole, certainly late 4th century in date; possibly also by Well 1046 immediately adjacent; and by the T-shaped corndrier (F1002) for which the only dating evidence was late 4th century. This, however, is the sum of the evidence: Pit 18 was the right date, but not necessarily in a field; other features in the middle of fields, such as the stone-lined pits (F1096, F1126, and F1169, which were presumably waterholes) were only datable to post c AD 250. Pit 1169 may in fact have been late 4th century on the basis of the similarity of its biological remains with those in F17 (see p 121).

The corndriers (Fig 19)

Corndrier 1002 was of the normal 3rd to 4th century type, but was of particular interest in two ways. Firstly the botanical evidence shows that it was used for dehusking as much as for drying the spelt wheat (see p104). From comparison with other examples where very few husks were found, such as at Barton Court Farm (Jones, in Miles forthcoming), it appears that these two operations in pre-paring the corn for milling may not always have been combined. Secondly, the other biological evidence indicates that the site was still largely grassland with no proof of arable agriculture, so that the corndrier and other evidence of cereals (the quernstones in Pit 47 and elsewhere and the threshing refuse in Pit 17) cannot be used as evidence for cereal growing on the site. It is reasonable, therefore, to assume that the wheat was brought to the site perhaps from fairly nearby, to be threshed, dehusked, dried, and presumably ground.

The other corndrier (F1058) was even less securely dated, and was less well preserved. Despite its very different appearance as excavated, it could originally have been the same type of drier but with no trace of the super-structure surviving. The hearth was at the opposite end from F1002, but such variations have been found else-where, eg at Barton Court Farm, Abingdon (Miles, forthcoming and 1977, fig 15). Again there was a hollow in the middle of the drier, presumably created by raking out the embers which had been pushed into the flue from the hearth to provide the heat. This hollow would naturally have been deepest at the hearth end of the drier. The gravel concretions might well have been added to provide a rough floor. Such a floor would have various advantages: firstly, it would make it easier to rake out the ashes; secondly, it would help to keep the embers evenly distributed when pushed into the drier, rather than collecting in the bottom of the hollow (which might result in uneven and inefficient heat transmission); thirdly, the floor would remain hot for longer after the firing was completed. It is impossible to say definitely whether the superstructure of this drier was T-shaped, but it is quite possible if one compares what would have been left of F1002 if another 200 or 300 mm had been lost from the top of it (Fig 19). The slot dug across the north-west end of F1058 cannot convincingly be interpreted as part of the arms of the T.

Pits 47 and 17 (Figs 6, 7)

These two features in Area I connected with grain have already been mentioned. Pit 47 was no more than an amorphous scoop of indeterminate purpose; but Pit 17 was of more interest. Originally it was probably a water-hole and, like F1033, had been redug when L17/2 was cut through. This recut would have re-exposed the gravel to provide a more rapid and deeper water supply. An alternative explanation, that L17/2 was a clay lining and that the profile of the bottom was formed merely by use, seems less likely. The bottom had silted up (L17/5) and the pit had then been used for rubbish, consisting firstly of the chaff from threshing (L17/4, see p110) and then, possibly after some deliberate back-filling (L17/3), of ordinary domestic refuse (L17/1), clearly datable to the late 4th century (p51 and p55).

The well and late 4th century occupation in Area I (Figs 19, 6, 7)

The cereal remains again need not be evidence for cereal growing on the site: apart from the fact that they were specifically threshing rubbish, the neighbouring contem-porary well (F43) produced good evidence for a grassland environment, as indeed did the non-cereal remains in Pit 17. Well 43 was larger, deeper, and better built than F1050 or F1046 and, on the basis of the biological evidence and the nature of the other late 4th century features nearby, it seems likely that it was in a farmyard and may have been for domestic as well as agricultural use.

The late 4th century domestic rubbish was certainly sufficiently abundant in Area I to suggest actual occupation, though no clear trace of any building was found. Apart from the well and Pit 17 the material was concentrated on the northern part of the Area. The layer of gravel (L31 and L57) was presumably laid down to form a firm surface above the earlier pits, and was then covered by a considerable amount of occupation material (L30). It was not clear what the amorphous group of small pits and scoops (F3) was: they were too irregular to be convincing as large postholes, and were clearly not rubbish pits as such. The relatively large number of associated coins in no way assists their identification. They appeared to mark the southern edge of the gravel layer (L31 and L57) and if they were postholes this could be taken as evidence for a building, such as a barn, with a gravel floor, but even so there was no evidence of a return to form an end wall.

The general layer of occupation material (L2) covering the penannular stockade was roughly contemporary and may even have been the same deposit as L30 and the fill of F3. The stakeholes (F8, F9, F67, F28, F27) filled with brown loam may also belong to the same period, though this is not certain, and there is no indication of what structure they represent. The stones found in L2, F3, and in the top of several other features, including the ends of the penannular slot, may have been dumped to consolidate the ground surface (they certainly did not seem to be building rubble).

The area seems to have been a farmyard, perhaps next to a domestic building. The absence of building stone, tiles, or slates suggests that any building would have been made of wood or turf and thatched (the tenon of a structural timber found in Well 43 might support the former suggestion). Salvage work was insufficiently thorough, and the contractors' methods too destructive for any detailed evidence to be retrieved from the immediate vicinity, though the general scatter of pottery continued in each direction. The biological evidence supports the farmyard interpretation and also suggests from the presence of box leaves the existence of some sort of garden nearby.

The area was still subject at least to occasional flooding according to the biological evidence from Well 43. In the last 100 years, the edge of the gravel terrace flooded quite frequently (see p6 and Fig 2) and this must also apply to the Roman period since the water table then cannot have been lower than the modern one: if it had been, the shallower wells (particularly F1050) would have been unusable, and the preserved organic remains in Pit 17 would not have survived up to the level of the modern water table, as they did. It is possible therefore that again the site was occupied only seasonally, but whether or not this is so it seems likely that the settlement was more permanent than that of the middle Iron Age; there is no botanical evidence to the contrary and the probable existence of box hedges and the presence of a properly constructed well both imply a fairly long-term settlement.

Phase IV: Medieval and later

Ridge and furrow (Figs 34, 4, 5)

Occupation on the site seems to have ceased at the end of the Roman period, and nothing more is known of its use until the arable farming of the Middle Ages when presumably the ridge and furrow was made. The two furrows excavated in Area II were widely spaced at 18 m apart, but this is not unusual and can be paralleled in surviving ridge and furrow in the neighbourhood. The furrows plotted from the air photograph just east of Area II were at half this spacing. This may be a genuine distinction since 18th and 19th century maps show a north-south field boundary between these two areas. The headlands presumably ran along the edge of the gravel terrace, because the furrows in Area II disappeared at their north end, presumably sloping upwards to meet the headland.

On the floodplain there was no sign of any ridge and furrow and the area remained unenclosed, known as Cumnor Meadow until the early 19th century (Cumnor enclosure award, 1814). The whole of the gravel terrace, however, seems to have been arable at one time or another, since traces of ridge and furrow are visible in vertical air photographs in many of the fields south and east of the main part of the site, as well as in the fields south of Lower Whitley Farm. Field work has shown that the hillside towards Cumnor was also very extensively ploughed.

Enclosures (Fig 3)

The open medieval fields had largely been enclosed before the parliamentary enclosure award of 1814 (Earl of Abingdon Estate map, 1808). Ditches 1003, 1136, and 1140 all appear on the map, but none of them produced any good dating evidence. The floodplain was re-enclosed with substantial drainage ditches as a result of the 1814 award.

Other modern features

Ditches 11 and 12 in Area I and Pit 1027 in Area III could be dated to the 19th century, but they were no more susceptible to convincing interpretation than many of their more ancient counterparts.

PART III : BIOLOGICAL EVIDENCE

Introduction

by Mark Robinson

Details of the geological setting of the Farmoor Reservoir site and its soils have already been given elsewhere in the report. These made the site particularly suitable for the preservation of a wide range of biological remains. The calcareous gravel meant that bones and molluscan remains survived in the dry archaeological deposits, while the shallow depth of the water table (c 1.5 m on the gravel terrace and less than 1 m on the floodplain) meant that the bottoms of many of the archaeological features were below it. Thus when they became filled by the clayey soil of the site they became sealed, and anaerobic, possibly acidic, conditions probably developed as trapped organic material began to decay. This would have slowed down further decay thereby preserving plant and animal remains ranging from seeds to insect cuticle. A result of the soil surface being basic to neutral is that all such remains which fell on the ground would have decayed within a few years unless they had become incorporated in a water-logged feature, so that there should be less trouble with residual material entering a deposit with its fill, a problem which soil pollen analysts have had to face on most archaeological occupation sites. Obviously the preserved remains have to be interpreted to give ecological information and again the site is most fortunately, indeed almost uniquely, situated. Beetle collecting was begun within a mile and a half of the site (2½ km) as early as 1819 by the Reverend F W Hope, then an undergraduate at Oxford. Various collectors worked in the area during the late 19th century, and from 1904 to 1938 an area of seven miles radius from the centre of Oxford (within which the site falls) was intensively worked for beetles by Commander J J Walker. Unfortunately there is no evidence that he collected in Cumnor Mead itself. The collections and some notes of Hope, Walker, and others are preserved in the Hope Department of Entomology, Oxford University. Walker published a series of lists of the beetles which had been caught within the seven mile radius (11 km) giving the habitats and localities where he had found them (Walker 1906, 1907, 1909, 1911, 1914, 1920, and 1929). By 1929, 2148 species of beetles, about 60% of the British fauna, had been caught in the Oxford district and there have been few additions since then.

The botany of the area is similarly well known. Systematic listing of its plants began in the 18th century with Sibthorpe and was completed by Druce at the end of the 19th century (Druce 1886; 1897). An extremely useful account for ecological information is given by Church (1922, 1925 a, 1925 b) and it is also the area from which Sir A G Tansley took many of his samples for his monumental work of 1939, *The British Isles and their vegetation* (Tansley 1965). The site is included by Bowen in his *Flora of Berkshire* (1968).

The site of the excavation is only one and a half miles (2½ km) away from the Wytham Estate which since 1943 has perhaps become, under the aegis of Mr C S Elton, the most intensively ecologically studied area in the country (Elton 1966). The proximity of Oxford University has also meant that much other ecological work has been carried out in the area around Farmoor.

It was against this background that the major programme of environmental archaeology developed at Farmoor. It began with a brief survey of the site before the excavation and continued with the presence of an environmental archaeologist (myself) on the site throughout most of the planned and salvage excavations from 1974 to 1976. By being thoroughly familiar with the site, all the best preserved or most stratigraphically useful organic deposits could be sampled as they appeared. It also meant that close cooperation with the director of the excavation was possible so that particular deposits could be sampled for archaeological reasons, or particular areas excavated to give more environmental information. During the excavation, lists of modern insects and plants from several different habitats in the vicinity were made, in the hope that they could be of some use in the interpretation of the results from the excavation. As the excavation progressed, some of the samples were analysed in the laboratory so that future sampling policy could be based on the early results.

The scope of the project enabled many biological groups to be studied. The following have been examined: pollen by Professor G W Dimbleby; mammal bones by Mr R Wilson; bird bones by Mr D Bramwell; mites by Mrs S Denford; ants by Mr C O'Toole; carbonized seeds initially by Mr M Jones, then by myself; waterlogged seeds, other plant remains, beetles, other arthropods and molluscs by myself; and also wood by myself, under the supervision of Miss J Sheldon.

In two instances the interpretation of the results required experimentation with modern material and details are given at the end of the report. It also required a further ecological survey to be made, especially of areas of permanent grassland still managed by traditional means at the edge of the Thames. There is not space to give the full results in this report but details are included where necessary. In addition to the archaeological deposits, a brief examination was given to some Pleistocene peat from the old river bed and the results are given at the end of the report.

For this work to take place, the assistance of many people was needed in the provision of sub-reports, facilities and advice; the due acknowledgements have been made at the beginning of the report (p2).

Plants and invertebrates: methods and results

by Mark Robinson with sections

by S Denford and M Jones

This section covers firstly the methods used for the analysis of deposits containing plant and invertebrate remains; secondly, the results obtained from these, including specialist reports for certain groups; and thirdly the interpretation of these results in the light of the archaeological evidence.

Methods

Sampling

Two types of samples were taken, bulk samples from deposits that were believed to have built up quite rapidly (which included all the waterlogged layers) and column samples through sequences of layers for molluscan analysis. Where possible, samples were taken as undisturbed blocks.

The bulk samples were all taken from levels with no apparent vertical change of composition. Where possible a spit's depth was confined to a few centimetres and followed any noticeable bedding planes. For the water-logged samples a quantity of between 3lb (1.36 kg) and 150 lbs (67.92 kg) was wrapped moist in three layers of clean Polythene with the air sucked out. If there was any region of the deposit in which preservation seemed best, a separate 5 lb (2.264 kg) sample specifically for seed analysis was taken and similarly wrapped. In addition, pollen samples of about 2 oz (50g) were taken from the freshly cleaned surface of some organic deposits with a clean trowel. These were again sealed in three previously unopened Polythene bags. From the dry deposits a quantity of the material was sealed inside a clean plastic fertilizer bag.

The column samples consisted of approximately 6lb (2.5kg) samples taken between the levels indicated and respecting changes in layer composition. They were sealed in plastic bags.

The samples

A description of each sample analysed and the quantity examined from each is given below and in Table 4 (this includes the samples analysed by Mrs Denford and Mr Jones whose reports appear on p103 to p106). Weights are for the wet samples; the sample numbers are those of their archaeological contexts.

The waterlogged bulk samples

F590/4 (see p12). Iron Age sump, Area II enclosures. Grey-black silt with very little apparent organic material.

F1007/1 (see p21). Iron Age gully sump, enclosure complex 1. Brown-black organic loam with some gravel, including a lens of plant material (in which Chenopodiaceae seeds were evident) and lumps of orange-yellow clayey silt.

F1009/1 (see p23). Iron Age gully sump, enclosure complex 1. Orange silty clay with a few grey blotches and some gravel. No apparent preserved organic material apart from a beetle elytron.

F1100/1 (see p23). Iron Age gully, enclosure complex 2. Dark brown to black silty organic clay with some plant fragments.

F1159 (see p25). Iron Age ditch, enclosure complex 3. Brown loam with a high organic content and remains of plant stems with some mats of plant material. Oxidized to a dark brown after exposure to the air.

F1172 (see p25). Iron Age occupation layer, enclosure complex 3. Grey gritty silty clay with a few orange flecks and some gravel. No obvious organic remains but many fragments of molluscan shells. This sample forms the bottom-most sample of Sample Column II (see below).

F1060/2 (see p33). Roman well.
Dark grey organic clayey silt with many light brown mats of plant stems. These rapidly oxidized to dark brown on exposure to the air. Many obvious pieces of wood and *Prunus* stones.

F43/10 (see p17). Roman well, Area 1.
Loose brown organic material with very little mineral content apart from a few fragments of limestone. Rapidly oxidized on exposure to the air. Consisted mostly of twigs and plant stems in a matrix of rather liquid organic silt with many water-filled spaces.

F17/4 (see p17). Roman pit, Area 1.
Hard, compacted, strongly horizontally laminated peat almost entirely composed of wheat chaff. Light brown when first exposed, very rapidly oxidizing to a dark brown. On splitting along the planes of fracture, leaves, compressed twigs, and insect remains were abundantly obvious. The only mineral content was the odd piece of limestone gravel which the acids of the peat had reduced to a cheese-like consistency and a few lenses of grey silt.

F1046/2 (see p32). Roman well.
Brown organic loam with some plant fibres.

F1074/4 (see p29). Roman ditch.
Brown peaty material made up of both plant stems and fibrous roots with grey silt and white gravel.

F1072 (see p29). Roman peat layer.

Table 4: The size of waterlogged samples

Sample No	Invertebrates and plant remains excluding pollen	Arthropods, twigs, wood etc.	Waterlogged cereal remains	Separate mite sub-sample	Separate pollen sub-sample
		Size of sub-samples examined for			
590/4	5 lb (2.264kg)	-	-	-	-
1007/1	5 lb (2.264kg)	31½lb (14.26kg)	-	-	+
1009/1	5 lb (2.264kg)	21½lb (9.74kg)	-	-	+
1100/1	5 lb (2.264kg)	23lb (10.41kg)	-	+	+
1159	5 lb (2.264kg)	154lb (65.66kg)	-	-	-
1172	5 lb (2.264kg)	-	-	-	-
1060/2	5 lb (2.264kg)	40lb (18.11kg)	-	-	+
43/10	5 lb (2.264kg)	31½lb (14.26kg)	-	-	+
17/4	5 lb (2.264kg)	31½lb (14.26kg)	1.5oz (40g)	+	+
1046/2	3 lb (1.358kg)	-	-	-	-
1074/4	5 lb (2.264kg)	-	-	-	-
1072	5 lb (2.264kg)	31½lb (14.26kg)	-	-	+
1169	5 lb (2.264kg)	-	-	-	-

Where a separate sub-sample was examined for waterlogged cereal remains or mites, these were not looked for in the other sub-samples from that sample.

Brown peat with much fine fibrous material, probably roots. Some silt and very little much eroded and softened limestone gravel. No well developed laminated structure, probably as a result of the roots. It contained a few much decayed plant rhizomes. A level of about 80 mm from close to the bottom of this layer was sampled. This was far enough from the bottom not to incorporate much gravel. F1169 (see p32). Roman water hole.
Black silt with a few preserved leaves.

The dry bulk samples
F1013/3 (see p19). Iron Age hearth pit.
Fine burnt black loam. About 6lb (2.7 kg) submitted for analysis of carbonized plant remains.
F1002/2 (see p34). Roman corndrier.
Burnt black sandy loam with some carbonized grain. About 60lb (27 kg) submitted for analysis of carbonized plant remains.

The column samples
Individual samples all weighed 5lb (2.264 kg) and were taken from between the levels indicated (zero being the bottom of the deposit) in Table 17. The layer within the columns were as follows:-
I (see p9f) Iron Age gully, Area II enclosures (Fig 5 Section K)

528/5	0-80	Dirty grey gravel with a little clay
528/4	80-280	Grey gravelly rather loamy clay with some iron panning
528/4	280-420	Grey gravelly clay loam with some iron panning
528/1	420-660	Dark brown clay loam with some gravel
528/1	660-720	Brown gravelly clayish loam

II (see p25) Iron Age alluvium, enclosure complex 3 (Fig 15, Section Q[111])

1172	0-70	Grey gritty silty clay with a few orange flecks and some gravel
1164	70-150	Grey somewhat gravelly clay with brown blotches
1164	150-450	Brown clay with grey flecks

III (see p25) Iron Age to modern alluvium, enclosure complex 3 (Fig.15, Section U[111])

Layer	Level (mm)	
1164	0-120	Grey gritty clay with a few orange flecks
1164	120-420	Grey-buff clay much orange-brown flecking
1164	420-620	Brown-buff silty clay
1164	620-680	Dark grey-brown humic clay loam

IV (see p23) Pre-Iron Age to modern (Fig.12 Section P[111])
No molluscan remains found so details not given.

In addition to the sample columns a single 5lb (2.264 kg) sample was examined from the pre-Iron Age soil close to Sample Column II, L1184 (see p25). It consisted of yellow sandy silt with a few grey flecks.

The size of sample

The size of sample examined has been determined partly by my experience with other sites (eg Robinson 1975, 161-4), partly by the amount of information which was wanted from a deposit, and partly by the results given by the first samples from the site to be examined. Obviously there is no reason why the size of sample required to give the range of species and an idea of their relative abundance in a deposit for one group should be the same as the size required for another. 5lb (2.264 kg) was found

to be suitable for seeds and molluscs and has been used for all but one samples (where the deposit remaining for sampling was not large enough). For insect remains total samples of 36.5lb (16.52 kg) gave sufficient specimens from some of the Roman deposits, but this weight was not large enough for the Iron Age ones. Therefore a very large sample (145lb, 67.92 kg) was examined from Ditch 1159.

Extraction

All analysis of the samples was carried out in the laboratory. Although on-site flotation might be the only way of dealing with large quantities of soil to be examined for carbonized remains, it is not at all practical for the recovery of any other plant or invertebrate fragments. Details will be given here of the methods used on the samples which I sorted. Where specialists sorted their own samples, details have been given in their reports.

The bulk samples
These were divided into two parts. One part, normally 5lb (2.265 kg), was to be examined for all invertebrate remains (except mites if a separate soil sample had been sent to Mrs S Denford) and all plant remains excepting pollen. In some instances a second, much larger part was examined only for arthropod remains (except mites again if Mrs Denford had examined a separate sample), and large plant remains such as pieces of wood and twigs.

The procedure for extracting the first part of the sample was as follows. The moist sample was first broken up by hand. Where possible it was split along obvious planes of fracture, so that fragile remains such as articulated insect skeletons, leaves, twigs, and snail shells could be removed. If the sample was very clayey (eg sample 1172) and breaking it up would result in severe damage to its contents, it was frozen and thawed a number of times. No obvious damage to specimens was caused by this process and it enabled many fragile and broken molluscan shells to be removed with all their pieces in situ.

After the sample had been broken apart it was placed in a bucket of hot water and gradually washed through a series of sieves down to an aperture size of 0.2 mm, enabling seeds as small as *Juncus* sp. and *Centaurium* sp. to be recovered. Clayey samples which had been frozen and thawed disaggregated much more easily in hot water than they would otherwise have done. The freezing not only did less damage than the use of reagents such as sodium hydroxide but was also more effective. Care was taken when washing the entire sample through the sieve to prevent fragile remains being damaged by pieces of stone or gravel. The residues on all the sieves down to an aperture size of 0.5 mm were sorted under water with the aid of a binocular microscope. The carbonized plant remains and the molluscs were dried; all other specimens were stored in 70% alcohol to await identification. As a result of the time it took to sort 2597 rush seeds from the 0.2 mm fraction of sample 1159, some of the subsequent samples had only one-tenth of the contents of this sieve examined. Where this was done, it has been indicated in the results.

Where a second part of the sample was to be examined for arthropod and larger plant remains alone, it was first of all broken up and placed in hot water as before, and was again washed through a stack of sieves but this time only down to an aperture size of 0.5 mm. The residue was then subjected to the paraffin flotation technique devised by Coope and Osborne and described in detail by Kenward (1974, 20). Briefly this method is as follows. The residue from the sieve which had been allowed to drain thoroughly but not dried was placed in a bowl. It was then thoroughly mixed with paraffin, the surplus paraffin was poured off, and the bowl filled with water. After the sediment had settled, the insect remains floating on the surface were poured off into a fine sieve (0.2 mm aperture). The process was then repeated until no more insect fragments were recovered. The flotant with the insect fragments was washed on the sieve with detergent and hot water. Sometimes this standard paraffin method was found satisfactory; in other instances a better extraction of all the insect remains was made by paraffin-floating small quantities of residue at a time in a jar. The flotant was sorted for arthropod remains which were stored in 70% alcohol. Any seeds or molluscs which happened to have floated with the insect remains, and were of species not recovered from the fraction of the sample which had been examined for them, were also saved. Pieces of wood and twigs were recovered from the residues left in the sieves before the paraffin flotation.

The normal procedure was modified for Sample 1159. It was realized that very few carbonized remains had been recovered from the Iron Age samples sorted for seeds, and therefore, after paraffin flotation a quantity (unfortunately unmeasured) of the residue and the flotant after the insect remains had been extracted was left to dissolve in concentrated nitric acid. After some weeks when almost all the organic remains had dissolved, it was sieved, washed, and then sorted for carbonized plant remains.

Sample 17/4 also required special consideration. It comprised almost entirely spelt wheat chaff and the individual spikelet fragments were extremely fragile. The peat was much too compressed for their separation without damage in the sieving of the ordinary 5 lb sample. Also the quantity of cereal fragments contained in a sample of that size would have been too considerable and would have taken up too much time to work on. Therefore a lump of peat in which the cereal preservation was at its best was cut down into a block about 80 x 80 x 40 mm. This was soaked in water, drained, and weighed. It was then placed under water in a dish and, using a binocular microscope, the individual spikelet fragments were carefully lifted off using a scalpel and a paint brush. At intervals the surface was cleaned by gently washing with water, which was allowed to overflow into a 0.2 mm aperture sieve. The remaining part of the block was drained and weighed, so that the weight removed could be calculated. The residue in the sieve was then sorted for any further cereal remains.

The column samples

Each sample was broken up as described for the first part of the bulk samples. The freezing treatment was particularly useful in breaking down the clay samples. They were then washed through a stack of sieves down to an aperture of 0.5 mm, apart from the bottom samples each of columns II and III where an aperture size of 0.2 mm was used, in case seeds were present. They had been preserved in Layer 1172, the bottom of column II, and this sample was then examined in the same way as the first part of the other bulk samples (and has been listed under them as well). The residues from all the other samples were dried and sorted for molluscan remains under the binocular microscope (no carbonized plant remains were present).

Reasons for extraction procedure

A wide range of views are held on how to extract plant and animal remains from soil samples, so here are the reasons for using the methods noted above. There would be little to dispute about the way in which the molluscs have been extracted; clearly nothing will induce slug granules or snail opercula to float out from a sieve residue containing limestone gravel. The smallest sieve used, with an aperture of 0.5 mm, is regarded by Evans (1972, 44) as suitable. The way in which the insect remains were recovered has been a standard technique in the Geology Department at Birmingham for some years now. Although it uses selective flotation, this property is based on a chemical difference between the insect cuticle and the other remains which affects their ability to absorb paraffin when they are moist. It is by no means completely effective and there is sometimes a tendency for soil-filled fragments to be too heavy to float, but normally virtually all the insect remains are recovered. Perhaps the finest sieve that was used for the preliminary sieving (0.5 mm aperture) was too coarse but when sieving the effective aperture of a sieve is rapidly reduced by clogging. Therefore, during the flotation, the float was caught on a 0.2 mm aperture sieve so that none of it should be lost. It is felt from the examination of the insect remains trapped by the 0.2 mm sieve, when the first part of a bulk sample was extracted, that few indentifiable fragments apart from aleocharine staphylinids (which I find impossible to identify to species) had been lost from the use of a 0.5 mm sieve on the second part of the bulk sample.

It is the extraction of seeds about which there is the most dispute. It must be said that the sample sizes required and the methods used to extract carbonized seeds efficiently need in no way be related to those required for the proper extraction of seeds preserved by waterlogging. Flotation machines, especially with the addition of frothing agents or paraffin, will rapidly give spectacular results when used on organic sediments which do not contain much other plant debris. Even then, extraction is by no means complete and can give dangerously misleading results. Certain marsh and aquatic plants, for example *Oenanthe* sp., *Lycopus europaeus* L., and *Ranunculus sceleratus* L., have seeds designed for dispersal by water. To this end they have spongey tissue attached to their seeds to act as floats. In my experience these seeds will float far more readily than most other sorts and so the results could be biased in favour of marsh and aquatic plants. When it comes to using flotation methods to extract seeds from peats, they are most unreliable. While the physical properties of, for example, Chenopodiaceae seeds would be different from those of most of the plant debris, many of the other seeds would be physically and chemically indistinguishable from the rest of the peat, such as a battered but still identifiable seed of *Zannichellia palustris* L. The use of flotation to extract waterlogged seeds is indeed a very different prospect from its use for the recovery of insect remains. It is unfortunate that RESCUE in its recent publication *First Aid for Seeds*, a booklet designed for use by archaeologists, should describe flotation as the conventional means of recovering waterlogged plant remains from archaeological sediments (Renfrew *et al* 1976, 16).

It was for these reasons that complete examination of the sieve residues or sub-samples from them for waterlogged plant remains was chosen.

Identification

All my identifications were made by direct comparisons with reference material at suitable magnifications under the microscope. It is important that an identification is only regarded as secure when all reasonable possibilities have been exhausted, not simply when a match is obtained. It may require a large number of specimens of a single species to be investigated so that its full range of variation can be seen. In the case of seeds, some modern specimens may need treatment with sodium hydroxide solution so that they resemble the eroded condition of the ancient ones. Wood must be thin-sectioned, often in three planes.

Identifications of seeds and insect remains were carried out with the specimens wet. Often the surface needed to be partly dried to show up extra details and this was achieved by allowing the specimen to begin drying on moist filter paper. Insect fragments were treated in this way rather than being examined mounted and dried on cards, simply out of personal preference, but fragile plant remains can be severely damaged and become unrecognizable if they are allowed to dry out completely. After identification the seed and insect remains were stored in a mixture of glycerol, alcohol, and formalin.

Insect identifications were made using the British Reference and General Collections in the Hope Department of Entomology, Oxford. Molluscs were identified by comparision with identified sub-fossil shells from various excavations in Oxfordshire, and the Dale Collection of Land and Freshwater Molluscs in the Hope Department. The Dale Collection is very comprehensive but not all the material in it is correctly identified, so in some instances it needed work on it before archaeological specimens could be identified from it. Seeds were identified by reference to the collection at the Institute of Archaeology, London, to sub-fossil specimens previously identified using the collection in the Botany School, Cambridge, to a collection made by M Jones and myself, to specimens obtained from the Weed Research Organisation, Yarnton, and to the collection of the Environmental Archaeology Laboratory, York Archaeological Trust. Wood was identified under the supervision of Miss J Sheldon using the slide collection at the Institute of Archaeology, London.

Further identification work has been done on all the samples since preliminary results were given in Limbrey and Evans (1978).

Results from the waterlogged bulk samples

Plant remains preserved by waterlogging

Pollen
The results of Professor Dimbleby's analyses are given in Table 5. He reports that Sample 17/4 contained many fungal spores as well as pollen.

Seeds
The results given in Table 6 are for all the waterlogged seed remains except cereal remains. Nomenclature follows Clapham et al (1962). Where the plants have vernacular English names, these have been given as well, because the archeological reader is likely to be familiar with many of them. The term 'seed' is used in a wide sense to cover the normal germinable unit so it will include fruits, nutlets, achenes, etc. The Umbelliferae 'seeds' were all single mericarps. The totals given are for the minimum numbers of seeds represented by the identified whole seeds and fragments. The fruit fragments of *Buxus sempervirens* have not been included in the total for Pit 17/4 as they cannot be easily related to the number of seeds which they enclosed. 'Varia' are those seeds which almost certainly belong to species not named in the list. In addition there are a number of unidentifiable seeds and fragments which could very well be from some of the species identified.

Along with identifications a short description of the habitats of each species is given. The habitat information has been taken from Bowen (1968); Church (1922, 1925a, 1925b); Clapham et al (1962); Tansley (1965); *The Biological Flora of the British Isles* (various volumes); and my own observation, both systematic and casual. It must be emphasized that many of the species can live in a number of different habitats and their presence could indicate any one of them. Unlikely habitats have been left out, for example, details that a species is coastal if it also has a perfectly respectable inland habitat. The habitat groups into which they have been divided are cultivated crops; aquatic; marsh; bankside or water's edge; disturbed ground (with a qualifier if its habitat includes arable); grassland; scrub or hedgerow; and woodland. Where necessary, additional information has been given. It must be remembered that a hedge with a ditch alongside will contain most of the above habitats, but under the scrub/hedge heading only those shrubs which make up the hedge itself, the climbers that scramble in it, and the 'woodland edge' herbs have been given. It must also be remembered that the habitat groups are very broad and that some plants showing the same heading are most unlikely to be found together. This will be discussed in the interpretation.

Cereal remains
The results of the extraction of cereal remains from a sub-sample of 17/4 and those recorded from the ordinary 5lb sample of 43/10 are given in Table 7.

Wood
Wood identification was only carried out on the samples given in Table 8. A total of 27 pieces of wood were identified, most being *Prunus*. A preliminary examination of the wood was made with a hand lens so that pieces could be selected for subsequent microscopic examination in an attempt to give the full range of species present in a deposit rather than taken at random. Only presence or absence of a species has been recorded because of the danger that some of the pieces had become fragmented into many parts, thereby giving no real idea of the amount of each species in a given deposit. The wood was not identified from the other bulk samples not included in Table 8. All of them contained wood except 1172 and they were all Roman except 1172.

The piece of wood identified as *Castanea* or *Quercus* from 1060/2 was probably *Quercus* but no large rays were found so *Castanea* cannot be eliminated. It was part of a large coppice stool from which about ten poles had been cut.

As they were not part of a bulk sample, the identifications of the wattles from Well 1060 have not been included in the Table. The uprights were *Quercus* and *Fraxinus*, the horizontals *Corylus* and *Fraxinus*. The *Quercus* uprights were made of fast-growing straight poles, one for example with a diameter of 75 mm, 7 years old, but with few large rays. This is the sort of wood produced by oak under coppice conditions.

The identification of the wooden artefacts is given in the archaeological finds section of the report.

Other plant remains
All waterlogged plant remains not listed in the previous Tables are given in Table 9. The details of habitat information are from the same sources as for Table 6.

Table 5: Results of pollen analyses

POLLEN AND FERN SPORES		Percentage of total pollen and fern spores					
		1007/1	1100/1	1060/2	43/10	17/4	1072
Acer	field maple	-	-	-	-	-	-
Alnus	alder	-	-	-	0.3	0.6	0.5
Betula	birch	-	-	-	0.3	-	-
Corylus	hazel	1.9	0.6	0.7	0.9	-	-
Fraxinus	ash	-	0.6	6.7	-	-	-
Pinus	pine	+	0.6	0.7	-	-	0.5
Quercus	oak	-	1.9	2.1	0.6	1.2	2
Rosaceae (*Prunus* type)	sloe, plum	-	-	0.7	-	-	-
Salix	willow	-	-	-	-	-	1.5
Gramineae	grass	42.1	45.5	45.5	43.8	12.2	44.7
Cereal type		2.3	1.9	0.7	0.3	59.9	-
Caltha		-	-	0.7	-	-	-
Caryophyllaceae		-	0.6	0.7	-	-	-
Chenopodiaceae	orache etc	9.3	1.9	0.7	1.6	1.2	-
Cirsium	thistle	-	-	-	-	0.6	2.5
Compositae Liguliflorae		12.2	20.0	9.7	6.5	3.5	1
Tubuliflorae		1.9	1.3	3.4	8.1	4.1	-
Cruciferae		2.3	-	-	1.2	0.6	-
Cyperaceae	sedge	0.5	9.1	2.1	3.4	-	35.3
Geranium	cranesbill	-	0.6	-	-	-	-
Hedera	ivy	0.9	-	-	-	0.6	-
cf. Orchidaceae	orchid	-	-	-	-	-	-
Plantago lanceolata L.	ribwort plantain	8.4	3.9	-	12.1	-	2.5
P. major L.	plantain	-	0.6	0.7	-	2.5	-
P. major L. or *media* L.	plantain	-	-	0.7	5.9	-	-
Plantago sp.	plantain	-	-	-	-	0.6	-
Polygonum cf. *aviculare* L.	knotgrass	0.9	-	-	0.3	-	-
P. cf. *convolvulus* L.	black bindweed	0.9	0.6	-	-	-	-
P. cf. *persicaria* L.	red shank	-	1.3	-	-	-	-
Ranunculaceae	buttercups etc	1.9	1.9	-	1.6	5.8	-
Reticulate Varia (cf. Cruciferae)		-	-	-	-	-	0.5
Rosaceae		-	1.3	-	-	-	-
Potentilla		-	-	-	0.3	-	-
cf *Rubus*		-	-	-	0.3	-	-
Rubiaceae		0.5	-	1.4	0.9	-	-
Rumex acetosa L.	sorrel	0.5	-	-	-	1.2	-
Rumex sp.	dock	-	cf 0.6	1.4	-	-	-
Tetrad?		-	-	0.7	-	-	-
Trifolium	clover	1.4	-	-	2.2	-	-
Umbelliferae		2.3	1.3	7.6	3.1	2.9	1.5
Urtica	nettle	0.9	0.6	2.8	-	-	2
Varia		7.0	1.3	6.2	5.6	5.2	1.5
Dryopteris		-	0.6	0.7	0.3	-	-
Polypodium		0.5	-	-	-	-	-
Pteridium	bracken	1.4	0.6	2.8	0.3	-	3
Number of pollen grains and fern spores		214	154	145	322	172	201

trees and shrubs: *Acer* – *Salix*
grass: Gramineae – Cereal type
herbs: *Caltha* – Rosaceae

82

Table 6: Results of seed analyses

SEEDS		590/4	1007/1	1009/1	1100/1	1159	1172	1060/2	43/10	17/4	1046/2	1074/4	1072	1169	Habitat
CHARACEAE															
gen. et sp. indet.		1	-	-	-	4	53	-	-	-	-	-	2	-	A
RANUNCULACEAE															
Caltha palustris L.	kingcup	-	-	-	1	2	-	-	-	-	-	-	-	-	M wet G and W
Ranunculus cf. acris L.	buttercup	-	1	-	-	2	-	-	3	5	4	1	-	-	G
R. cf. repens L.	buttercup	16	23	9	4	48	-	3	32	7	21	28	-	-	damp G and W, D(a)
R. arvensis L.		-	-	-	-	-	-	-	-	2	-	-	-	-	Da
R. parviflorus L.	buttercup	-	-	3	-	-	-	-	-	-	-	-	-	-	dry Da and G
R. flammula L. or reptans L.	lesser spearwort	-	1	-	-	5	-	-	-	-	-	-	-	-	M
R. S. Batrachium	water crowfoot	1	1	3	341	2	83	1	-	-	-	-	242	-	A
Thalictrum flavum L.	meadow rue	-	-	-	-	2	-	-	-	-	-	2	1	1	M wet G
PAPAVERCEAE															
Papaver rhoeas L., dubium L., lecoquii Lamotte or hybridum L.	poppy	-	1	1	2	28	-	-	-	-	-	-	-	54	Da
P. argemone L.	poppy	-	2	-	15	2	-	-	2	-	2	-	-	-	Da - esp dry sandy soils
Chelidonium majus L.	greater celandine	-	-	-	-	-	-	-	-	-	-	-	-	126	D esp hedgerows and waste places near human habitation
FUMARIACEAE															
Fumaria sp.		4	5	-	3	3	-	5	2	-	3	-	-	3	Da
CRUCIFERAE															
Brassiceae sp.		-	-	1	-	-	-	-	2	-	-	-	5	-	Da B C
Coronopus squamatus (Forsk.) Aschers	swine-cress	-	-	-	-	-	-	-	1	-	-	1	-	-	D - esp trampled muddy places
Thlaspi arvense L.	penny-cress	-	4	-	-	2	-	3	5	2	2	-	-	-	Da
cf. Capsella bursa - pastoris (L.) Medic.	shepherd's purse	-	2	-	-	-	-	-	3	-	-	-	-	-	Da
Rorippa nasturtium-aquaticum (L.) Hayek	watercress	-	-	1	-	1	-	-	-	-	-	-	-	-	at edge of clean water
cf. Sisymbrium officinale (L.) Scop.	hedge mustard	-	-	-	-	-	-	-	2	-	-	-	-	-	Da
cf. Descurainia sophia (L.) Webb	flixweed	-	-	-	-	-	-	1	-	-	-	-	-	-	Da
gen. et sp. indet.		-	10	50	2	5	-	-	32	-	2	-	1	1	
VIOLACEAE															
Viola spp.	violet	-	10	-	11	6	-	-	-	-	-	-	-	-	M G S W Da
HYPERICACEAE															
Hypericum sp.	St. John's wort	-	-	-	-	-	-	-	-	1	-	-	-	1	M G S W
CARYOPHYLLACEAE															
Lychnis flos-cuculi L.	ragged robin	-	6	3	2	11	-	-	5	-	-	-	-	-	M wet G and W
Agrostemma githago L.	corn cockle	-	-	-	-	-	-	-	5	-	-	-	-	-	Da
Stellaria media gp.	chickweed	1	42	20	171	65	-	3	87	4	29	2	-	11	Da
S. cf. graminea L.	stitchwort	-	1	-	-	1	-	-	-	-	-	4	-	-	G W
? Stellaria sp.		-	3	-	-	-	-	-	48	-	-	-	-	-	
? Sagina sp.	pearlwort	-	-	-	-	5	-	-	3	-	-	-	-	-	G bare places
? Arenaria sp.		-	1	-	-	5	-	-	-	-	-	-	-	-	Da
Spergula arvensis L.	corn spurrey	-	-	-	1	-	-	-	-	-	-	-	-	-	Da-acid often sandy soil
Scleranthus annuus L.		-	-	-	4	1	-	-	-	-	-	-	-	-	Da-sandy often acid soil
gen. et sp. indet.		3	27	7	3	86	-	3	1	-	3	-	-	31*	
PORTULACEA															
Montia fontana L. cf. ssp. chondrosperma (Fenzl) Walters—blinks		2	2	1	2	4	-	-	-	-	-	-	-	-	M G Da and W all wet and usually acid soil

83

Table 6: Results of seed analyses (cont)

	590/4	1007/1	1009/1	1100/1	1159	1172	1060/2	43/10	17/4	1046/2	1074/4	1072	1169	Habitat
CHENOPODIACEAE														
Chenopodium bonus-henricus L. — good king henry	-	-	-	-	-	-	-	-	-	-	-	-	-	C D G
C. cf. polyspermum	-	-	-	2	-	-	2	2	1	-	-	-	-	Da
*C. album L. — fat hen	1	42	19	7	35	-	24	11	-	-	-	2	26	Da
C. cf. urbicum L. — goose foot	-	-	1	-	2	-	-	1	1	-	1	-	-	Da
C. rubrum L. or botryodes Sm. — goose foot	1	461	23	27	70	-	26	1	10	193	-	2	3	Da - esp heavy soils, at water's edge
Atriplex sp. — orache	-	120	17	9	55	-	35	20	1	79	-	2	23	Da
gen. et sp. indet.	-	-	-	-	121	-	-	11	-	-	-	-	-	Da
MALVACEAE														
Malva sylvestris L. — common mallow	-	-	-	-	18	-	-	-	-	10	-	-	4	D - esp roadsides (G.)
LINACEAE														
Linum usitatissimum L. — flax	-	14	9	7	-	-	-	9	-	-	-	-	-	C
L. catharicum L.	-	-	-	-	43	-	7	4	1	2	-	-	-	G - esp calcareous
BUXACEAE														
Buxus sempervirens L. — box (fruit fragments)	-	-	-	-	-	-	-	-	14	-	-	-	-	S - on chalk and limestone soils C
ROSACEAE														
Filipendula ulmaria (L.) Maxim — meadow-sweet	1	-	3	3	7	-	-	5	-	-	4	1	-	M wet G and W
Rubus fruticosus agg. — blackberry	87	4	1	1	+	-	6	1	1	1	3	2	79	W S D
Potentilla anserina L. — silverweed	4	2	2	23	193	1	1	2	-	1	7	-	-	G - esp damp and grazed D
P. cf. reptans L.	1	20	6	16	144	1	10	10	-	-	-	-	1	G D
Potentilla sp.	-	3	-	-	2	3	-	1	-	-	-	-	-	M G D S W
Agrimonia eupatoria L. — common agrimony	-	-	-	-	1	-	2	2	-	-	-	-	-	S and D -esp hedges and roadsides G
Aphanes arvensis agg. — parsley piert	7	3	-	5	23	-	3	-	-	-	-	-	-	Da and G - mostly on dry and rarely on clay soils
Sanguisorba officinalis L. — burnet	-	-	1	-	3	-	-	1	-	1	-	-	-	G - wet and usually meadowland
Rosa sp. — rose	-	-	-	-	-	-	-	1	3	-	-	-	-	S W
Prunus spinosa L. — sloe	-	-	-	-	-	-	1	2	-	1	-	-	-	S W
P. ? spinosa L. — sloe	-	-	-	-	-	-	-	-	1	-	-	-	-	S W
P. domestica L. cf. insititia — bullace	-	-	-	-	-	-	8	-	-	-	-	-	-	C (S)(W)
P. domestica L. cf. domestica — plum	-	-	-	-	-	-	-	-	+	-	-	-	-	C
P. cf. avium L. — cherry	-	-	-	-	-	-	1	-	-	-	-	-	-	W C
Crataegus sp. — hawthorn	-	2	-	-	-	-	-	-	2	-	-	-	-	S W
Malus sylvestris Mill. — (crab) apple	-	-	-	-	-	-	-	-	1	-	-	-	-	S W C
HIPPURIDACEAE														
Hippuris vulgaris L. — mare's-tail	1	-	-	2	1	-	-	-	-	-	-	-	-	A - usually muddy margins
HYDROCOTYLACEAE														
Hydrocotyle vulgaris L. — pennywort	1	-	-	-	-	-	-	-	-	-	-	1	-	bogs, fens and M usually on acid soil
UMBELLIFERAE														
Chaerophyllum temulentum L.	-	1	-	-	53	-	-	-	1	-	-	-	42	S and D - esp hedges (G)
*Anthriscus caucalis Bieb.	-	-	-	-	-	-	2	-	-	1	-	-	-	Da - often dry or sandy
Torilis sp.	-	2	-	1	3	-	9	2	-	-	-	-	-	Da
Coriandrum sativum L. — coriander	-	-	-	-	-	-	-	-	1	-	-	-	-	C
Conium maculatum L. — hemlock	263	-	-	-	-	-	-	3	+	-	-	-	-	B W S and D - all damp
Apium nodiflorum (L.) Lagg. — fool's watercress	-	-	-	-	-	-	-	-	-	-	42	28	1	A M
Berula erecta (Huds.) Coville — water parsnip	-	-	-	-	-	-	-	-	-	-	1	1	-	A
*Oenanthe cf. aquatica (L.) Poir — water dropwort	9	1	-	2	-	-	-	-	-	-	-	-	-	A M
Oenanthe sp.	-	-	-	-	-	-	-	-	5	-	-	8	-	A M
Aethusa cynapium L. — fool's parsley	-	5	-	6	1	-	12	2	14	21	-	-	3	Da
Anethum graveolens L. — dill	-	-	-	-	-	-	16	1	-	1	-	-	-	C
Pastinae sativa L. — (wild) parsnip	-	-	-	1	1	-	9	2	112	-	1	-	1	D and G on calcareous soil C
Daucus carota L. — (wild) carrot	-	6	-	1	-	-	21	-	-	3	2	-	33	(D) and G on dry calcareous soil C
gen. et sp. indet.	-	-	-	-	-	-	-	-	-	-	-	-	-	

esp nitrogen rich soils

Family / Species	Common name													Notes
POLYGONACEAE														
Polygonum aviculare agg.	knotgrass	6	71	151	261	77	1	2	31	3	47	3	4	Da
P. persicaria L.	red shank	-	9	3	460	3	-	2	1	-	-	1	-	M (G) B and Da - all damp
P. cf. lapathifolium L. or *nodosum* Pers.		-	2	-	41	-	-	1	4	-	-	-	-	Da and B - damp
P. convolvulus L.	black bindweed	-	1	-	8	4	-	1	-	-	-	1	-	Da
Polygonum sp.		-	-	-	7	-	-	-	-	-	-	-	1	
Rumex spp.	dock	22	23	7	125	-	18	56	11	28	11	-	-	Da G M S W
URTICACEAE														
Urtica urens L.	small nettle	3	107	34	116	282	1	-	23	-	-	-	-	Da - often dry light soils
U. dioica L.	stinging nettle	10	17	3	24	54	3	241	160	58	1766	9	674	D W S and B - often nitrogen and phosphorus rich soils
CORYLACEAE														
Corylus avellana L.	hazel	-	-	-	-	-	-	-	-	-	-	-	-	S W
PRIMULACEAE														
Anagallis arvensis L.	scarlet pimpernel	-	3	-	2	-	3	1	-	-	1	1	4	Da
OLEACEAE														
Fraxinus excelsior L.	ash	-	-	-	-	-	1	-	3	-	-	-	-	S W
GENTIANACEAE														
Centaurium sp.	centaury	-	-	-	1	-	-	-	-	-	-	-	-	G
MENYANTHACEAE														
Menyanthes trifoliata L.	bogbean	-	-	-	-	-	-	-	-	-	-	2	-	A - shallow water M
BORAGINACEAE														
Myosotis sp.	forget-me-not	-	-	-	1	1	-	-	-	-	-	-	-	B M G W
SOLANACEAE														
Hyoscyamus niger L.	henbane	7	5	2	12	12	3	-	3	-	-	-	2	D - esp nutrient rich soil
Solanum sp.		-	-	-	2	2	2	-	1	-	2	1	-	Da S W B (A)
SCROPHULARIACEAE														
Veronica sp.		-	-	-	-	-	-	2	-	-	-	-	-	(Da) G
Rhinanthus sp.	yellow rattle	-	-	2	2	-	5	-	-	2	2	2	-	Da G
Euphrasia sp. or *Odontites verna* (Bell.) Dum.		-	-	1	4	4	-	1	-	-	10	10	-	
LABIATAE														
Mentha sp.	mint	11	-	-	-	2	6	2	-	-	9	161	-	G and W - wet Da M A
Lycopus europaeus L.	gypsy-wort	7	3	-	-	-	2	-	-	-	2	69	-	M B
Prunella vulgaris L.	self-heal	3	6	2	-	48	5	5	20	12	1	1	-	G
Ballota nigra L.	black horehound	-	-	-	-	-	3	3	1	1	7	-	-	D - esp roadsides and hedges
Lamium sp.	deadnettle	-	1	4	-	5	5	3	-	-	4	-	2	Da
Galeopsis tetrahit agg.	hemp-nettle	-	1	1	-	1	1	-	-	-	1	2	-	Da (M) (W)
Glechoma hederacea L.	ground ivy	-	2	-	-	2	2	2	1	-	-	1	3	G S W
gen. et sp. indet.		-	-	-	-	-	-	-	5	-	6	-	-	
PLANTAGINACEAE														
Plantago major L.	plantain	12	11	6	12	29	1	2	38	-	20	20	-	G - short or grazed Da
P. media L. or *lanceolata* L.	plantain	-	-	-	-	-	1	-	-	-	-	-	-	G
CAPRIFOLIACEAE														
Sambucus nigra L.	elder	1	-	1	-	+	36	24	16	31	13	8	4	S W and D -esp base and nitrogen rich soils
VALERIANACEAE														
Valerianella rimosa Bast.	lamb's lettuce	2	11	1	5	3	-	1	1	-	-	-	-	Da - basic soil
V. dentata (L.) Poll.	lamb's lettuce	-	11	5	3	3	-	1	-	-	-	-	-	Da - dry basic soil
gen. et sp. indet.		-	1	3	-	-	-	-	-	-	-	-	9	Da G M W

Table 6: Results of seed analyses (cont)

Species	Common name	590/4	1007/1	1009/1	1100/1	1159	1172	1060/2	43/10	17/4	1046/2	1074/4	1072	1169	Habitat
DIPSACACEAE															
Dipsacus fullonum L.	teasel	-	-	-	-	-	-	-	-	-	-	-	-	-	B S D
Succisa pratensis Moench	devil's-bit scabious	-	-	-	1	-	-	-	1	-	-	-	-	-	M damp G and W
COMPOSITAE															
Senecio sp.	groundsel or ragwort	-	-	-	1	-	-	8	2	66	-	-	-	-	Da M G
cf. Pulicaria sp.	fleabane	-	-	-	-	-	-	-	-	-	1	-	-	-	M wet G
Anthemis cotula L.	stinking mayweed	-	-	-	-	-	-	-	25	31	-	-	-	-	Da - esp base rich heavy soil
Tripleurospermum maritimum (L.) Koch	scentless mayweed	-	-	-	-	-	-	1	2	2	2	-	-	-	Da
Chrysanthemum leucanthemum L.	ox-eye daisy	1	-	3	13	4	-	26	2	6	11	-	-	-	G
Arctium sp.	burdock	-	-	-	-	+	-	-	-	-	-	-	-	-	D S
Cirsium spp.	thistle	5	47	-	14	19	-	-	-	3	-	-	-	-	Da M G S
Carduus or Cirsium spp.	thistle	4	3	6	16	14	2	2	-	29	-	3	2	-	Da M G S
Onopordum acanthium L.	cotton thistle	16	-	1	5	4	-	18	2	-	-	-	-	-	D?C
Centaurea cf. nigra L.	knapweed	-	-	-	-	-	-	-	-	-	4	-	-	-	G
Centaurea sp.		-	-	-	-	-	-	-	-	1	-	-	-	-	Da G
Lapsana communis L.	nipplewort	-	-	-	-	1	-	5	2	2	2	2	-	11	Da
Leontodon sp.	hawkbit	-	-	-	5	17	-	-	-	1	-	-	-	-	G
Picris echioides L.		-	-	-	-	-	-	-	-	131	-	-	-	-	Da
cf. P. hieracioides L.		-	-	-	-	-	-	-	-	1	-	-	-	-	G D
Sonchus arvensis L.	sow-thistle	-	2	-	1	-	-	-	2	-	-	-	-	-	(M) B Da
S. oleraceus L.	sow-thistle	-	2	-	-	-	-	-	-	1	-	-	-	5	Da
S. asper (L.) Hill	sow-thistle	-	16	7	5	5	-	17	10	75	1	1	1	-	Da
Taraxacum sp.	dandelion	-	-	-	-	2	1	1	1	-	1	-	-	-	D M G
gen. et sp. indet.		-	3	1	-	11	-	1	1	20	-	-	-	-	
ALISMATACEAE															
Alisma sp.	water-plantain	2	-	-	-	1	-	-	1	-	-	1	10	-	A B
cf. Sagittaria sagittifolia L.	arrow-head	-	1	-	-	-	-	-	-	-	-	-	-	-	A
POTAMOGETONACEAE															
Potamogeton sp.	pondweed	2	-	-	1	-	1	-	-	-	-	2	2	-	A
ZANNICHELLIACEAE															
Zannichellia palustris L.		2	-	-	4	6	24	-	-	-	-	2	2	-	A
JUNCACEAE															
Juncus spp.	rush	760*	166	346	164	2597	40	38	198	57	70*	80*	153	220*	esp M and wet G
IRIDACEAE															
Iris pseudacorus L.	yellow flag	-	-	-	-	-	-	-	-	-	-	-	8	-	A M B
LEMNACEAE															
Lemna sp.	duckweed	112	-	-	103	391	9	-	1	-	-	-	150	3	A
SPARGANIACEAE															
Sparganium sp.	bur-reed	1	-	-	-	-	-	-	-	-	-	-	-	-	A M - ungrazed
CYPERACEAE															
Eleocharis S. Palustres	sedge	28	10	6	29	20	3	2	78	5	1	1	5	1	A- shallow water M G - wet all open vegetation
Carex spp.	sedge	13	31	12	4	59	6	3	26	8	-	4	112	8	esp wetter soils
GRAMINEAE															
gen. et sp. indet.	grass	4	4	27	5	33	1	19	30	8	13	-	2	3	A
Varia		4	6	4	2	6	-	8	4	19	6	2	6	4	
Total		1442	1402	802	1347	4932	237	678	1040	804	739	2017	1028	1398	

Habitat information: A, aquatic; B, bankside; C, cultivated; D, disturbed ground; Da, disturbed ground including arable; G, grassland; M, marsh; S, scrub; W, woodland. Less usual habitats given in brackets. All samples 5 lb except 1046/2 which was 3 lb.

* against number of a species from a particular sample indicates that it has been derived from a tenth sub-sample. + indicates presence in insect but not seed sample. * against species name means there are no modern records of the plant in National Grid Square SP 40.

Table 7: Results of analyses of cereal remains

UNCARBONIZED CEREAL REMAINS	43/10	17/4
Cereal size Gramineae caryopses	1 cf. *Triticum* (wheat) 1 cf. *Bromus* (a large seeded grass)	4 cf. *Triticum*
Triticum spelta L. (spelt wheat) glumes	-	38 pairs of glumes, some with rachis and remains of lema and palea but none with caryopses; one pair still attached to pair above. 216 single glume bases with some or most of glume attached.
Triticum sp. (wheat) glumes	-	16 pairs of glumes. 50 single glume bases.
Cereal straw	-	some fragments present but in very poor condition.

Results of 17/4 from special 1.5 oz sample, and of 43/10 from the ordinary 5 lb seed sample. No uncarbonized cereal remains present in any of the other deposits examined.

Table 8: Results of wood analyses

WOOD		590/4	1007/1	1009/1	1100/1	1159	1060/2	43/10	17/4	1072
Alnus or *Corylus*	alder or hazel	-	-	-	-	-	-	-	-	+
Castanea or *Quercus*	chestnut or oak	-	-	-	-	-	+	-	-	-
Corylus	hazel	-	-	-	-	-	-	?	-	-
Fraxinus	ash	-	-	-	-	-	-	-	+	-
Prunus	sloe, plum	-	+	-	-	-	+	+	+	+
Quercus	oak	-	-	-	-	-	-	+	-	-
Rosa	rose	-	?	-	-	-	-	-	+	-
Salix	willow	-	-	-	-	-	-	+	-	+
Sambucus nigra	elder	-	-	-	-	-	-	+	-	-

Sample sizes various, see p78.

Table 9: Results of analyses of other plant remains

OTHER PLANT REMAINS	590/4	1007/1	1009/1	1100/1	1159	1172	1060/2	43/10	17/4	1046/2	1074/4	1072	1169	Habitat
Bryophyta (moss) stem with leaves	-	-	+	-	-	-	-	+	+	+	-	-	-	
Bud Scale	-	-	-	-	+	-	+	+	+	+	+	-	-	SW
Bruxus sempervirens L. (box) leaf, shoot	-	-	-	-	-	-	-	-	+	-	-	-	+	C
Crataegus or *Prunus* sp. (hawthorn or sloe) thorny twig	-	-	-	-	+	-	+	+	+	+	+	+	+	SW
? Glyceria maxima (Hartm.) Holm (reed-grass) rhizome	-	-	-	-	-	-	-	-	-	-	-	+	-	A
Leaf Abscision Pad	-	-	-	-	+	-	+	+	+	-	+	-	-	SW
Pteridium aquilinum (L). Kuhn (bracken) frond fragment	-	+	?	-	-	-	-	-	-	-	-	-	-	GSW - esp light acid soils
Quercus sp. (oak) leaf	-	-	-	-	-	-	-	+	-	-	-	-	-	SW
Rosa sp. (rose) prickle	-	+	-	-	-	-	+	+	+	-	-	-	-	SW
cf. *Trifolium* sp. (clover) calyx	-	-	-	-	1	-	9	5	3	2	-	-	-	G
cf. *Vicia* sp. (vetch) seedpod fragment	-	-	-	-	-	-	+	-	+	-	-	-	-	DaGSW
cf. *Prunus* sp. (sloe,plum) fruit stalk	-	-	-	-	-	-	12	-	-	-	-	-	-	CSW
cf. *Rubus fruticosus* agg. (blackberry) prickle	-	-	-	-	-	-	-	-	-	-	-	-	+	SWD

Habitat information: A, aquatic; C, cultivated; D, disturbed ground; Da, disturbed ground including arable; G, grassland; S, scrub; W, woodland. All samples 5 lb except 1046/2 which was 3 lb.

Table 10: Results of analyses of carbonized seeds

CARBONIZED SEEDS	590/4	1007/1	1009/1	1100/1	1159	1172	1060/3	43/10	17/4	1046/2	1074/4	1072	1169	Habitat
CHENOPODIACEAE														
Chenopodium sp. — fat hen etc	-	-	-	-	-(1)	-	-	-	-	-	-	-	-	Da
Atriplix sp. — orache	-	-	-	-	-	-	-	-	-	-	-	-	2	Da
gen. et sp. indet.	-	-	-	-	-	-	-	-	-	-	-	-	12	Da
PAPILIONACEAE														
Vicia or *Lathyrus* sp. — vetch	-	-	2	-	-(2)	-	-	-	-	-	-	-	1	Da M G S W
? gen. et sp. indet.	-	-	-	-	-	-	-	-	-	-	-	-	-	
ROSACEAE														
Prunus spinosa L. — sloe	-	-	-	-	-(1)	-	-	-	-	-	-	-	-	S W
POLYGONACEAE														
Polygonum aviculare agg. — knotgrass	-	-	-	-	-	-	-	-	-	-	-	-	4	Da
P. convolvulus L. — black bindweed	-	-	-	-	-	-	-	-	-	-	-	-	1	Da
Rumex sp. — dock	-	-	-	-	-	-	-	-	-	-	-	-	11	Da G M S W
SOLANACEAE														
Hyoscyamus niger L. — henbane	-	-	-	-	-(1)	-	-	-	-	-	-	-	1	D
RUBIACEAE														
Galium sp. — bedstraw	-	1	-	-	3(19)	-	-	-	-	-	-	-	1	Da M G S W
COMPOSITAE														
Anthemis cotula L. — stinking mayweed	-	-	-	-	-	-	-	-	-	-	-	-	13	Da - esp base rich heavy soil
Tripleurospermum maritimum (L.) Koch — scentless mayweed	-	-	-	-	-	-	-	-	-	-	-	-	20	Da
GRAMINEAE														
cf. *Bromus* sp.	-	-	-	-	-(1)	-	-	-	-	-	-	-	-	Da G
Triticum spelta L. — spelt wheat	-	-	-	-	-	-	-	-	1	-	-	-	-	C (Da)
Triticum sp. — wheat	-	-	-	-	-	-	-	-	1	-	-	-	7	C (Da)
Hordeum vulgare L. emend. — six-row hulled barley	-	-	2	-	-	-	-	-	-	-	-	-	-	
H. vulgare L. emend. or *distichon* L. — hulled barley	-	-	-	-	-(1)	-	-	-	-	-	-	-	1	C (Da)
Avena sp. — oats	-	-	-	-	-(1)	-	-	-	-	-	-	-	2	C (Da)
cf. *Avena* sp. — oats	-	-	3	-	-	1	-	-	-	-	-	-	3	C Da
Cereal indet.	-	-	1	-	-(3)	-	-	-	-	-	-	-	-	C Da
gen. et sp. indet. — grass	-	-	-	-	-	-	-	-	-	-	-	-	2	C Da
varia	-	1	-	-	2(7)	-	-	-	-	-	1	-	15	
Total	0	2	8	0	5(37)	1	0	0	2	0	1	0	96	

Number of Seeds

Habitat information: B, bankside/water's edge; C, cultivated; D, disturbed ground; Da, disturbed ground including arable; G, grassland; M, marsh; S, scrub; W, woodland. Less common habitats given in brackets.

All samples 5 lb except 1046/2 which was 3 lb and 1159 where the numbers from a larger sample have been given in brackets alongside the numbers from the ordinary 5 lb sample (see p 80).

Table 11: Results of analyses of other carbonized plant remains

OTHER CARBONIZED PLANT REMAINS		Number of Fragments													Habitat
		590/4	1007/1	1009/1	1100/1	1159	1172	1060/2	43/10	17/4	1046/2	1074/4	1072	1169	
Avena sp. (oats)	awn fragments	–	–	–	–	–	–	–	–	–	–	–	–	13	C Da
cf. *Avena* sp. (oats)	palea fragment	–	–	–	–	–	–	–	–	–	–	–	–	1	C Da
Hordeum vulgare L. emend. (six-row barley)	rachis node	–	–	–	–	1(1)	–	–	–	–	–	–	–	1	C (Da)
Triticum spelta L. (spelt wheat)	glume bases	–	–	–	–	–(1)	–	–	–	2	–	–	–	199	C (Da)
Triticum sp. (wheat)	glume base	–	–	–	–	–(1)	–	–	–	–	–	–	–	1	C (Da)
Triticum sp. (wheat)	rachis fragments (some attached to the glume bases)	–	–	–	–	–	–	–	–	–	–	–	–	21	C (Da)
cf. *Triticum* sp. (wheat)	awn fragments	–	–	–	–	–	–	–	–	–	–	–	–	8	C (Da)
cf. *Vicia* (vetch)	seed pod	–	–	–	–	–	–	–	–	–	–	–	–	1	Da M G S W

Habitat information and sample sizes as for Table 10.

Plant remains preserved by carbonization

Carbonized seeds
These are listed in Table 10. The details of nomenclature, minimum number of seeds present, and habitat information are from the same sources used for Table 6.

Other carbonized plant remains
These are listed in Table 11. Some of the spelt glume bases were double and these have been counted as two in the total. Nomenclature and habitat information are from the same sources used for Table 6.

No wood charcoal was present in any of these samples; in fact the only potentially identifiable wood charcoal from the site came from House Circle 1007 and was used unidentified for a radiocarbon determination.

Molluscs

Table 12 gives the minimum number of individuals represented by the molluscan fragments from each of the samples except for *Arion* sp. Nomenclature follows Kerney (1976a) for the freshwater molluscs and Walden (1976) for the land snails. The habitat information has been taken from Boycott (1934; 1936), Evans (1972), and Sparks (1959-60). For freshwater molluscs the habitat groups given in Sparks have been used. Those species not included by him have been assigned a group using Boycott (1936). Slum species are those able to live in water subject to stagnation, drying up, and large temperature variations. Catholic species can tolerate a wide range of conditions except the worst slums. Ditch species require clean, slowly moving water, often with abundant aquatic plants. Moving water species require no more than a clean stream a few yards wide with a slow current. Some individuals in the last two groups are also able to live in large enclosed ponds, if they are clean, but certainly not small ponds. Marsh snails have been divided into those which are obligatory marsh dwellers and those terrestrial species which to a greater or lesser extent occur in marshes. The preferences of marsh and terrestial species for open or shady habitats are indicated if they are known to exist.

Insects

Coleoptera (beetles)
The minimum number of individuals represented by the fragments identified is given in Table 13 except for aleocharine staphylinids where it is thought that many of them have been lost through the sieves. The families follow Crowson (1956). The nomenclature follows Kloet and Hincks (1945) except for Carabidae after Lindroth (1974); *Helophorus* S. *Meghelophorus* after Angus (1970); Staphylinidae after Tottenham (1954); Histeridae after Halstead (1963); and Scarabaeidae after Britton (1956).

Sufficient information on habitats has been hard to find so a wide range of publications has been used. They are as follows: Allen (1958, 1965); Angus (1964); Balfour-Brown (1940-58); Donisthorpe (1939); Drummond (1956); Easton (1966); Fowler (1887-1913); Freude *et al* (1964-1974); Greenslade (1965); Greenslade and Southwood (1962); Hickin (1963, 1975); Hinton (1940-41, 1945); Hofman (1950, 1954, 1958); Horion (1941-67); Jennings (1915); Joy (1932); Landin (1961); Luff (1965); Moore (1955); Morris (1965a, 1965b); Munro (1926); Nash (1971); Paulian (1959); Raw (1951-2); Reitter (1908-16);

Table 12: Results of analyses of molluscs

MOLLUSCA	Habitat	1169	1072	1074/4	1046/2	17/4	43/10	1060/2	1172	1159	1100/1	1009/1	1007/1	590/4
								Minimum Number of Individuals						
GASTROPODA														
PROSOBRANCHIA														
VALVATIDAE														
Valvata cristata Müll.	D	-	-	1	-	-	1	-	17	5	4	-	-	-
BITHYNIIDAE														
Bithynia tentaculata (L.)	F	-	1	-	-	-	-	-	16	3	2	-	-	-
Bithynia sp.	F	-	-	-	-	-	-	-	-	2	-	-	-	-
EUTHYNEURA														
ELLOBIIDAE														
Carychium sp.	(M)s	2	-	-	-	-	-	-	-	-	-	-	-	-
LIMNAEIDAE														
Lymnaea truncatula (Müll.)	S M	-	-	-	-	-	1	-	7	4	3	-	-	-
L. palustris (Müll.)	C M	-	-	-	-	-	-	-	6	-	-	1	-	-
L. peregra (Müll.)	C	-	-	-	2	-	-	-	6	1	-	-	-	-
Lymnaea sp.	M S D C F	-	-	2	-	-	-	-	6	2	2	-	-	-
PLANORBIDAE														
Planorbis planorbis (L.)	D	-	-	6	-	-	-	-	7	2	4	1	-	1
Anisus leucostoma (Mitt.)	S	-	-	2	-	12	-	-	4	1	-	-	-	1
Bathyomphalus contortus (L.)	C	-	-	1	-	-	-	-	1	-	-	-	-	-
Gyraulus albus (Müll.)	C	-	-	-	-	-	-	-	-	-	-	-	-	-
Armiger crista (L.)	C	-	-	2	-	-	-	-	12	3	-	2	-	2
SUCCINEIDAE														
Succinea sp.	Mo	-	-	-	-	-	-	-	1	1	-	-	-	-
COCHLICOPIDAE														
Cochlicopa sp.	(M)	5	-	-	-	-	-	-	-	-	-	-	-	-
VERTIGINIDAE														
Vertigo pygmaea (Drp.)	(M)o	-	-	-	-	1	-	-	-	-	-	-	-	-
PUPILLIDAE														
Pupilla muscorum (L.)	T o	1	-	-	-	-	-	-	-	-	-	-	-	1
VALLONIIDAE														
Vallonia costata (Müll.)	T o	45	-	-	-	1	2	8	2	2	-	-	-	-
V. pulchella (Müll.)	(M)o	4	-	1	-	-	5	-	1	2	-	-	-	-
V. excentrica Sterki	T o	6	-	-	-	-	-	2	1	-	1	-	-	2
V. pulchella (Müll.) or excentrica Sterki	(M)o	23	-	-	2	-	3	2	-	1	1	-	-	-
Vallonia sp.	(M)o	-	-	-	-	1	-	-	-	1	-	-	-	-
ARIONIDAE														
Arion sp.	(M)	+	-	-	-	-	-	-	-	-	-	-	-	-
ZONITIDAE														
Vitrea sp.	(M)s	18	-	-	-	-	-	2	-	-	-	-	-	-
Oxychilus cellarius (Müll.)	T s	8	-	-	-	-	3	-	-	-	-	-	-	-
LIMACIDAE														
Limax or Deroceras sp.	(M)	7	-	-	-	-	3	-	-	-	-	-	-	-
HELICIDAE														
Trichia hispida (L.)	(M)	17	-	2	3	1	5	4	-	-	-	-	-	-
Cepaea sp.	(M)	1	-	-	1	-	-	-	-	-	-	-	-	-
Helix aspersa Müll.	T	1	-	-	-	-	-	2	-	-	-	-	-	-
BIVALVIA														
SPHAERIIDAE														
Pisidium sp.	M S D C F	1	-	-	-	-	-	-	-	-	-	-	-	-
Total		140	1	17	8	16	41	18	96	29	17	5	0	5

Habitat information: C, 'catholic' aquatic; D, 'ditch' aquatic; F, flowing water aquatic; M, obligate marsh dweller; (M), terrestrial species which can live in marshes; S, 'slum' aquatic; T, terrestrial. Qualified by: o, open habitat; s, shaded habitat.
All samples 5 lb except 1046/2 which was 3 lb.

Table 13: Results of analyses of beetles

COLEOPTERA	590/4	1007/1	1009/1	1100/1	1159	1172	1060/2	43/10	17/4	1046/2	1074/4	1072	1169	Habitat or Food
CARABIDAE														
Carabus violaceus L.	—	—	—	—	—	—	—	—	1	—	—	—	1	T - often woodland
Leistus spinibarbis (F.)	—	—	—	—	—	—	—	2	1	1	—	—	—	T - usually woodland
Nebria brevicollis (F.)	—	1	1	—	5	—	—	9	5	—	—	—	—	W G D
Nebria sp.	—	—	—	—	—	—	—	—	—	—	—	—	—	W G D
Notiophilus sp.	—	—	—	1	1	1	—	1	—	—	—	—	—	M W G D
*Blethisa multipunctata (L.)	—	—	—	—	—	—	—	2	—	—	—	—	—	M B - at edge of water
Elaphrus cupreus Duft.	—	—	—	1	—	—	—	1	—	—	—	—	—	M B - at edge of water
Loricera pilicornis (F.)	—	—	—	—	1	—	—	3	3	3	—	—	—	M W G D
Clivina fossor (L.) or collaris (Hbst.)	1	—	2	1	11	—	—	2	—	—	—	—	—	moist B W D and G - often under dung
Dyschirius globosus (Hbst.)	1	—	1	—	2	—	—	2	—	—	—	—	—	T - moist ground, M
Dyschirius sp.	—	—	—	—	—	—	—	1°	—	—	—	—	—	T - moist ground, M
Trechus quadristriatus (Schr.) or obtusus Er.	1	14	7	4	13	—	1	4	2	3	—	—	—	B W G D (cut vegetation)
T. micros (Hbst.)	—	—	—	—	6	—	—	1	—	—	—	—	—	B - usually of flowing water
Bembidion lampros (Hbst.)	—	—	—	—	1	—	—	—	—	—	—	—	—	G and D - dry open soil (W)
B. properans Steph.	—	—	1	—	5	—	1	9	—	—	—	—	—	T - less dry open clayish soil and mud
B. obtusum Ser.	—	—	—	—	3	—	—	—	—	—	—	—	—	T - open, clayish
B. dentellum (Thunb.)	—	—	—	—	—	—	—	1	—	—	—	—	—	(G) and M - well vegetated
B. cf. articulatum (Pz)	—	—	—	—	2	—	—	—	—	—	—	—	—	B - esp on open mud
B. gilvipes Strm.	—	—	—	—	—	—	—	1	—	—	—	—	—	(W) B also wet meadowland
B. assimile Gyll. or clarki Daws.	—	—	—	—	1	—	—	4	—	—	—	—	—	M - well vegetated and close to water
B. quadrimaculatum (L.)	—	—	—	—	1	—	—	2	—	—	—	—	—	W M - also open drier places
B. biguttatum (F.)	—	—	—	—	1	—	2	2	6	—	cf. 1	—	1	B G and W - usually near water
B. lunulatum (Geof. in Fouc.)	—	—	—	—	—	—	—	—	—	—	1	—	—	(W) D B and M - well vegetated often clayish soil
B. guttula (F.)	—	—	—	—	—	—	—	—	1	—	—	—	—	M G and W - moist (in manure heaps)
B. guttula (F.) or unicolor Chaud	—	—	1	—	6°	—	—	2	2	—	1	—	—	M G and W - moist (in manure heaps)
Bembidion spp.	2°	—	1°	2°	6°	1	1°	1°	5°	—	1°	3	1°	mostly in wet or marshy places
Pterostichus cupreus (L.)	—	—	1	1	—	—	—	3	3	—	—	—	—	G D and (W) - moist, sometimes near water
P. versicolor (Strm.)	1	—	—	—	—	—	—	2	—	—	—	—	—	G D
P. cupreus (L.) or versicolor (Strm.)	—	—	1	—	3	—	1	—	—	—	—	—	—	G D (W)
P. vernalis (Pz)	—	—	—	—	—	—	—	3	2	—	—	—	—	(W) and G - moist, often near water
P. melanarius (Ill.)	—	2	5	—	1	—	—	6	3	—	2	—	—	D G (W)
P. nigrita (F.)	—	—	—	—	—	—	—	5	—	—	—	—	—	M B
P. anthracinus (Ill.)	—	—	—	—	—	—	—	—	1	—	—	—	—	M and B - shaded
P. minor (Gyl.)	—	—	—	—	—	—	—	—	—	—	—	—	—	M and B - both wooded and open
P. stenuus (Pz)	—	—	—	—	—	—	—	—	—	—	—	—	—	W G D and B - often near water
P. madidus (F.)	—	—	—	1°	—	—	3°	—	2°	—	—	—	—	W G D and C
Pterostichus spp.	1°	—	—	—	—	—	—	1°	—	—	—	—	—	M T
Abax parallelopipedus (Pill)	—	—	3	2	3	—	—	5	—	—	—	—	—	W (G) (D) (C)
Calathus fuscipes (Goez.)	—	—	—	—	6	—	1	4	—	—	—	—	—	W D and G - often in meadowland
C. melanocephalus (L.)	—	—	—	—	4	—	—	—	—	—	—	—	—	(W) G D
Calathus sp.	—	—	—	—	—	—	—	—	—	—	—	—	—	T
Synuchus nivalis (Pz)	—	—	—	—	1	—	—	1	—	—	—	—	—	G and D - often in sandy or gravelly places (W)
Olisthopus rotundatus (Pk.)	—	—	—	—	—	—	—	—	—	—	—	—	—	G D
Agonum marginatum (L.)	—	—	—	—	—	—	—	4	1	—	—	—	—	M B and G - usually wet
A. muelleri (Hbst.)	—	—	—	—	1	—	—	4	—	—	—	—	1	(W) M G D
A. viduum (Pz.)	—	—	—	1	—	—	—	4	2°	—	—	—	—	B - rich vegetation (W)
A. dorsale (Pont.)	—	—	2°	—	—	—	—	3	3°	1	—	—	—	G and D - usually open
Agonum spp.	1	—	—	—	—	—	—	5	—	—	—	—	—	mostly wet habitats
Amara cf. aenea (DeG.)	—	—	1	—	—	—	—	1	—	1°	—	—	—	T - dry open ground
A. aulica (Pz.)	1°	—	2°	—	2	—	—	2°	3	—	—	—	—	G and D - often feeding on seeds of Compositae
Amara spp.	—	—	—	—	—	—	—	—	—	1°	—	—	—	T
cf. Zabrus tenebrioides (Goez.))	—	—	—	—	—	—	—	—	—	1	—	—	—	G D

Minimum Number of Individuals

91

Table 13: Results of analyses of beetles (cont)

	590/4	1007/1	1009/1	1100/1	1159	1172	1060/2	43/10	17/4	1046/2	1074/4	1072	1169	Habitat or Food
Harpalus aeneus (F.)	-	-	-	-	2	-	-	2	-	-	-	-	-	D G (W)
H. cf. punctatulus Duft.	-	-	-	-	-	-	-	-	-	-	1	-	-	T - open
H. azureus (F.)	-	-	-	1	-	-	1	1	-	1	-	-	-	D and G - short vegetation
H. S. Ophonus sp.	-	-	-	-	1	-	2°	3°	-	-	-	-	-	T - mostly dry and open
H. rufipes (Deg.)	1	-	-	-	-	-	-	17	-	-	-	-	-	D - often cultivated (G)
Harpalus spp.	-	-	-	-	2	-	-	-	-	-	-	-	-	T
Acupalpus luridus Dej or exiguus Dej	-	-	-	-	-	-	-	-	-	-	-	-	-	B - moist and shady
cf. Acupalpus sp.	-	-	-	-	-	-	-	-	-	-	-	-	-	mostly wet places
Chlaenius vestitus (Pk.)	-	-	-	-	-	-	-	-	-	-	-	-	-	M B - often on mud
Lebia chlorocephala (Hoff.)	-	-	-	-	-	-	-	-	-	-	-	-	-	G - larvae mostly on Hypericum feeding Chrysomelids
Dromius linearis (Ol.)	-	-	-	-	-	-	2	-	-	-	-	-	-	G (M)
D. quadrimaculatus (L.)	-	-	-	-	-	-	-	-	-	-	-	-	-	W - often on trees
*D. cf. notatus Step.	-	-	-	-	-	-	-	-	1	-	-	-	-	T - dense vegetation
Dromius sp.	-	-	-	-	-	-	-	-	-	1°	-	-	-	T
Metabletus obscuroguttatus (Duft.)	-	-	-	-	1	-	1	1	-	-	-	-	-	V
Brachinus crepitans (L.)	-	-	-	-	1	-	-	3	-	-	-	-	-	G - dry open, often on chalk
HALIPLIDAE														
Haliplus sp.	-	-	-	-	-	-	-	-	-	-	1	-	-	A
DYTISCIDAE														
Hygrotus inaequalis (F.)	-	-	-	-	-	-	-	-	-	-	-	1	-	A - ponds, slowly moving water often with detritus bottom
H. impressopunctatus (Schal.)	-	-	-	-	-	-	2	2	-	-	1	-	-	A - stagnant water, often with silty bottom
Hydroporus spp.	-	-	-	1	-	-	1	1	-	1	3	-	-	A
Agabus bipustulatus (L.)	-	-	-	-	-	-	-	-	-	-	-	2	-	A - ponds, puddles and ditches
Agabus sp.	-	-	-	-	-	-	-	-	-	-	-	-	-	A
Ilybius sp.	-	-	-	-	-	-	-	-	-	-	-	-	-	A
Rantus sp.	-	-	-	-	-	-	-	-	-	-	1	-	-	A
Colymbetes fuscus (L.)	-	-	-	-	1	1	-	-	-	-	1	1	-	A - stagnant water, ponds and ditches with much vegetation
HYDRAENIDAE														
Ochthebius dilatatus Steph.	-	-	-	-	2	-	-	-	-	-	-	-	-	A - standing water B - mud and decaying vegetation at water's edge
O. minimus (F.)	-	-	-	-	2	-	-	-	-	-	1	-	-	A - often stagnant
Ochthebius spp.	1	4	2	4	19	-	1	1	6	1	4	2	-	A - mostly standing water B - mud at water's edge
Hydraena testacea Curt.	-	-	-	-	-	cf. 1	17	6	-	-	-	-	-	A - esp duckweed covered stagnant water, sometimes running water
HYDROPHILIDAE														
Helophorus nubilus F.	1	-	2	-	2	-	1	-	-	-	-	-	-	T
H. rufipes (Bosc.)	-	1	2	-	2	-	-	-	-	-	-	-	-	T - often on Cruciferae
H. porculus Bed.	-	-	-	-	-	-	-	-	-	-	-	-	-	"
H. rufipes (Bosc.) or porculus Bed.	-	-	-	-	-	-	-	-	-	-	-	-	-	"
H. grandis Ill.	5	2	-	-	7	-	3	15	8	2	1	-	-	A - puddles, ponds, rarely flowing water
H. aquaticus (L.)	-	-	-	-	4	-	-	3	-	-	-	-	-	A "
H. grandis Ill. or aquaticus (L.)	2	1	1	1	-	-	-	-	-	-	3	-	-	A "
Helophorus spp. (brevipalpis size)	11	11	4	7	89	-	7	8	9	3	10	7	-	A - but sometimes spend much time out of water
Coelostoma orbiculare (F.)	1	1	-	-	-	-	3	3	-	-	2	-	-	V - esp in wet places, often at water's edge A - ponds
Sphaeridium bipustulatum F.	-	-	-	-	2	-	-	-	-	-	2	-	-	F V C
S. scarabaeoides (L.) or lunatum F.	-	-	-	-	-	-	-	-	-	-	-	-	-	F - esp cow dung (V)
Cercyon lugubris (Ol.) or atomarius (F.)	-	-	-	-	-	-	1	2	-	-	-	-	-	F V C
C. terminatus (Marsh.)	-	-	-	-	2	-	-	4	8	-	-	-	-	F V
C. quisquilius (L.)	2	-	-	-	2	-	1	4	8	-	-	-	-	F V
Cercyon spp.	2	19	11	2	31	-	17	27	143	6	4	3	2	F V C - some species on mud at water's edge
Hydrobius fuscipes (L.)	1	-	-	2	4	-	12	1	8	9	2	-	-	A - stagnant water often with detritus bottom
Anacaena globulus (Pk.)	-	-	1	-	1	-	-	-	7	-	-	-	-	G and W in wet places, V A
Anacaena sp.	-	-	-	-	1	-	-	-	3°	1	-	2	-	"
Laccobius sp.	-	-	-	-	-	-	-	-	-	-	-	-	-	A
Helochares sp.	-	-	-	-	5	-	-	-	-	-	-	-	-	A - ponds and ditches

92

HISTERIDAE — STAPHYLINIDAE

The data columns (1–7) are counts from successive samples; the right-hand column gives habitat notes.

Taxon	1	2	3	4	5	6	7	Habitat notes
HISTERIDAE								
Hister quadrimaculatus L.	1	–	–	–	–	–	–	F V C
H. bissexstriatus F.	1	–	–	–	–	–	–	F V
Margarinotus spp.	5	–	–	–	–	–	–	F V C
Atholus duodecimstriatus Schr.	3	–	–	–	–	1	–	F V
Onthophilus striatus (Forst.)	2	–	–	–	–	1	–	F V C
Abraeus globosus (Hofn.)	–	–	–	–	–	–	–	rotten wood
Acritus nigricornis (Hofn.)	–	1	–	–	1	–	–	V – often haystack refuse
Gnathoncus nannetensis (Mars.)	1	1	–	1	–	–	–	C V – esp rotten fungi F – often bird droppings, bird's nests
Saprinus aeneus (F.)	–	–	–	–	–	–	–	F C (V)
ANISOTOMIDAE								
Choleva or *Catops* spp.	–	–	2	2	1	1	–	V – often leaf litter or fungi in woods C (G)
SCYDMAENIDAE								
gen. et sp. indet.	–	–	2	2	2	–	1	T V
SILPHIDAE								
Silpha obscura L.	–	–	1	1	1	–	–	C
Phosphuga atrata (L.)	–	1	1	–	1	1	–	mostly under bark or in rotten wood (G) (D) (V)
MICROPEPLIDAE								
Micropeplus fulvus Er.	–	2	1	10	2	1	–	V – often straw or hay (B – on mud)
STAPHYLINIDAE								
Metopsia gallica (Koch)	–	–	7	3	1	1	–	G V
Omalium spp.	–	–	2	3	2	–	1	V – all sorts C F T
Acidota crenata (F.)	3	–	4	–	3	1	6	W – under leaf litter M
Lesteva sp.	1	–	13	3	3	–	–	B – often at water's edge M
Carpalimus bilineatus (Step.)	45	–	2	–	–	–	–	B – on wet mud (G V and F on wet soils)
Aploderus caelatus (Gr.)	3	–	–	–	–	–	–	V F
Oxytelus sculptus Gr.	11	2	11	6	56	4	1	V F (C)
O. sculpturatus Gr.	1	8	6	–	–	–	1	V F C (also G D)
O. nitidulus Gr.	12	1	5	11	3	–	1	V F C (M)
O. rugosus (F.)	1	–	5	–	3	–	–	V F (C)
Oxytelus sp.	13	1	4	7	7	–	5	mostly V F and C
Platystethus arenarius (Geof.)	33	5	1	79	–	1	–	F V
P. cornutus (Gr.)	1	–	–	–	–	–	–	M and B – often on mud (V F)
P. cornutus (Gr.) or *alutaceus* Th.	9	–	–	–	1	6	–	"
P. nitens Sahlb.	2	–	2	–	–	–	–	F V B
Stenus sp.	–	–	–	–	–	1	–	W G D M
Paederus litoralis Grav.	2	–	2	–	–	–	–	G and D – mostly dry
Lathrobium sp.	13	–	4	6	–	–	–	W G D M V (C)
Leptacinus sp.	3	–	–	–	–	–	–	F V
Xantholinus fracticornis (Müll.)	–	2	2	11	2	1	–	V F (C)
X. angustatus Step.	–	–	2	2	–	–	–	V – sometimes at water's edge
X. fracticornis (Müll.) or *atratus* Heer	1	–	3	3	–	–	–	F V (C) also ant's nests
X. glabratus (Gr.)	–	–	3	4	–	–	–	G D F V
X. linearis (Ol.)	10	1	6	5	–	–	–	W G V (F)
X. longiventris Heer	3	2	3	1	–	–	–	W G V (F C)
X. linearis (Ol.) or *longiventris* Heer	–	–	–	–	–	–	–	W G C (F C)
Philonthus intermedius (B.& L.) or *laminatus* (Cr.)	6	–	–	1	–	–	–	W G V F C
Philonthus spp.	2	2	1	14°	15°	1	1	V F C (W G D)
Gabrius sp.	–	–	2	–	–	–	–	W G V F C
Staphylinus pubescens DeG.	–	–	2	2	–	2	–	V F C
S. olens Müll.	2	–	–	1°	–	2	–	W G
S. aeneocephalus DeG. or *cupreus* Ross.	–	–	1	1	–	–	–	W G
Staphylinus sp.	–	–	–	–	–	–	–	T
Ontholestes tessellatus (Geof.)	1	–	1	1	9	–	–	F V C (G W)
Quedius sp.	–	–	–	1	–	–	–	T
Tachinus sp.	–	1	9	5	5	–	–	T
Leucoparyphus silphoides (L.)	–	–	1	1	–	–	–	F V
Aleocharinae gen. et sp. indet.	+	+	+	+	+	+	–	

93

Table 13: Results of analyses of beetles (cont)

Taxon	590/4	1007/1	1009/1	1100/1	1159	1172	1060/2	43/10	17/4	1046/2	1074/4	1072	1169	Habitat or Food
LUCANIDAE														
Lucanus cervus (L.)	-	-	-	-	-	-	-	-	-	-	-	-	-	larvae in dead and decomposing wood esp oak stumps
GEOTRUPIDAE														
Geotrupes spiniger (Marsh.)	-	2	2	-	-	-	-	-	-	-	-	-	-	F
Geotrupes sp.	1	2	1	-	2	-	1	1	1	-	-	-	1	F
SCARABAEIDAE														
Onthophagus ovatus (L.)	-	-	-	-	-	-	1	-	-	-	-	-	-	F C V
O. coenobita (Hbst.) or vacca (L.)	-	1	-	-	-	-	-	1	1°	-	-	-	-	F - mostly
Onthophagus spp.	-	-	1	-	3	-	-	12	9	-	-	-	-	F(C)
Oxyomus sylvestris (Scop.)	1	-	-	-	2	-	-	1	-	-	-	-	-	V C F - mostly as dung heaps
Aphodius erraticus (L.)	-	-	-	-	2	-	-	1	1	1	-	-	-	F(C)
A. fossor (L.)	-	-	-	-	1	-	1	-	-	-	-	-	-	F
A. luridus (F.)	-	2	-	-	1	-	-	-	-	-	-	-	-	F
A. rufipes (L.)	1	-	-	-	-	-	-	-	-	-	-	-	-	F
A. equestris (Pz.)	-	-	-	-	-	-	-	3	16	-	-	-	-	F
A. contaminatus (Hbst.)	4	4	16	14	17	-	3	4	4	-	-	-	-	F
A. cf. prodromus (Brahm.)	2	2	2	1	8	-	3	23	-	-	-	-	-	F V
A. cf. sphacelatus (Pz.)	-	2	2	-	-	-	-	4	-	-	2	-	-	F V (C)
A. porcus (F.)	1	-	-	-	1	-	-	1	-	-	-	-	-	F - in Geotrupes burrows
A. fimetarius (L.)	-	-	-	-	1	-	4	4	-	-	-	-	-	F V
A. scybalarius (F.)	8	8	2	-	7	-	6	6	-	-	-	-	-	F V
A. lividus (Ol.)	-	-	-	-	-	-	-	-	-	-	-	-	-	F V
Aphodius spp.	2°	17°	12°	9°	161°	1	4	364°	9°	3	4°	2°	1°	mostly F
Serica brunnea (L.)	-	-	-	-	1	-	-	-	-	-	-	-	-	larvae on grass roots in sandy places
Homaloplia ruricola (F.)	-	-	-	1	1	-	-	-	-	-	-	-	-	larvae G - usually dry, chalky; adults on trees as well
Melolontha sp.	1	1	-	-	-	-	1	1	-	-	-	-	-	larvae on roots of trees and grasses
Phyllopertha horticola (L.)	-	-	-	-	5	-	-	-	-	-	-	-	-	larvae on roots in permanent grassland
HETEROCERIDAE														
Heterocerus sp.	-	-	-	-	1	-	1	-	-	-	-	-	-	B and M - on mud at water's edge
DRYOPIDAE														
Dryops sp.	-	-	-	1	-	-	-	2	-	-	3	2	-	B A and M - in or close to water (V)
ELATERIDAE														
Melanotus rufipes (Hbst.)	-	-	-	-	-	-	-	-	-	-	-	-	-	rotten wood
Athous hirtus (Hbst.)	-	-	-	-	1	-	1	1	1	-	-	-	-	W G - esp meadowland
A. haemorrhoidalis (F.)	-	-	-	-	-	-	-	3	3	-	-	-	-	W G - esp meadowland
A. bicolor (Geolz.)	-	-	-	-	-	-	-	3	cf. 1	-	-	-	-	(W) G - esp meadowland
Agriotes pallidulus (Ill.)	-	-	-	-	-	-	-	-	-	-	-	-	-	larvae mostly on the roots of grassland plants, adults esp in meadowland, also on trees, bushes and sometimes decaying vegetation
A. sputator (L.)	1	-	-	-	3	-	-	-	-	-	2	-	-	
A. lineatus (L.)	2	-	-	-	2	-	-	-	-	2	-	-	-	
A. obscurus (L.)	-	-	-	-	-	-	-	-	-	-	-	-	-	
Agriotes sp.	-	-	-	-	7°	-	-	-	3°	5	-	1	-	G and trees often close to water
Adrastus nitidulus (Marsh.)	-	-	-	-	1	-	-	-	-	-	-	-	-	
TRIXAGIDAE														
Trixagus obtusus (West. in Curt.)	-	-	-	-	-	-	-	-	-	-	-	1	1	inc rotting wood G
CANTHARIDAE														
Cantharis rustica Fall. or nigricans Muel.	-	-	-	-	-	-	-	1	1	1	-	-	-	
C. cf. rufa L.	-	-	-	-	-	-	-	-	-	-	-	-	-	
Cantharis sp.	-	-	-	-	4	-	-	1	-	-	-	-	-	
Rhagonycha fulva (Scop.)	-	-	-	-	-	-	-	-	-	1	-	-	-	Adults often on flowers of herbs and shrubs
R. testacea (L.) or limbata Th.	-	-	-	-	-	-	-	-	-	-	-	-	-	
Rhagonycha sp.	-	-	-	-	-	-	-	-	-	-	-	-	-	

Taxon	1	2	3	4	5	6	7	8	9	10	11	12	13	Habitat / notes
ANOBIIDAE														
Stegobium paniceum (L.)	–	–	1	21	7	11	–	1	–	–	–	–	–	P - flour, bread, grain (in open on poplars?)
Anobium punctatum (DeG.)	2	–	–	–	–	–	–	–	–	–	–	–	2	dead wood
PTINIDAE														
Tipnus unicolor (P. & M.)	–	–	8	8	9	8	–	–	–	–	–	–	–	straw and bird's nests (old wood) P
Ptinus fur (L.)	–	10	29	–	9	9	2	–	–	–	–	–	–	straw and bird's nests etc P - grain (C old wood)
Ptinus sp.	1	–	–	–	–	–	1	–	–	–	–	–	–	mostly V
LYCTIDAE														
Lyctus fuscus (L.)	–	–	–	–	–	–	1	–	–	–	–	–	1	wood - dead hardwood, not standing trees
MELYRIDAE														
Malachius marginellus Ol.	–	1	–	–	1	1	–	–	–	–	–	–	–	adults often on flowers of herbs and shrubs
M. bipustulatus (L.)	–	1	–	–	–	–	–	–	–	–	–	–	–	"
NITIDULIDAE														
Meligethes sp.	1	1	4	1	–	1	–	1	–	–	–	–	–	herbs and trees - mostly on flowers
Omosita discoidea (F.)	–	–	–	–	–	–	–	1	–	–	–	–	–	C - dry
O. colon (L.)	–	1	1	–	–	1	–	–	–	–	–	–	–	C - dry
Epuraea sp.	–	–	–	–	–	–	1	–	–	–	–	–	–	larvae in fungi, Scolytid burrows and at sap; adults also on flowers
RHIZOPHAGIDAE														
Monotoma sp.	–	–	2	1	–	–	–	–	–	–	–	–	–	V (manure, C)
PHALACRIDAE														
Phalacrus sp.	–	1	1	–	1	–	–	–	–	–	–	–	–	larvae on grass and *Carex* smuts, adults on flowers
Olibrus sp.	–	1	1	–	1	–	1	–	–	–	–	–	–	adults and larvae on flowers of Compositae
Stilbus testaceus (Pz.)	1	–	2	–	2	–	–	–	–	–	–	–	1	in dry grass and hay
CRYPTOPHAGIDAE														
gen. et sp. indet.	–	10	9	9	–	1	–	–	–	–	–	–	4	V - of all sorts T
COCCINELLIDAE														
Scymnus frontalis (F.)	–	1	1	–	1	–	–	–	–	–	–	1	–	G - esp dry, sandy
Anisosticta novemdecimpunctata (L.)	–	–	–	–	–	–	–	–	1	–	–	–	–	M B
Coccinella sp.	–	1	–	–	1	–	–	–	–	–	–	1	–	T
LATHRIDIIDAE														
Lathridius sp.(*Enicmus minutus* agg.)	18	6	19	17	104	–	1	4	1	–	–	–	–	V also manure (C G W)
Enicmus transversus (Ol.)	–	–	–	–	1	–	–	–	–	–	–	–	–	V (G W)
Corticaria pubescens (Gyll.)	–	–	2	2	1	–	–	–	–	–	–	–	–	V
Corticaria, Corticarina or *Melanophthalma* sp	2	8	12	4°	14°	2°	–	–	–	–	–	4	–	mostly V
gen. et sp. indet.	–	–	2	3	–	1	–	–	–	–	–	–	–	mostly V
COLYDIIDAE														
Aglenus brunneus (Gyll.)	–	–	–	–	–	–	–	3	–	–	–	–	–	V
MYCETOPHAGIDAE														
Mycetophagus quadriguttatus Muel.	–	–	2	2	–	–	–	–	–	–	–	–	–	hay and straw refuse, tree fungi (P)
Typhaea stercorea (L.)	–	–	1	2	–	–	–	–	–	–	–	–	–	V - esp hay and straw ref P
TENEBRIONIDAE														
Crypticus quisquilius (L.)	–	–	–	–	–	–	–	3	–	–	–	–	–	T - open sandy places
Tenebrio molitor L.	–	–	2	–	–	–	–	2	–	–	–	–	–	P - grain, flour etc also bird's nests and old trees
PYROCHROIDAE														
Pyrochroa serraticornis (Scop.)	–	–	–	1	–	1	–	–	–	–	–	–	–	larvae on rotten wood esp oak, adult on flowers
ANTHICIDAE														
Anthicus antherinus (L.)	–	–	1	–	1	–	–	2	–	–	–	–	–	V

95

Table 13: Results of analyses of beetles (cont)

	590/4	1007/1	1009/1	1100/1	1159	1172	1060/2	43/10	17/4	1046/2	1074/4	1072	1169	Habitat or Food
CERAMBYCIDAE														
Phymatodes testaceus (L.)	-	-	-	-	-	-	-	4	-	-	-	-	-	recently dead hardwood with the bark on esp Quercus
P. alni (L.)	-	-	-	-	-	-	-	1	-	-	-	-	-	decaying or recently dead hardwood with the bark on
BRUCHIDAE														
Bruchus cf. luteicornis Ill.	-	-	-	-	-	-	4	-	-	-	-	-	-	on Papilionaceae
gen. et sp. indet.	-	-	-	-	-	-	-	-	2	-	-	-	-	"
CHRYSOMELIDAE														
Donacia sp.	-	-	-	-	-	-	-	-	1	-	-	-	-	various aquatic plants
Plateumaris affinis (Kunz.)	-	-	-	-	-	-	-	-	-	-	-	8	-	Iris pseudacorus L. and Carex spp.
Donacia or Plateumaris sp.	-	-	1	-	2	-	-	-	-	-	-	-	-	various aquatic plants
Lema sp.	-	-	-	-	-	-	-	-	1	-	-	1	-	various herbs and shrubs
Chrysolina polita (L.)	-	-	-	-	-	-	-	-	-	-	-	-	-	Labiatae often in marshes
Gastrophysa polygoni (L.)	-	1	-	-	2	-	2	-	1	1	2	-	-	Rumex and Polygonum spp.
Phaedon sp.	-	-	-	-	2	-	1	3	-	-	-	-	-	various herbs
Hydrothassa aucta (F.)	-	-	-	-	2	-	1	-	1	-	1	-	-	Ranunculus spp.
Prasocuris phellandrii (L.)	-	-	-	-	-	-	2	2	-	-	1	-	-	aquatic Umbelliferae
Timarcha tenebricosa (F.)	-	-	-	-	-	-	-	-	-	-	-	-	-	esp Galium spp. in grassy places
Phylletreta vittula Redt.	-	1	-	2	12	-	3	1	5	2	2	-	-	Cruciferae and Reseda sp.
P. nemorum (L.) or undulata Kut.	-	-	-	-	-	-	1	-	3	1	1	-	-	
P. cf. exclamationis (Thun.)	-	-	-	3	-	-	3	1	3	-	3	-	-	
P. atra (F.)	-	-	-	-	2	-	3	-	-	-	-	-	-	
P. cf. diademata Foud.	-	-	-	-	-	-	-	-	-	-	-	-	-	
P. nigripes (F.)	-	3	1	1	2	-	2	3	2	1	2	-	-	Iris pseudacorus L.
Phylloreta spp.	-	-	-	-	4°	-	-	-	-	-	-	-	-	various herbs
Aphthona coerulea (Geof.)	4	-	-	-	-	-	5	3	4	-	3	-	-	includes Lythria, Corylus, Salix, Calluna, Rumex, Sanguisorba
Longitarsus spp.	3	-	6	-	15	-	5	5	-	-	3	-	-	and Epilobium spp.
Haltica spp.	-	-	-	-	-	-	6	6	-	-	2	-	-	Salix and Poplus spp.
Chalcoides sp.	-	-	-	-	-	-	-	-	-	-	-	-	-	Podagrica feeds on mallows
Haltica or Podagrica sp.	-	-	-	-	-	-	-	-	1	-	4	-	-	Rumex spp.
Mantura rustica (L.)	-	-	-	-	-	-	1	1	-	-	4	-	-	Polygonaceae esp P. aviculare L.
Chaetocnema concinna (Marsh.)	5	1	-	33	9	-	9	10	17	9	4	-	1	various herbs including Eleocharis spp.
Chaetocnema sp.	-	-	-	-	2°	-	2°	2°	-	-	2	2	-	Cruciferae, Papaver spp. and perhaps other herbs
Psylliodes cf. cuprea (Koch.)	-	-	1	-	-	-	2	2	-	-	-	-	-	Carduus spp. and perhaps other herbs
P. cf. chalcomera (Ill.)	-	-	-	-	2	-	-	-	-	1	-	-	-	various herbs
Psylliodes sp.	-	-	-	-	-	-	-	-	-	-	-	-	-	various herbs
Cassida sp.	-	-	-	-	-	-	-	-	-	-	-	-	-	
ATTELABIDAE														
Caenorhinus sp.	-	-	-	-	-	-	-	-	1	-	-	-	-	various trees and Rosaceous plants
Rhynchites caeruleus (DeG.)	-	-	-	-	-	-	1	-	-	-	-	-	-	Roseceous trees and shrubs, Quercus sp. Agrimonia sp.
APIONIDAE														
Apion cf. marchium Hbst.	1	-	-	-	-	-	-	1	1	-	-	-	-	Rumex acetosella L.
*A. malvae (F.)	-	-	-	-	1	-	1	1	-	-	-	-	-	various Malvaceae
A. aeneum (F.)	-	-	1	-	-	-	-	-	-	-	-	-	-	
A. radiolus Kirb.	-	-	-	-	-	-	-	-	-	-	-	-	-	
*A. urticarium (Hbst.)	-	-	-	-	-	-	2	2	cf. 1	2	1	-	-	Urtica dioica L. U. urens L.
A. pisi F. or aethiops Hbst.	-	-	-	-	-	-	1	-	2	1	-	-	-	larvae Medicago spp. and Onobrychis viciifolia Scop. adult - Papilionaceae
A. craccae (L.)	-	-	-	-	-	-	2	2	2	-	1	-	-	Vicia and Lathyrus spp.
A. cerdo Ger.	-	-	-	-	-	-	2	-	cf. 1	-	-	-	-	larva Vicia cracca L. adult Vicia and Lathyrus spp.
A. pommonae (F.)	2°	-	1°	-	-	-	3	-	2	-	1°	-	1°	larva on various Papilionaceae adult on trees esp Quercus and herbs
Apion spp.	2	2	1°	-	11°	-	42°	3°	48°	-	1°	1	1°	various herbs

96

CURCULIONIDAE / SCOLYTIDAE

	77	165	119	114	804	14	411	950	699	116	136	78	23	Habitat or food
CURCULIONIDAE														
Otiorrhynchus ligustici (L.)	–	–	–	–	–	–	–	–	–	–	1	–	1	Papilionaceae
Trachyphloeus bifoveolatus (Beck.)	–	–	–	1	–	–	–	–	–	–	–	–	–	T
Trachyphloeus sp.	–	–	–	–	–	–	–	–	–	–	–	–	–	T
Phyllobius sp	–	–	–	–	–	–	2	–	–	1	–	–	–	trees, grasses and *Urtica* sp
Barypithes sp.	–	–	–	–	–	–	–	–	1	–	–	–	–	T
Strophosomus sp.	–	–	–	–	–	–	–	–	–	–	–	–	–	T
Barynotus sp.	–	–	–	–	–	–	–	–	–	–	–	–	–	T
Sitona puncticollis Step. or lepidus Gyll.	–	–	–	–	2	–	–	–	1	2	2	–	–	Papilionaceae
Sitona spp.	–	–	3	–	6°	–	6	5	9	2	2	–	–	Papilionaceae - esp *Trifolium* spp.
Bagous or Hydronomus sp.	–	–	–	–	–	–	–	–	–	–	–	–	–	aquatic plants
Tanysphyrus lemnae (Pk.)	–	–	–	–	1	–	–	1	1	–	1	–	–	*Lemna* sp.
Notaris bimaculatus (F.) or scirpi (F.)	3	–	–	3	6	–	–	9	2	–	–	–	–	aquatic grasses, sedges and *Typha* sp.
N. acridulus (L.)	–	–	–	–	–	–	1	–	–	–	8	–	–	larva esp *Glyceria maxima* H; adult also *Polygonum amphibium* L. and *Eleocharis* sp.
Orthochaetes setiger (Beck)	–	–	–	–	–	–	–	–	–	–	–	–	–	T
Tychius sp.	–	–	–	–	2	–	–	–	1	–	–	–	–	mostly Papilionaceae
Alophus triguttatus (F.)	–	–	–	–	1	–	–	–	–	–	–	–	–	various herbs
Phytonomus austriacus (Schr.)	–	–	1	–	2	–	–	1	–	1	–	–	–	Papilionaceae - esp *Trifolium* spp.
Phytonomus spp.	–	–	–	–	–	–	–	1°	–	–	–	–	–	various herbs
Acales turbatus Boh.	–	–	–	–	–	3	3	–	4	4	–	–	–	dead *Crataegus, Corylus* and *Poplus* spp. esp in hedges
Baris lepidii Germ.	–	–	–	–	–	1	–	4	–	–	–	–	–	various Cruciferae in marshy places
Limnobaris pilistriata Step.	–	–	–	–	–	–	–	–	–	–	–	–	7	larvae - esp *Schoenoplectus* sp. adults - other Cyperaceae and *Juncus* spp. as well
Ceuthorhynchus pyrrhorhynchus (Marsh.)	–	–	–	–	–	–	–	–	–	–	–	–	–	*Sisymbrium officinale* (L.) Scop and prob other Cruciferae
C. pollinarius (Forst.)	–	1°	–	1	–	–	2	1	1	–	–	–	–	*Urtica dioica* L.
C. erysimi (F.)	1°	–	–	1°	–	–	–	5	–	–	–	–	–	Cruciferae
Ceuthorhynchinae gen. et sp. indet.	–	–	–	–	11°	–	4°	8°	12°	3	3	–	1	various herbs
Mecinus pyraster (Hbst.)	–	–	–	–	1	–	1	–	1	1	1	–	–	*Plantago lanceolata* L. and *P. media* L.
Gymnetron labile (Hbst.)	–	–	–	–	–	–	1	–	–	–	–	–	–	*P. lanceolata* L.
G. pascuorum (Gyll.)	–	–	–	–	–	–	1	–	2	–	–	–	–	*P. lanceolata* L.
SCOLYTIDAE														
Scolytus rugulosus (Ratz.)	–	–	–	–	–	–	1	–	2	–	–	–	–	Rosaceous trees and shrubs
Hylesinus oeleiperda (F.)	–	–	–	–	–	–	–	–	2	–	–	–	–	mainly *Fraxinus* twigs
Leperesinus fraxini (Pz.)	–	–	–	–	–	–	4	4	–	–	–	–	–	mainly *Fraxinus* sp. also other trees
Anisandrus dryographus (Ratz.) or saxesini (Ratz.)	–	–	–	–	1	–	–	–	–	–	–	–	–	various trees, often *Quercus* spp.
Total	77	165	119	114	804	14	411	950	699	116	136	78	23	

Habitat or food information: A, aquatic; B, bankside/water's edge; C, carrion; D, disturbed/bare ground; F, dung; G, grassland; M, marsh; P, pest of stored farinaceous foods; T, terrestrial (but no detailed habitat information known); V, decaying plant remains; W, woodland or scrub. Less usual habitats given in brackets.

Sample sizes various, see p78. * against species name means there are no modern records from the Oxford District. °against number of a genus not identified to species from a particular sample means that it includes other species than those named to species in that sample. + indicates present but uncounted.

97

Table 14: Results of analyses of Hemiptera

HEMIPTERA	590/4	1007/1	1009/1	1100/1	1159	1172	1060/2	43/10	17/4	1046/2	1074/4	1072	1169	Habitat or Food
						Minimum Number of Individuals								
HETEROPTERA														
CYDNIDAE														
Sehirus bicolor (L.)	-	-	-	-	-	-	-	1	-	-	-	-	-	*Lamium album* L. / *Ballota nigra* L.
PENTATOMIDAE														
Dolycoris baccarum (L.)	-	-	-	-	1	-	-	-	-	-	-	-	-	often at woodland margin
COREIDAE														
Syromastus rhombeus (L.)	-	-	-	-	-	-	-	-	1	-	-	-	-	dry often sandy places on Caryophyllaceae
LYGAEIDAE														
Heterogaster urticae (F.)	-	-	-	-	2	-	-	23	1	1	5	-	-	*Urtica dioica* L.
Stygnocoris fuligineus (Geof.)*	-	1	-	-	-	-	-	-	1	-	-	-	-	
Scolopostethus sp.	-	1	-	-	-	-	-	4	-	-	-	-	-	often *Urtica dioica* L.
CIMICIDAE														
Anthocorinae gen. et sp. indet.	-	-	-	-	-	-	1	-	3	1	1	-	-	
HETEROPTERA gen. et sp. indet.	-	-	-	-	-	-	3	-	1°	1°	-	-	-	
HOMOPTERA														
CICADELLIDAE														
Aphrodes bicinctus (Schr.)	-	-	-	1	-	-	3	7	3	-	-	-	-	
A. albifrons (L.) or *fuscofasciatus* (Goez.)	-	-	1	-	-	-	3	1	1	-	-	-	-	
A. histrionicus (F.)	-	-	1	-	-	-	1	-	1	-	-	-	-	
APHIDAE														
gen. et sp. indet.	-	13	2	2	5	-	-	2	4	-	-	-	-	
HOMOPTERA														
gen. et sp. indet.	-	1	3	-	1	-	1	6	3	5	3	1	1	
Total	1	15	6	3	9	0	12	44	18	8	9	1	1	

Sample sizes various, see p78. °against number of a genus as for Table 13.

98

Table 15: Results of analyses of Formicidae

Sample sizes various, see p.78.

FORMICIDAE		590/4	1007/1	1009/1	1100/1	1172	1159	1060/2	43/10	17/4	1046/2	1074/4	1072	1169	Habitat
								Minimum Number of Individuals							
Myrmica sp	worker	–	–	–	–	–	1	–	–	2	–	–	–	–	Nests under large stones or tree roots in shady woodland or hedgerows
Stenamma westwoodi West.	female	–	–	–	–	–	–	30	1	7	6	–	–	1	Nest under stones and at the roots of trees in limestone pasture or open dry woodland
S. westwoodi West.	female	–	–	–	–	–	–	–	–	–	–	–	–	–	
Myrmecina graminicola (Lat)	female	–	–	–	–	–	–	–	–	–	2	–	–	–	
M. graminicola (Lat.)	female	–	–	–	–	–	–	–	–	–	–	–	–	1	
Formica rufa L. (Wood Ant)	female	–	–	1	–	–	1	–	1	–	–	1	–	–	Nests in leaf and twig litter mounds in pine and oak woods
F. cunicularia (Lat.)	worker	–	–	–	–	–	–	–	–	–	4	–	–	1	Nests in old pasture and at the edge of woodland
Lasius flavus (F)	worker	–	–	–	–	–	–	–	2	–	–	–	–	–	Nests in old trees, stumps, hedges, old walls and sand dunes
L. fuliginosus (Lat.)	worker	–	–	–	–	–	5	–	2	–	–	–	–	–	
L. fuliginosus (Lat.)	female	–	–	–	–	–	–	–	–	–	–	–	–	–	
L. niger (L.)	worker	–	–	–	–	–	–	1	7	1	1	–	–	–	Nests in soil or under stones; in woodland, cultivated fields and grassland
L. niger (L.)	female	–	–	–	–	–	–	–	–	–	–	–	–	–	
L. umbratus (Nyl.)	worker	–	–	–	–	–	–	–	4	–	–	–	–	–	Nests in soil at the base of old trees, under decaying wood and under boulders
Total		0	0	1	0	0	7	31	17	10	13	1	0	3	

Table 16: Results of analyses of other insects

Sample sizes various, see p.78.

OTHER INSECTS	590/4	1007/1	1009/1	1100/1	1172	1159	1060/2	43/10	17/4	1046/2	1074/4	1072	1169
DERMAPTERA													
Forficula auricularia L.	–	2	–	1	–	1	7	26	10	4	1	–	–
TRICHOPTERA													
larval cases	–	–	–	–	3	–	–	–	–	–	–	–	–
HYMENOPTERA													
adult heads (other than Formicidae)	2	4	4	2	–	23	41	79	14	10	3	3	–
DIPTERA													
Chironomid larval head capsules	few	many	many	many	some	many	some	few	present	–	many	few	–
Diptera puparia	1	5	2	5	–	42	2	3	8	7	–	–	–
Diptera adult heads	–	3	1	2	–	7	6	4	7	1	6	–	–

Table 17: Results of analyses of other Arthropods

Sample sizes various, see p.78.

OTHER ARTHROPODS	509/4	1007/1	1009/1	1100/1	1159	1172	1060/2	43/10	17/4	1046/2	1074/4	1072	1169
CRUSTACEA													
Branchiopoda - *Daphnia*	some	many	many	some	–	some	very many	very many	present	many	many	some	–
Ostracoda	–	–	few	few	present	many	many	many	–	some	–	–	–
ARACHNIDA													
Araneae	–	–	1	6	6	3	39	6	6	2	2	–	–

and the Royal Entomological Society (1953-75). In addition, information was also gained from unpublished work by Dr M R Speight (pers comm); an interleaved volume of offprints of the *Preliminary list of Coleoptera observed in the neighbourhood of Oxford* (Walker, 1906-29) with annotations by the author, which is in the Hope Department Library; the Wytham Ecological Survey; and my own limited observations. The habitat groups into which the Coleoptera have been divided are aquatic; marsh; bankside or at water's edge; disturbed or bare ground; grassland; and woodland including scrub. Where a beetle is terrestial, as opposed to marsh or aquatic, but there is not sufficient information to say more about its habitat, this has been indicated. There are also some Coleoptera that have very specialized and limited terrestial habitats, such as carrion and stored farinaceous foods. These have been given as additional habitats. Those beetles which feed on a limited number of species of plants have had their food named instead of the habitat information being given. As with the habitat information for the plants, the categories are very broad and there are some species placed in the same habitat group which are most unlikely to live together. A particular problem is that some beetles have been caught in several different habitats, even feeding in them, but it is not known whether they are capable of breeding in them all. Problems of this sort will be discussed in the interpretation.

Not included in Table 13 is a single carbonized specimen of *Chaetocnema* sp. from Sample 1169. The rest of the insect remains have been preserved by waterlogging.

Hemiptera (bugs)

The minimum number of individuals represented by the fragments identified is given in Table 14. Nomenclature follows Kloet and Hincks (1964) whilst food and habitat information is from Southwood and Leston (1959).

Formicidae (ants)

Table 15 gives the results received from Mr C O'Toole for the ant remains passed to him for identification. As before, minimum numbers are listed. It has been thought worthwhile listing the fertile females and the workers separately (no males were found) because only the former can fly. Nomenclature and habitat information is from Boulton and Collingwood (1975) with additional habitat information from Donisthorpe (1927). Mr O'Toole reports that all have been found in Oxfordshire this century.

Other insects

Minimum numbers of individuals represented by the other insect remains are listed in Table 16.

Other Invertebrates

Remains of other invertebrates apart from mites are listed in Table 17. Where no sample had been given to Mrs Denford for mite analysis, the mites recovered from the same samples as the rest of the invertebrates were passed on to her and have been included in her report (p104).

Results from the dry bulk samples

Plant remains preserved by carbonization

These samples were examined by Mr M Jones for carbonized plant remains and the results are given in his report (p103).

Results from the column samples

Molluscs

The mollusca from the column samples are listed in Table 18, giving the minimum number of individuals represented by the remains from each sample except for the slugs of the genus *Arion*, where the presence of granules is simply indicated. Sample Column IV is not included in the results because no biological remains were found in it. However, it is worth stating that unlike the samples from the other columns, the mineral residues after sieving the samples from Column IV contained very little limestone gravel. Perhaps this is not unconnected with the lack of molluscan remains. The nomenclature and habitat information in Table 18 follows that used in Table 12.

Other biological remains

A number of other biological remains were found from the column samples. Sample 0-70 mm of Column II was the only one to contain seed and insect remains and it was therefore treated as if it was one of the bulk samples, a finer sieve used and the results included with them as well. Valves of ostracods and the calcareous oospores of Characeae occurred sporadically throughout Columns II and III but they have not been listed as the sieves used were too coarse to catch anything but a small fraction of them. No carbonized remains were found in any of the column samples.

The illustrations and notes on identifications

A number of the plant and animal remains which were recovered have been illustrated in Fig 36 to give an idea of the range of material which was present. Notes are also needed about some of the identifications.

Seeds which have been referred to as *Oenanthe* cf. *aquatica* (Fig 36,1) were present in three of the Iron Age samples. As the only reference material available was sub-fossil seeds, which had previously been identified using the reference collection in the Botany School Cambridge and it no longer grows in this region (Perring and Walters 1962, 164), a tentative identification only has been given. It is of interest, however, that seeds of this species were recovered from a post-glacial alluvial deposit by the Thames at Oxford (Brown in Durham 1977).

Three types of *Eleocharis* S. *Palustres* nuts seem to be present. One is smaller than the other (Fig 36, 10) and on the basis of its size is probably *palustris* ssp. *palustris* (L.) Roem & Schult (Clapham *et al* 1962, 1064; Walters 1949, 194). Of the other two types that are illustrated in Fig 36,9 has a rather smooth shiny surface with a high proportion of oblong epidermal cells, while the type shown in Fig 36,11 presented a rough surface with smaller, mostly isodiametric epidermal cells. It is quite likely that these two types of nut represent the fruits of *E. palustris* ssp. *vulgaris* S M Walters and *E. uniglumis* (Link) Schult, but it is not possible to be certain which is which. (The style bases were not complete on the specimens so any decision must be on epidermal cells alone.) Godwin (1975, 389) refers to Bell on noting that the small cells of the nutlet surface in *E. uniglumis* are responsible for the shiny appearance that distinguishes them from the punctate

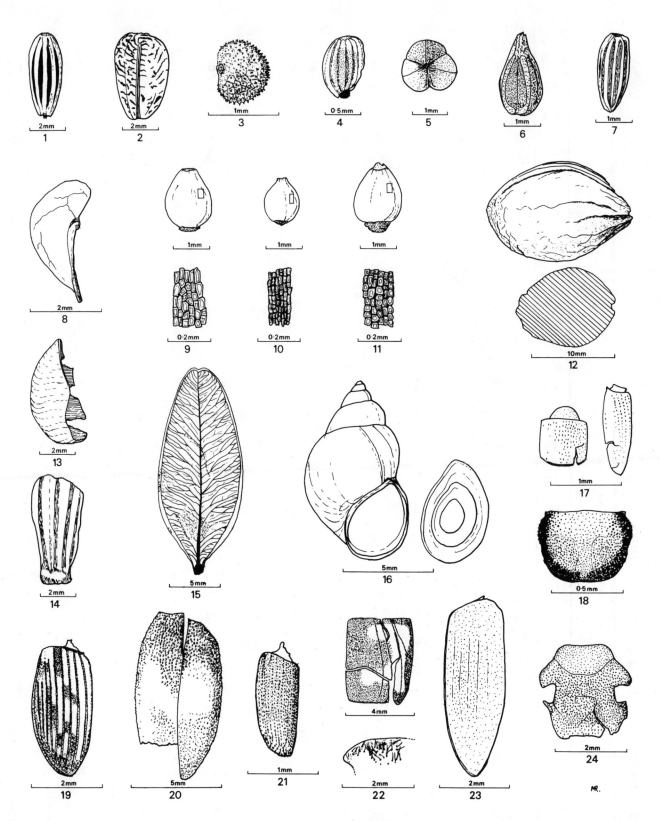

Fig 36 Biological identifications: 1. Oenanthe *cf.* aquatica *mericarp (590/4); 2.* Onopordon acanthium *achene (590/4); 3.* Lychnis flos-cuculi *seed (1159); 4.* Lemna *sp. seed (1159); 5.* Valerianella rimosa *fruit, end on view (1007/1); 6.* V. dentata *fruit (1007/1); 7.* Chrysanthemum leucanthemum *achene (1060/2); 8.* Filipendula ulmaria *achene (43/10); 9-11.* Eleocharis S. palustris *nuts with details of cell patterns (43/10); 12.* Prunus domestica *stone (1060/2); 13.* Buxus sempervirens *fruit fragment (17/4); 14.* Triticum spelta *glume fragment (17/4); 15.* Buxus sempervirens *leaf (17/4); 16.* Bithynia tentaculata *shell and operculum (Sample Column III 12-22 cm); 17.* Aglenus brunneus *pronotum with head and left elytron (1159); 18.* Carpalimus bilineatus *pronotum (1159); 19.* Aphodius equestris *left elytron (17/4); 20.* Otiorrhynchus ligustici *paired elytra (1072); 21.* Scolytus rugulosus *left elytron (1060/2); 22.* Hister quadrimaculatus *right elytron and left underside of the front of the pronotum (1159); 23.* Crypticus quisquilius *left elytron (1159); 24.* Tenebrio molitor *head, elytral fragments also found (17/4).*

101

Table 18: Results from the column samples - Molluscs

Minimum Number of Individuals

MOLLUSCA	Layer 1184	II 0-7	II 7-15	II 15-25	II 25-34	II 34-45	III 0-12	III 12-22	III 22-32	III 32-42	III 42-52	III 52-62	III 62-68	I 0-8	I 8-12	I 12-19	I 19-28	I 28-42	I 42-49	I 49-56	I 56-66	I 66-72	Habitat
GASTROPODA																							
PROSOBRANCHIA																							
VALVATIDAE																							
Valvata cristata Müll.	–	17	30	24	41	59	17	12	31	2	13	12	2	–	–	–	–	–	–	–	–	–	D
V. piscinalis (Müll.)	–	–	–	–	2	–	–	–	43	7	5	3	–	–	–	–	–	–	–	–	–	–	F
POMATIIDAE																							
Pomatias elegans (Müll.)	–	–	–	–	–	–	–	–	–	–	–	–	–	–	–	1	–	–	–	1	–	–	T
BITHYNIIDAE																							
Bithynia tentaculata (L.)	–	16	21	20	25	61	20	14	3	4	4	–	–	–	–	–	–	–	–	–	–	–	F
Bithynia sp.	–	0	7	35	69	105	6	42	10	–	–	–	2	–	–	–	–	–	–	–	–	–	F
EUTHYNEURA																							
ELLOBIIDAE																							
Carychium sp.	–	–	–	–	–	–	–	–	–	1	–	–	–	–	–	–	–	–	–	–	–	–	(M)s
PHYSIDAE																							
Aplexa hypnorum (L.)	–	–	–	–	–	–	3	–	–	–	–	–	–	–	–	–	–	–	–	–	–	–	S
LYMNAEIDAE																							
Lymnaea truncatula (Müll.)	–	7	7	31	36	26	17	58	28	3	25	19	8	–	–	–	–	–	–	–	–	–	S M
L. palustris (Müll.)	–	6	7	5	10	36	16	14	12	1	4	2	–	–	–	–	–	–	–	–	–	–	C M
L. peregra (Müll.)	–	6	11	7	15	53	35	32	12	–	–	–	–	–	–	–	–	–	–	–	–	–	C
Lymnaea sp.	–	6	11	29	71	127	113	63	20	–	–	–	–	–	–	–	–	–	–	–	–	–	M S D C F
PLANORBIDAE																							
Planorbis planorbis (L.)	–	7	11	12	19	55	34	46	20	1	–	–	1	–	–	–	–	–	–	–	–	–	D
Anisus leucostoma (Milt.)	–	4	17	22	30	51	38	18	15	6	66	32	3	–	–	–	–	–	–	–	–	–	S
A. vortex (L.)	–	–	2	1	2	4	3	6	–	–	–	–	–	–	–	–	–	–	–	–	–	–	D
Bathyomphalus contortus (L.)	–	–	–	–	1	7	–	1	–	–	–	–	–	–	–	–	–	–	–	–	–	–	C
Gyraulus albus (Müll.)	–	1	–	2	2	3	3	–	1	–	–	–	–	–	–	–	–	–	–	–	–	–	C
Armiger crista (L.)	–	12	14	23	63	228	67	112	58	1	1	–	–	–	–	–	–	–	–	–	–	–	C
Hippeutis complanatus (L.)	–	–	–	1	–	–	–	1	–	–	–	–	–	–	–	–	–	–	–	–	–	–	C
Planorbarius corneus (L.)	–	–	1	–	–	–	–	–	–	1	–	–	–	–	–	–	–	–	–	–	–	–	S D C
Planorbis sp.	–	–	1	–	–	–	6	5	–	–	–	–	–	–	–	–	–	–	–	–	–	–	
SUCCINEIDAE																							
Succinea sp.	–	–	–	1	2	1	–	1	1	1	31	20	11	–	–	–	–	–	–	–	–	–	M o
COCHLICOPIDAE																							
Cochlicopa sp.	–	–	–	–	–	–	–	–	–	–	1	1	–	–	–	–	–	–	–	–	–	–	(M)
VERTIGINIDAE																							
Vertigo pygmaea (Drp.)	–	–	–	–	–	–	–	–	–	–	1	1	–	–	–	–	–	–	–	1	–	–	(M) o
Vertigo sp.	–	–	–	–	–	–	–	–	–	–	–	–	–	–	–	–	–	–	–	1	1	–	(M)
VALLONIIDAE																							
Vallonia costata (Müll.)	1	–	–	–	–	–	–	–	–	–	3	2	–	–	–	–	–	–	–	1	1	–	T o
V. pulchella (Müll.)	–	–	–	–	–	–	–	–	–	–	–	2	–	–	–	–	–	–	–	–	–	1	(M) o
V. excentrica Sterki	–	–	–	–	–	–	–	–	–	–	3	–	–	–	–	–	–	–	7	1	1	5	T o
V. pulchella (Müll) or *excentrica* Sterki	1	–	–	–	–	–	–	–	–	–	2	1	–	–	–	–	–	–	6	1	3	11	(M) o
Vallonia sp.	1	–	–	–	–	–	–	–	–	–	1	1	–	–	–	–	–	–	–	–	–	–	(M) o

Sample Column II = intervals 0-7 to 34-45; Sample Column III = intervals 0-12 to 62-68; Sample Column I = intervals 0-8 to 66-72.

Mollusc table (rotated, left of page). Habitat qualifier shown in the right-hand column for each taxon.

Family / Species		Habitat
ENDODONTIDAE	Punctum pygmaeum (Drp.)	(M)
ARIONIDAE	Arion sp.	(M)
VITRINIDAE	Vitrina sp.	(M)
ZONITIDAE	Oxychilus cellarius (Müll.)	Ts
LIMACIDAE	Limax or Agriolimax sp.	(M)
FERUSSACIIDAE	Cecilioides acicula (Müll.)	T
HELICIDAE	Candidula intersecta (Poir.)	T
	Trichia hispida (L.)	(M)
	Cepaea sp.	(M)
	gen. et sp. indet.	(M)
BIVALVIA SPHAERIIDAE	Pisidium sp.	
Total		**M S D C F**

Total row (column totals): 3 96 149 218 395 848 384 430 319 37 160 98 35 1 2 1 34 16 8 30

Habitat information: C, 'catholic' aquatic; D, 'ditch' aquatic; F, flowing water aquatic; M, obligate marsh dweller; (M), terrestrial species which can live in marshes; S, 'slum' aquatic; T, terrestrial. Qualified by: o, open habitat; s, shaded habitat. Levels in centimetres above bottom of deposits. All samples 5 lb.

fruits of *E. palustris*, in which the cells are larger and present concavities at the surface of the nutlet. Clapham *et al* (1962, 1063-4) describe the nut of *E. palustris* to be finely punctate or nearly smooth, while that of *E. uniglumis* is usually rather coarsely punctate-striate. Other workers have had problems separating the seeds of these two species and van Zeist (1974, 281) points out that conflicting statements have been published as to which of the two species has oblong as well as isodiametric cells. He does not think that they can be identified to species. As no reliably named reference material was available, the nuts have been identified to the subgenus only and the record of *E. uniglumis* from Alchester (Robinson 1975, 164-5) which was for the type of nut illustrated in Fig 36,9 cannot be regarded as definite.

The stones of two sorts of plum were present in the Roman samples (see p.120). One sort of stone which was present in quantity in Well 1060 (illustrated in Fig 36, 12) resembled a modern variety of damson, being rather larger than wild bullace, so has been referred to as *Prunus domestica*, cf. ssp. *insititia*. The other, represented by a single stone in the beetle sample from Pit 17, had a larger, flatter stone (20.5 x 13.0 x 9.0 mm) and has been referred as *P. domestica* cf. ssp. *domestica*.

There was only a single seed of *Malus sylvestris* (identified on epidermal cell pattern) in the sample from Pit 17 examined for seeds, but the beetle sample contained a flattened apple 'core' consisting of pairs of seeds enclosed by the endocarp.

Curious woody fragments of plant material were found in Sample 17/4 (Fig 36, 13) and after leaves of *Buxus sempervirens* were identified from this sample they were matched with the parts of box fruits which enclose each seed.

Most of the wheat chaff from Pit 1169 is from *Triticum spelta* (see Table 11) but a few of the rachis fragments consist of short jointed internodes which could well indicate that they are from *T. aestivocompactum* Schiem (bread wheat).

The fragment of *Lucanus cervus* (stag beetle) identified from Pit 17 is a pronotum and its shape shows that it is from a female beetle.

Plant remains from the dry bulk samples
by Martin Jones

Methods and results

Two samples of soil from the Farmoor excavation were screened by flotation on the suspicion that they contained carbonized seeds. This suspicion was substantiated for one sample, from a Roman corndrier (L1002/2), while the other sample, from an Iron Age feature (L1013/3), was found to be barren of seeds.

The corndrier sample, after being floated and decanted through a 0.5mm mesh, yielded 70 gm of floated material, rich in carbonized plant remains. This being rather too large a sample for complete analysis, it was randomly divided into two sub-samples. The first sub-sample of 10 g received thorough analysis, and all the plant remains except for charred wood were picked out, identified, and counted. The second sub-sample of 60 g received a less thorough analysis, and only seeds of species not encountered in the first sub-sample were picked out, identified, and counted. Both sub-samples were scanned for analysis under x 20 magnification.

The results are given in Tables 19 and 20.

Table 19

Dry carbonized seeds	1002/2
Cereals	
Triticum (wheat)	
Hexaploids:- *T. spelta*	11
NFI	8
NFI	35
Cereals NFI	19
Total Cereals	73
Weeds	
Avena sp. (oats)	1
Chenopodiaceae (goosefoot family)	7
Polygonum convolvulus (black bindweed)	1
Ploygonum sp. (knotgrass)	1
Rumex acetosella (sheep's sorrel)	1
Rumex sp. (dock)	9
Labiatae (dead-nettle family)	1
NFI	5
Total Weeds	26

Other dry carbonized plant remains	
Triticum spelta glume bases	346
Avena sp. awns	numerous fragments
cf. *Triticum* sp. awn	1

Plant remains from the 10 g sort. NFI, not further identified.

Discussion

The carbonized sample from the Roman corndrier is very rich in chaff. In an unthreshed sample of spelt wheat, one would expect the number of glume bases to be the same as, or up to 30% less than, the number of grains. However, in this sample there are four to five times as many glume bases as there are grains.

The sample is therefore best considered as debris from the final stage of threshing in which the husks were removed. A possible function of corndriers is the parching of grain prior to this process, and one might therefore suppose that the husks were being removed in the vicinity of the corndrier, and that readily available chaff was being used to kindle the corndrier fire.

Bearing in mind the composition of the chaff, the cereal grains are probably all of spelt wheat, .

In comparison with other chaff-rich samples from the region, this sample has a low proportion of weed seeds, which suggests that the sample of spelt wheat was relatively pure, even in the unthreshed state, perhaps resulting from the method of harvesting involved, or from a crop cleaning process prior to threshing.

Table 20

Dry carbonized seeds	1002/2
Anthemis cotula (stinking mayweed)	4
Caryophyllaceae (chickweed family)	1
Centaurea cyana/nigra (cornflower/knapweed)	1
Eleocharis sp. (spikerush)	1
Galium aparine (goosegrass)	1
Galium sp. (bedstraw)	2
Hyoscyamus niger (henbane)	1
cf. *Poa* sp. (meadowgrass)	5
Tripleurospermum maritimum (L.) Koch (scentless mayweed)	3

Additional species from remaining 60 g.

Most of the weed seeds in the sample are of species commonly associated with arable ground, without any ecological preference within that habitat. *Eleocharis* (spikerush) and *Anthemis cotula* (stinking mayweed), however, are both associated with damp habitats. The former is commonly associated with grazed marshland (Walters 1949), the latter with poorly drained arable fields on clay (Kay 1971), and both have a preference for basic soils. These species occur in samples from a number of sites that have recently been studied in and around Abingdon, sometimes as major components of the samples, and one would suppose that the drainage of Iron Age and Roman arable fields was commonly poor enough for them to flourish.

The mites
by Susan Denford

Methods and results

A number of mites collected from samples of some of the Iron Age and Roman deposits at Farmoor were studied. The samples were of various sizes, and the mites were collected either during paraffin flotation for the extraction of insect remains (from sieves of 0.5 mm or 0.2 mm), or by wet sieving and flotation in saturated magnesium sulphate solution with a sieve size of 0.05 mm (see Table 21). The latter method is more suitable for mite extraction. The number of mites collected per sample is therefore somewhat misleading, particularly with regard to the smaller species, ie those less than 0.5 mm in length.

Table 21: Origin of samples and method of mite collection

Sample no	Period	Deposit	Sample size	Collection method
590/4	Iron Age	Well or sump	-	Paraffin, 0.5 mm sieve
1007/1	"	Sump- hut-circle ditch	-	"
1009/1	"	Sump-enclosure ditch	-	"
1100/1	"	Hut-circle ditch	1.8 l	Saturated MgSO4 solution, 0.05 mm sieve
1159	"	Sump-enclosure ditch	5 lb	Paraffin, 0.2 mm sieve
17/4	Roman	Pit	1.0 l	Saturated MgSO4 solution, 0.05 mm sieve
43/10	"	Well, stone-lined	-	Paraffin, 0.5 mm sieve
1046/2	"	"	3 lb	Paraffin, 0.2 mm sieve
1060/2	"	Well, wattle-lined	-	Paraffin, 0.5 mm sieve
1072	"	Peat	-	"
1074/2	"	Droveway ditch	-	"

Table 22: Mites

ACARI	590/4		1007/1		1009/1		1100/1		1159		17/4		43/10		1046/2		1060/2		1072		1074/2		Habitat Groups
	No	R.A.	No	R.A.	No	R.A.	No	R.A.	No	R.A.	No	R.A.	No	R.A.	No	R.A.	No	R.A.	No	R.A.	No	R.A.	(see text)
CRYPTOSTIGMATA																							
Damaeus onustus C.L.K.	–	–	–	–	–	–	–	–	–	–	–	–	1	–	9	–	13	12.1	–	–	–	–	4
Belba sp.	–	–	–	–	–	–	–	–	–	–	2	–	–	–	–	–	–	–	–	–	–	–	–
Astegistes pilosus (C.L.K.)	–	–	–	–	–	–	1	–	–	–	–	–	–	–	3	–	–	–	–	–	–	–	1
Ceratoppia bipilis (Herm.)	–	–	–	–	–	–	–	–	–	–	–	–	–	–	–	–	–	–	–	–	–	–	–
Tectocepheus sarakensis Träg.	–	–	–	–	–	–	–	–	–	–	1	–	–	–	–	–	–	–	–	–	–	–	–
T. velatus (Mich.)	–	–	–	–	–	–	4	–	–	–	–	–	–	–	3	–	–	–	–	–	–	–	5
Oppia ?clavipectinata (Mich.)	–	–	–	–	–	–	2	–	–	–	111	12.8	–	–	–	–	–	–	–	–	–	–	5
O. nitens (C.L.K.)	–	–	–	–	–	–	–	–	–	–	577	66.8	–	–	–	–	–	–	–	–	–	–	3
Hydrozetes sp.	–	–	1	–	–	–	–	–	–	–	–	–	–	–	–	–	–	–	–	–	–	–	1
Ameronothrus maculatus (Mich.)	–	–	–	–	–	–	4	–	–	–	–	–	–	–	–	–	–	–	–	–	–	–	4
Micreremus brevipes (Mich.)	–	–	–	–	–	–	–	–	2	–	2	–	–	–	–	–	–	–	–	–	–	–	1
Scutovertix minutus (C.L.K.)	–	–	–	–	–	–	30	15.7	–	–	–	–	–	–	–	–	–	–	–	–	–	–	5
Liebstadia humerata Sell.	–	–	–	–	–	–	–	–	–	–	39	–	–	–	–	–	–	–	–	–	–	–	–
L. similis (Mich.)	–	–	4	7.2	–	–	–	–	–	–	9	–	–	–	4	–	–	–	–	–	–	–	4
Phauloppia lucorum C.L.K.	–	–	1	–	1	–	18	9.5	3	–	19	–	7	11.7	–	–	4	–	1	–	–	–	2,4
Scheloribates laevigatus (C.L.K.)	–	–	5	9.1	–	–	–	–	4	–	–	–	–	–	–	–	–	–	–	–	–	–	2
S. latipes (C.L.K.)	2	–	–	–	–	–	–	–	35	26.5	–	–	–	–	–	–	–	–	–	–	–	–	1
Zygoribatula terricola v.d.H.	–	–	22	40.0	2	–	110	56.7	15	12.3	1	–	–	–	30	12.7	–	–	–	–	–	–	–
Chamobates schützi (Oudms.)	–	–	–	–	–	–	–	–	–	–	2	–	–	–	15	6.3	–	–	–	–	–	–	–
Euzetes globulus (Nic.)	–	–	–	–	–	–	–	–	–	–	3	–	7	11.7	7	–	24	22.4	–	–	–	–	4
Diapterobates humeralis (Herm.)	–	–	2	–	–	–	–	–	–	–	–	–	9	15.0	–	–	6	–	–	–	–	–	4
Humerobates rostrolamellatus Grandj.	–	–	1	–	–	–	–	–	3	–	1	–	15	25.0	2	–	30	28.0	–	–	1	–	4
Trichoribates incisellus (Kr.)	1	–	2	–	1	–	4	–	4	–	46	5.3	–	–	8	–	1	–	1	–	–	–	1,4
T. trimaculatus (C.L.K.)	–	–	15	27.2	–	–	11	5.8	44	33.3	5	–	17	28.3	119	50.2	25	23.3	–	–	–	–	1,4
Minunthozetes semirufus (C.L.K.)	–	–	–	–	1	–	2	–	–	–	–	–	–	–	–	–	–	–	–	–	–	–	2
Punctoribates punctum (C.L.K.)	–	–	–	–	–	–	–	–	–	–	1	–	–	–	6	–	–	–	–	–	–	–	2
Pelops sp.	–	–	–	–	–	–	1	–	–	–	–	–	–	–	–	–	–	–	–	–	–	–	–
Pelopiulus montanus Hull	–	–	–	–	–	–	1	–	2	–	2	–	3	5.0	1	–	2	–	–	–	–	–	1
P. phaenotus (C.L.K.)	–	–	3	5.5	–	–	1	–	17	12.8	2	–	–	–	2	–	–	–	–	–	–	–	1
Oribatella berlesi (Mich.)	–	–	–	–	–	–	–	–	–	–	–	–	–	–	6	–	1	–	–	–	–	–	–
Galumna lanceatus Oudms.	–	–	–	–	–	–	–	–	–	–	1	–	1	–	–	–	–	–	–	–	–	–	–
MESOSTIGMATA																							
Pergamasus nr. longicornis Berl.	–	–	–	–	–	–	–	–	–	–	1	–	–	–	1	–	–	–	–	–	–	–	–
P. ?robustus (Oudms.)	–	–	–	–	–	–	–	–	–	–	–	–	–	–	–	–	–	–	–	–	–	–	–
Pergamasus spp.	–	–	–	–	–	–	–	–	1	–	9	–	–	–	1	–	1	–	–	–	–	–	–
Pachylaelaps spp.	–	–	–	–	–	–	–	–	–	–	–	–	–	–	1	–	–	–	–	–	–	–	–
Uropodidae	–	–	–	–	–	–	–	–	–	–	31	–	–	–	6	–	–	–	–	–	–	–	5
Total	3		56		5		190		132		865		60		224		107		3		4		

Habitat groups see p106. Figures are numbers per sample and relative abundance (RA). RA is expressed as a percentage and is given where the species accounts for 5% or more of a sample containing over 50 specimens.

Most of the specimens were in extremely good condition (due to the waterlogged state of the deposits), retaining many of the body setae and, in a few cases, leg segments. This allowed identification to species level to be made, and the results are shown in Table 22. Many mite species are fairly restricted in their choice of habitat, and the distribution of a species at the present day may be used to define the original environment. The mites from Farmoor fall into five habitat groups (See Table 22), as follows:

1 Damp sites with little surface vegetation other than mosses or lichens. *Z. terricola, S. minutus* and *T. trimaculatus* are particularly common in this habitat.

2 Wet grassland. *P. punctum* is frequently found in grassland habitats together with *M. semirufus*. It is unfortunate that both these species are rather small, being 0.3. to 0.4 mm in length, and are therefore probably under-represented.

3 Aquatic.

4 Aerial vegetation. All these species occur in vegetation, and are in some cases specially adapted to the drier above-ground environment. *D. onustus* and *H. rostrolamellatus*, for example, use a tracheal method of respiration which allows the development of a thicker cuticle, so decreasing water loss. *D. humeralis* is a fairly rare species, the adults of which are found particularly on tree branches. It is interesting to note that *D. onustus, P. lucorum, D. humeralis,* and *H. rostrolamellatus* tend to be associated with the trunk and branches of the tree, rather than the leaves.

5 Plant refuse. *O. nitens* and *O. clavipectinata*, in contrast to most *Oppia* species, occur frequently in plant refuse. *O. nitens* has been recorded from grain stored on farms, in compost, and in other plant debris, while *O. clavipectinata* was first recorded in straw used for thatching.

The majority of the deposits sampled represent accumulations of material from different sources, and the mite fauna clearly reflects this. However some conclusions as to the original nature of the site can be drawn from the mite species present.

The Iron Age environment (mites)

Of the five deposits studied from this period, only the hut-circle ditch (Sample 1100/1) can be said to contain an *in situ* as opposed to a derived fauna (mites tend to be fairly limited in movement and normally reflect the immediate environment of a deposit rather than a wide area). In 1100/1, the species belong mainly to Group 1, being associated with damp sites and a vegetation cover of mosses or lichens, so are quite consistent with a ditch environment.

Scutovertex minutus, for example, which accounts for 15% of the fauna, has been recorded from damp ditch sites at the present day. There are also a few species characteristic of a wet grassland habitat, suggesting that the area surrounding the ditch was probably grassland. The ditch sumps (1007/1, 1009/1, and 1159) all contain these two elements, together with a number of species more commonly found in vegetation (Group 4). It is possible that these were brought into the deposits with flood debris as the Iron Age settlements are all situated on the flooplain and lower first gravel terrace of the Thames, which would probably be subject to flooding. This explanation is further supported by the fact that the species represented are those usually found on living wood (not structural timbers), occurring on larger branches rather than on small twigs and leaves. An aquatic mite was also collected

from 1007/1. Any flooding would have been temporary, on the evidence of the ditch fauna, which contains no aquatic species (which would be present with standing water), although the ditch was clearly damp.

The mite material therefore seems to argue for a periodically flooded, wet grassland environment at Farmoor during some part of the Iron Age.

The Roman environment (mites)

Three wells (43/10, 1046/2, and 1060/2) were examined from the Roman settlement, and one in particular (43/10) contained a large number of mites associated with aerial vegetation, with over 80% of the species belonging to Group 4. These were present to a lesser degree in 1062/2, a wattle-lined well. 1046/2 contained mostly species of moss or lichen (Group 1), together with a few grassland mites. The former group could have been derived either from the walls of the well, which was lined with stone, or from the immediate (and possibly trampled) area around the well. Samples from peat overlying the end of the droveway (1072), and from the droveway ditch (1074/2), contained very few mites, mainly species of Group 1 and Group 4. The small number from the peat sample is surprising, and could merely reflect the difficulty of extracting mites from peat by paraffin flotation. The last Roman sample studied (17/4) was from a pit, and species associated with plant refuse (Group 5) formed over 80% of the mite fauna. Both *Oppia clavipectinata* and *O. nitens*, the most numerous species, have been found on farms and in crop refuse, and are in agreement with the evidence that the pit contained cereal remains. A few mites of aerial vegetation and moss and lichen were present, which would suggest a mixture of material consistent with an interpretation of grain refuse rather than grain storage. It is impossible to say from the mite fauna whether or not the grain was grown on the site.

The environment during the Roman period was clearly still grassland, with the suggestion of a few trees or scrub in the immediate vicinity of the wells. The possible presence of crop refuse could indicate cultivation, or the processing of crop material on the site.

Plants and invertebrates: interpretation
by Mark Robinson

Reliability of results

Before the results are interpreted their reliability must be discussed. All the deposits sampled showed no obvious signs of disturbance which could have contaminated them. For the organic remains to have been preserved as well as they were, they must have been below permanent water table ever since they were deposited. Thus they would have remained undisturbed by burrowing mammals and earthworms. This need not be true for the dry bulk samples or the column samples apart from the bottom of Column II. However, the quantity of carbonized remains from 1002/2 in relation to the surrounding soil, and the vertical differences within the column samples, both of the soil and of the molluscs present, shows that serious mixing had not taken place. What it does mean is that conclusions cannot be drawn from single specimens because they could have been moved by limited action of burrowing animals.

The reasons for the extraction methods used for the different groups have already been given. Apart from those mites which were not extracted by a magnesium sulphate flotation process (see p104), it is not thought that any of the results were biased at this stage.

Details of identifications have been given and the number of specimens which remained completely unidentified with no name given to them was low. No beetle or molluscan fragment that remained could definitely be said to come from a species not given in the Tables (although it is very likely that there were other species present). Those seeds which fitted this category have been entitled 'varia'; their numbers are very low in relation to the total number of specimens identified. However, it is unfortunate that a more comprehensive seed reference collection was not available, because quite a significant proportion of the seeds have not had their identifications taken very far.

Keeping these considerations in mind an attempt can now be made to interpret the results. It will be divided into three parts. Firstly, those species no longer found in the area and any implications that the results as a whole might have about climatic change will be considered, and those species previously believed to have been later introductions will also be mentioned. Secondly, the way in which the particular assemblages may have arisen in the deposits will be discussed. Finally, the results will be used to try to give a picture of the Iron Age and Roman environments and some aspects of human activity on the site.

Distributions, ancient and modern

It is hardly surprising, given the small amount of other work which has been undertaken on waterlogged organic remains from archaeological sites of this date on basic soils in southern England, that the results should include some species which have not previously been found from Iron Age or Roman deposits in this country. Equally it is only to be expected that some of the species found can no longer occur in the locality of the site.

The site of Farmoor lies within the 10 km National Grid Square SP40. Those seeds from plants given as no longer known to occur within that square by both Bowen (1968) and Perring and Walters (1962) have been indicated in Table 6 (apart from obviously cultivated plants and *Sagittaria sagittifolia* which I have found growing just inside it at grid reference SP499054 near the junction of the Seacourt and Hinksey streams). Excluding the tentative identifications, only two of the species found, *Anthriscus caucalis* and *Valerianella dentata*, have never been recorded from the square. They are annuals of disturbed ground which are rare and have sporadic distributions within the new county of Oxfordshire. Both species are known to have suffered recent declines in the area but have been found in adjacent 10 km squares within the last 45 years (Perring and Walters 1962, 154, 267; Bowen 1968, 249). Further consideration will be given to them when other, now rare, disturbed ground weeds from the site are discussed in relation to the past environment (see p113).

The only mollusc in Table 12 not recorded as found in grid square SP40 after 1950 is *Anisus leucostoma* (Kerney 1976a). However, shells of it with the periostracum still intact were recovered from Thames flood refuse deposited in December 1976 within that square (p143).

Despite the large number of beetles identified from Farmoor, they represent no more than about 13½% of the number of species listed by Walker from within seven miles of Oxford (Walker 1929). However, the percentage from Farmoor would be somewhat greater if all the specimens had been identifiable to species. Almost three-quarters of the species from Farmoor have been recorded a mile and a half away in the Wytham Estate, and, excluding the tentative identifications, only twelve species are not included in Walker's lists for the Oxford district (Walker 1906-29). Of those twelve, *Malachius marginellus* was subsequently caught by Walker in Summertown (Walker 1939); there is a specimen of *Apion cerdo* from his Oxford District Collection in the Hope Department of Entomology which he had not recognized; and I caught several specimens of *Gymnetron pascuorum* on Pixey Mead in June 1974.

Details of the remaining species are as follows:

Blethisa multipunctata L.
This species is widely though locally distributed within the British Isles and lives in open marshy places at the edge of water, normally with soft soil, often with moss and *Carex* vegetation (Lindroth 1974, 32). There are no records for it from Oxfordshire or Berkshire (Moore 1957, 171-2).
Hister quadrimaculatus L.
It is a very rare southern English species (Halstead 1963,9) with a distribution which tends towards being coastal.
Silpha obscura L.
This carrion beetle has a local distribution in England (Joy 1932, 468) but was found from Roman deposits at Appleford (Robinson, forthcoming).
Acidota crenata (F.)
It is described by Tottenham (1954, 32) as rare and very local, but widely distributed.
Homaloplia ruricola (F.)
This is a rare species occurring in southern England on chalky soils as far north as Norfolk (Britton 1956, 13; Joy 1932, 255). It has been taken in Oxfordshire at Ewelme (Aubrook 1939, 125).
Apion malvae (F.)
It is a local species occurring as far north as Derby (Joy 1932, 164).
A. urticarium (Hbst.)
This is a rare southern English species, occurring no more further north than Leicestershire (Joy 1932, 164). The nearest locality to Farmoor from which it has been caught is Streatley, Berkshire (specimens in the Hope Department). It is of special interest because it has now been found from three Roman sites in Oxfordshire and one in Gloucestershire (Robinson 1975, 167).
Otiorrhynchus ligustici (L.)
This is the most interesting beetle to be identified from Farmoor. It is a very rare British beetle and only one has been caught in this country in the last 50 years at Wenlock Edge, Salop (Morris 1965a). There was evidently a colony of them at Ventnor, Isle of Wight, and there are three specimens caught there in 1922 in the Hope Department collections. The only other locality in which it has been found this century is Matlock, Derbyshire, where a single specimen was caught. Its supposed food plant in this country is *Anthyllis vulneraria* L. but none was present near the Shropshire find and it has been reared experimentally on a wide range of herbs including *Rumex* sp., *Daucus carrota* and several species of Papilionaceae, (Morris 1965a.) In France it is sometimes a pest on forage Papilionaceae (Hoffman 1950, 142).

While there are no other records for it from archaeological sites it has been quite a frequent find amongst warm faunas from glacial deposits, eg Isleworth (Coope and Angus 1975, 373).
Gymnetron labile (Hbst.)
It is locally distributed in Britain (Joy 1932, 222) and it has been found in a Roman deposit at Appleford (Robinson, forthcoming).

It can be seen that the fauna and flora from the site contained very few species which are not found in the vicinity today. Indeed Hope recorded in an interleaved copy of Marshman's *Entomologia Britannica: Coleoptera,* now in the Hope Department Library, the capture of 157 species of beetle at Oxford between 1819 and 1822. Of these, 19 species have never been taken since in the Oxford district. Two of them, *Necrophorus germanicus* L. and *Platycerus caraboides* L., both taken at Wytham, are no longer regarded as native in this country, although there are specimens of them in several old British collections. It is not even as if there is anything to suggest that Wytham Wood was 'special' like, for example, the ancient woodland of Sherwood or Windsor Forests (Donisthorpe 1939, 5). It might almost seem that the present fauna of the Oxford District is more similar to that of Roman and Iron Age times than 150 years ago, though in fact this is probably not the case. Hope does not record the locality of all his captures and his list for Oxford is hardly a balanced one which would result from random collecting, even allowing that most collectors of his day tended to concentrate on the larger, more spectacular, species. He was trying to build up a collection rather than list the species in a particular locality. Therefore his 19 exclusive species were out of a sample considerably larger than 157 species, but he would have discarded some and not recorded others. While he notes that he caught some of the 19 species himself including *Obera oculata*, which is now very rare and confined to the Fens, he makes no claim to the capture of the two species from Wytham which are no longer British. He describes the specimen of *Necrophorus* as being sent to him. It is possible that these two specimens were not British but that they had been sold to him as British.

There were certainly some specimens of dubious origin in his collection and a rather scurrilous article in *The Entomologists' Weekly Intelligencer* (written in 1857 when Hope was still alive) suggested that Shropshire (where Hope lived) was the place where one could capture Alpine and Southern European species and that one of them had actually been found ready pinned. The anonymous author (writing in a style identical to that of T V Wollaston who used to write on Coleoptera in the *Intelligencer* around that date) urges coleopterists to go to Shropshire and *hope* for the best — *spes nunquam fallit* (Stainton 1857, 118-19).

The flora from the Farmoor site contains some elements that are English rather than British, and some of these species become rather rare in northern England. The fauna, however, has some definitely southern English elements and no northern species at the edge of their range. For example, the bug *Syromastus rhombeus* is only found south of a line from South Wales to Suffolk and is more common south of this area (Southwood and Leston 1959, 61). A few examples of beetles with southerly distributions not already mentioned are: *Metabletus obscuroguttatus, Brachinus crepitans, Lucanus cervus, Aphodius equestris, Anthicus antherinus,* and *Phymatodes testaceus* (Britton 1956, 16; Joy 1932, 242, 306, 373, 381; Lindroth 1974, 134) Of these the stag beetle *(Lucanus cervus)* has a reliably known distribution because it is very conspicuous after flight if it has landed on a path or roadway, so that members of the public find them and tend to bring them to museums. There are very few records for the Oxford district, the last specimen being caught in Oxford in 1924 (Taylor 1941). The main range of the beetles is to the south-east of Farmoor (Clark 1966), the nearest known breeding locality being about thirteen miles (21 km) away in that direction at Brightwell (Osborne 1955).

Both the Roman and Iron Age faunas indicate that the climate (most critically the mean summer temperature) at least could not have been much colder than today. But could it have been any warmer? Several of the species not now found in the Oxford district are simply rare species with a scattered distribution. Whilst *Otiorrhynchus ligustici* can be common in France (Hoffman 1950, 142), which is probably due to climatic factors, it is a curious species for it is parthenogenetic (Morris 1965a, 169-71). This would enable populations to survive at a very low density in favoured localities even if a favourable climate were required for it to reach them (it is probably flightless). Therefore the single find from Farmoor, within its known range, is no indication of changed climatic conditions. The only beetle which might be indicating a climatic change since the Roman period is the weevil *Apion urticarium* (Robinson 1975, 170), for it persistently occurs in low numbers from Roman deposits in the area. It is common in France (Hoffman 1958, 1538) and its rarity in this country can hardly be due to a lack of its food source for it feeds on nettles, both *Urtica urens* and *U. dioica* (Fowler 1891, 142).

There is one plant which might indicate warmer conditions. Although *Lemna* spp. (duckweed) occur over much of the British Isles, their fruiting is infrequent and irregular, only occurring in hot summers in Britain now (Godwin 1975, 378, 432). I was not able to find any fruiting plants at all in 1975 and I only managed to obtain them in the hot summer of 1976. In July of that year the flow of the Cherwell was reduced to a mere trickle, and it became covered with a mat of *Lemna gibba* L. At Hampton Gay a small proportion of the plants in the pools and covering the stones of the largely dried up river bed were fruiting. The quantity of *L. gibba* growing there, however, was immense, and while it took a long time examining disgusting slime under the microscope to obtain a few seeds, the total crop from that area would have been very large. It would be quite possible that the Iron Age and Roman duckweed seeds were merely the result of the occasional hot summer out of the many ordinary and a few plants fruiting when most of the population did not.

A number of seeds were found at Farmoor from plants which have no Flandrian record given by Godwin (1975). These are *Ranunculus arvensis, Valerianella rimosa,* and *Dipsacus fullonum.* There are some more plants which he has not recorded from Flandrian contexts earlier than Roman that occurred in the Iron Age deposits. They are as follows: *Ranunculus parviflorus, Papaver argemone, Malva sylvestris, Valerianella dentata,* and *Onopordon acanthium* (Godwin 1975, 479). There is nothing particularly surprising about the discovery of any of these species. From the point of view of date, they are all plants which tend to be dependent on man to provide a bare earth surface for them to colonize. Some of them, especially *Ranunculus arvensis,* are cornfield weeds (Clapham *et al* 1962, 72). Some of them were probably introduced to the country by man, but only when considerably more archaeological deposits have been subjected to botanical analysis can any date be given with certainty. A few of the species are of particular ecological interest and will be discussed later.

It is probable that some of the insect remains have not previously been recorded from deposits of their date but only two are of particular archaeological interest. Both are species which tend to be dependent on man to a greater or lesser extent for the provision of their habitat. The first is *Tenebrio molitor,* a minor stored-products pest which is normally associated with buildings (Brendell 1975, 14). However, it does occur out of doors in decaying trees and birds' nests, in this country as well as Europe, and can distribute itself by flight (Freude *et al* 1969, 260, Wytham

Ecological Survey). Previously the only species of the genus to be recorded from archaeological deposits, usually with other grain beetles, is *T. obscurus* F., eg at Alcester (Osborne 1971, 162-3) and York (Kenward, pers comm). *T. obscurus* is now by far the rarer of the two species (Brendell 1975, 14) and it seems strange that it was the reverse in Roman times now that there is evidence for the presence of both of them in the country then. The other species of interest is *Aglenus brunneus*, represented by three specimens in an Iron Age deposit. It has been the subject of much discussion by Kenward (1975a; 1976b) who gives the previous earliest record for it in this country as Roman. It is now almost entirely restricted to man-made habitats, eg manure heaps, rotting straw, and mill refuse, probably feeding on fungus. In this country it seems unknown away from decaying remains of some sort left by man but there are a very few records of it in the wild in Europe (Kenward 1975a, 63, 65-7). The beetle may require temperatures above those found in natural habitats in Britain today (Kenward 1975a, 68). *A. brunneus* is blind and flightless which would present no problem in its possible natural habitats, fungi or buried wood in forests, but would imply that it was probably brought to the Farmoor site by man, even if it subsequently prospered in a manure heap.

A single specimen of the snail *Candidula intersecta* was found in an Iron Age context (Sample Column I, through the ditch of the Area II enclosure). This species may not be indigenous over most if not all of its present range in Britain, and is regarded as perhaps a post-medieval introduction (Evans 1972, 179; Kerney 1966, 11). The sample containing it was reasonably well stratified within the ditch, being from under a stone (see Section K, Fig 5) but the deposit was not below the water table so that it is quite possible that it was introduced by a burrowing animal. Other, less well stratified, specimens of this species were found in a Bronze Age ring ditch on the Thames gravels at Abingdon, Oxon (Robinson in Parrington 1978, 93) and other prehistoric finds are discussed by Thomas (1977).

Origin of the assemblages

The assemblages are divided into those animals which entered the deposits under their own power, and the plant parts and animals which were in some way transported to them. Once there, some will have flourished and reproduced, others will have found the conditions unsuitable and simply died. Some may have been introduced dead.

The samples are from contexts of two different sorts. Column Samples II and III along with Bulk Sample 1072 are from habitats which are likely to have been uniform (or showing the same sorts of variation) over quite same distance, while the others are all from particularly localized habitats such as ditch bottoms, wells, etc., with surrounds which were presumably quite different. This obviously affects greatly the way in which the results can be interpreted.

Column Samples II and III

The molluscs from Sample Column II and part of Sample Column III (0-420 mm) are largely aquatic, which serves to confirm that the deposit which covered the Iron Age occupation complex was alluvium. Above 420 mm in Sample Column III the proportion of obligate non-aquatics begins to increase. It is quite likely that this represents a slowing down in the rate of deposition.

The organic remains from the bottom of Sample Column II (Bulk Sample 1172) present a similar picture to the molluscs. Most of the seeds are from aquatic plants and the only non-aquatic plant represented in large numbers is *Juncus* spp. (rush). The insect remains were few.

Bulk Sample 1072

Bulk Sample 1072 contained a rather different range of remains. The nature of the deposit itself, a rather rooty peat from which the rotted traces of a rhizome resembling that of *Glyceria maxima* were found, suggests that it formed under water. It is unlikely to have been a peat which formed with the water table far below the surface because a large number of seeds of the aquatic plants *Ranunculus, S. Batrachium*, and *Lemna* sp. were present, and that would mean that the seeds had been introduced by flooding. Ombrogenous peat requires acidic conditions to develop but the floodwaters of the Thames are basic. Only about 5% of the seeds are from plants of dry ground but 20% of the total number of beetles could not have lived in the water below which the deposit was forming, or the aquatic plants above it, or the marsh at its edge. This illustrates the greater dispersive powers of Coleoptera.

Column Sample I

Turning now to the more localized deposits, the mollusca from Column Sample I are all terrestrial species and there is nothing to suggest that any of them lived anywhere other than in the ditch or around its edge.

The Iron Age sumps and gullies

The next group of samples (590/4, 1007/1, 1009/1, 1100/1, and 1159) were all from the sumps or deep parts of gullies belonging to Iron Age enclosure complexes. 1007/1 and 1009/1 come from different parts of the same complex; the others are from separate ones. Apart from 590/4, the gully systems were traced back in their entirety and found to be self-contained (plans Figs 11, 13, 14). All but 1007/1 contained aquatic molluscs, but this in itself need not imply that they had been introduced by flooding. Species of aquatic gastropods of the sub-class Euthyneura have lungs and are probably partly amphibious. A wide range of aquatic molluscs occur in isolated dew ponds and it is suggested that they reached them as eggs attached to the water weed draped around birds' legs (Reid 1889-94, 279, 204). An even stranger means of transport has been shown to take place. Species of *Pisidium* and *Sphaerium* have been found nipped to the legs of aquatic insects and a specimen of *Dytiscus marginalis* L. was caught in flight carrying one (Rees 1965, 272-3). There is also the possibility of transport to the gullies on the feet of cattle or in a dirty bucket. What is important in using the molluscs to indicate flooding is that the ecological conditions in the gullies would not have been suitable for some of the species to flourish.

Bithynia tentaculata found in both 1100/1 and 1159 is included by Sparks in his flowing water group of molluscs and Boycott (1936, 139-40) states that the freshwater operculates live almost exclusively in running water, with *B. tentaculata* never occurring in small closed ponds. *Valvata cristata*, another operculate, occurred in those two samples. Even if an unusual means of transport had introduced the above species into the gullies, it is most unlikely that they would have been able to breed and establish themselves in sufficient numbers so that several individuals would be present in samples 1100/1 and 1159. Therefore flooding is regarded as the only likely explanation of their introduction.

The seeds (and oospores) of *Characeae, Ranunculus S. Batrachium, Rorippa nasturtium-aquaticum, Potamogeton* sp. *Zannichellia palustris* and *Lemna* sp. could have entered the deposits, even though other methods are quite plausible, ranging from introduction in the faeces of ducks (Gillham 1974, 94) to cows with muddy feet. Once in the gullies, if they contained standing water, some of them could have flourished.

However, the evidence of flooding raises quite a serious problem. What is there to prevent all of the organic remains in these Iron Age deposits from being seen as flood refuse? The results from the modern flood refuse show how the river can carry a collection of seeds, a large proportion of which come from non-aquatic plants. The results of Easton (1947, 113-5) show how the same can be so for beetles. The nature of the fill of the gullies suggests that a large proportion of the remains entered by other means. They contained much debris of human occupation in the form of pottery, animal bones, and fine particles of charcoal. This sort of deposit was probably accumulating at a time when the site was occupied and there is every reason to suggest that plant and insect remains were accumulating in the gullies at the same time.

It is very hard to show whether these sumps and gullies contained standing water when the river was not in flood because of what flooding may have introduced. This consideration is relevant here because Mrs Denford regards the mite fauna of 1100/1 as an *in situ* damp ditch fauna. The water table must have been more or less on the surface of these deposits or above them as they formed, otherwise the wealth of remains discovered would not have been preserved. Perhaps these mites were a fauna which lived on the edge of the gully rather than on the bottom.

Roman wells and waterholes

The Roman deposits 1060/2, 43/10, 1046/2, and 1169 will be discussed as a group. All but the last were from features that were certainly wells, the last was probably a well. Two of these wells, 43/10 and 1169, contained aquatic bivalves of the genus *Pisidium* with a freshwater operculate, *Valvata cristata,* in 43/10 as well. The continual extraction of water combined with not much direct sunlight reaching the bottom could well have resulted in them being able to live there, even though the area of water was small. Both wells also contained a few seeds of *Lemna* sp. Modern flood records suggest that these two wells would have been inundated about once every three years (see p6), but the evidence from the preserved biological remains for them flooding is not as reliable as that from some of the Iron Age deposits since all the aquatic species may have been able to flourish in the wells.

The other molluscs in all four wells are largely terrestrial species which probably fell over the edge or were introduced with soil.

All the other plant remains in the wells were presumably introduced from outside, perhaps by dropping off plants overhanging the well, blowing in, or being dumped there by man. A very good example of the latter is given by 1169. Unlike any of the other waterlogged deposits this contained a large quantity of carbonized plant remains. When the species and numbers of carbonized and water-logged seeds are compared they can be seen to be quite different. To a certain extent this must be due to differential preservation by the two means, but even when remains known to have been preserved by both means on this site are compared, there is still little correspondence between the species represented. The three most common carbonized remains, 199 *Triticum spelta* spikelet fragments, along with *Tripleurospermum maritimum* and *Anthemis cotula* seeds, fall into this category yet none were preserved by waterlogging in 1169. There were 674 waterlogged *Urtica dioica* seeds and 228 *Chelidonium majus* seeds but none preserved by carbonization. (Although no carbonized *U. dioica* or *C. majus* seeds were found at Farmoor, there is no reason to suggest why they should not be preserved by this process). Clearly, the carbonized seeds had resulted from a pile of burnt threshing debris brought to the vicinity by man, whilst the other seeds were perhaps from plants growing around the well.

It may be assumed that some of the insects walked or flew into the wells and that others were attached to rubbish or bits of wood which fell or were dumped into them. Presumably these were also the means, combined with water transport, that resulted in the presence of the insect remains in the Iron Age gullies and sumps. Few of the species of water beetles from the wells were represented in any large number, and as individuals of all the species must have entered the wells from outside the non-numerous species are best regarded as indicative of aspects of the environment elsewhere. All the numerous species, *Hydraena testacea, Helophorus grandis, H. cf. brevipalpis,* and *Anacaena globulus,* could probably have bred in the wells but they all leave water quite readily for new habitats and can colonize in quite large numbers. *H. brevipalpis* is well known for swarming (Benham 1975) and a canvas tank of water in an Oxford garden half a mile (1 km) from a river had over 100 beetles in it 24 hours after filling (Greenstead 1939). The insects were mostly *H. brevipalpis,* and were observed freely flying in and out of the water.

The wells seem to have supported their own populations of aquatic Crustacea in the form of *Daphnia* and ostracods. Their means of dispersal are obscure but they are very effective at reaching even the smallest and most isolated bodies of water.

Pit 17

Pit 17 was a curious feature and the origins of Layer 17/4, the organic deposit in it, must be considered separately from the other Roman samples. From the exceptional preservation of the remains in the layer of peat, the top of which corresponded with the modern water table, it is probable that the water level had never been any lower since their deposition. The bulk of the peat was spelt wheat chaff, but it contained a wide range of other plant and animal material. Although some of it is consistent with the plant remains and insects which might be expected to abound in a pile of threshing debris, most of them clearly had other origins. It is suggested that the pit was left open, at least for a short time, enabling the other remains to enter and become mixed with the wheat chaff.

The pollen sample from 17/4 gave a most curious result. Over 60% of the pollen was cereal-type yet the major European cereal crops are generally known for their poor pollen dispersal. Values this high are hardly ever recorded from ancient deposits. Therefore it seems highly significant that this result should have been obtained from a deposit containing cereal debris. An experiment was devised to investigate whether the pollen could remain enclosed within the husks of a hulled cereal, and the result proved positive. (Brief details are given on p143; for further details and its implications see Robinson and

Hubbard 1977). It is most likely that some pollen has remained enclosed by the lemma and palea either entering the deposit with the chaff or with those few grains which had survived unthreshed. If cereal-type pollen is excluded from the pollen sum, the percentage of the other types of pollen present assume values rather similar to those from the other two Roman wells (Wells 1060 and 43) suggesting that much of the non-cereal pollen in Pit 17 could have been derived from the background pollen rain.

Ditch 1074

Sample 1074/4 was from a Roman droveway ditch and the mollusca indicate that it must have had water in it at least for some of the year.

The problem of 'background' faunas and statistical interpretation

It is hoped that the above discussion has demonstrated how an appreciation of the way in which different biological specimens accumulate in a feature is vital to the interpretation of that information. The most fundamental point is that there are clearly two distinct elements — the general surrounding environment and the environment of particular deposits. Kenward (1975b, 1976a), by collecting beetle remains from places unsuitable for them to complete their life cycles (a drain sump in a concrete yard and on roof tops), demonstrates the existence of a distant component, the 'background' fauna in death assemblages. He suggests that it may seriously detract from the accuracy of the use of such remains to reconstruct past ecological conditions (Kenward 1976a, 7). At Farmoor most of the samples give almost entirely background information; the only exceptions are Column Sample I, the top of Column Sample III, Bulk Samples 1072 and part of 17/4, and in other bulk samples a few molluscs, mites, common aquatic invertebrates, and perhaps common seeds of aquatic plants. If they did not grow in the deposits, clearly the specimens entered from the different surrounding environments. Undoubtedly some of those remains may indicate environmental conditions a very considerable distance away, just as one of the beetles in Kenward's roof assemblages, *Helophorus tuberculatus* Gyll., had flown or travelled inside a bird's gut a distance of tens of kilometres. The single specimen of *Homaloplia ruricola* from Sample 1159, for instance, could well have flown to the site from the Downs, 17 km away. It is a powerful flyer which seems confined to chalky districts (Britton 1956, 13). Unlike Kenward's samples, however, the Farmoor ones were not collected in an ecological desert. There is every reason to think that there would have been a substantial plant and invertebrate background population living right up to the edge of the particular deposits from which the samples were taken (see p.113) It can be assumed that the part of the background fauna which came from some distance away would have become almost completely swamped by that which lived closer to the deposit, except where a substantial part of it had been transported by flooding.

The problems of statistical interpretation of pollen and molluscan evidence have partly been overcome as a result of the considerable amount of work which has been done on those remains. Seeds and insects from rural archaeological sites, however, are still a rather unfamiliar subject. It is proposed that the interpretation of these results will largely avoid statistics but will try to take into account the biological characteristics of the species involved. There seem to be too many problems of non-randomness for simple statistics; for example some beetles tend to occur in swarms, and a high level of seeds of a particular species may only mean that a single plant was overhanging the edge of the deposit, rather than that there were a large number of them a little further away. With both seeds and insects, their dispersive powers vary greatly. Kenward (1976a, 13-14) has pointed out that beetles from some habitat groups, for example woodland species, show less dispersive ability than those from other groups. Different species of plants vary considerably in their level of seed production and there will be the same problem with population levels of different species of insect being very diferent in their respective habitats.

Much use will be made of the comparison of results from different deposits, but using only very simple statistics. The statistics used by Pearson (1959-60, 66) on Pleistocene beetle deposits, the coefficient of community and the percentage similarity, seem to be influenced too much by the above considerations, as well as the sample size, to be relied upon.

The early Iron Age environment (Phase I)

There is very little evidence for the earliest Iron Age. The early Iron Age pits on the first gravel terrace may have been for grain storage or rubbish, but neither is certain (see p65). The one sample which was examined for carbonized seeds (1013) did not contain any (p103) and a small quantity of burnt daub was found to have been bonded only with grass. On what becomes the modern river floodplain, the sample from the soil which preceded the later Iron Age deposits there contained few molluscan remains, all of which could have been terrestrial (Layer 1184, Table 18).

The middle Iron Age environment (Phase II)

Flooding

It is for the middle Iron Age occupation of the site that much environmental evidence survived. The most interesting piece of evidence is that two of the Iron Age enclosure complexes on the floodplain, groups 2 and 3, were suffering flooding while they were in use, as suggested by the presence of a certain aquatic molluscs in their gullies (Samples 1100/1 and 1159) (see p109) The remaining enclosure compled on the floodplain, group 1 (Sample 1007/1 and 1009/1, did not produce convincing evidence for flooding, but this may have been how seeds of aquatic plants entered these deposits. Further evidence for flooding while the complexes were in use is given by Layer 1172, the occupation layer of the southernmost enclosures. It clearly was an occupation layer from the quantity of pottery, small flecks of charcoal, and other debris of human activity, but the large number of aquatic molluscs from it, including *Bithynia tentaculata* and *Valvata cristata,* as well as many seeds from aquatic plants, show its origins to be partly alluvial. They could not have been derived from the very early or pre-Iron Age soil, Layer 1184, for no remains of aquatic animals or plants were found in it (see above).

There is no evidence from Column I of Iron Age flooding on the gravel terrace itself although there is some evidence for Roman flooding, and the edge of it has flooded in recent times (p6). The molluscs from Sample Column 1 contain no obligate marsh or freshwater species, and one of the species, *Pomatias elegans,* never occurs in marshy habitats (Evans 1972, 133).

General environment—its flora

It is evident from the results of pollen analysis of the two Iron Age samples that clearance had been very thorough by this time. Tree and scrub made up only 1.9% of the pollen from 1007/1 and 3.8% of the pollen from 1100/1. It is hoped that future work elsewhere will show what the pre-clearance woodland of the Thames Valley was, but the ease with which trees can colonize the modern alluvial floodplain as in some of the Cherwell meadows provides good evidence that Farmoor was at one time wooded.

The major ecotype indicated by the pollen seems to be grassland, with high values for Gramineae, *Plantago lanceolata* and *Liguliflorae.* The waterlogged seeds are predominantly from plants of disturbed ground; it is the rather less numerous seeds of grassland plants that will give an idea of what plants made up the main ecotype indicated by the pollen. From the Iron Age samples there are seeds of about 35 species which could have grown in such grassland (Table 6) but it must be remembered that some of them have non-grassland habitats as well.

A number of the species are restricted to wet habitats, such as *Caltha palustris* (kingcup); *Thalictrum flavum* (meadow rue); *Lychnis flos-cuculi* (ragged robin); *Filipendula ulmaria* (meadow-sweet); most *Juncus* spp. (rushes); and *Eleocharis* S. *Palustres.* Few, however, are confined to dry places when they occur in grassland; these are *Ranunculus parviflorus* and *Daucus carota* (carrot).

Comparison with modern grassland

There are many examples of alluvial grassland undamaged by modern agricultural techniques still surviving in the area and all but the two dry grassland plants mentioned above can be found on them. These meadows and pastures are characterized by a diverse herb flora and make a colourful contrast with the other grassland in the region during early summer. Their flora is by no means uniform and this variation seems to be dependent partly on management and drainage, for they still flood quite frequently. Baker (1937) gives lists of the plants growing in one grazed and one group of mown flood-meadows bordering the Thames only a few miles away from Farmoor. Port Meadow is a single open field of about 400 acres (160 hectares) which has been almost continuously pastured at least since Domesday by horses and cattle. Yarnton, Oxey, and Pixey Meads have for centuries been regularly mown for hay and then the aftermath grazed. Out of the 95 species occurring in them, only 30 are common to both.

The Farmoor lists however cannot simply be compared with Baker's lists to decide whether the grassland was grazed or mown. There are many ways in which the grassland could have been managed and all these would have had their effects on the composition of the flora. For example, it is possible to obtain a second crop of hay off the alluvial grassland in September (Church 1922, 68). While *Lychnis flos-cuculi* is restricted to the hay meads in Baker's study, it is as common in the pastures as the meadows in the flood-lands by the Cherwell. Once tussocks of rush form in a pasture (perhaps related to drainage problems and a past period of neglect) a tall vegetation environment somewhat similar to that in a hay-meadow is created. A mile and a half (2½ km) down the Thames from the Farmoor site, near Swinford Bridge, there is a pasture in which *Sanguisorba officinale* (burnet) can be found flowering in many of the clumps of rushes and *Succisa pratensis* flowers in a few of them. Similarly *Vicia cracca* (tufted vetch) and *Chrysanthemum leucanthemum* (ox-eye daisy) have been found flowering in tussocks in a pasture by the Cherwell. These species are normally regarded as indicative of meadow-land. On the whole, the plants generally regarded as indicative of pasture seem more reliable. Perhaps this is because they are prostrate species which cannot stand the competition of taller plants shading them, and meadows tend not to have regions of very short vegetation.

Two obvious problems remain with using seeds to indicate the type of grassland: most of the herbs in a hay meadow only set seeds if the cutting is left very late and many of the herbs in a pasture will be prevented from flowering by grazing; once seeds have been set, there is still the problem that not all will be preserved in a recognizable condition in a waterlogged deposit.

Despite the above problems there does seem to be some evidence for short, probably grazed pasture around the Iron Age settlements. *Potentilla anserina* (silverweed) is very common on Port Meadow and other alluvial pastures in the area and I have never found it in a hay meadow. It is well represented in the Iron Age samples. A rather weedy species, it flourishes especially when the ground's surface has been broken, and is capable of withstanding much trampling, so perhaps it was favoured by conditions around the site.

Another plant which gives useful information about the grassland is *Eleocharis* S. *Palustres.* It is thought (p100) that the forms represented definitely included *E. palustris* ssp. *palustris* and one, perhaps both of *E. palustris* ssp. *vulgaris* and *E. uniglumis. E. palustris* is a plant of shallow ponds, marshes, and wet grassland on basic to slightly acidic soils with no competition from tall species. *E. uniglumis* is a plant of more restricted habitats and when growing away from the coast can be found in the same places as *E. palustris* except that is does not occur on acid soils or in water (Walters 1949, 193, 196, 204). It is not listed by Baker as growing on Port Meadow, which seems a most suitable habitat for it. On looking for it in June 1976, however, I found *E. palustris* to be very common on the wetter part of Port Meadow, growing in company with *Potentilla anserina* and *Myostis scorpioides* L. Church (1925a, 65) mentioned it as growing at the wettest end of Port Meadow so perhaps Baker missed it. Walters (1949, 197, 205) notes that in heavily grazed pasture it is extremely difficult to detect and I only noticed it because flowering spikes were present. *E. palustris* requires water at or above soil level for rhizome growth in the spring but can tolerate drier conditions during the rest of the year. Intolerance of shade is one of the most important limiting factors for both species, normally confining it to reed swamp, wet pastures and marshes, all subject to grazing. However, it is an early colonizer, so would perhaps survive for a few years before being displaced by taller species in a newly created habitat (Walters 1949, 196-7). Walters (1949, 197-8) gives as an example of a suitable habitat some grazed marshy pasture in a similar Thameside position two and a half miles away at Hagley Pool. There, *E. palustris* and *E. uniglumis* were growing in company with *Carex* spp., *Filipendula ulmaria, Iris pseudacorus, Juncus* sp., *Ranunculus repens* and various grasses. Perhaps the Iron Age alluvial grassland was not unlike some of the modern riverside pastures, but presence of hay meads in the vicinity or a mixed treatment for the whole area cannot be eliminated. Many pasture plants have substantial roots which would enable them to carry sufficient food reserve to survive perhaps alternate years of hay cropping. Possibly one part of the floodplain at Farmoor was the traditional occupation site, even if the individual settlements did not last long (see below p114), with continual trampling and the grazing of a few tethered animals creating a small area suitable for pasture plants whilst the rest of the floodplain was hay meadow.

The cut-off river channel and seeds of aquatic plants

As well as some of the wet grassland plants indicated above which are able to occur in wetter habitats, all the Farmoor Iron Age deposits contained seeds from plants liking very marshy and aquatic conditions. It has been explained above (p110) how it is thought that flooding could have introduced some of these seeds into the Iron Age gullies and once there, some of the plants, especially *Lemna* sp. (duckweed) could have flourished even if there were only a little water in the gully bottoms for much of the year. There may have been a closer source for these seeds than the main river itself, in the cut-off river channel which was less than 25 m away from Complex 3 (Sample 1159) and was perhaps connected to Sump 590. The stratigraphic evidence (see p141) suggests that the channel may still have been an open pool with a marshy area at its edges. Perhaps it resembled Hagley Pool, a detached backwater of the Thames which now has no more than a trickle of water entering and leaving it through a flowing ditch. A list of plants for Hagley Pool is given by Tansley (1965, 588) and from the seeds present in Samples 590/4 and 1159 it is possible to envisage a similar community. With the evidence given above for grazing it is likely that the very shallow water at the edge had low plants similar to those listed by Tansley (1965, 682) for the grazed Thames edge of Port Meadow. Seeds of suitable plants found include: *Mentha* sp. (mint); *Rorippa nasturtium-aquaticum* (watercress); *Apium nodiflorum* (fool's watercress); and *Eleocharis* sp. In slightly deeper water, away from the pressures of grazing perhaps there was a tall reedswamp, suggested by the presence of the following suitable species: *Carex* spp. (sedges); *Oenanthe* sp. (water dropwort); *Hippuris vulgaris* (mare's tail); and *Sparganium* sp. (bur-reed). The last named species is readily eaten by cattle and cannot stand much grazing (Cook 1962, 251). Seeds from open waterplants include *Ranunculus* S. *Batrachium* (water crowfoot); *Potamogeton* sp. (pondweed); and *Zannichellia palustris*. Of course their origin could have been the main river.

The Iron Age ground surface sloped down towards the cut-off river channel. Perhaps, as the ground surface approached the water table, conditions became rather marshy and the wetter grassland plants became more important. Sample 1159 contained considerably more rush seeds than any of the other deposits, which is consistent with the deposit being close to an area with tussocks of rush, a zone of *Juncetum effusi* (Tansley 1965, 537-4). Such conditions exist in some places between the braided streams of the Thames just below Oxford as well as more locally in many of the riverside pastures.

The weeds around the settlements

Moving to the conditions which existed around the settlements themselves, and the more local effects of man than the maintenance of grassland, there is a wide range of seeds from plants of disturbed ground which presumably grew around the settlement. If the surface of the grassland had been much broken by the trampling of cattle, a few of the species would have been able to establish themselves away from the settlements as well. This damage is most likely to happen on the wettest soils. It is probably the reason that *Polygonum persicaria* (redshank) can be found growing in some of the Cherwell floodmeadows. However, it is described as always occurring in disturbed communities (Simmonds 1945-6, 122).

There is evidence that the turf had been stripped in enclosure group 3 (p70) but even the trampling of man and his animals would have provided sufficient bare ground for the weeds to flourish in profusion. The collection of weeds is rather a strange one. There are those annual plants which would be expected on seasonally wet, perhaps rather heavy soil, for example *P. persicaria; P. aviculare* (knotgrass); *Sonchus* spp. (sow thistles); *Chenopodium album* (fat hen); and *Atriplex* spp. (orache). There are also rather weedy grassland plants including *Plantago major* (plantain); *Ranunculus repens* (buttercup); and *Rumex* spp. (docks) (though most of these are in no way confined to moist habitats).

Along with this group, however, there are seeds from annual weeds normally associated with light dry soils, such as *Papaver* spp. (poppies) and *Urtica urens* (small nettle) (Bowen 1968, 44; McNaughton and Harper 1964). It is perhaps with them that it is possible to explain how seasonally flooded land could be a suitable place to live. These plants are annuals and complete their life cycles in only a few months. It is only during those few months that the soil condition influences the growth of the plant. In the summer months the ground surface of Port Meadow is dry, sometimes so dry that most plant growth ceases and the grass becomes bleached over all but the wettest part (as observed in 1976). Magdalen Meadow in Oxford floods quite often, but in the summer the water table can be three feet or more below the ground surface (Tansley 1965, 570). Since the level of the Thames is kept artificially high in the summer by locking, this effect would probably have been more extreme in Iron Age times. The excavation showed that the Iron Age soil on top of the gravel was quite thin on the floodplain; where undisturbed, the bottom of it was rather sandy. With the stripping of only a thin layer of soil, a well-draining surface would therefore be revealed. The evidence that the ground had been stripped to bare gravel over most of the enclosure formed by Ditch 1159 makes it possible that the annuals of dry sandy soils mostly grew during the summer months over the thin soil and bare gravel of the stripped areas, whilst the weeds of heavier wetter soils tended to grow on those places where the ground surface had not been stripped, but merely disturbed. *Kickxia spuria* (L.) Dum. was able to establish itself and set seed quite soon after some bare gravel, which had been under water, became exposed during construction work on the Farmoor Reservoir. It is described as a plant of arable land, usually cornfields on light soils (Clapham *et al* 1962, 681).

Several of the plants of disturbed ground tended to be associated with nutrient rich soil, for instance on and around dung heaps, but better evidence for the presence of dung is given by the Coleoptera, and will be presented later. Some of the plants of bare ground represented in Sample 1159 may have grown on bare mud exposed as the water level in the old river bed became lower in the summer. It is a common habitat of *Chenopodium rubrum* (Williams 1969, 835) and 1159 was the only Iron Age sample in which it occurred.

Unusual weeds

Even allowing for the variation in soils on the floodplain from wet clay to dry sandy gravel, the species of weed seeds

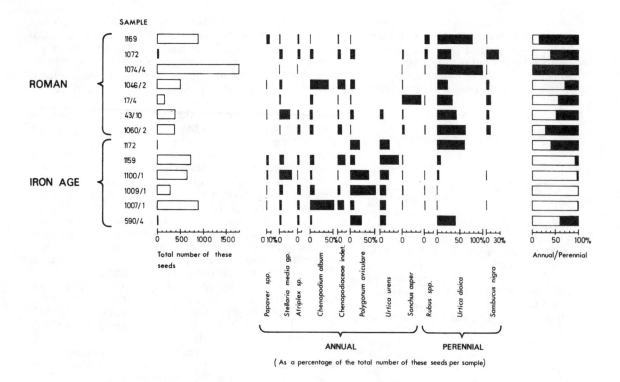

SAMPLE

ROMAN
- 1169
- 1072
- 1074/4
- 1046/2
- 17/4
- 43/10
- 1060/2

IRON AGE
- 1172
- 1159
- 1100/1
- 1009/1
- 1007/1
- 590/4

Total number of these seeds

0   500   1000   1500

0 10%0   0   0   50%0   0   50%0   0   0   0   0   50   100%0 30%

Papaver spp.
Stellaria media gp.
Atriplex sp.
Chenopodium album
Chenopodiaceae indet.
Polygonum aviculare
Urtica urens
Sonchus asper
Rubus spp.
Urtica dioica
Sambucus nigra

ANNUAL   PERENNIAL

(As a percentage of the total number of these seeds per sample)

Annual/Perennial

0   50   100%

Fig 37   Percentages of various weed seeds from disturbed ground plants which do not also occur in grassland. The total numbers of seeds of those species are all for 5 lb samples, the total for 1046/2 being estimated from the number in a 3 lb sample

found include some rather unexpected plants and omit others. *Hyoscyamus niger* (henbane) seeds were found in all the Iron Age deposits. Its requirements of disturbed, usually nutrient rich soil would have been met around the settlements but it is described as rare, sporadic and decreasing in this area (Bowen 1968, 229). It was not always rare, however, and in the 16th century was described as occurring almost everywhere by highways, in borders of fields, and about dunghills (Salisbury 1961, 49). There is no immediately obvious reason for its decline. *Valerianella rimosa* and *V. dentata* were both present even though they are now mostly confined in the region to arable on the chalk (Bowen 1968, 249). *Anthriscus caucalis* is now rare and sporadic in the area, having suffered a recent decline (see p107). The reasons for the decline of these plants could well be changing agricultural practices and perhaps they were only particularly viable in a certain habitat. While they were flourishing they could have 'subsidized' populations in less suitable habitats; for example, a plant which grows on dungheaps would have a continual supply of its seeds sent out to arable fields. If conditions became unsuitable in its 'key' habitat, it would cause a decline in the others as well. An example of the weed which has declined as a result of known changes in agricultural practice is that of *Agrostemma githago*, the corn cockle (see p120).

The problem of the rarity of some perennial weeds

Two species of disturbed ground plant which are particularly common in nutrient-rich ground around settlements, and whose seeds are normally found in large numbers from archaeological deposits, are *Urtica dioica* (stinging nettle) and *Sambucus nigra* (elder). They were certainly present in the area during the Iron Age, but their

seeds were found in much greater numbers in the Roman deposits. Similarly high numbers were recovered from the Roman site on the first gravel terrace at Appleford, Oxon (Robinson in Hinchliffe, forthcoming). Few waterlogged Iron Age archaeological deposits have been examined for seeds, but the results from Fisherwick, a site on the Tame gravels, Staffs (J R A Greig, pers comm) show that seeds of both species can be common on wet Iron Age sites. It would be thought that the conditions around the Iron Age settlements at Farmoor would be ideal for their growth, certainly the evidence from the Chenopodiaceae and also the insects would suggest suitable nutrient - rich soil from dung and refuse around the enclosures. *U. dioica* and *S. nigra* are both capable of growing on the alluvial flood-plain today. Both species, however, are perennials not normally found in grassland, though once given the opportunity to invade, *U. dioica* can survive for many years (Greig-Smith 1948, 345).

S. nigra must be several years old before flowering and *U. dioica* does not flower in its first year (Greig-Smith 1948, 349) which perhaps gives a clue to the low numbers of their seeds. The proportions of the seeds from the more common species of disturbed ground plants as a percentage of the total number of seeds of those species in each deposit are compared in Fig. 37. Only disturbed ground plants not normally occurring also in undisturbed grassland have been included, thus excluding plants such as *Ranunculus repens* (buttercup). Also, they were all species which were found from both the Iron Age and Roman deposits, so that there can be no problem with plants being unable to colonize a suitable habitat simply because they did not occur in the area. It can be seen that although most of those plants which are annual weeds are common in both the Iron Age and Roman deposits, the seeds of those which do not flower in their first year only reach high numbers from the Roman samples. This difference is not due to the different nature of the deposits; the Iron Age samples were mostly from sumps in gullies and the Roman samples mostly from wells. The sample which had the highest proportion of *U. dioica* seeds was from a Roman ditch (Sample 1074/4).

A possible reason for this difference is that the Iron Age settlements were temporary whilst the Roman ones were permanent. There would be a few of these weed seeds present in the grassland before a settlement was founded, but once the activities of man had left disturbed nitrogen-rich soil around his dwellings, colonization would begin. In the first year, of course, only the annuals would produce seed. In the second year, there would still probably be a preponderance of annual weed seeds because the only perennials setting seed would be those few plants which had arrived from outside as seeds in the first year. The annuals would have mostly arisen from locally produced seeds of the previous generation. Over the next few years the perennials would gradually establish themselves in number and begin to produce seeds in bulk, while continued human activity would provide newly disturbed ground, ensuring that the annuals were never completely replaced. If the Iron Age settlements were abandoned after only a few years of use, grassland plants would be likely to re-establish themselves before the perennials had reached high numbers. Even had the perennials managed to establish themselves in quantity, abandonment would result in the waterlogged bottoms of the features becoming filled in, perhaps before they had received many of the perennials' seeds. Certainly the Roman features must have been open while perennial weed seeds were being produced in quantity nearby, but there is nothing to suggest that this was so when the Iron Age deposits were accumulating.

Crops and collected plants

When considering crop plants from archaeological deposits, they can be divided into three groups. Firstly, there are those plants which must be cultivated crops. These are recognized either as alien to the region in which they were found and only able to survive there under conditions of agricultural management, or as having morphological differences from their ancestors as a result of selective breeding. Secondly, there are those species with varieties which can be crops but whose wild ancestors are able to grow in the same vicinity and whose remains are indistinquishable from the cultivated variety. Sometimes the wild forms are also usable to man, sometimes they are not. Thirdly, there are those plants which could grow wild in the vicinity, which are not recognized as crops by us, but could conceivably be used if cultivated by man. In the first group will be some alien crops which can also grow as weeds of other crops, but which could not survive outside cultivated habitats; and allied to this will be those alien weeds which can only survive under cultivated conditions. The only problem with this grouping is that a few morphologically distinct cultivars, eg *Prunus domestica* (plum), are able to survive outside cultivation. Running parallel to the first group and merging with the last two will be wild plants deliberately collected by man; firstly, aliens to the district; secondly, obviously useful wild plants which could have grown locally; and thirdly, local wild plants, not obviously useful (to us). As more is known about the habits of ancient man, so it may become possible to deduce which plants were regarded as useful. The only reason for regarding remains of plants from the last two groups as indicating cultivation or collection is if there is something unusual about the context or quantity of the find.

The only species to fall into the first group (definitely cultivated plants) from Iron Age deposits at Farmoor are *Triticum* sp. (wheat), *Hordeum vulgare* (six-row hulled barley), and cf. *Avena* sp. (oats). They were all represented by carbonized remains, that in itself implying human attention to them, but the numbers were so low that only one of the species might have been the crop and the others could have been its weeds. Although the carbonized remains indicate that the Iron Age community at Farmoor used grain, they do not indicate whether or not the people at the site grew it themselves. The presence of a *Prunus spinosa* (sloe) stone amongst the carbonized seeds shows that by no means all of them are burnt threshing debris. The few grains of cereal-type pollen could have been brought to the site enclosed by the bracts of hulled cereals (see p143) and, as its separation from other grass pollen was on the basis of size, there remains a slight possibility that it was from wild grasses with large pollen grains (Dimbleby, pers comm). The floodplain would hardly have been suitable for the cultivation of cereals, so that if the inhabitants of the Iron Age enclosure complexes grew their own grain, presumably their fields were on the first gravel terrace, in which case the siting of the settlement on the floodplain seems surprising (see p134). The column sample through the enclosure gully on the gravel terrace (Column Sample I) contained no carbonized remains and Sample 590/4 from a waterlogged feature on the edge of the terrace contained no cereal remains. Unfortunately there were no other waterlogged Iron Age deposits on the gravel terrace, but 590/4 produced a similar range of seed to the other Iron Age samples indicating disturbed ground, grassland, marsh, and aquatic habitats.

The only plants worth considering as entering the second group of cultivated crops with indistinquishable wild varieties are *Daucus carota* (carrot) and species of Brassicae (which includes cabbage and turnip). There is nothing to suggest that the seeds were anything other than the wild varieties. Even if such vegetables were grown, only a few would probably be allowed to run to seed for the next year's crop. The seeds of other edible plants are *Rorippa nasturtium-aquaticum* (watercress), *Mentha* sp. (mint), and *Rubus fruticosus* agg. (blackberry). Although they are all cultivated at present, it would be unlikely that man would have done so in the Iron Age at Farmoor. If blackberries had been collected for food, seeds would have been expected in much higher numbers; as for the other two species, if parts of these plants had been brought back to the site for food, they would not have included the seeds. There is not space even to begin discussing those plants indicated at Farmoor which have had an accepted medicinal use at one time or another, but there is nothing to indicate such a use from the circumstances of discovery.

Amongst the remaining plants there are those which are sometimes collected and eaten (the third group) but, as a recent book on their cookery advises for many of them, '...it is probably prudent not to eat large quantities regularly' (Mabey 1975, 90). A particular favourite amongst archaeologists trying to suggest what the occupants of their sites ate, *Chenopodium album* (fat hen, melde), was present. There are reliable examples of its use as a food (eg Johnston 1962) but it can prove poisonous to humans (Forsyth 1954, 61). On the basis of its preferred habitat it would be surprising if its seeds had not been found at Farmoor.

There are only three species of the third group of plants from the Iron Age deposits which seem likely to have been deliberately collected or cultivated. The first is the stone of *Prunus spinosa* (sloe) from Sample 1159 because it has been carbonized. The second is *Onopordum acanthium* (cotton thistle) which is rarely seen in this area today, even though it is more common in the east of England (but growing in such places as on railway embankments). The only reason to suspect its cultivation or collection is that seeds of it were found in five Iron Age deposits, one containing sixteen, whereas there were none from the Roman samples, and it seems rather unlikely to be growing on the site in the first place (but see *Hyoscyamus niger* etc above, p113). Perhaps its down or large seeds were put to some use. The third species is *Pteridium aquilinum* (bracken). It does not seem very likely that it could have grown on the site, but it grows on the nearby hills of Wytham and Cumnor Hurst. This could account for the natural occurrence of the few spores in both the Roman and Iron Age pollen samples, but not for the fragments of fern matching bracken which were found from Samples 1007/1 and 1009/1 (enclosure group 1) *Pteridium* mainly occurs on light acid soils (Clapham *et al* 1962, 16). Experimental work has shown that the plants themselves grow well in the presence of calcium salts but that young plants are frequently killed by fungal attack. This is perhaps a limiting factor in the establishment of sporelings on basic soil (Conway and Stephens 1957). It thus seems very unlikely that it was able to grow on the floodplain or the gravel terrace and cannot be found in either locality today. Bracken does, however, manage to grow on basic soils over limestone, calcareous grit, and even Oxford Clay on Wytham Hill (Osmaston 1959, 17-21), although acidic colluvial sands are at the surface in some places and it is not known what the state of the soil would have been when the bracken first became established. There is also evidence which might be interpreted as indicating areas of rather acidic soil on the floodplain at Farmoor (p124). Despite these two considerations *Pteridium* still seems an unlikely plant to be growing around the Iron Age settlements. There is evidence of prehistoric man bringing bracken to sites elsewhere, perhaps as litter for animals (Dimbleby and Evans 1974, 132).

Beetles—comparison with other faunas

The Coleoptera from the Iron Age samples are rather hard to interpret because there has not been the systematic compiling of lists for localities on the river floodplain, even though there has been much random collecting. To build up as complete lists for the Coleoptera of Port Meadow and Pixey Mead as Baker (1937) did for the plants would probably require intensive collecting over several years, with weekly visits during the summer.

The list of species from the Iron Age deposits at Farmoor quite closely resembles those which have been obtained from flood refuse in the area (Easton 1947; Walker 1908; Walker's diary). These flood deposits were sampled immediately they had been stranded by the river and amongst the organic debris was found a large number of beetles, mostly live terrestrial species which had been washed out of their hiding places. Sudden floods normally provide the best catches. The reason for the resemblance, however, need not be that the Iron Age Coleoptera were deposited by flooding: the flooding would catch a comprehensive range of beetles from the floodplain and the Iron Age deposits would collect this fauna as well. Walker's diary gives a full list of species identified from a deposit made by the Cherwell on Sparsey Bridge (just above Oxford) on 1 and 2 May 1908. About two-thirds of the 152 species of Iron Age beetles from Farmoor are included in his massive total of 337 species. Those remaining from Farmoor do not fall into any particular habitat group not included at Sparsey Bridge, and some of

them are in any case riverbank and aquatic species. Similarly there are no ecological groups from the Sparsey list not represented at Farmoor. One of the reasons for the greater length of the Sparsey list is simply that, because he was dealing with whole insects, he was able to identify most of them to species, especially a wide range of aleocharine staphylinids which I cannot identify from sclerites at all. The Farmoor list compares in the same sort of way to a list of a Thameside flood deposit at Shillingford Oxon. (Easton 1947), with no obvious ecological group in either which is not shared. The Shillingford report gives the number of individuals found for each species and when these are compared with the Farmoor Iron Age results there is a good agreement for some groups. For instance both lists give high numbers for dung beetles of the genus *Aphodius* and also for beetles of the genus *Cercyon*.

A comparison of the Farmoor Iron Age Coleoptera with lists from archaeological and geological deposits in other environments shows how faunal lists can be influenced by habitat. The Farmoor results bear no resemblance to those from Roman to Viking urban contexts in York. Those faunas tend to be dominated by 'filth' and synanthropic species, often grain beetles. They certainly do not have the range of Carabidae, Chrysomelidae and Curculionidae (Kenward, pers comm). In the results from the peats of the Somerset Levels the terrestial group at Farmoor is largely absent and, while both sites produce marsh and aquatic groups, the species that make them up are mostly different (Girling 1976). Comparison with a woodland fauna from an alluvial deposit at Shustoke, Warwickshire (Kelly and Osborne 1964), emphasizes how different the Iron Age environment at Farmoor was, with so few of the Coleoptera being dependent on trees or timber. Most of the Chrysomelidae and Curculionidae from the Shustoke 'A' deposit must feed on the foliage of trees whereas none needs do so from the Farmoor Iron Age samples. Even from the Shustoke 'B' deposit which was regarded as indicating an open environment (though with some secondary woodland and scrub) there are far more tree-dependent Coleoptera than in the Farmoor Iron Age samples. For example, the single sample of the Shustoke 'B' deposit contained five Scolytidae of three species whereas there was only one specimen from all the Farmoor Iron Age samples. The Farmoor samples on the other hand contained a greater proportion of Coleoptera that are dependent on dung or decaying vegetable matter than either of the Shustoke samples. Another fauna to compare the Farmoor Iron Age Coleoptera with is that provided by the Bronze Age shaft at Wilsford, Wiltshire (Osborne 1969, 557-60), with which it shows some affinities in terms of broad ecological groupings rather than individual species. The environment was regarded as being predominantly open grassland with few trees and the presence of many grazing animals. Both faunas contain a large proportion of dung beetles and each only has a single beetle associated with trees which could not have lived on structural timbers. The difference is that the wide range of species and high numbers of marsh and aquatic beetles present in Farmoor Iron Age samples were not present in the Wilsford fauna. A final comparison can be made with the Farmoor Roman Coleoptera. There is a good overlap of species between them, about two-thirds of the Iron Age beetles also occurring in the Roman samples. There is also a tendency for the more numerous Iron Age species to be numerous in the Roman deposits. There do not seem to be any ecological groups present in the Iron Age which were not also present in the Roman period, but two extra groupings seem to occur in the Roman samples. Firstly, there is a synanthropic group of about six species that occur in straw or stored grain, none of which occur in the

Iron Age samples; secondly, there are beetles which feed on trees or wood other than structural timbers, including three species of Scolytidae and two Cerambycidae as well as several species which feed on rotten wood. The Iron Age samples contained only a single scolytid.

Simply, from these comparisons it is possible to say that the Coleoptera indicate a landscape with few trees, some pasture, and some marsh, and that such a fauna would not be out of place in some of the flooded grassland in the locality today. This interpretation has been arrived at without any of the problems of over-representation of particular habitat groups distorting the results which can occur if the fauna is simply split into ecological groups with the largest group taken to represent the predominant habitat.

Grassland beetles

Thus the Coleoptera support and supplement the results from plant remains in general but also more specifically. There are wireworm beetles (*Agriotes* spp.) which would have occurred at the roots of the grassland plants and the weevils (Curculionoidea) which would have fed on them above ground. Some additional plants, which have seeds that do not preserve well, are indicated, such as *Trifolium* sp. (clover) by *Sitona* spp. The grazed nature of the grassland inferred from the seeds is confirmed by the presence of a large number of dung beetles.

Dung beetles

Dung beetles can present rather a problem with their interpretation. Some species are by no means confined to dung and can complete their life cycle in other habitats, especially decaying plant remains (of which, after all, dung is only a specialized form), eg *Cercyon* spp. Others can live in manure heaps as well as dung in the field (eg *Oxyomus sylvestris*). Even those species which are confined to breeding in dung in the field may be attracted to a manure heap by its smell or visit decaying vegetation. If they are then collected from these habitats some confusion is caused as to what their true habitat is. Luckily, some of the species of dung beetle from the Iron Age samples do seem to be confined to the dung of large herbivores (ie domestic mammals) in the form of cowpats, etc. *Geotrupes* sp. takes dung into tunnels it excavates in the soil beneath; *Aphodius contaminatus* burrows in it. Several of the less numerous species of *Aphodius* identified and probably most of those species which made up the large number of unidentified *Aphodius* are also restricted to dung in the field. The numbers in which the dung beetles were found would imply the presence of domestic animals in quantity close to the deposits, and therefore indicate that at least some of the grassland was grazed.

Beetles of disturbed ground

It is hard to infer directly the presence of disturbed or bare ground from Coleoptera alone. All the species from Farmoor which occur in that habitat can also occur in grassland, as will be seen from the habitat information given in Table 9. Some of the large Carabidae (such as *Nebria brevicollis, Pterostichus melanarius,* and *Harpalus rufipes*) occur in much higher numbers where there is bare earth between plant stems at ground level, but they do occur in low numbers in grassland along with those carabids more usually associated with it (such as *Calathus*

fuscipes and *C. melanocephalus*). Indirectly there is the evidence from those beetles which feed on plants of disturbed ground. *Chaetocnema concinna* tends to feed on *Polygonum aviculare* (seeds of which were present) but can also eat other species of Polygonaceae; *Apion aeneum* feeds on mallows (seeds of *Malva sylvestris* were present); and many of the Ceuthorhynchinae feed on weeds of the family Cruciferae. None of the plant-feeding beetles from the Iron Age samples are, however, entirely confined to plants of disturbed ground, although there is a species of bug, *Heterogaster urticae*, which mostly feeds on nettles.

Tree, shrub, and wood dependent beetles

Although many of the Iron Age beetles found can occur in woodland, none of them is confined to it. The few seeds of *Crataegus* sp. (hawthorn), the twigs of *Prunus* (blackthorn etc) along with remains of *Rosa* sp. (rose) and *Rubus* sp. (blackberry) show that woody species of plants were not entirely absent but only a few of the beetles found are dependent on wood. *Anobium punctatum* and *Lyctus fuscus* were present in low numbers, but they only attack dead wood including structural timbers (Hickin 1963, 21, 46; 1975, 35) and need not indicate the presence of the trees. *Phyllopertha horticola* has larvae which feed on roots in grassland with a high diversity of flowering plants but some authors give the food of the adult as leaves of trees and shrubs (eg Horion 1958, 229). Indeed it does sometimes feed on them, but it has been shown that it can still breed if the adult eats grass or does not eat at all (Raw 1951-2, 644-5). The only beetle that requires living or dead wood with the bark in place is the scolytid *Anisandrus* sp. (Hickin 1975, 292). The Coleoptera in general thus agree well with the pollen in showing a general lack of trees.

Marsh beetles

There is a good range of beetles that live in marshy places or at the edge of water, especially from Sample 1159, which could have lived around the cut-off river channel. These include *Chlaenius vestitus;* the rare *Agonum marginatum*, and several species of Bembidiini. There is one species, *Trechus micros*, which is usually found on the banks of running water (Lindroth 1974, 44). A number of the Staphylinidae occur on wet mud at the edge of the water, for example *Carpelimus bilineatus* and *Platystethus cornutus*, but they are not all restricted to this habitat. There is no way of telling whether the *P. cornutus* from Sample 1159 lived in exposed mud on which *Chenopodium rubrum* was growing at the edge of the cut-off river channel or whether the beetle was living in a rather wet manure heap on which the same plant was growing. Several of the beetles feed on aquatic or marsh plants, including Prasocuris phellandrii (mostly on *Oenanthe* sp.) and *Notaris acridulus* (on *Glyceria maxima* and *Eleocharis* sp. amongst others).

Beetles of decaying plant material

So far the Coleoptera have only been used to confirm or amplify details of habitats already indicated by the plant remains, but they show the presence of one extra habitat, namely decaying vegetable material. Some of the species which live in dung in the field can also live in places such as compost heaps or piles of manure (eg *Oxytelus sculpturatus, Platystethus arenarius,* and *Philonthus* sp.) There are no species from Farmoor which occur in manure heaps without also living on cow pats etc, but there are a few beetles of decaying vegetable remains that tend to avoid dung altogether, such as *Xantholinus linearis* and *X. longiventris* (Horion 1965, 100-1). Several of these 'filth' species are found reasonably frequently away from decaying remains, but the numbers in which they were recovered from the Iron Age samples would suggest accumulations of rotting vegetation and perhaps manure in the vicinity of the enclosures.

Other habitats

There are no other significant habitats indicated by the Coleoptera. There are only three individuals of a single synanthropic species, the enigmatic *Aglenus brunneus*. While it might have required man to introduce it to the site (see p109) it would have been capable of living in one of the 'filth' habitats described above. The numbers of species restricted to carrion are low, and the odd specimen of *Osmosita colon* could easily have been picking the bones of a dead wild animal. The presence of *Crypticus quisquilius* is interesting for it normally occurs in sandy coastal habitats, but one of its few inland localities at present is about five miles away at Frilford Heath near Tubney where it lives in sandy fields in the company of other seaside beetles (Walker 1926, 189-190). Perhaps the Farmoor specimens lived in a sandy place on the Lower Corallian or Lower Greensand near the site.

Other invertebrates

The other invertebrate remains add little information about the environment which has not been indicated by the plants, molluscs, and beetles. The Formicidae (ants) can live in some of the habitats interpreted from the other groups, for instance *Lasius flavus* will nest in marshy ground (Donisthorpe 1927, 256). The *Daphnia*, ostracods, and chironomid larvae could have all lived in temporary puddles in the ditch bottoms and, apart from the problem as to whether Gully 1100 was water-filled (see p110), the Acari (mites) serve only to confirm the other evidence for the Iron Age environment.

Post Iron Age alluvium

Some time after the Iron Age sites on the floodplain had ceased to be occupied, the nature of the flooding changed. Rather than being the sort of flooding which occurs on Port Meadow today, depositing mostly flotsam with very little mineral material (see p142), a much greater mineral load was deposited causing a build up of alluvium over the Iron Age enclosure complexes, especially group 3 (see Section U[111] Fig 15). Either it meant that the severity of flooding had increased or that the water carried a heavier sediment load, and it is quite possible that the first caused the second. This alluvial deposition filled in the cut-off river channel and had the effect of levelling the floodplain. Perhaps the type of flooding was already beginning to change when complex 3 was in use, for its occupation layer (1172) was a similar clay to the alluvium above it and had the same proportions of aquatic molluscs. The filling in of the cut-off river channel must have altered the drainage pattern of the floodplain and the preservation of organic material in Layer 1172 would suggest that the water table rose on this part of the site. The presence of a greater proportion of obligate non-aquatic snails in the upper part of the alluvium would suggest that the rate of

deposition had by then become slower resulting in a greater proportion of the molluscs being of local origin (see p109). There is no good dating evidence for the slowing down of alluvial deposition, but the main build up of alluvium must have been substantially complete by the 4th century AD. The peat of Layer 1072 (see Fig 17) would not have been able to form nearby at its relatively high level unless the alluvium had been present to the north of it to prevent the water draining away.

The Roman environment (Phase III)

The Roman samples were all from the gravel terrace itself, there being no traces of Roman occupation on the floodplain.

There is evidence which might suggest that the part of the settlement which was on the edge of the gravel terrace sometimes flooded, but it is not as convincing as that for the Iron Age. It is based on the presence of *Pisidium* sp. in two of the wells (Samples 43/10 and 1169) and *Valvata piscinalis* in one (Sample 43/10), but flooding is not the only way in which they could have been introduced (see p109).

General environment—its flora

The pollen analyses of the Roman samples show that grassland was again predominant and there was little tree pollen. The highest value was 11.6% of the pollen in Sample 1060/2 being from woody species. The results from the other samples were much lower, being 2.1% woody species pollen from 43/10; 4.4% from 17/4 (if cereal-type pollen is excluded from the total: see p111); and 4.5% from Sample 1072.

The waterlogged seeds are also predominantly from plants of disturbed ground (apart from those of Sample 1072 which will be considered separately). There is almost the same range of grassland species which made up the background environment, but those plants which live in damp habitats tend to be confined to the deposits which were located on the edge of the gravel terrace, especially Well 43. *Filipendula ulmaria* (meadow sweet) and *Lychnis flos-cuculi* (ragged robin) only occurred in samples less than about 25 m away from the terrace edge, while seeds of *Juncus* sp. (rushes), *Carex* sp. (sedges) and *Eleocharis* sp. occurred in rather low numbers from Samples 1046/2 and 1060/2, which were more than 50 m from the edge of the terrace.

Types of grassland

Grazed pasture is again indicated as in the Iron Age by the presence of *Eleocharis* S. *Palustres* (see above, p112), but its seeds were not common in all the Roman samples and it is left to the Coleoptera (see below, p122) to support the evidence. Seeds from some meadowland plants, for example *Rhinanthus* sp. (yellow rattle) and *Chrysanthemum leucanthemum* (ox-eye daisy), are more common from the Roman than the Iron Age samples. They are both, according to Stapledon, species characteristic of old meadows (Tansley 1965, 567) and in the study by Baker (1937) of Thameside hay meadows and pastures they were only present in the hay meads. It would be rash, however, to say that the greater numbers of their seeds represented an increase in meadowland; an example has already been given of *C. leucanthemum* flowering in a grazed pasture

118

(see above, p112), although it more commonly occurs in meadows and is much more abundant in them. Also, the Roman samples are mostly from a drier part of the site than the Iron Age ones, and different plants would tend to be dominant in both haymeadow and pasture. There is no reason why these plants should produce seeds in the same number as the plants they replaced.

The rarity in the Roman samples of the species taken to indicate grazing of the Iron Age grassland may indicate not less pasture but drier pasture. It has already been stated how the seeds of some species taken to indicate grazed grassland (eg *Eleocharis* S. *Palustres*) were commoner in the Roman samples close to the edge of the gravel terrace than from those further onto it, and it would therefore be safer to say that the grassland plants suggest that meadow and pasture elements were both present, and that reliable evidence of grazing comes from fewer of the Roman than the Iron Age deposits. Any apparent difference between the use of the Roman and Iron Age grassland, however, could be due to different species compositions dependent on wetness alone.

Vegetation at the north end of the droveway

Although the cut-off river channel between the gravel terrace and the alluvial floodplain had been filled in and probably raised almost to the level of the rest of the flood-plain, it was still quite a wet area, perhaps with a stream flowing through it. Thus, where the droveway led up to the edge of the gravel terrace to give access to the floodplain, a layer of peat (1072) built up under water over the surface of the droveway after it had ceased to be maintained at the end of the 4th century AD. Reasons have been given above as to why it is thought that this layer built up under water (see p109). The plant remains would suggest that the vegetation was a reedswamp with *Glyceria maxima* (reed grass), several species of *Carex* (sedge), *Alisma* sp. (water plantain), and *Iris pseudacorus* (yellow flag). At the water's edge probably grew *Lycopus europaeus* (gypsy wort). There are also seeds from plants of shallow water and water's edge which perhaps grew where the vegetation was less dense, eg *Mentha* sp. (mint) and *Apium nodiflorum* (fool's parsley). *Menyanthes trifoliata* (bogbean) can also be regarded as belonging to this group because it grows poorly in closed communities (Hewett 1964, 729). Possibly grazing pressure kept down the taller reedswamp vegetation in places along the water's edge. The open water plants, *Ranunculus* S. *Batrachium* (water crowfoot) and *Potamogeton* sp., could have grown in places where the reedswamp vegetation was absent or had their seeds introduced when the Thames flooded.

There is little evidence for the environment of this part of the site earlier in the Roman period, when the droveway was definitely in use, but the presence of aquatic molluscs in the first of the droveway ditches at this point (probably dating from the 2nd century; Sample 1074/4) shows that it contained water for at least some of the year. There were not very many seeds of aquatic and marsh plants from this sample perhaps due to the maintenance of the droveway ditches, keeping water levels lower than after abandonment, and also frequent use preventing much vegetation from growing on it. The eastern droveway ditch had been replaced three times at this place and a new gravel surface had been laid down where a track probably crossed on to the floodplain.

Plants of disturbed ground

Seeds from plants of disturbed ground were just as prevalent from the waterlogged samples (apart from 1072) as they had been in the Iron Age. A similar range of annual weeds was present, but in addition the seeds of two perennials, *Sambucus nigra* (elder) and *Urtica dioica* (stinging nettle), occurred in much higher numbers. A comparison between numbers of seeds of perennial weeds from the Iron Age and Roman samples suggests that the Iron Age enclosures were only used for a short period of time (see p114). The presence of these perennial weeds, however, cannot be taken to indicate long-term occupation of the Roman site, for they are not dependent solely on disturbed ground caused by human habitation and will grow in hedgerows and scrub. Only archaeological evidence can be used to show that the Roman site was in use for a long period of time resulting in the rather different conditions under which the plants of disturbed ground would have grown. This evidence is provided by the wide range of dates for the archaeological features, the number of times that the droveway ditches were recut, and the very existence of such a laid-out field system with occupation areas.

From the very low numbers of seeds of plants of disturbed ground present in Sample 1072 from the peat over the Roman droveway, it has been assumed that the majority of the seeds in the sample came from plants growing in the immediate vicinity of the deposit (see p 109). This idea seems to be confirmed by the falling off in the number of seeds from wet grassland plants in the deposits further on to the gravel terrace (p118). It is thus likely that the differences between the weed species present in the different samples reflect very local differences in the habitat around the deposit. Sample 1169 had large numbers of seeds of *Chelidonium majus* (greater celandine), *Rubus fruticosus* agg. (blackberry), and *U. dioica* (stinging nettle). This group of plants can frequently be found in hedgerows and are often common on waste ground near human habitation which has been left undisturbed for some years. In contrast to Sample 1169 the greater celandine and blackberry seeds were lacking from Sample 1046/2 and there was a much greater proportion of seeds from plants of freshly disturbed ground eg *Atriplex* sp. (orache), *Stellaria media* gp. (chickweed), and *Polygonum aviculare* agg. (knotgrass), all plants which might be found growing on arable land, or the spoil from a recently dug ditch. Despite such differences between the samples, however, none had seeds from one sort of disturbed ground habitat alone; Sample 1169 also had many seeds of *Papaver* sp. (poppy) while *S. nigra* was well represented in Sample 1046/2.

Arable weeds

One group of weeds is of special interest because the species seem particularly dependent on arable agri-culture. The following seem to show the most association: *Ranunculus arvensis* (corn buttercup), *Agrostemma githago* (corn cockle), and perhaps *Anthemis cotula* (stinking mayweed). They are all plants which are likely to have been introduced to this country and only one of them has been found in a pre-Roman Flandrian context in Britain. Carbonized seeds of *A. githago* were present in quantity at the bottom of a late Iron Age pit near Abingdon, Oxon M Jones, pers comm). *A. cotula*, although being abundant as a cereal weed and not being found on waste ground, is sometimes common in farmyards and occasionally occurs at roadsides (Kay 1971, 625) and therefore cannot be taken to indicate arable agriculture on its own. It is likely that the other two species are entirely dependent on arable agriculture for their survival in this country, even though they may also grow in places where threshing debris has been discarded. Church (1925 b, 20) gives a list of two dozen weeds he found growing on a threshing waste heap along with wheat, barley and oats in a Cowley smallholding. This might have been the way in which seeds of *A. cotula* and *A. githago* ended up in Well 43, since there were virtually no cereal remains in the sample (only a single waterlogged cereal grain and no chaff at all). No such explanations need be found for the presence of waterlogged *A. cotula* and *R. arvensis* in Sample 17/4 for this peat deposit consisted largely of spelt wheat chaff. *A. cotula* was found in two other Roman samples, 1002/2 from the corndrier (see p 104) and Sample 1169. In both of these it had been preserved by carbonization along with carbonized spelt wheat chaff.

Cereals

Leaving the weeds for an examination of the crops themselves, unlike the Iron Age samples, three Roman samples contained a significant quantity of cereal remains. In all the samples the remains represent the debris from the threshing of spelt wheat *(Triticum spelta)*. Spelt does not have free-threshing grains and requires parching over a corndrier to render the glumes brittle, unless a sophisticated mill is to be used (Helbaek 1953, 233). It has been assumed that the carbonized remains from inside the corndrier (Sample 1002/2), which contained five times as many glume bases as cereal grains, were from grain which had been subjected to this process, threshed, and then the winnowings perhaps used to kindle the corndrier fire (p104). Sample 1169 contained 199 carbonized spelt glume bases to 7 carbonized wheat grains and probably represents similar debris which had been burnt. The carbonized remains of other species of cereal, *Hordeum vulgare* (six-row hulled barley) and *Avena* sp. (oats), are present in such low numbers in the above two samples that they were probably only growing as weeds in those two particular crops. The carbonized weed seeds in those two samples would be from weeds which had been harvested with the crop and then removed in the winnowing. Mr Jones believes that the weeds from the corndrier sample suggest that the crop had been grown on a rather damp soil (p104). The carbonized weed seeds in Sample 1169 are particularly interesting because seeds had also been preserved by waterlogging. There is little overlap between the common species preserved by the different means, even those for which both carbonized and waterlogged seeds have been identified from the Farmoor deposits (see p110). This suggests completely separate origins for the two groups, the carbonized seeds having come ultimately with the crop from the arable fields, and the waterlogged seeds presumably from those plants which were growing in the more immediate vicinity of the well. This emphasizes that, while the cereal remains, their weeds, the corndriers and quern fragments shown that the Roman settlement was using the products of arable agriculture, they provide no indication of whether the arable fields were close to the site. Indeed there is no proof that the community was growing its own cereals; the occupants of the site could simply have been buying wheat threshed from the ear, parching it to thresh the grain from the chaff, and milling it themselves.

The third deposit which contained a significant quantity of cereal remains, Pit 17, was most unusual because the remains had been preserved by waterlogging and consisted largely of spelt wheat chaff (p110). Again the lack of caryopses (grains) suggests that the chaff had a similar origin to the two carbonized deposits apart from the burning. The weeds present in the crop cannot be established because the deposit did not consist entirely of threshing debris and they do not obviously stand out by being carbonized. The chaff in Pit 17 represents the threshing of only a small quantity of grain. If it is assumed that there was one grain of spelt for each glume base, on the basis of the $1^1/_2$ oz (42.4 gm) examined for cereal remains out of the total content of about 150 kg of Layer 17/4 in the pit, the debris would represent the threshing of over 1.3 million grains. Taking Percival's figure of 5 g for the weight of 100 caryopses (grains), they would have weighed about 65 kg. Using the productivity figure of 1600 lb per acre for spelt wheat, the contents of the pit would represent the crop of only about 0.03 hectares (0.07 acres) (Percival 1974, 327, 330). Therefore, the contents of the pit alone do not indicate extensive arable agriculture, although they do not exclude it either.

Although it is not known where the arable fields were, a little more can be said about them. They would have differed from modern ones in their weed flora as well as their cereal crops. *Hyoscyamus niger* (henbane) is hardly a modern arable weed, yet carbonized seeds of it were present in two of the Roman samples (see p113). *Agrostemma githago* (corncockle) seeds were found in Well 43 and it has been suggested that they were ultimately derived from arable agriculture (see p119). Corncockle is now extremely rare, yet up until the end of the last century it was a common cornfield weed and seeds of it have been identified from all the Roman sites in Oxfordshire from which samples have been analyzed. Its decline was probably because its seeds retain their viability in the soil for a short period only and were therefore easily dealt with by improved seed screening (Salisbury 1961, 36). It is thus interesting to find the plant persisting as late as 1925 in cereal crops around Oxford, being described as a conspicuous and common weed (Church 1925a, 62; 1925b, 7).

Other cultivated plants

Apart from the cereals there are the seeds of four other species from Roman Farmoor which fall into the category of definitely cultivated crops as defined above (p115). They are *Linum usitatissimum* (flax), *Prunus domestica* (plum), *Anethum graveolens* (dill), and *Coriandrum sativum* (coriander). One more species stands out as cultivated even though it was hardly a crop, *Buxus sempervirens* (box).

Flax seeds have also been found in small numbers from the Roman site at Appleford, Oxon, and the Roman villa at Barton Court, Abingdon, Oxon (Robinson in Hinchliffe forthcoming). The presence of its seeds, however, need not mean that it was growing in the vicinity because they can be used for oil or eaten as well as its stems being retted for fibres (Pliny XXVIII, xiv).

Two varieties of plum were found in the Roman samples, one with stones the size and shape of a variety of damson, the other from a larger-fruited variety (see p103). There is some evidence to suggest that a tree of the smaller-fruited variety overhung Well 1060. In all, 105 plum stones were recovered from the samples sieved from that deposit. Plum stones were so much in evidence when the feature was excavated that it is probable that several hundred more were discarded. The 5 lb sample examined in detail for plant remains contained eight plum stones, but also twelve fruit stalks which resembled those of plum. All the Roman samples from which the wood was identified included twigs of *Prunus* sp. but 1060/2 was the only one to produce *Prunus*-type pollen and *Scolytus rugulosus,* a beetle described as feeding on fruit trees (Joy 1932, 232) or plum, sloe, and rose (Reitter 1916, 272). This circumstantial evidence perhaps suggests that there was a plum tree close to the well which dropped its fruit into it rather than that the stones had simply entered the well with rubbish. These 105 plum stones would represent about 0.7 kg (1½ lb) of fruit on the basis of the weight of the modern damsons which had stones resembling them.

The single seeds of coriander and dill are pleasing finds but there is no way of knowing whether they were grown on the site or not. Coriander seems to be a common find on Roman sites, for example the town of Alchester, Oxon (Robinson 1975, 167). Dill has been identified from several Roman sites (Willcox 1977, 272-8).

The box leaves and shoots from Samples 17/4 and 1169, along with the *Buxus* fruit fragments from Sample 17/4, represent the most interesting plant remains from Farmoor. Box is a plant of chalk and limestone scarps which is regarded as native to this country (Piggot and Walters 1953). It is now extremely rare growing in its original habitat, occurring in only three 10 km grid squares all of them in southern England (Perring and Walters 1962, 98). The nearest one to the site is SU67, to the west of Reading. It is probable that box was once more widespread in Berkshire for at SU428715 is the village of Boxford and there is a reference of Asser, in the 9th century, to *'Berrocshire: quae paga taliter vocatur a Berroc Silva ubi buxus abundantissime nascitur'* (Gelling 1973, 1). It is now, of course, much cultivated and is often self-sown (Bowen 1968, 175). Box is quite capable of growing on the Thames gravels as the gardens of Oxford demonstrate and there is a bush of it growing on the bank of the Cherwell in the Oxford University Parks which is flooded every year. Despite this, however, it does seem a most unlikely plant to be growing wild at Farmoor. Apart from yew and holly it is the only native evergreen hedging plant and Pliny describes its use for ornamental hedges (XVI, xxviii). This would seem to be its most likely use at Farmoor although it is unfortunate that it is not possible to say whether the shoots and leaves had been removed from the bushes by clipping.

Excluding trees which may have been managed by coppicing, there are ten species of plants from the Roman samples which fall into the second group of crop plants, perfectly respectable crop species but with remains morphologically indistinguishable from wild forms which might grow in the locality (see above p115). There are the same five species which were regarded as unlikely to have been cultivated in the Iron Age (p115) and in addition *Chenopodium bonushenricus* (good King Henry); *Prunus cf. avium* (sweet cherry); *Malus sylvestris* (apple); *Pastinaca sativa* (parsnip); and *Corylus avellana* (hazel). There is nothing about the context of any of the remains that would suggest cultivation, and all but the parsnip could have been collected from the wild in a suitable form if the occupants of the Roman site were indeed eating them. The apple from Pit 17 is perhaps the most likely of the above remains to have reached the deposit as a result of deliberate human activity. *M. sylvestris* ssp. *sylvestris* (crab apple) is common in coppices on the Oxford clay near the site at present. While parsnip in the wild is not of much use, it is claimed that parsnips of a very large size can be produced by growing wild parsnip in good soil and by selecting seed from the larger rooted individuals over a period of about ten years (Mabey 1975, 63).

There is just as great a range of species from the Roman period as the Iron Age which fall into the group of plants which are unlikely to have been cultivated or collected but which could conceivably be of use to man (see p115). There is nothing about the nature of the remains that would suggest any of them had been so used.

Trees, shrubs, and thorn hedges

It has already been stated that tree pollen was low in frequency in the Roman samples, but macroscopic remains of woody species were not uncommon and, combined with the evidence from the insect remains, suggested that possibly there were thorn hedges on the Roman site. Whereas there is only a single piece of *Prunus* wood from an Iron Age sample, those Roman features from which the wood was examined contained many pieces. In addition all the Roman deposits contained thorny twigs of the blackthorn/hawthorn *(Prunus spinosa/Crataegus)* type. There was one Iron Age sample which contained seeds of *Crataegus* sp. (hawthorn) and *Rosa* (rose) prickles whilst another contained bud scales, leaf abscision pads, and thorny twigs. As can be seen from Table 6 seeds of *Crataegus* sp., *Fraxinus excelsior* (ash), *P. spinosa Rosa* sp. occurred in several of the Roman deposits. Table 9 shows that bud scales and leaf abscision pads were present in the majority of the Roman samples whilst there were *Rosa* prickles in several. A single specimen of *Anisandrus* sp. is the only beetle from an Iron Age sample which does not invade structural timbers but attacks living or recently dead wood with the bark in place. There are 23 individuals of six species limited to such a food source from the Roman samples: the Scolytidae, the Cerambycidae, and *Acales turbatus* (Hickin 1963, 50; 1975, 251-5, 292, 301: Hoffman 1958, 1389). In addition there are some species only from the Roman samples such as *Pyrochroa serraticornis* and *Melanotus rufipes* which attack very rotten wood, and others such as *Chalcoides* sp. and *Rhynchites caeruleus* which tend to eat leaves of trees or shrubs. Some of these beetles are confined to trees or shrubs other than those belonging to the Rosaceae (Hickin 1975, 251-5, 301) and there were a few pieces of non-rosaceous wood in the Roman samples.

Unlike in the Iron Age, therefore, there seems to be abundant evidence from the macroscopic remains for trees or shrubs, especially those belonging to the family Rosaceae, growing on the site in Roman times. The presence of such plants is also suggested by the ants and mites (see p123). Yet the evidence from the seeds and Coleoptera is for a mostly open environment and there is little evidence of trees or shrubs from the pollen. How can this be so? A possible explanation is as follows. The Rosaceae are insect-pollinated plants which do not cast much pollen to the wind and therefore are poorly represented in pollen analyses. There is evidence for the presence of trees from other families which are wind-pollinated but there is little pollen from them in the samples. Had the site become overgrown by scrub, much of it would probably have been *P. spinosa* and *Crataegus monogyna* initially, but other species would have established themselves after a while and would have contributed to the pollen rain, thereby presumably being evident from the pollen samples. There is nothing from the archaeological evidence to suggest that the site had been abandoned to scrub; indeed its occupation seems to have been at its most intensive during the late Roman period. If scrub was present, it would have to be a very artificial form in which only the rosaceous components were able to flower in quantity; in other words these results may possibly indicate the presence of thorn hedges. If there were *P. spinosa* (blackthorn) hedges there would have been all the evidence from the thorny twigs etc for the presence of woody species on the site without any tree pollen. Had there been some trees, for example *F. excelsior* (ash) established in the hedges, they would have provided suitable habitats for some of the boring beetles but the frequent cutting or the occasional pollarding could have prevented them from producing much pollen.

The Roman economy of Farmoor perhaps included trees managed for their wood. The *Quercus* (oak) uprights of Well 1060 may have grown under coppice conditions and in the same well was part of a large coppice stool, probably oak, from which about 10 poles had been cut (see p81). There is no way of telling whether there were deliberately coppiced trees present in hedges on the site or managed woodland elsewhere from which supplies were obtained. The pollen evidence does not suggest the presence of woodland in the area nearby.

Timber-feeding beetles

In the Roman period there was a large rise in the number of beetles which are capable of invading structural timbers as well as dead wood in the wild compared with the Iron Age. All but one of the Roman samples contained specimens of *Anobium punctatum*, giving a total of 56 as opposed to 3 from the Iron Age samples which also contained 2 specimens of *Lyctus fuscus*, a beetle of not too dissimilar habits. *A. punctatum* may have been living in dead wood in the Roman hedges along with *Acales turbatus,* which seems to be recorded most frequently from hedges (eg Walker 1911, 10), but unlike *A. turbatus, A. punctatum* can and commonly does infest woodwork in buildings (hence its common name of the furniture beetle). The worked pieces of wood (see p59) suggest that its domestic habitat may also have been present.

Synanthropic species of beetles

The other group of beetles, apart from those associated with wood or trees, which are present in number from the Roman but not the Iron Age samples are the synanthropic species. The following species are regarded as falling under this heading: *Stegobium paniceum; Tipnus unicolor; Ptinus fur; Mycetophagus quadriguttatus; Typhaea stercorea;* and *Tenebrio molitor.* All but *S. paniceum* certainly have habitats in this country away from human influence, a particular favourite being birds' nests. Even *S. paniceum* has been caught in circumstances which would suggest that it is capable of leading an independent existence (Allen 1965, 115). Perhaps the grouping might be thought rather arbitrary because many of the other beetles in the species list are ones which benefit from special localized habitats created by man, *(eg A. punctatum)* but all the same it is useful. All these synanthropic species are, or have been regarded as, pests of stored farinaceous materials, although some in fact feed on fungi which have infested the stored food rather than the food itself such as *T. stercorea* (Green 1952). The presence of all these species in Pit 17 is presumably related to the presence of so much spelt wheat chaff. *T. unicolor, P. fur,* and *M. quadriguttatus* were found in debris in the corners of an old mill at Cothill, Oxon (Walker 1916), and all the other species are known from granary refuse or flour. Only three of the above species occurred in the other samples, *T. stercorea, S. paniceum,* and *P. fur.* Of these three, only *S. paniceum* is more commonly found in grain or stored foods than in other habitats, and there is a single specimen of it from Well 1046. *P. fur* occurred in some numbers from all but two of the Roman samples and is

omnivorous on rather dry decaying animal and vegetable matter (Hinton 1940-41, 368) including straw and hay waste (Horion 1961, 265). *T. stercorea* is similarly often associated with straw and hay waste (Horion 1961 68). It is quite possible that the last two species were occurring in thatch or haystacks on the site.

Even though these six synanthropic species were not present in the Iron Age samples at all, their numbers must be regarded as rather low when compared with some Roman town sites. In particular the numbers of those species which are most often found infesting grain are low and none of the species seem to be obligate grain beetles. As a comparison, beetle faunas from Roman York can be entirely dominated by grain beetles (Kenwood, pers comm). These results would suggest that while there may have been more grain stored on the site or more cereal refuse present than in Iron Age times, it was not present at Farmoor in anything like the quantity that it was in some of the Roman towns. Even Sample 17/4 only had three individuals of two species *(S. paniceum* and *T. molitor)* which can be regarded as grain beetles. The presence of *P. fur* in most of the samples might suggest that there was rather more relatively dry decaying plant debris present on the site than in Iron Age times, though the presence of thatched buildings would provide a suitable habitat.

Grassland beetles

All the other ecological groups of Coleoptera from the Roman samples were also present in the Iron Age deposits, with quite a tendency for the same groups of species to be numerous from both sets of samples. As before there are the weevils which feed on grassland plants (eg *Gymnetron pascuorum* on *Plantago lanceolata* (ribwort plantain), and *Sitona* spp. mostly on *Trifolium* spp. (clovers)). There is a group belonging to the genus *Apion* which feed on *Vicia* and *Lathyrus* spp. (vetches) from Well 1060 and many of the unidentified species of *Apion* from that deposit also feed on Papilionaeceae. It is interesting that the only two samples (17/4 and 1060/2) to contain fragments of seed pods which matched *Vicia cracca* (tufted vetch) were the only two to contain the beetle *Apion craccae,* the larvae of which seem to be confined to that species of vetch (Hoffman 1958, 1480-1). They were also the only two samples with specimens of Bruchidae, which often feed on vetch seeds. The Roman samples were the only ones to contain elaterids of the genus *Athous.* Their larvae are especially common on the roots of grassland plants but the adults often occur on flowering shrubs, a requirement perhaps met by the suggested hedges, though it is not known how essential adult feeding is to the beetle (see *Phyllopertha horticola* p117). The grassland beetles from the Roman period seem to have a greater meadowland element than those from the Iron Age samples, but they cannot be used to infer the presence of extensive haymeadows. Some of the tall vetches, eg *Vicia cracca,* could have been scrambling up shrubs in hedges rather than climbing up long grass.

Dung beetles

The large group of dung beetles belonging to the genus *Aphodius* was as evident from the Roman samples as it was in the Iron Age. The plants do not provide such good evidence for pasture as they did in the Iron Age, but it would be safe to say from the beetles that there was much dung of large herbivores in the form of cow pats etc. around the Roman site and therefore, presumably, grazed pasture.

Insects of disturbed ground

The same species of large carabids which tend to prefer soil without too much vegetation at ground level to hinder their movements *(Nebria brevicollis, Pterostichus melanarius* and *Harpalus rufipes)* were present in reasonable numbers, but as stated for the Iron Age (p117) they cannot be used by themselves as indicators of bare or disturbed ground. There are, however, many phytophagous beetles which feed on weeds of disturbed ground, such as *Chaetocnema concinna* mostly on *Polygonum aviculare* (knotgrass), and *Ceuthorhynchus pollinarius* on *Urtica dioica* (stinging nettle). There are also some heteropteran bugs (listed in Table 14) from the Roman samples which feed on weeds of disturbed ground, such as *Sehirus bicolor* which feeds on *Lamium album* (white deadnettle) and *Baollota nigra* (black horehound). Seeds from all these weeds are present. The bug *Heterogaster urticae,* which is given as feeding on *U. dioica* (stinging nettle) but occasionally feeds on other plants (Southwood and Leston 1959, 79; Kenward pers comm), was represented by 2 individuals from the Iron Age samples, but by 29 from the Roman samples which correlates well with the larger number of *U. dioica* seeds from the Roman deposits.

Marsh and aquatic beetles

There is as wide a range of marsh and aquatic beetles from the Roman samples as from the Iron Age. Probably a marshy area with some flow of water through, it had reestablished itself on the floodplain at the edge of the gravel terrace, despite the cut-off river channel being filled in with alluvium to the level of the rest of the floodplain. This was probably the origin of the peat deposit which built up over the droveway in this wet area (Sample 1072). Most of the beetles are aquatics which would have lived in the shallow water here, phytophagous species which would have fed on the plants growing out of the water, and marsh species from the water's edge. The aquatic beetles are all species of slowly moving to stagnant water, eg *Hygrotus inaequalis* and *Colymbetes fuscus.* The seeds have already indicated a wealth of marsh and aquatic plants and there is a suitable range of beetles which could have fed on them (eg *Plateumaris affinis* on *Iris pseudacorus* (yellow flag) and *Carex* spp. (sedges); *Chrysolina polita* on *Mentha aquatica* (water mint), *Lycopus europaeus* (gypsy wort) and other species; and *Limnobaris pilistriata* on *Schoenoplectus* (bullrush) and other aquatic Cyperaceae). The species from the marshy water's edge include *Elaphrus cupreus* and *Pterostichus anthracinus.*

Good evidence is afforded for this marshy area, possibly with water flowing through it continuing eastwards along the edge of the gravel terrace. Samples 43/10 and 17/4 have a range of bankside and marsh species which tend to be absent from Wells 1060 and 1046 further onto the gravel terrace. There is a wide range of Carabidae from marsh or bankside habitats including *Blethisa multipunctata, Pterostichus vernalis, P. nigrita, Agonum* spp., and a number of Bembidiini. Some of them, such as *Bembidion assimile* or *clarki* and *Agonum viduum* (Lindroth 1974, 58, 84), suggest that there was rich vegetation at the water's edge. The phytophagous beetles again indicate what some of this vegetation was composed of, eg *Prasocuris phellandri* on aquatic Umbelliferae; *Apthona coerulea* on *Iris pseudacorus* (yellow flag) and *Notaris acridulus* which could have been feeding on *Glyceria maxima* (reedgrass) in a reedswamp, or *Eleocharis* spp. growing in shallow water

or a marshy grassland.

There are about ten species of aquatic beetles from the Roman wells and pits: while some may have been living in the water at the bottom of them (eg the 17 *Hydraena testacea* from Sample 1060/2), each species must have come in from an aquatic habitat elsewhere. None of the species requires clean flowing water or large expanses of water and all could have had their origin in the stream along the edge of the gravel terrace. However, many water beetles fly readily and could in any case have come from some miles away.

The same species of Staphylinidae which often occur on wet mud or in decaying vegetation at the edge of water (eg *Platystethus cornutus*) were present as in the Iron Age. No doubt they found suitable habitats in rubbish dumped on the marshy ground at the edge of the gravel terrace, as well as in the vegetation there as it decayed and any exposed mud at the edge of the water.

Beetles of decaying plant material

General 'filth' species (eg *Cercyon* spp. and *Philonthus* spp.) formed a significant part of the Roman fauna. Presumably some lived along with the *Aphodius* species in dung on the field and others were present in manure or rubbish heaps in the yards of the settlement itself. There are also those 'filth' species which tend to be confined to rotting plant remains, eg compost heaps, that were present in the Iron Age (see p117).

Other habitats

There are some beetles from the Roman samples which occur in habitats which have not been mentioned above (eg *Silpha obscura*, a carrion beetle), but none were found in sufficient numbers for there to be anything unusual about their presence. Many of the beetles from Farmoor from both Iron Age and Roman deposits can occur in woodland, but only from the Roman samples are there species which usually occur in it (though even so, they are by no means confined to such a habitat), eg *Leistus spinibarbis* (Lindroth 1974, 26), *Choleva* or *Catops* spp., and *Phosphuga atrata*. It is quite possible that they were able to find suitable places too in the bottoms of the hedges which are believed to have been present on the site.

Ants and mites

It is for the Roman period that the Formicidae and Acari make a useful contribution. The most numerous of the ants is *Stenamma westwoodi*, which, with a total of 46 individuals, occurred in all but one of the Roman samples. It nests under large stones or amongst the roots of trees in shady woodland or hedgerows (Boulton and Collingwood 1975, 22). Several of the other species which were represented by workers nest in old tree stumps, hedges, etc., and the impression given by the ants is of an environment with many trees, since large stones were notably absent from the site.

Similarly, a large proportion of the mites from Wells 1060 and 43 were species associated with trees, many living on tree trunks (see p106). According to what habitat information there is, they are indeed restricted to trees. Grassland mites may be under represented from these two samples because small enough sieves were not used (see p106) but the tree species still must have been present in some numbers.

It is possible that the apparent discrepancy of the ants

and mites from some of the other evidence is due to different dispersive powers. Mites tend to be animals of fairly limited movement, and the worker ants would tend to forage quite near to their colonies. If there were a few trees close to some of the Roman wells it is possible that they would have had their faunas of mites' and ants' nests at their roots. With their poorer dispersive powers than some of the other groups there would be less of a tendency for their numbers to be diluted in the deposits by species from elsewhere. It has already been suggested that there may have been a plum tree very close to Well 1060 (see p120): possibly it had a colony of *Stenamma westwoodi* at its roots and mites on its branches. Nor should the evidence from the mites and ants be seen as conflicting with that from the pollen; pollen shows the overall environment to be open and without those wind-pollinated trees that produce pollen which is preserved in quantity, while the ants and mites show that trees or bushes were at least locally present. This would be in agreement with the evidence for a hedged landscape which has been given above (p121).

The other ants and mites fit in with the results interpreted from the other evidence without any problems. For instance the mites from Sample 17/4, the threshing debris, are mostly those which tend to live in decaying plant remains and have been found in crop refuse (see p106).

The single female head capsule of *Formica rufa*, the wood ant, is interesting because it is a true woodland species. Being a female, it would have had wings and could have flown from a great distance away. It used to be common around Tubney and Appleton, about 2 miles (3.2 km) to the south of the site, but now the nearest colony is 14 miles (22.5km) away at Shabbington Wood (information from Mr C O'Toole).

The Iron Age and Roman soils

The surviving soils

Some of the plants and insects from the site are rather specific about the sort of soils on which they occur, and it is worth combining this evidence with that from the surviving soils. The only soil which could be shown stratigraphically to be pre-Iron Age on the gravel terrace itself was a fine reddish-yellow silty loam which remained in a few hollows in the limestone gravel of Area II. It was not generally distributed. No Roman ground surface survived. The topsoil of the gravel terrace was a brown sandy clay loam. Along the edge of the terrace it contained very much more clay, and it was also clayey to the south, where it overlay a clay colluvial deposit presumably derived from the Oxford Clay of Cumnor Hill. In some places in the centre of the gravel terrace a layer of sand was present on the surface of the gravel and then the soil was much deeper and sandier, being a sandy loam. Where the soil overlay clay or sand, a layer of calcium carbonate had precipitated at depth. The topsoil of the gravel terrace was generally quite well drained and had been subjected to ploughing. It probably corresponded to the Badsey Series given by Jarvis (1973, 174-80).

The soil through which some of the Iron Age features were cut on the floodplain varied from a thin layer of yellow clay (enclosure group 2) to a yellow sandy silt (enclosure group 3). As has been described above (p70) the soil had been stripped to the gravel in much of enclosure group 3. During the Iron Age a gleyed grey alluvial clay built up over the stripped area. After the Iron Age sites had been abandoned, a considerable quantity of

alluvium, a grey-buff gleyed clay, was deposited in some areas (p25). The Roman floodplain soil is thus likely in places to have been well above the Iron Age level. The rate of deposition slowed, with a dark grey-brown humic clay loam forming the modern topsoil. It was poorly drained and showed no signs of ever having been ploughed. It corresponded to the Thames Series of Jarvis (1973, 181-2).

No pH measurements of the soils were taken because of the danger that they had subsequently changed, especially those sealed in waterlogged anaerobic conditions. It is from the biological remains that this information must be inferred.

The Iron Age soils

The majority of the Iron Age seeds are from plants of neutral to basic soils or those which show little preference at all. One of the plants typical of calcareous grassland is *Linum catharticum*, seeds of which are common in several of the samples. These are the plants that would be expected on the floodplain, because of its thin soil covering over calcareous gravel and flooding by the basic waters of the Thames which has a pH of about 8 (Baker 1937, 412). There are, however, a few seeds from plants which normally live in acid soils. The single seed of *Spergula arvensis* (corn spurrey) which is a calcifuge weed common on light sandy soils (New 1961, 206) could have been brought to the site by flooding. Another species, *Scleranthus annus*, which is more common on acid soils is by no means absent from those with calcium carbonate (Salisbury 1961, 248). *Montia fontana* (blinks), however, presents rather more of a problem. It is present from five of the Iron Age samples and it is a plant of water and wet places on acid soils (Clapham *et. al*, 1962, 267-9). It is always possible that it was growing at the edge of streams on the acid sands further upriver and had been deposited by flooding, but it does occur in all but one of the Iron Age samples.

There is a chance that acidic conditions could have existed in some areas in the floodplain. The pre-Iron Age soil in the region of enclosure group 3 was calcareous, containing some limestone gravel and fragments of molluscan shell in quite good condition. Column Samples IV in the pre-Iron Age ground surface at enclosure group 2 did not contain any molluscan remains and, on testing with hydrochloric acid, the gravel remaining in the sieves proved not to be calcium carbonate. On one area of Port Meadow where the limestone gravel has a covering of alluvium, the soil has been leached and there is a pH of 6.6-6.8 near the surface. This has occurred because it is an area which does not flood very frequently and the water table is lower than the southern area where the flood waters remain longest. (The pH at the surface of the southern area is 7.7-7.9 (Baker 1937, 413)). Enclosure group 2 was on one of the highest places on the Iron Age floodplain at Farmoor. If such locally non-basic areas existed, perhaps some of the plants with calcifuge tendencies could have lived on them.

Another plant of interest relating to the Iron Age soils is *Hydrocotyle vulgaris* (pennywort). In the Oxford district it is described as being confined to central wet swamps, tending to boggy conditions (Church 1925b, 9). It often occurs on peat and possibly peat was building up in some places in the cut-off river channel in the way that it did in Roman times over the north end of the droveway (see p119). The Roman peat became acidic enough below the surface to soften the limestone gravel to the consistency of cheese.

The Iron Age seeds from the floodplain samples

included plants from both wet clayey soils and better drained sands (see p113). This has been explained as perhaps due to the stripping of topsoil by man in some places (notably enclosure group 3) to leave a relatively sandy layer on top of the gravel which with the probably low water table in the summer would create suitable well-drained sandy localities.

The presence of Mollusca including *Pomatias elegans* in the ditch of the Area II enclosure group (Column Sample I) has been taken to indicate a basic soil on the gravel terrace during the Iron Age. *P. elegans* only occurs on the most calcareous of soils (Boycott 1934, 29).

None of the Iron Age Coleoptera from Farmoor are associated with acid soils. A number, such as *Bembidion properans* (Lindroth 1974, 54), tend only to occur on rather clayey soils. There are also a few from sandy soils, eg *Serica brunnea* (Britton 1956, 13), but these need not have lived on the site (see *Crypticus quisquilius*, p118).

The Roman soils

The Roman soil on the floodplain would have been a varying depth of alluvial clay or clay loam over the gravel. Above enclosure group 3 it would probably have been at least 0.5 m deep, probably more, and must have been basic because it contained many molluscan shells. Over enclosure group 2 it would only have been 0.3m thick and might not have been very calcareous because of the absence of Mollusca from Sample Column IV.

There are no Roman seeds from plants of acid ground. All are from plants of neutral to basic soils or show little preference. The seeds of wet grassland and marsh plants tended to be confined to those Roman deposits along the edge of the gravel terrace with the floodplain (see p118). This would be in agreement with the modern soil at Farmoor being more clayey and wetter along the edge of the gravel as it sloped down to the floodplain. It is also of interest that waterlogged seeds of *Tripleurospermum maritimum* (scentless mayweed) only occurred in the two wells furthest on the gravel terrace, whilst waterlogged *Anthemis cotula* (stinking mayweed) seeds were only present in two samples, both close to the edge of the gravel. (The specimens in Sample 17/4 could easily have been transported along with the cereal remains from wherever the arable fields were.) *A. cotula* occurs most often on heavy base-rich clay soils and it is not uncommon for a heavy soil on which the plant is abundant to be replaced a few metres away by a light soil with no *A. cotula*. It is sometimes replaced by *T. maritimum* on lighter soils (Kay 1971, 625).

The Coleoptera include species of both clay and sandy soils. Several of the species of *Bembidion* normally occur on clay soils, as does *Agonum muelleri*. The species of sandy soils include *Synuchus nivalis, Olisthopus rotundatus* and *Aphodius equestris* (Britton 1956, 16: Lindroth 1974, 80, 83).

One species of beetle which was present in two Roman and one Iron Age samples is *Brachinus crepitans*. Several specimens were found from another Roman site on the Thames gravels at Appleford (Robinson in Hinchliffe, forthcoming). It is usually found on chalkland (eg Lindroth 1974, 134) but the finds seem too frequent to regard it merely as a stray like *Homoloplia ruricola* (see p111). It is, however, by no means unknown on other soils (Allen 1947).

The environment and man at Farmoor

So far, the activities of man have only been considered in so far as they affect the environment. These ranged from the clearance of woodland and the maintenance of an open landscape to agricultural practices which resulted in *Agrostemma githago* growing as a cornfield weed and being brought to the site. The environments thus indicated combined with the archaeological evidence, however, give considerable information as to how man used the area and what his activies were on the site at different times.

The Iron Age (Phases I and II)

Phase I
Very little is know about the earliest Iron Age environment other than that the site was inhabited and that its occupants dug pits on the gravel terrace (see p111).

Seasonal occupation (Phase II)
The most striking aspect about the later Iron Age settlements is that those on the floodplain were suffering flooding *at the time when they were in use*. This can only imply that they were being occupied seasonally. The Iron Age enclosure complexes could have been situated on the gravel terrace nearby where they would have been above the normal winter flood level, yet one of the complexes was as close to the gravel terrace as it could be without being upon it. This shows that the occupants were not concerned by the prospect of flooding. However, the resource which the floodplain had to offer, the grassland, would have only been available in the late spring, summer and early autumn. Summer floods do occasionally occur after heavy rainfall at present (the farmer on the other side of the river recalled to me how his hay bales were washed away one year). Perhaps this disadvantage was outweighed by the soil of the floodplain containing much more clay and being more consolidated than that on the gravel terrace. If the houses were of turf or clay block construction, considerably better building materials would have ben available on the floodplain. Elsewhere in this report it is described how the soil had been stripped to the gravel around one of the enclosure complexes in Iron Age times and how an experimental hut was rapidly built out of clay blocks (p70).

The evidence from the weed seeds suggest that the hut sites on the floodplain were not in use for many years (p114). Probably after about five years, some of the perennial weeds would have been represented in high numbers, but it may have been longer. This is a point which requires experimental verification. The recutting of all the gullies could have occurred in a single year if it had been wet and animals were confined in the enclosures, or they could have been cleared out annually. This evidence for short-term occupation is rather what might be expected, if the structures survived reasonably intact after mild floods and were worth repairing until worse flooding one year caused more severe damage. Then it might have been easier to rebuild elsewhere.

The use of the grassland (Phase II)
It has been suggested that the attraction of the floodplain to man was its grassland. The advantage that floodplain grassland has over other grassland in the area is that its high water table enables the grass to continue growing throughout the summer and not become parched. If the grass is being mown for hay this means that it is possible to make two cuttings per year, one at about the end of June and the other in about mid-September. The first crop is normally better than the second, but should there be late spring flooding which would spoil the first cut, the second is improved. The winter flooding might mean that grass

starts growing on the floodplain later than in other localities but it will have its nutrients replenished from the river (Church 1922, 70; 1925a, 66-7; 1925b, 13). The alluvial grassland need not have two hay crops taken from it; a mowing can be made in June and then the aftermath grazed until the winter as is the practice on Pixey and Oxey Meads at present. Alternatively it can be permanent pasture as Port Meadow is, or left for hay some years and grazed others, as Magdalen Meadow used to be.

The botanical and entomological evidence from the floodplain enclosure complexes indicates pastureland, but this need not mean that the whole floodplain was always grazed (see p112). The main advantage of using the floodplain for pasture is that the grass would be growing throughout the summer unless it was exceptionally dry, whereas, on the gravels, for example, growth normally ceases for part of the summer. It might be better to use the gravels for the haycrop, leave them through the summer to recover and then graze them in the winter. This explanation is rather too simple, though, because there are other soils in the area, all with their own characteristics, and the Iron Age farming policy would have taken them all into account.

Unfortunately, dung beetles tend not to be confined to the dung of a particular large herbivore, so that they are no use in establishing what animals were grazing the floodplain pasture. The animal bones obviously reflect what was being eaten on the site rather than what was grazing there. However there does seem to be a trend when comparing Iron Age sites in the Thames Valley for cattle bones to predominate, with the proportion of sheep bones becoming lower as the sites become wetter. Farmoor shows the extreme of this trend so far. Horse bones were rather more prevalent at Farmoor than on these other sites (see p133). This trend follows the suitabilities of the various sites to the different animals.

Whatever animals were kept at Farmoor, conditions on the floodplain would not have been very suitable for sheep. The snail *Lymnaea truncatula* which carries the sheep liver fluke was present in several of the enclosure gullies and also Layer 1172 inside enclosure 3.

The use of Phase II enclosures

If the most perfect circle in each of the enclosure complexes is interpreted as the hut site, the others might have been compounds into which cattle could have been herded (although the gullies would have to have been combined with some other sort of structure to make them animal proof). Each enclosure in group I had its own sump and therefore water supply which would fit the suggestion that they were used for animals. The dung beetles support such an interpretation.

Some of the possible uses of these enclosures have been considered elsewhere (p71). The only one worth mentioning here is their use for temporary haystacks. All that can be said is that although the beetle fauna included some species of rotting vegetation which are often found in haystack bottoms, by no means all the sort of species which would be expected were present. The species of rotting vegetation tended to be those of wet habitats. Numbers of the Lathridiidae, one family which could be expected in quantity from a haystack, are low and those synanthropic species of rather dry decaying vegetation which normally abound in haystacks, eg *Typhaea stercorea,* are absent. Still, the suggestion is for a temporary hay collecting site and it would take time for an appropriate beetle fauna to develop. Seeds found from haymeadow plants are extremely few, but the hay is ready for cutting before the seeds of most of them would have matured, and it deteriorates if left standing longer. The problem of haystacks is therefore left unsolved.

Other possible activities of man in the Middle Iron Age

It seems unlikely that occupants of the floodplain sites were practising much arable agriculture themselves. There was no evidence which would suggest it and the floodplain itself would be unsuitable. If there were arable fields nearby on the gravel terrace it would seem slightly strange to live on the floodplain. However, as will be seen for the Roman period, while it is very easy to demonstrate that a community used grain, it is almost impossible to prove that it was grown nearby unless the physical remains of the arable fields themselves survive.

The only other biological evidence of relevance to the way in which man used Farmoor in the Iron Age is rather negative. There is nothing to suggest that the land had in any way been enclosed by hedges, which is consistent with the lack of any field system ditches. Compared with the Roman period there are few beetles of the sort which can be common about human habitations infesting the timbers, thatch, and stored foods. Indeed, the impression tends to be gained that, other than the maintenance of grassland by preventing woodland from regenerating, Iron Age Man's impact on the environment at Farmoor was rather slight. The enclosure complexes were merely temporary islands, with their disturbed ground and quantities of decaying organic material in a sea of grassland.

The alluvial deposit and man

It is not possible to link the Iron Age abandonment of the floodplain sites to whatever change in the river regime caused the sudden deposition of a considerable quantity of alluvium. It might, however, be possible to link this deposit sediment with the activities of man. Its presence is by no means unique. Iron Age pottery was found at Wallingford and Bray under a layer of alluvium by the Thames *(Berkshire Archaeol J* 1960, 55-9) as was a Beaker burial in Oxford (NJ Palmer, pers comm). Perhaps a change in agricultural practice was responsible for extensive alluvial deposition in the Upper Thames Valley during the Iron Age. It has been suggested that soil erosion following large-scale clearance and arable agriculture was reponsible for a sudden change in the type of alluvium being deposited in the lower Severn-Avon valley at about 600 BC (Shotton 1978). Clearance could result in a more rapid run-off of water from the ground. If more extensive clearance at the end of the Bronze Age or early Iron Age were combined with the introduction of winter-sown cereals (thus causing the soil surface to be left bare and unconsolidated by stubble over the winter), the subsequent erosion may have resulted in considerable alluvial deposition on river floodplains (S Limbrey, pers comm.)

The Roman site (Phase III)

The Roman use of the site was rather different from the Iron Age. The settlement was confined to the gravel terrace and was of a much more permanent nature. Even so, there is evidence that the edge of it might have suffered occasional flooding, so it might not have been a very comfortable place to live in the winter. Neither the archaeological nor the biological evidence can show whether the site was occupied all the year round, but purely from its layout, siting, and permanence it seems likely that it was.

The biological evidence suggesting thorn hedges in the Roman period (but not the Iron Age) agrees very well with archaeological evidence for the presence of Roman, but not Iron Age, field ditches. The division of the gravel terrace into small hedged fields implies a more intensive use of the land and probably a much more varied use, especially as neighbouring fields could have been managed in completely different ways (making the biological evidence from them much more difficult to interpret).

Grassland

The function of the Roman site is likely to have been at least partly the same as in the Iron Age: the exploitation of the alluvial grassland, for it was to the floodplain which the droveway led. No real idea can be gained of what sort of grassland it was because the nearest evidence is from the edge of the gravel terrace. One can speculate as to whether the hay scythe (p61) had been discarded, broken, where the droveway met the floodplain on the way back from mowing. Pasture and perhaps haymeadow were present on the gravel terrace, but apart from the scythe the evidence for hay growing is very tentative (p118).

Arable

There is considerably more evidence for the involvement of the settlement in arable agriculture, but its location is problematic. The products of arable farming could equally well have been brought a considerable distance to the site as grown on it. Threshing was not an activity which could be carried out in the fields because spelt wheat requires parching over a corndrier to release the grains. Cereal straw would also have had many uses on a habitation site. Evidence from pollen is not a reliable indication of nearby cereal cultivation because, as has been shown (p143), cereal pollen can become enclosed in quantity within the bracts of hulled cereals. The beetle fauna of an arable field is rather different from that of an ordinary piece of disturbed ground. Both have a large population of big carabid ground beetles, but the latter will have a much wider range of phytophagous species feeding on the greater number and variety of weeds. Unfortunately, though, the beetle remains in the samples are from many different habitats including weedy ground so the presence of arable crops would not be noticed. All likely pest species on growing crops would also be able to feed on wild species.

The corndriers and wheat chaff show that the site was probably involved in processing grain in some quantity, but it need not have been any more than the grain supply for the settlement itself. The Roman period was a time when cereals would have provided man with his main source of carbohydrate, so consumption would have been high. If the grain were only for consumption on site the inhabitants of Farmoor might not need to be growing at all. They could have been bringing in hulled grain and processing it themselves. Unknown economic factors would determine whether it was better for the people to use the site for pastoral or arable farming and, if it were used primarily for pastoral, whether it was worth also growing grain for their own consumption.

There is some danger that because arable agriculture cannot be proved to have taken place on the site, it will be assumed that it did not. The first gravel terrace is perfectly suitable for growing cereals and part of the area could easily have been given over to arable. The small fields lining the droveway seem unlikely to have been for arable because of the pits and wells, but this does not exclude the presence of more open arable land behind and between these paddocks and yards.

Apart from the gravel, the nearest soil as easily cultivated is on the Corallian limestone on the tops of Wytham and Cumnor hills. It is not unreasonable to assume that the territory of the Farmoor settlement extended that far, thereby providing the settlement with land other than the gravel terrace which was suitable for

arable. (It would seem rather perverse to be ploughing the difficult Oxford Clay when the gravels had not been taken into cultivation as well.) There is just not sufficient evidence.

Gardens?

It is quite possible that some of the small ditched fields were not paddocks or corn plots but gardens for the cultivation of fruit and vegetables. There is evidence from Well 1060 which might suggest that a plum tree grew close to it, but unfortunately there is no evidence for the cultivation of any other fruit, vegetables or herbs. Indeed, most of the plants which fall into these categories for which seeds were found need not have been cultivated or used by man at all (see p121). Apart from the cereals and the plums only flax *(Linum usitatissimum)*, dill *(Anethum graveolens)*, and coriander *(Coriandrum sativum)* are species which, if they were not cultivated on the site, were probably brought to it for human consumption.

The best evidence for the use of part of the site as gardens is given by the presence of box leaves *(Buxus sempervirens)* in two of the Roman deposits. Box is a good hedging plant but bushes of it take a long time to grow and box hedges are not very animal proof. Box hedges were postulated for the Roman palace at Fishbourne (Cunliffe 1971, 128); evidence for them was found in the form of clippings from Winterton Roman Villa, Lincs (R Goodburn, pers comm), and from the town of Silchester (Reid 1903, 426; 1909, 485); but these are very different sorts of sites from Farmoor. Its occurrence at Farmoor ought not to be entirely surprising because there is enough modern evidence for people in very poor communities growing a few flowers as well as purely functional crops. There is no other evidence of ornamental plants at Farmoor, but given the species of shrubs and herbs represented by seeds, it would be possible to construct a very pretty garden with roses, ox-eye daisy, blue flax, and some of the other species present, all of them being grown for their flowers in modern English gardens. However, all these species could have, and almost certainly were, growing wild or cultivated as useful crops.

Disturbed ground

It is easy to envisage that the droveway, the ditch edges, and the areas around the settlement were disturbed ground on which weeds grew. Near the buildings there were probably farm yards with piles of manure or compost heaps of domestic rubbish in which filth beetles live, and neglected corners where greater celandine *(Chelidonium majus)* and elder *(Sambucus nigra)* grew.

Possible buildings

There is plenty of archaeological evidence in the form of the domestic rubbish and stone lined wells that people lived on the site, but very little evidence as to what they lived in. There is room for debate as to whether the penannular gully (F5) and F7 represent a circular hut or merely a stockade (see p73) and this point is still disputed between the two authors of this report. Otherwise there is only part of an oak tenon joint from one of the wells (which could have been from a structural timber) and some burnt daub. The Coleoptera give a much stronger indication of human occupation on the site than in the Iron Age with more synanthropic and wood-boring species. It would be easy to imagine wooden houses and barns with thatched roofs which left no other trace apart from the beetles which infested their woodwork and those which ate the decaying thatch and the few grains of cereal that remained in the ear on it. However, the beetles would be equally happy living in dead wood in the hedges, in the cereal refuse in Pit 17, and in haystacks. The biological evidence remains as inconclusive as the archaeological evidence, although there must have been some reason for the increased numbers of synanthropic beetles compared with the Iron Age.

Other activities

The animal bones, as well as reflecting eating habits, suggest that the occupants of the site may have performed ritual practices with horses (see p130). The presence of oyster shells in some of the Roman features (p133) emphasizes that not all the meat which was eaten came from animals that lived at Farmoor. Apart from this the only other biological evidence for human activity is that concerning timber. Both reasonably substantial timbers and coppice poles were used on the site but there is no evidence as to where they might have been obtained from.

Later uses of the site

Human activity on the site in the Saxon period is unknown and there are no remains which suggest that it was ever inhabited subsequently. Traces of ridge and furrow show that the gravel terrace was ploughed in the medieval period, but the floodplain presumably remained grassland, although further down the river (at Grid ref SP 443083) what are apparently arable ridges extend onto the floodplain. They do not seem to be water meadow ridges. Presumably they are a result of the same pressures which caused the rather difficult Oxford Clay to be ploughed in medieval times. After enclosure until the construction of the reservoir the gravel terrace was used for mixed farming. The floodplain, although drained, remained as open grassland in the form of Cumnor Mead and was only divided relatively recently. The permanence of the grassland on the floodplain, probably for hundreds of years, is shown by the fact that fritillaries (*Fritillaria meleagris* L). used to grow on it until they were destroyed by the construction of the first reservoir in 1962 (information from a villager). These flowers, once so common in the Thameside meadows, which were 'hunted over by children for the first snake-heads' even in the first quarter of this century (Church 1925a, 34), have all but disappeared. They are very sensitive to changes in grassland management and 'improvements'.

The vertebrates
by Bob Wilson with a section by Don Bramwell

Methods and results

The Farmoor bones are moderately well preserved but

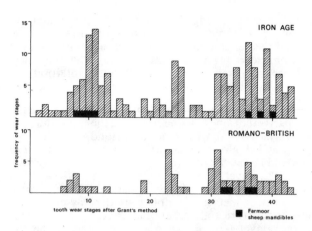

Fig 38   Comparison of Farmoor sheep mandibles with Abingdon age data

badly fragmented. 590 bones or their reunited portions (if newly broken) were identified of some 1460 remains. In addition part skeletons of two horses, two sheep, and a dog were examined. 50-70% of the identified and 65-80% of the unidentified bones in the various feature groups were newly broken (cf Wilson in Parrington 1978). Consequently on this site, percentages of gnawed and burnt bone would not be reliable. Burnt bone is uncommon in the sample except from F15 and F1013. 'Weathering' appears related to the leaching of bones above the water table or their preservation below it.

Bone fragment numbers are given in Table 23 and minimum numbers of individuals (Chaplin 1971, 70-5) per species are given for some samples in Table 24. Areas I and II provide the most reliable samples. The frequencies and percentages of grouped skeletal elements were given in the Ashville report but the Romano-British sheep proportions are now augmented by material from F37: cranial debris 44-51%, limb extremities 13-25%, and other body bone 31-36% depending whether part skeletons are included or not (Wilson in Parrington 1978, Table 4).

Age data

Grouped age data are recorded in Table 25. Early fusing epiphyses include those fused in modern pigs by two years, in modern sheep, cattle and horses by one and a half years and in modern dogs by one year of age. The three part skeletons of sheep (F15, 34, and 37) would add 20 early fused and 11 late fused epiphyses to the Romano-British totals, the pelvic extremities in F15 not being counted in my epiphyseal record. The mandibles and epiphyses of the dog (F1054) and the horse skeletons were not included.

Table 23: Bone fragment and oyster shell frequency at Farmoor

| Species | Early Iron Age Pits | Mid Iron Age enclosures | | | | | IA Total | Romano-British | | RB Total |
	Area III	Area II	F1045 F1019	group 1	group 2	group 3		Area I	Area III	
cattle	19	20	5	15	16	14	89	134	70	204
sheep	18	21	2	5	7	16	69	90**	16	106**
pig	6	2	1	3	3	4	19	10	6	16
horse	3	14	-	3	7	9	36	11*	20	31*
red deer	2†	-	-	-	-	-	2†	2	2†	4†
dog	2*	3	-	-	-	2	7*	-	2	2
oyster	-	-	-	-	-	-	-	4	1	5
Total	50	60	8	26	33	45	222	251	117	368

* excluding part skeletons of sheep F15 (27) and F34 (43), dog F1054 (20) and horse F37   † excluding antler fragments except pedicles.

Species	Early Iron Age Pits	Mid Iron Age enclosures				IA Total	Romano-British	RB Total
	Area III	Area II	group 1	group 2	group 3		Area I	
cattle	3	2	2	2	3	8	4	7
sheep	2	3	1	2	2	7	4	4
pig	3	2	1	1	1	4	2	2
horse	1	2	1	2	2	3	5	8
red deer	1	-	-	-	-	1	1	1
dog	2	1	-	-	1	2	-	1
oyster	-	-	-	-	-	-	3	4
sample size (fragment no)	50†	60	26	33	45	222†	251†	368†

† Minimum numbers include considerations of part skeletons

Two other 'mature' mandibles, F15 and F37, could be added to the Romano-British tally. This additional material is listed to maintain a distinction between part skeletons and the usual bone scatter providing such data.

The age-staged sheep mandibles are compared (Fig 38) with the distributions from sites in Abingdon (Hamilton in Parrington 1978, 129) and the kill-off patterns may have been similar. Seasonal killing is a possibility in the Iron Age summer to winter period but ageing methods are not shown to be reliable as yet. Also lambing could have been in February-March (Higgs and White 1963) or as late as May as occurs in Soays at Butser Hill, Hampshire (P Reynolds, pers comm).

Red deer antlers

A large pedicle base and antler (c 200mm in circumference above the coronet) from an early Iron Age feature (F1053) indicates that the stag was killed between late summer and spring before antler loss in March. Two proximal tines and the main beam were sawn through, saw cuts being made from four or five sides in each case. Chopping has cut into the pedicle and also planed off part of the coronet. Parallel knife cuts occur in the midline of the frontal bones. Another broken antler tine from F1053 is sawn as above; both antler pieces appear to be waste. An antler strip (F1062) of the same period is sawn at both ends and trimmed flat.

Six antler fragments of varying size including two cast off bases occurred on the surface of the Roman droveway (L1075). One base has a circumference of 157 mm. Five tine points are worn and one seems burnt.

Articulated remains

Early Iron Age dog

From F1054, 20 bones of a dog were recovered. Epiphyseal fusion in the femur indicates that it was a mature animal and at least 1½ years of age (Silver 1969, 289). A tibia length of 180 mm gives an estimated shoulder height of 535 mm which lies within the 290-580 mm range calculated for Iron Age dogs (Harcourt 1974, Table 9).

The right distal humerus has an incompletely healed fracture line 18 mm in length from the medial to lateral edges of the articulation surface. From this, a second fracture crack to 1 mm wide runs proximally (Plate X). Unfortunately the radius and the ulna are missing and the extent of the elbow fracture is unknown. The humerus has healed without deformity.

Mid Iron Age horse skulls

From the southern butt end of F1100 parts of a cranium include well worn molar teeth. The squamosal is fused with the parietal and suggests that the horse was more than 12 years of age. Nicks and fine cuts occur around the orbit indicating skinning or meat removal. Tongue removal and separation of the mandibles is indicated by two fine cuts in front of the pterygoid hamulus.

From the northern butt end of F1100 there is a fragmented premaxilla and three permanent premolars. The incisors indicate an age of around five years, although

Table 25: Grouped age data

		Early and late fusing epiphyses f = fused, u = unfused (see text)									
		cattle		sheep		pig		horse		dog	
		f	u	f	u	f	u	f	u	f	u
Iron Age	early	21	2	4	-	-	2	8	-	-	-
	late	16	3	4	12	-	-	5	4	1	-
Romano-British	early	34	-	5	-	-	1	16	-	-	-
	late	21	2	4	2	-	-	2	1	-	-

		mature (m) and immature (i) mandibles (M3 in wear or not)									
		cattle		sheep		pig		horse		dog	
		m	i	m	i	m	i	m	i	m	i
Iron Age		-	1	4	5	2	3	3	-	1	-
Romano-British		2	1	4	-	1	-	1	-	1	-

Table 26: Bone measurements of the double horse burial (F37)

		upper horse (H1)			lower horse (H2)		
		TL (mm)	LL (mm)	HT (m)	TL (mm)	LL (mm)	HT (m)
femur (to top of head)	L	361	393 est	1.379	-	-	-
tibia	L	360	328	1.430	-	-	
metatarsal	L	272	266	1.417	287	277	1.476
	R	272	264	1.407	287	277	1.476
calcaneum	L	103	-	-	112	-	-
	R	104	-	-	-	-	-
1st phalanx	L	-	-	-	87	-	-
	R	78	-	-	87	-	-
2nd phalanx	both	46	-	-	50	-	-

by tooth wear this horse would be younger than 'horse 1' in the Roman double horse burial (see below). The presence of slightly worn canines indicates a male or castrate. Several knife cuts indicate skinning around the muzzle.

Romano-British double horse burial
(Fig 8, Pl V1)

Two partly dismembered horse skeletons lay one on top of the other in F37, a small round-bottomed pit to the east of the Romano-British gully (F5) in Area I. The entire front limbs, some sacral and all caudal vertebrae were missing from both skeletons and the uppermost skeleton lacked mandibles. Extensive damage to the bones is a result of soil leaching, recent fragmentation from the passage of earth-moving machinery, and the difficulties of removing the bones from the hard adhesive clayey fill of the feature.

The skull, backbone, and pelves of the lower horse, designated H2, lay in a reverse S across the pit (Fig 8). The left hind leg was dislocated at the hip and lay across the posterior rib cage. The right hind leg crossed above the left, the right hock lay outside the posterior rib cage, while the metatarsal was wedged between two vertebrae of the anterior rib cage.

Most of the backbone and ribs of the uppermost horse, H1, lay on their right side and against the anterior rib cage and above the neck vertebrae of H2. The backbone was bent and dislocated between the first lumbar and last thoracic vertebrae, and between the third and fourth last thoracic vertebrae. The skull and neck were separated from the thoracic portion of the spine and lay on their dorsal side and on top of the rib cage and the legs of H2. Dislocation occurred between the atlas and the axis. Both femur heads lay outside their pelvic sockets and with the spinal dislocations seem unlikely to have resulted from soil pressure alone. Both back legs of the upper horse, H1, were folded in the pit and lay on the skulls of both horses.

Age
The teeth best indicate an age of over five and under six years for H1 and four to four and a half years for H2 (Silver 1969, 293). In the latter, however, M3 is in wear while I3 had yet to erupt, suggesting that tooth wear was greater than allowed by modern age data. Alternatively I3 erupted nearer five years, but this disagrees even more with the pelvic and femur evidence below. The wear of the teeth of H1 seems unreliable (see pathology).

Fusion in the parietal and occipital sutures seems to confirm the above estimates but the pubic portions of the pelves are unfused in the midline for both horses. One proximal epiphysis is separated from the femur shaft in H2 but soil leaching and mechanical damage may have contributed to this separation. Epiphyseal fusion could have been delayed by fodder shortages and by possible castration (below). Nevertheless, the epiphyses indicate younger ages than do the teeth. H1 almost certainly was aged four to five and a half years and H2 three to four and a half years old, perhaps four and a half to five years and three and a half to four years respectively. The year difference in these estimates seems genuine and the developmental differences are difficult to explain in any other way.

Sex
Both pelvic sets appear to have a character which is intermediate between more obvious male and female pelves in a range of 14 local Iron-Age and Romano-British specimens. Although development is incomplete, the medial pubic portions had yet to fuse, I do not think that the horses were stallions since the skeletal range includes well developed male pubes at this pre-fusion stage. However the pubis is thicker than expected for mares.

The upper canines of H1 and one of H2 are lost; from memory they were less erupted than a slender pointed canine erupted 6 mm from the bone of H2. Better developed lower canines are present in H2. Baker (pers comm) says that stallions and geldings have fully formed teeth apart from occasional maleruption or delayed eruption of a canine tooth. From my description Baker and Tutt (pers comm) consider that the horses were males even though Sisson (1953, 399-40) stated that a small proportion of modern mares have upper canines or canines in upper and lower jaws. I suggest that these horses were geldings but do not rule out a possibility that they were mares.

Measurements (Table 26)
For total length (TL) the bones were placed on their posterior or posterio-ventral surfaces along the longitudinal axis of an osteometric board, apart from the calcanea which were laid on their lateral sides. Lateral length measurements (LL) are those of Kieserwalter (Boesneck and von den Driesch 1974, 334).

Some measurements were prevented by bone damage. This is unfortunate since the height estimates (HT) from the lateral lengths vary. The measurements show why they are bound to be inaccurate. In H2 the metatarsal estimate is 5% greater than the tibial which could mean a height difference of half a hand. The means of the tibial and metatarsal estimates are c 1.42 m for H1 and c 1.44m for H2, ie about 14 hands at the shoulder. The femur estimates for H1 indicates a lesser mean at 13.2 hands. A crude comparison of the broken femurs indicates that the height of H2 would also be somewhat less than given by the lower leg bones.

Pathology
The right upper M1 of H1 is very shallowly rooted, lies askew, and is worn irregularly (Pl XI). Part of it or another obstruction has impacted against the P4 which is lipped over it (Pl X1). Displacement of the M1 by a milk or supernumerary tooth may not seem to explain the shallow tooth root so its early damage from other injury is possible. The later erupting P4 was partly obstructed by this trauma. Horse bit wear on the premolars does not seem to occur.

Small opposed pits up to 4 mm in diameter occur at the interface of the third and central tarsal bones in the hock of H2. This interface and that of the proximal metatarsal and the third tarsal have slight, irregular bone depositions in both legs of H2 and the right of H1. This seems to be the beginning of osteoarthrosis. Probably H2 was affected by lameness for this is not always related to the degree of joint fusion.

Butchery
At least one transverse cut occurs on three first phalanges of H1 and 2, five occur around the fourth (H1), and single cuts occur on both proximal sesamoids of the right leg of H2. On the left lacrimal of H1, two parallel cuts occur in front of the eye socket. A parallel cut marks the malar above the facial crest. Cuts occur near the proximal ends of two rib fragments in the 7-10th rib area of H2.

The midshaft of the right femur of H2 has been chopped from about 45° above its distal end (Pl VI). Several fragments from this blow lay *in situ*. Some of the parietal fragments have angular ancient breakages, as does the third phalanx of H1.

All the knife cuts on the distal leg bones and the skull, and the absence of some body parts, eg the tail vertebrae, indicate that the skins were removed from both horses. Gutting is also likely in order to have fitted the remains into the pit. Butchery did not proceed as far as on some carcasses, for instance the marrow bones and the brains were not removed. The hyoid and therefore the tongue remained with the skull of H2 but the headmeats of H2 were probably removed with its mandibles. Absence of the forelimbs and perhaps of the tails shows that some of the other meat was stripped off. The cuts on the ribs seem to have been made as the front limbs were removed.

One may compare with these skeletons a forelimbless sheep which had been gutted and probably skinned at the Iron Age Ashville Trading Estate site. Such limb removal was interpreted as an early stage in carcass dismemberment (Wilson in Parrington 1978, 124).

Associated sheep bones
Near the centre of the bottom of the pit, a right sheep mandible lay under the backbone of H2. Left and right scapulae and pelves (female) and left forelimb bones (humerus, ulna, and radius articulating at the elbow, metacarpal, TL 123mm, and two phalanges) and five rib and two vertebral fragments were also scattered on the bottom of the pit. In the mandible M3 seems late erupting or wear on M1 and M2 is greater than usual, the latter confirmed by wear on P4. It is probably at Stage E (Payne 1973, 293). Butchery seems likely to have fractured the pelves and midshaft of the humerus.

These bones could be from one individual, a ewe older than three years (fused distal radius), possibly less than four, and of a withers height around 600 mm.

Placement of the horses
The skeleton, possibly carcass, of H2 was laid on its back across the pit and the backbone was bent into the reverse 'S'-shape to accomodate the head and pelves in the pit. Possibly both legs had been laid over the rib cage before the backbone was bent. The other skeleton was laid on its right beside the anterior thorax and over the neck of H2. The neck of H1 was bent and broken, perhaps by chopping against the femur of H2 before H1 was shifted to its excavated position (Pl VI). The dislocations in the lower spine and in the upper neck may have occurred about this time. Then the back legs were brought into the pit to lie on the skulls of both skeletons, probably after disarticulating the legs at the hips.

Discussion
We have two geldings or mares around 14 hands in height (ie of modern pony size), dying or slaughtered around four or five years of age. The carcasses were almost certainly skinned and part, but not all, of the meat was removed before the remains were put into the pit.

The burial is difficult to date (p74) but the size of the horses renders them less likely to be of the Iron Age. The season of killing could only be guessed at present.

The horses died at ages when they were least likely to be vulnerable to disease. Any such disease symptoms do not seem to have affected the taking of the hides or meat; sometimes sheep skeletons show no sign of butchery except occasional probable skinning marks suggesting they died of disease and were not eaten, eg F34 at Berinsfield (Wilson in Brown and Miles forthcoming) and Barton Court Farm (Wilson in Miles forthcoming).

Articulated bones might be more common on sites were it not for dogs and other scavengers destroying bones. Consequently the butchery of the horses could have been regarded as complete even though, in general, prehistoric and Roman butchery often seems to have proceeded beyond this stage (eg to extract the brains and possibly the marrow) or proceeded differently in disjointing the carcass (eg the sheep in F15). A surplus of exploitable edibles is implied if the horse flesh was removed for eating.

What was placed in the pit seems to have been waste; the skeletal dislocations, the separation of the rib cage of H2, and the small size of the pit give an impression of debris being crammed into it. Thus, even temporary meat storage in the ground, like that of venison, seems dubious: the inferred removal of skins would require a pit lining to avoid gritty meat, and better methods of preservation seem obvious. It is possible that the pit had ceased to function for other purposes and became a convenient disposal place for rubbish. Such disposal possibly implies habitation nearby, otherwise the ultimately odious rubbish need not have been buried rather than being left for dogs and scavengers.

So far the burial has not been viewed as necessarily unusual, but any implication of normal rural processes conflicts with the probability that these horses were slaughtered almost simultaneously. This would double any intended effort of meat preservation and would have caused some wastage, unless all the meat was immediately consumed. Fresh meat could have been available at a later date if the killing of the second horse was delayed. Any purely subsistence economy would have been set back by a double killing.

Fatal horse disease has been regarded as an improbable explanation (see above). Horse stealing and banditry are other 'abnormal' possibilites which might lead to the concealment of incriminating waste which might otherwise be left to scavengers, but the evidence for such explanations is totally lacking.1g.

The other main explanation of the burial which seems

possible is that it was associated with some ritual practice. This could have required the killing of two horses, and moreover their death occurred at an age when their economic value should have been increasing, and when mortality was normally low. In comparison to the age at death of cattle, sheep, and pigs (Wilson in Parrington 1978, 119) it appears that horses were reared for purposes other than primarily as a food supply, eg as working animals. Although carcasses do show signs of butchery, this could imply either that the meat was eaten as a part of the normal diet or that it was involved in some ritual activity. The ages of the horses compare well with those of potentially ritual horse burials of Iron Age date. Horse A at Blewburton Hill, which had bizarre associations for the excavator (Collins 1953, 30-31), was aged around five years (Collins 1953, 59) and one skull in F1100 at Farmoor has a similar age estimate. Another skull of similar age was buried in a pit at Appleford (Wilson in Hinchliffe, forthcoming). This evidence, admittedly from Iron Age contexts, perhaps stengthens the argument for ritual killing at around this age, but these examples span a wide range of archaeological contexts, none of which had unquestionable ritual connotations. No close parallels are known, and the most obvious type of double horse burial, the chariot burial, is clearly inapplicable; apart from the obvious dissimilarities the ages of the horses and the absence of bit wear would argue against it (though possibly bit wear might not be evident in young horses).

Without good parallels, in terms of both anatomical details and the type of deposit, it is impossible to reach any firm conclusion. At present it seems that the burial is a rubbish deposit and as such it gives only indirect evidence of the original treatment of the horses.

Romano-British sheep skeleton

In F15,27 bones seem to have come from one individual, a polled sheep of moderate size (prox tibia width 28mm) and about three to three and a half years as aged from the epiphyses (Silver 1969).

The lateral processes on the right hand side of three near-complete lumbar vertebrae are cut off close to their bodies and similar chopping has cut off the right hand side of the sacrum (Pls XII and XIII). Chopping appears to have begun on the third sacral vertebra and continued forward along the backbone and indicates that the carcass was divided in half. The right-hand side of the skull has been cleft off also but by a dorsal chop cutting down as far as the occipital condyles (Pl XIV), the head perhaps being detached previously since the halving of the carcass seems best done from the ventral side, and most conveniently (but not necessarily so) if it was hung by the back legs rather than by supporting it on a block. Possibly the symmetry of the division indicates a right-handed farmer-butcher avoiding cutting through the bulk of the backbone and also his left holding hand!

The left pelvis and possibly the whole leg was severed from the backbone by chopping through the lateral and ventral sacrum (from the ventral midline). This ought to have occurred after the halving of the carcass. Two anterior ribs are cut through 10 mm below the condyle and two more posterior ribs are cut through 20 and 50 mm below the condyle (medial blows). This may represent another cutting line on the carcass. Another is indicated by a chop through the midshaft of the humerus.

Several other vertebrae have been chopped up into at least seven fragments after the midline cleavage, since one fragment has a broad body and would occur between the complete vertebrae and the sacrum bearing the apparently continuous line of chopping marks. The sacrum is almost certainly chopped through between the third and fourth vertebrae, but the place of this in the butchery sequence is not clear.

Possible Romano-British sheep

In F34, 43 bones were recovered from a recently fragmented skeleton (with fused femur epiphyses), possibly a ewe, with an estimated withers height of 0.66-8 m (lengths of metatarsal, 147 mm est, calcaneum 57 mm and astragalus 30 mm, cf Teichert 1975, 68). This burial is not dated (see p 00) but the size of both sheep burials (F15 and F34) appears to be outside the range of Iron Age sheep and they are probably Roman or later in date. No obvious butchery marks were present on this second skeleton.

Further butchery notes

(Iron Age butchery marked†; Romano-British marked*)

On the skull
Horizontal chop below* and a vertical chop in front* of cattle horn cores (removal of horns; cf Wilson in Parrington 1976, 68). Horizontal cuts above cattle temporal condyle* (meat removal). Cuts on great cornu of sheep hyoid†, medial horizontal cuts on mid-ramus of pig

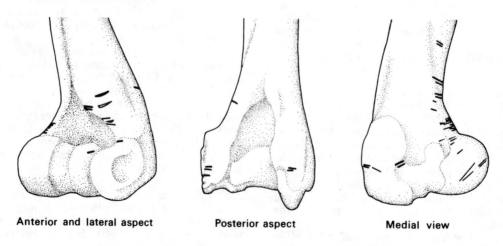

Anterior and lateral aspect   Posterior aspect   Medial view

Fig 39   Cut marks on distal humerus of cattle (approx 1/4)

mandible*, medial diagonal cuts under M3 and P4 of pig mandible† (all tongue removal) and diagonal cuts rising toward the incisors on the lateral forejaw of same pig mandible (skinning?). This mandible is split through the symphysis. Both occipital condyles chopped through vertically on cattle skull*, trimmed occipital condyle of sheep* (decapitation; cf Wilson in Parrington 1978, 119).

On the backbone
Transverse cuts on ventral body and one on dorsal anterior articulation surface of partly fused sheep atlas*, cf transverse cuts on both sides of dorsal anterior articulation surface of sheep atlas† (decapitation from the ventral side). Transverse cuts on ventral side of lateral processes of sheep lumbar vertebra† (from posterior - a common Iron Age mark suggestive of flank removal and not carcass division as in F15 skeleton*). First and second thoracic vertebrae, the second halved transversely by ventral chop (ie between second and third rib) the first vertebra trimmed on both sides from ventral direction.†

On some limb bones
Knife cuts on the distal humerus of cattle are recorded in Fig 39*†. These marks are very similar to those at Ashville (Wilson in Parrington 1978, fig 75). Transverse cuts around the two cattle phalanges* (skinning or hoof removal).

Pathology

The lower lateral shaft on an Iron Age cow metatarsal is enlarged by bone deposition probably as a result of infection or contusion rather than fracturing from a blow (F503). Other details of pathology have already been dealt with (teeth and hock joints of horse, see double horse burial; elbow fracture of dog, see skeleton description p 129).

The bird bones
by Don Bramwell

F5, stockdove femur, F43, corncrake sternum. Both bones are Roman in date, c 3rd to 4th centuries AD. The stockdove is a very edible bird favouring old parkland which usually nests in tree holes. The corncrake is a summer migrant once widespread in Britain on farmland such as cornfields and meadows. The sternum is slightly immature, possibly a bird captured during reaping operations about September.

Discussion

The Iron Age

Some idea of local animal populations will be gained from the Ashville results (Wilson in Parrington 1978, 133) which give a wider range of information than here. The results at Farmoor indicate that about equal numbers of cattle and sheep were kept, fewer sheep perhaps on the lower alluvial levels, although the proportion of sheep seems subject to underestimation. As elsewhere, pigs were less common and horses and dogs less common again.

An emphasis on keeping cows rather than castrates or bulls is indicated but unproven by Farmoor metapodials (Wilson in Parrington 1978, Table 11). If herds were small this could be related to reproductive potential as much as to dairying purposes. By contrast a greater proportion of

castrates as steers or oxen occurred in the samples from Croft Ambrey and Ashville; draught oxen almost certainly were present at Ashville (pathological metatarsal) which helps to confirm arable farming there.

Sheep appear relatively less important than cattle compared to sites on the second terrace and this may result from pastoral conditions favouring cattle rather than sheep (see liver fluke snail host, p126, and Wilson in Parrington 1978, 136). The bone data are scarcely useful for seasonal trends, though the deer antler (p129) may be evidence of winter occupation on the higher first terrace in the early Iron Age. As there is evidence of seasonal occupation of the floodplain enclosures (p125), the bone data are even less adequate to discuss the possible complexity of animal husbandry in this sort of settlement than they would be for the type of relatively self-contained economy which is often implicitly assumed in discussion of dietary remains on rural sites. At present I feel it is necessary to substantiate, by excavation of similar wetland sites, the observed ratios of sheep to cattle and cows to castrates as evidence of local differences between settlements.

Romano-British changes

Compared to the Iron Age, there appears to be either an increased proportion of cattle and horses raised or a decrease in that of sheep. This is also (at least superficially) true at Appleford (Wilson in Hinchliffe forthcoming). Disease factors or marketing demands may be involved. Changes in breeding stock are hinted at by the presence of polled sheep and a greater variation in the size of the domestic species (Wilson in Parrington 1978, 133-4). A 3rd to 4th century AD deposit of cattle horn cores from Kingston Bagpuize contained only male and castrate cores (Armitage in Parrington 1976, 68-9). Such results from this nearby hill country are difficult to interpret, although they contrast with the Iron Age evidence of the cattle sexes. The presence of oyster shells demonstrates trade and indicates a diet changing from that in the Iron Age.

PART IV: CONCLUSIONS AND DISCUSSION

Conclusions

by George Lambrick and Mark Robinson

It seems evident from the work at Farmoor that in both main phases of occupation, Iron Age and Roman, the environment was predominantly grassland and that in both periods the economy of the site was largely based on pastoral agriculture. Despite these overall similarities, however, there were important changes in settlement pattern and in detailed land use, which appear to reflect differences between the respective economies.

Early Iron Age

In the earliest period, although the site was clearly occupied, and there is evidence for iron working and weaving, information is totally lacking for the economic basis or organization of the settlement. The bone evidence is insufficient to show anything definite, though it is not inconsistent with a pastoral economy based mostly on cattle. The other environmental evidence adds nothing to this (see p111). The length of life of the settlement and its permanency are uncertain, although its position on a slightly higher part of the relatively dry gravel terrace may reflect a deliberate attempt to be clear of winter flooding (Figs 34, 2).

Middle Iron Age — gravel terrace enclosures

The changes in pottery and in type of feature between the early and middle Iron Age follow the pattern of the Mount Farm and Ashville sites (Myres 1937; Parrington 1978); although it seems reasonable that it indicates a definite change in the communities inhabiting these sites, there is no detailed explanation for this, and it can only be regarded in the traditional terms of the change from Iron Age 'A' to Iron Age 'B', or from La Tène I to La Tène II.

The Iron Age enclosures on the edge of the gravel terrace may represent a separate phase of occupation, and their position sets them apart from the floodplain settlements (Fig 34), but even the results from Area II are tantalizingly inconclusive. The biological evidence again suggests a pastoral economy, but there is no firm evidence either way of flooding or of the duration of occupation. The settlement may have been similar to the floodplain farmsteads, but the major recuttings of the ditch and the presence of the palisade and post-built 'workshop' may indicate a more permanent settlement, though this is far from clear. There is no definite evidence that the economy was not entirely different: although there was no arable agriculture in the immediate vicinity it might have been practised at some distance from the enclosures, whose position does not suggest the sort of specialization evident in the floodplain groups (see below).

Middle Iron Age—floodplain enclosures

The farmsteads on the floodplain were certainly subject to flooding, and there can be little doubt that their occupation was seasonal, especially as there was drier ground more suitable (though by no means ideal) for permanent settlement so close at hand (Figs 34, 2). The idea of seasonal occupation has been expounded by Case who suggested that the low-lying Iron Age sites on Port Meadow could not have been occupied in the winter because of flooding. He gave the following as one possible way in which the region could have been used in prehistoric times (Case 1963, 51):

> Winter folds and huts, corn-plots and burial-places on the Summertown-Radley terrace well above the floods; in summer some members of the community ranging with cattle over the meadows of the floodplain from other folds and huts, others possibly making for springs near the limestone uplands with sheep and others moving ubiquitously on the fringes of woodland with swine.

The results from the Iron Age floodplain enclosures at Farmoor are in complete agreement with the relevant part of this picture, and it cannot be argued that the river regime was different and that the sites used not to flood, since contemporary flooding has been proved at Farmoor.

The biological evidence suggests not only a grassland ecology, but also that near the farmsteads at least it was predominantly pasture. These seasonal, self-contained pastoral farm units must have been established for the primary purpose of minding the grazing herds. Indeed it is reasonable to suggest that this was virtually their only concern, and from the bone evidence (p133), that it may have been chiefly dairy farming. The few carbonized cereal grains show that the occupants of the site certainly used grain, but it was probably not produced on the site. There is no evidence for arable land in the vicinity: the floodplain itself is unsuitable, and it is unlikely that farmsteads based on mixed agriculture would be seasonal. Since a suitable locality for permanent settlement and arable agriculture existed nearby on the gravel terrace itself, the siting of the enclosures on the floodplain suggests a much more specialized economy, making the most of the rich summer grazing. The availability of good hay may also have been exploited though it would not have been necessary to estabish summer farmsteads on the floodplain for this.

Another important point about these farmsteads is that the enclosures were used for perhaps only about four or five summers, emphasizing the transitory nature of the settlement.

These conclusions have wider implications. Firstly, there must have been a permanent settlement or winter encampment elsewhere. None has yet been located, but the nearby hills provide possibilities (Fig 1). Iron Age pottery (not all of the same date) has been found on Wytham Hill and on its westward spur, Beacon Hill. The latter in particular would be a good place for a permanent settlement: it is a small, steep-sided hill divided from Wytham Hill by a saddle, and as its name implies, it has wide clear views. It also overlooks the crossing point of the Thames at Swinford, lying at the bottom of its western slopes. No trace of earthworks has been found on either hill, but they need not be expected, and anyway this could in part be due to extensive small-scale quarrying. No trace at all has been found of Iron Age settlement on the hills round Cumnor or on Boars Hill, though in the latter case the name Youlbury on the crest of the hill has been thought suggestive (Gelling 1974, 463).

Settlement on the clay hillsides cannot be ruled out, but apart from the hills the gravel terraces either side of the river seem the most likely possibility. Extensive Iron Age occupation is known round Stanton Harcourt and Cassington, and in the latter case the similarity of the pottery and the convenience of Swinford as a crossing point have already been noted (p6).

The second major implication of the nature of the floodplain settlements concerns their wider economic setting. The floodplain was clearly marginal land in terms of occupation sites, and this is reflected in the seasonal short-lived nature of the settlements; the corollary of this, however, is that the very existence of such marginal settlements with so specialized a purpose demonstrates that economically the land was very far from being marginal. The purpose of the farmsteads was to maximize the value of the floodplain grassland, and the specialization which is clearly apparent in them is evidence for a more complicated economy than one based on individual mixed farming.

The structure of the society and the exact form of its economy, however, are not clear, since various widely differing arrangements could produce the same results. It is possible, for example, that there were herdsmen who moved with their families and animals between summer and winter pastures, leading an independent existence bartering their produce or selling it at local markets to obtain the provisions they did not produce themselves. Equally a more complex society and economy might be reflected which involved considerable organization in the division of labour to exploit natural resources by this sort of specialization. Even then it is possible to envisage various ways in which such specialization might occur, from a deliberately imposed policy to the exploitation of complicated grazing rights of which we know nothing.

The layout of the floodplain enclosures, a penannular house gully with attached compounds, seems to be quite a common feature of Iron Age sites of this date in the Thames Valley, and the Farmoor examples do not stand out as exceptional. Such enclosures have been excavated on the second gravel terrace at Ashville, Abingdon, and much less extensively on the floodplain on Port Meadow, Oxford (Atkinson 1942), and many similar, but undated, examples can be detected from aerial photographs.

In general the enclosures fall into Harding's category of 'open settlements' (Harding 1974, 26-7). These unprotected farms seem fairly common in the area, for example around Stanton Harcourt (see Fig 1; Benson and Miles 1974, Maps 21, 22). The possible existence of fields marked by intermittent lengths of gully or palisades (Riley 1946, 38 and fig 9; Williams 1951, 15 and fig 7) associated with these second gravel terrace occupation sites suggests more permanent settlement on the higher ground.

Because of the very short-lived nature of the settlements, their individual abandonment cannot have been caused by the general worsening of flooding indicated by the alluvial build-up over the enclosures. If modern records are a reliable comparison, the levels of floods would have varied considerably from year to year, and it is in any case flooding unusually late in the spring or early in the autumn and occasionally occurring in mid-summer that should be considered, since it is only these which would have affected the seasonal occupation. The only possible results of the general worsening of flooding would be the siting of new enclosures (perhaps the northern group) on the slightly higher part of the floodplain, and eventually perhaps the abandonment of the

practice of summer occupation of the floodplain generally.

Exceptionally bad individual floods on the other hand might have led to the abandonment of particular enclosures: each year the house could have been repaired and reoccupied until it was no longer worth repairing. However, this is not the only possible explanation of the short-term occupation of the farmsteads since there may have been social and economic reasons again unknown to us.

Iron Age - Roman transition

There was no occupation of the site between the middle Iron Age and the Roman periods, but this does not mean that the grassland did not continue to be exploited. The landscape would have remained similar in general terms until the creation of the Roman field system, but the great increase in alluvial deposition is likely to have altered the floodplain's detailed appearance quite considerably. The Iron Age settlements were covered and probably largely levelled off, the cut-off river channel must finally have silted up (though possibly a stream may have continued to flow on the same course), and the natural undulations in the floodplain must to some extent have been levelled up. The causes of increased alluviation are uncertain, but one possibility is that it was the result of increased clearance, or changes in the cultivation process causing greater run-off and consequently increased levels of silt suspension in the river (see p126).

Roman

The overall picture of the site in the Roman period is reasonably clear (Fig 34) although there are considerable difficulties in detailed chronological interpretation (see p72). Once again the settlement was probably concerned with the exploitation of grassland, but it was achieved by different means and unlike the Iron Age other agricultural activities were probably important as well.

The basic environment seems to have been grassland and it appears that it was predominantly pasture though there was also some evidence for hay meadows. The droveway and enclosed fields, possibly with thorn hedges, are clear indications of a more careful control in the use of the land, exploiting its natural advantages in a different and probably more intensive way than the Iron Age practice. It is likely that one of the purposes of the fields was to control the use of pasture by moving the animals between them to allow rapid regeneration of the grass when they were not in use. Perhaps the floodplain was used as a hay meadow (as suggested by the presence of the scythe) and the animals could have been turned out on to it after haymaking in June to graze the aftermath. The grass would be growing well on the floodplain throughout the summer at a time when lack of water slows down growth or brings it to a halt on the gravel terrace. The animals could have been brought back to the gravel terrace at the onset of flooding in the autumn, by which time the pasture there would have regenerated. Obviously other models can also be postulated, especially if a larger-scale organization involving the clay hillsides is envisaged.

The droveway presumably provided access between the small enclosed fields, the floodplain, and other parts of the field system. It may also have served a farm or other settlement somewhere south of the site. Behind the enclosures along the droveway may have been large areas of unenclosed land, as seems apparent from aerial photographs of a similar Roman site at Long Wittenham

(Benson and Miles 1974, Map 35). Alternatively, these areas may have been divided into larger fields, the boundaries of which remained undetected. Whatever the details it is probable that the use of the grassland was sufficiently controlled to enable the land to support more animals than in the Iron Age, especially during winter.

The evidence for fruit trees, corndriers, and perhaps gardens suggests a more varied land use than for the Iron Age. Although the existence of arable in the southern part of the site is not ruled out by the biological evidence, the presence of pits and waterholes in that area makes it seem unlikely. For the possibly unenclosed land on the gravel terrace behind the small fields along the droveway there is no firm evidence, and since it is very difficult to show that arable agriculture took place in a given locality without physical evidence of ploughing (see p127), it would be a mistake to rule out the possibility merely because its presence cannot be proved. Nevertheless, although the background economy was clearly mixed agriculture (because of the evidence for cereal processing on the site in the late Roman period), the impression from the other evidence is that the contemporary environment was predominantly grassland, and it would be quite reasonable for wheat to have been brought to the settlement for processing.

The details of the settlement as opposed to the field system are less clear. In the 4th century around Area I there was a farmyard where probably the corn was threshed and ground; there was almost certainly some sort of building, perhaps of timber and thatch, though no direct evidence was found; and there also seems to have been a garden, inferred from the presence of box fruits and leaves.

The field system predated the excavated occupation site which was thus probably a subsidiary farmyard added to a more complicated agricultural settlement, perhaps a 'native settlement' or an estate attached to a villa. The actual form of the social and economic structure is again open to speculation: nothing positive is known about the form of the buildings and the surprising quality of some of the finds could be explained in several very different ways. Once again, to clarify these broader considerations it would be necessary to locate and investigate any other contemporary settlements in the vicinity.

There is nothing out of the ordinary about the layout of the Roman site or the sort of remains recovered from it. Droveways with attached small fields are common throughout the Roman period on the first gravel terrace in Oxfordshire. Parts of rather larger systems were excavated at Appleford (Hinchliffe forthcoming) and at Northfield Farm, Long Wittenham (Gray 1970, 107-9); there are many plans of similar, but undated, sites from aerial photographs (Benson and Miles 1974, Maps 34, 35, etc). Such sites also occur on the higher gravel terraces, but none is known to extend on to the floodplain. So far as the evidence goes from these other sites (and some biological investigation was undertaken at Appleford) it agrees with the results from Farmoor. It is likely that some of the more unexpected discoveries about the environment were simply the result of the scope of the investigation rather than that they were peculiar to Farmoor.

Comparison of the Iron Age and Roman settlements and economies

The transitory nature of the Iron Age floodplain enclosures contrasts with the permanence of the Roman field system and its settlement. This permanence is suggested for the settlement by its confinement to the gravel terrace above normal flood levels, and by the evidence for box hedges; in the field system it is evident from some dating evidence, the probable existence of thorn hedges, and indeed simply from the existence of such a field system.

The contrast should not be taken too far, however, especially in social and economic terms. The well in Area I suggests that the Roman farmyard was liable at least to occasional flooding and there is nothing to show that occupation was not seasonal, or that the inhabitants of the site were not living in buildings of a similar standard to those of the Iron Age. Moreover, though the Roman field system is evidence of stable land use, the absence of such evidence for the Iron Age in no way indicates that the land use and economy (rather than the settlements) then were any less stable; the very existence of farmsteads in such a marginal settlement area demonstrates its considerable economic importance and it is most unlikely that the value of such land was not also exploited before and after the farmsteads existed.

The comparison thus shows up detailed differences of land use and settlement pattern exploiting in different ways the natural advantages of the site. More basic differences may have existed, but it is not possible to demonstrate them from the evidence of this site alone; it would be necessary to locate and possibly excavate associated settlements. At present it remains possible that in both periods there was a more permanent settlement elsewhere based on mixed farming and that in each case the site at Farmoor was used for specialized pastoral agriculture. In such broad terms there could be considerable similarities between the two settlements. Indeed some continuity of land use may be suggested by the alignment of the row of Iron Age farmsteads on the floodplain and the gravel causeway across the old river channel persisting into the Roman period with the laying out of the droveway on the same line.

Comparison of the Iron Age and Roman environments

There are also basic similarities between the environments of the two periods, especially in comparison with the change which must have occurred with the clearance of primeval woodland from the site. Both landscapes owed their original appearance to the activites of man, and the similarity persisted in the maintenance by him of grassland for domestic animals. There were, however, notable differences between the two environments.

The Iron Age farmsteads on the floodplain were set in an expanse of grassland which was probably pasture, and habitats associated with the human occupation seem to have been few and minor. By contrast the permanence of the Roman settlement resulted in two new habitats being created. Firstly, there was the more enduring disturbed ground of the farmyard, probably rich in nutrients, where plants such as elder and stinging nettle flourished; secondly, buildings may have provided in their thatch and timbers a habitat for some of the synanthropic species of beetles. Other new habitats were also created: the scrub, probably in the form of hedges, resulted not only in the appearance of the woody species themselves but also provided a habitat for hedgerow plants and a whole new range of insects and birds. New habitats would also have been presented by the cultivation of part of the Roman site as a garden, and even if cereals were not extensively grown on the gravel terrace, their processing resulted in the creation of a habitat for grain beetles. There may also have been differences of detail in the background grassland environment. There still seems to have been a large grazed grassland component in the Roman period, but if, for instance, the floodplain was annually mown for hay instead of being permanent pasture the effect would have been substantial.

The impression seems to be that none of the habitats making up the Iron Age environment were lost in the Roman period, but that several new ones were created, probably resulting in a more diverse fauna and flora. These environmental changes must have created a very different landscape for man even if his presence on the site at both periods was for the same basic purpose. If these changes were widespread in the Thames Valley, the consequences could have stretched far afield, not only for man but also for the fauna and flora including, for example, migratory birds such as the redwing and fieldfare which feed on hedgerow berries (Elton 1966,180).

The medieval and later environment

A more marked change in the use of the site came in the Middle Ages when the gravel terrace was converted to unenclosed arable land. This probably reflects only the pressure on land which necessitated the extension of arable to maximize cereal production. The floodplain remained grassland throughout its archaeological existence.

Discussion

by George Lambrick and Mark Robinson

Very many points of interest emerged from the excavations and biological studies at Farmoor: they are apparent in most aspects of the work and include both details and more general points. This discussion is intended to consider these aspects further and to assess their implications.

Waterlogged cropmark sites and the value of biological information

The existence of much of the site, particularly the Iron Age enclosures on the floodplain, had not even been suspected. Where floodplains are not cultivated (as is common) there is relatively little chance of detecting sites by aerial photography and virtually none of finding them from pottery scatters. Earthworks may be visible and pasture marks may be good for aerial photography as on Port Meadow (Atkinson 1942, Pls I, II and III), but this case may be exceptional and it is reasonable to expect that other such sites remain undetected. Only more careful survey work or a continued increase in the cultivation of floodplains are likely to show any more clearly whether many such sites exist.

An important consideration is that the nature of the land which makes the detection of such sites difficult is also what makes them potentially more informative than those on the higher gravel terraces where organic biological remains are less well preserved. The biological work done at Farmoor has shown how much more it can add to the ordinary archaeological interpretations. Some of the conclusions based on the biological evidence could have been guessed, but hardly any could have been put forward with any confidence, while others would not have been thought of at all. Even a very poor cropmark site which is waterlogged can thus yield more information than a nonwaterlogged site, and the value of such sites is

also increased by their rarity, whether it is genuine or merely reflects the difficulties of finding them.

The value of 'environmental archaeology' is at last becoming generally recognized by archaeologists, but too often as an afterthought. At Farmoor the interrelation of the archaeological and biological results was most important. For example, it was only by combining the two that not very unusual Iron Age enclosure complexes could be shown to have been seasonally flooded and therefore seasonally occupied; likewise the archaeology enabled what were mostly not very unusual lists of plants and animals to be related to their true context in a landscape which showed much human influence.

The attempt to examine evidence from as many biological groups as possible proved invaluable when trying to resolve some problems: for example, it would not have been possible to suggest that hedges were present on the Roman landscape without the consideration of several different types of evidence.

Modern experimentation and observation also proved essential for the proper understanding of the biological remains recovered from the site, and one of the experiments, that of analysing hulled cereal for pollen, produced results relevant for the interpretation of all cereal pollen from archaeological sites and may substantially alter some earlier conclusions which have been drawn from its presence. In addition, because of the incompleteness of modern ecological information on some species, it was also essential to undertake field work not only on the site itself, but also in those habitats which seemed most similar to those indicated by the results.

The work at Farmoor has shown the value of thorough biological work in general, but in particular it has shown that this can be as valuable (or more so) in conjunction with extensive salvage excavation as when used for pure research work. Even though many of the features at Farmoor could not be interpreted in detail archaeologically because of what had already been lost, it was still possible to produce a fairly full picture of the background environment and economy of the settlements. In anything other than salvage conditions it would in fact have been extremely difficult (and costly) to locate and excavate in detail features covering as large an area, especially those not revealed by cropmarks.

Aspects of the Iron Age settlements

Iron Age chronology

The dating of the main Iron Age phases is not very clear because the small amount of diagnostic pottery and the small number of radiocarbon samples do not provide a very secure basis for establishing a watertight chronology.

Farmoor has, however, provided another instance of the division between the early and middle Iron Age settlements, though in adding little to what is already known about the early settlements it only helps to confirm the difference and underline the need for more work to locate associated structures and to elucidate the character of such settlements.

Pits

On a low-lying site with high water table, such as Farmoor, grain storage below ground even on the gravel terrace would probably have been unsatisfactory, and of the other possible functions of the pits, rubbish disposal seems the most likely. The objection that rubbish pits would have been a 'hygienic luxury' (Harding 1974, 79) seems spurious, and the succeeding argument that rubbish would in any case have been spread on the land may be inapplicable to pastoral settlements in the Iron Age (though cf Pliny XVII, vi, 54). Similarly Harding's argument that open pits would have been too dangerous is also weak: storage pits later used for rubbish would have presented exactly the same problem when the grain or other material was removed from them. On the whole the idea of Iron Age rubbish pits has tended to be dismissed too lightly, if it is considered at all (cf Cunliffe 1974, 170).

The form and function of small enclosures

The enclosure phase at Farmoor has provided useful information but also raises points for discussion. The form of such enclosures has to be treated with caution. The penannular gullies for round houses seem readily identifiable as a type, but the purpose of the other enclosures is by no means clear, despite useful biological evidence. Parallels do not necessarily help since even at Farmoor the exact layout of the subsidiary enclosures varied. Furthermore such annexes are clearly not confined to any single type of settlement, nor do they have any single definite purpose. Functions such as animal pens, work compounds, gardens and storage areas are all possible and have already been considered. What is clearly dangerous is to assume either that any one function can be applied to all examples, or that each was not used for several different purposes.

Enclosure gullies

At Farmoor the gullies were undoubtedly for surface drainage, and mostly would not in themselves have been animal-proof: turf walls, fences or banks would have been needed in addition. Where Iron Age houses with associated enclosures built out of stone have survived, it can be seen that the compound boundaries form true physical barriers (Cunliffe 1974, 183-4, and Fig 12:3). Evidence for proper barriers seldom survives on gravel sites, but their probable existence remains an important consideration.

The biological evidence for short-term use of the floodplain enclosures at Farmoor shows that the gullies must have been recut almost annually (or even more frequently), and even given much slower rates of silting elsewhere it is probably dangerous to assume on other sites that three or four recuts imply occupation lasting for several decades, unless there is positive dating evidence to support it (cf Erith and Holbert 1970, 17).

The penannular gullies at Farmoor were unquestionably open, certainly not all foundation slots. The difference between the two has been made quite clear at Mucking (Jones 1974, fig 5) and is illustrated by the difference at Farmoor between the floodplain gullies and the palisade (F560) in Area II or the stockade (F5) in Area I. The interpretation of flat-bottomed gullies as wall foundation trenches, as at Milton Common (Rowley 1973, 32 and fig 4) or Gun Hill (Drury and Rodwell 1973, 53-54, and fig 8 and 9, Nos 17 and 21), often seems unreliable, especially when the supposed uprights would have had the diameter of telegraph poles. A palisade type of fence or wall is an extravagant use of timber even if the

posts are small or can be made out of split logs; one made out of tree trunks is almost inconceivable for any domestic use.

Turf buildings

The possible use of turf walls may have been underestimated through lack of positive evidence. At Farmoor there is some evidence, but it is indirect and uncertain. Even so the availability and the convenience of turf as a building material are sufficient to suggest that its use should be considered as much as that of other materials wherever no definite constructional evidence survives. Only on soils where suitable turf would not have been available can it be excluded with much certainty. Positive evidence for turf buildings may be difficult to obtain, though there are some possible but very dubious examples at Danebury (Cunliffe 1976, 205).

Evidence for turf stripping is more common, especially on upland sites (Avery et al 1967, 225; Jobey 1959, 235; Wheeler 1943, 96; Hogg 1960, 17; etc) and there is some evidence for turf-cored banks (Clark and Fell 1953, 6). On gravel sites, however, it has seldom been remarked upon although some evidence has been recorded. Locally at both Langford Downs and Heath Farm there were areas of natural gravel apparently trodden into a hard surface (Williams 1946, 53; Rowley 1973, 31 and fig 3). If these interpretations are correct, the corollary must be that the turf had first been removed. How much was removed and what was done with it remains a mystery, but if the Heath Farm house had been built of turf it would provide one adequate explanation for the absence of structural evidence from which the excavator felt forced unconvincingly to conclude that the penannular gullies held the walls of the house (Rowley 1973, 32). Conclusive evidence from this region is likely to be elusive, but on Port Meadow some of the enclosures surviving as earthworks have distinct internal mounds which could be the remains of collapsed turf buildings (Atkinson 1942, fig 4).

Semicircular structures

The other main point of interest at Farmoor concerning Iron Age buildings is the probable semicircular building in Area II. Harding has suggested an alternative interpretation of the Beard Mill house as successive drying racks (Harding 1972, 37), but the Ivinghoe example (Cotton and Frere 1968, fig 3) is rather more convincing, and the Farmoor one may be the most plausible case yet found, though there are still problems of interpretation. There are two basic types of possible semicircular buildings, the kind suggested by gullies or wall slots, and those indicated by postholes. For the former it is as necessary to be sure that the slot held posts as it is with the latter to be sure that the other semicircle of posts never existed. With either sort other interpretations such as their having been windbreaks must be considered. There is an enigmatic parallel in this respect at Twywell, Northamptonshire (Jackson 1975, 54 and Fig 17). The excavator was not certain whether more postholes had existed, but if there were only the semicircle, it would be plausible as a windbreak: its arc faced south-west and on the supposed leeward side there were traces of hearths, a possible two-post drying rack and even clay and cobbled flooring as evidence of a working area. These associations are not certain and there is little evidence for the structure definitely not being part of a round house except the absence of larger postholes for a south-east entrance.

Another possible example which again might alternatively be a circular or semicircular building was found at Weakley by the same excavator (Jackson 1976, 74 and fig 3), and there were Bronze Age examples at Chalton, Hampshire (Cunliffe 1970, 3-6 and fig 3).

The Farmoor case seems more straightforward in being neither complicated by a mass of other postholes as at Beard Mill, nor thrown into question by the possible existence of more as at Twywell, while its position seems to preclude its use as a windbreak. Even so its interpretation as a building is not certain since the posts could have been free-standing (see p67). Although on the whole the evidence for semicircular buildings is growing, and this interpretation still seems most likely for Farmoor, caution must be observed in making over-confident identifications; no unassailable examples have yet been found.

Aspects of the Roman settlement

Field systems on the first gravel terrace

For the Roman period the layout of the field system and its function are the most obvious aspects of interest. Such systems are common on the first gravel terrace and from aerial photographs they seem to have various characteristics in common with the Farmoor example: they normally consist only of small rectangular enclosures lining a droveway rather than an extensive grid of fields; the droveway and fields always appear to stop short of the floodplain; the droveways frequently cross the gravel terrace to meet the edge of the floodplain at right-angles; the small fields often seem to contain pits and wells. The Farmoor example has a few extra features which may also occur in the others. The droveway turned to run along the edge of the floodplain; there appeared to be gateways between one or two of the small fields; the fields seemed to contain many waterholes ranging in type from unlined pits to proper wells; there were corndriers in two of the fields; according to the biological evidence, the field boundaries were probably hedges. The biological evidence has also shown that the Farmoor system was probably based on pastoral agriculture, which work at Appleford (Robinson in Hinchliffe forthcoming) shows may apply to other cases.

A major problem, however, remains with the interpretation of these droveway sites. The large blank areas which seem evident between these clusters of fields might represent the main arable and grassland fields on the gravels. They may have been left unenclosed, but it must be remembered that it is possible to have field boundaries which leave no physical trace. In the pre-Belgic Iron Age there are only scanty lengths of ditch, shallow gullies, possible palisades, and the odd pit alignment to divide up the land mostly on the higher gravels. Possibly whatever method of land division was used in the Iron Age survived into the Roman period in these apparently 'blank' areas and simply is not evident from air photography or salvage excavation.

The small fields attached to the droveway could have been the gardens, working yards and paddocks of the settlements themselves and it is noticeable that in most instances where areas have been excavated pits containing some domestic rubbish have been found within them suggesting human occupation nearby.

Buildings

A further point of interest is the absence of substantial buildings associated with these field systems, although there is ample evidence for human occupation. The odd posthole and pieces of daub are as much evidence as has yet been found for buildings, and so far no plan of a Roman building has been recovered, unless the penannular 'stockade' in Area I was in fact a building. Roof tiles have so far proved very scarce on first terrace sites, and there is no real evidence for the suggested villa at Penn Copse near Appleford (D Miles, pers comm; Benson and Miles 1974, fig 34). If there were substantial buildings they were built mostly of destructable materials.

By contrast, on the second gravel terrace safe above the level even of exceptional floods, a number (admittedly not large) of substantial buildings, probably villas or small farms, have been found, such as near Lechlade (Benson and Miles 1974, Map 2); at Barton Court Farm, Abingdon (Benson and Miles 1974, Map 31 and fig 19; Miles forthcoming); and at Drop Short near Drayton (Benson and Miles 1974, Map 33). This contrast needs confirming by more fieldwork, but at the moment seems valid and may reflect something of the background economy (see p136). Until there is evidence to the contrary it seems fair to assume that the Roman inhabitants of the first gravel terrace were living in houses no more substantial than those of their Iron Age counterparts.

Gardens

The evidence for gardens is an interesting additional detail which could only be discovered through the biological evidence. In some respects it adds a new dimension to established concepts of Roman rural life, for while gardens might be expected for large villas and town houses (and indeed have been shown to have existed), they have not formed part of most accepted ideas of minor rural settlements. There should be no surprise, however, for the absence of gardens in the past has only been based on lack of evidence, and it is more reasonable to expect that most people living in the country then would have had gardens as they do now.

Cereal processing

The biological work has revealed useful information about the threshing and drying of grain which is clearly widely applicable. By putting this evidence in its wider context of a grassland environment, it has wider implications for the interpretation of evidence for cereal processing. In the past the existence of corndriers and quernstones has frequently been taken as evidence for settlements practising, or even being based on, arable agriculture. This is largely because apart from animal bones these features are usually the only evidence available to illustrate the type of agriculture. The wider biological evidence has revealed a more complex picture, and it is clear that the more superficial archaeological evidence of the usual sort is fairly indirect and can easily disguise or distort the true picture.

The Iron Age and Roman settlements: general considerations

The specialized pastoral agriculture evident for the middle Iron Age at Farmoor suggests a more sophisticated, or at least a more complex, economic and social pattern than has often been assumed for the Iron Age. The standard model of mixed subsistence farming may have to be modified, whether the Farmoor floodplain settlement was part of a wider organized economy or the result of semi-nomadic occupation. The possibility that such specialization was common in any community based on mixed farming cannot be ignored, and may apply to very many sites.

The floodplain settlements reflect the importance of economic factors in determining the siting of settlements, and also thereby the economic importance of the existing environment. A similar exploitation of the floodplain by the Saxons has been suggested (Sturdy 1963, 95-8) and it is reasonable that in a relatively primitive society trans-humance between areas of high economic advantage would have been easier than the deliberate creation or improvement of the economic potentialities of areas most suited to settlement. There is no positive evidence to show that this was not common in lowland Britain, and while the distinction between 'mobile northern pastoralists' and 'more sedentary cultivators of the south' (Cunlifee 1974, 203) may remain valid as a very broad generalization, it should not be forgotten that it probably disguises an even more complex and varied economy than perhaps has been fully realized.

The evidence for increased alluvial deposition and, by inference, flooding from about the Iron Age has important implications for floodplain and first gravel terrace sites both earlier and later in date. The possibility that prior to the Iron Age the water table was lower and the floodplain did not flood so frequently is of relevance to the presence of Bronze Age ring ditches on Port Meadow and in other low-lying areas. The recent build-up of alluvium is reflected on later sites in Oxford, at the Blackfriars Priory (Robinson in Lambrick and Woods 1976, 227), and at St Aldates (Durham 1977) and clearly influenced their use.

The extent and the causes of the increased silting need much further investigation, but if a major change in cereal cultivation is shown to be the reason (see p126) the implications are even more important, since it would be reasonable to postulate a rapidly expanding population both demanding and encouraged by more productive arable agriculture. The importance of this for our under-standing of prehistoric Britain is clearly considerable.

The type of Roman field system in the area on the gravels is already well attested and the Farmoor excavations throw little light on the basic social and economic background; despite the contrast between settlements on the first gravel terrace and those on the second (see p139), there is still no way of knowing whether this site was part of a large villa estate or merely a native settlement. Although on some sites such a system of small fields or paddocks has been related to its basic farm unit, such as with the small villa at Barton Court, Abingdon (Miles forthcoming), the relationship with apparently more distant fields and possible subsidiary farmyards is still not clear and needs elucidation. In most such cases it has not been possible to distinguish definite areas of pastureland and areas of arable. The arable land supplying the Farmoor settlement, for example, need not have been on the site or even in the valley: possibly the rights of the settlement or the land of any estate to which it belonged extended onto the fertile soil of the Upper Corallian ridge around Cumnor (see Fig 1).

The distinctions between the Iron Age and Roman settlements are of interest, but it is unfortunate that evidence was not found to indicate when the change occurred between the two patterns of land use, from the small enclosures or compounds in a fairly open landscape to enclosed fields and paddocks. At Farmoor the contrast between the Iron Age floodplain settlement and the Roman gravel terrace settlement is very marked, but so far it is only one example, and the pattern may not be repeated everywhere. On Port Meadow, for example, remains of Bronze Age, Iron Age, and Roman dates all exist on the floodplain and the pasture marks indicate a much greater variety of features than was found at Farmoor (Benson and Miles 1974, Map 28). In fact, one of the interesting implications of Farmoor is the light which it throws on Port Meadow. Any unploughed prehistoric and Roman valley settlement is rare; one with surviving earthworks and considerable potential for intensive biological analysis, combined with such an extent, number, and date range of features is probably unique (Benson and Miles 1974, Map 28; Atkinson 1942).

The results from Farmoor, however, may also be significant outside the Thames Valley since similar settle-ment patterns have been found on river gravels elsewhere in Britain (cf RCHM 1975). At Tallington, Lincs, in the Welland Valley, for example, there seem to have been isolated house enclosures in the Iron Age whereas in the Roman period there were rectangular enclosures laid out against a droveway system. Pollen analysis presented a similar picture of a rather treeless landscape (Simpson 1966, 15-25).

The work at Farmoor has been valuable at several different levels: it has made a useful contribution to the study of the development of river floodplains, it has shed light on several details of interpretation, both archaeolog-ically and biologically, and it has provided important new evidence for the environment and economic background of Iron Age and Roman settlements in the area, which should be useful for Iron Age and Roman archaeology beyond the Oxford region.

APPENDICES

Appendix 1: The fluvial and alluvial deposits

by John Martin

The old river channel

On the basis of a very brief field examination and study of the layers in the section measured, drawn and described by Messrs Lambrick and Robinson (Fig 40) it is possible to confirm that this section represents a profile through a fluvial channel (see Figs 2 and 3 for course of channel and position of trench).

While it is difficult to establish the relationship between the channel infill and the gravel of the Thames floodplain terrace, it appears that downcutting of the channel, exposing the Oxford Clay in places, took place after deposition of the bulk of the gravel sheet.

Active erosion of the southern bank is suggested by the steep contact between Layers 16-18 and the gravel. These layers appear to represent a fairly coarse lag deposit.

Reduction of current strength and discharge resulted in the deposition of finer-grained sediments with an important organic component.

It is not possible to estimate on geological grounds the time-span over which channel formation and abandonment took place, but certain archaeological evidence throws light at least on the later stages of the process (see p118).

It is probable that some flow took place along the channel for a long period after it had ceased to be important, and as a topographic marshy depression it might have been under standing water for long periods during flooding of a later developed channel.

Deposition of alluvium from flood-water would have been enhanced by the entrapment of wind-blown material.

The alluvial deposits on the floodplain

Iron Age features exposed during excavation were sealed by Layer 1172, silty alluvium with abundant small limestone pebbles. It is not clear how this alluvium related to the channel sequence described above, although it is suggested that the main alluviation occurred after abandonment of this channel, and was caused by flooding of the floodplain terrace as a whole, rather than by a local event. The difference in colour between Layer 1184 (the pre-Iron Age soil) and Layer 1172 (the Iron Age and post-Iron-Age alluvial deposit) could have resulted from a general heightening of the water table in the later period; but this need not be so and it could equally well be explained by the difference in particle size.

Layer 1172:
dark grey/brown silty clay containing abundant sand/gravel grade sub- to well-rounded limestone pebbles; also shell and ? root fragments. Typical river overbank deposit.

Layer 1184:
orange/brown silty sand. The great majority of the clastic fragments are calcareous. Probably represents river overbank deposit. It is possible that some colour mottling may represent pedogenic processes.

Appendix II: A late Devensian peat deposit from the cut-off river channel

by Mark Robinson

The geology of the cut-off river channel and how it remained open until the Iron Age have already been described above. There were no peat deposits in the channel when it had attained its final form at the point of the published section across it (Fig 40) even though there

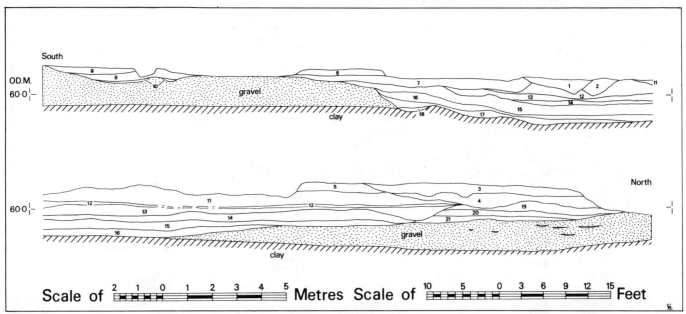

Fig 40 Section through old river channel:
1. brown loam (modern field ditch); 2. dark brown loam (modern field ditch); 3. very dark grey brown clay; 4. grey brown clay; 5. dark grey brown clayey loam; 6. dark brown peat (cf L1072); 7. hard packed gravelly peat with plant stems etc; 8. medium grey brown gravelly clay (droveway ditch); 9. very dark blue-grey gravelly silt (droveway ditch); 10. orange gravel; 11. orange brown clay with traces of iron panning; 12. purplish grey clay; 13. blue clay, some iron panning, becomes more orange northwards; 14. streaky grey bedded fine to medium sand; 15. very silty bluish grey clay with many decayed roots; 16. streaky grey to yellow bedded silt/sand/gravel; 17. orange gravel; 18. yellow gravel; 19. orange sand; 20. light grey-blue sand; 21. streaky grey bedded sand and silt.

were some small lenses of peat laid down in the gravel as it was eroding its way southwards. However, about 350 metres to the west were three layers of peat sandwiched between layers of sand at the bottom of it. A sample of the lowest layer of peat was taken and examined in the hope that it would provide information on the pre-clearance vegetation of the site. It proved, however, to be of much older date than had been expected, so only limited details will be given.

The plant remains included fruits of *Betula nana* L. (dwarf birch) and calyces of *Armeria maritima* (Mill) Willd. (thrift). *B. nana* is a circumpolar arctic-alpine plant and apart from a relict population in Upper Teesdale it is restricted in the British Isles to northern Scotland. *A. maritima* is at present restricted to coastal sites and mountains in Britain but during the Devensian period was common inland (Godwin 1975, 257-8, 306-7).

The insect remains included the weevil *Otiorrhynchus nodosus* (Muel.) which only occurs in England north of the Humber, and two non-British species, *Helophorus glacialis* Villa. and *H. obscurellus* Popp. They are both arctic-alpine species, *H. glacialis* occurring in the far north of Europe at the edge of melting snow patches and on mountains elsewhere in Europe (Angus 1973, 317). *H. obscurellus* occurs in arctic Russia, the Lena river in Siberia, and the Altai and Tien Shan mountains (Coope 1970, 105).

There were no warm elements in the flora and fauna which is clearly glacial. The first gravel terrace through which the channel cut is believed to have been deposited during the last glaciation. *H. glacialis* is typical of late Devensian deposits of pollen zone III but is rare in earlier deposits (Angus, pers comm) and several specimens were present in the minute sample which was examined.

Peat from a channel deposit elsewhere on the Farmoor reservoir site was examined for Coleoptera by Angus and Coope at Birmingham and their fauna was very similar to this one. Its radiocarbon date was 10,600 ± 250 bp (Coope 1976, 20-22). It seems possible that both deposits were from the same channel.

Appendix III: The faunal remains from the gravel

(identified by Philip Powell)

A number of bones of prehistoric animals were recovered from fluvial deposits in the gravel, but in no case was the exact stratigraphical position recorded. The date of the old river channel indicated by the biological remains (see Appendix II) would, however, be later than that of the animals given below, which are more likely to have been deposited during the accumulation of the gravel sheet. A few bones, the only ancient remains of interest that were recovered from the first stage of the reservoir, were also identified.

Stage 1 Mammoth teeth (2)
      Right humerus of ox or bison
      Left radius of rhinoceros
Stage 2 Mammoth teeth (possibly a pair) with remains of mandible (2)
      Almost complete mandible of mammoth with teeth
      Horn of bison
      Top of skull and horns of bison
      Proximal end of scapula (including glenoid cavity) of bison
      Right rib (*c* 4th) of rhinoceros
      Part of pelvis of rhinoceros

Appendix IV: Modern flood refuse from Port Meadow, Oxford

by Mark Robinson

As there are only published lists of Coleoptera from modern river flood deposits, it was thought worthwhile to examine flood refuse for plant and molluscan remains so that an idea could be gained of the range of species likely to be carried by it.

A 1 oz sample was collected on 5 December 1976 which had been stranded close to a probable Iron Age house enclosure at Grid ref SP492082. The main flooding had occurred a few days earlier. It consisted of bits of grass, duckweed (*Lemna* sp.), a few decaying remains of aquatic plants, a couple of cypress (Cupressaceae) clippings, insects, a piece of bark, seeds, and molluscan shells. There

Table 27

SEEDS		
RANUNCULACEAE		
Ranunculus cf. *repens* L.	buttercup	4
R. sceleratus L.	crowfoot	49
CRUCIFERAE		
gen. et sp. indet.		1
CHENOPODIACEAE		
Atriplex sp.	orache	10
ROSACEAE		
Filipendula ulmaria L.	meadowsweet	3
Potentilla anserina L.	silverweed	29
P. cf. *reptans* L.		1
Crataegus monogyna Jacq.	hawthorn	5
LYTHRACEAE		
Lythria salicaria L.	purple loosestrife	1
ONAGRACEAE		
Epilobium sp.	willow-herb	6
UMBELLIFERAE		
Berula erecta (Huds.) Coville	water parsnip	2
Oenanthe sp.	water dropwort	3
Angelica sylvestris L.	wild angelica	4
POLYGONACEAE		
Polygonum aviculare agg.	knotgrass	4
P. convolvulus L.	black bindweed	1
Rumex hydrolapathum Huds.	dock	4
Rumex sp.	dock	76
URTICACEAE		
Urtica dioica L.	stinging nettle	11
BETULACEAE		
Betula sp.	birch	35
Alnus glutinosa (L) Gaertn.	alder	94
LABIATEAE		
Mentha sp.	mint	8
Lycopus europaeus L.	gipsywort	172
Scutellaria galericulata L.	skullcap	24
RUBIACEAE		
Galium sp.	bedstraw	1
CAPRIFOLIACEAE		
Sambucus nigra L.	elder	2
COMPOSITAE		
Bellis perennis L.	daisy	1
Tripleurospermum maritimum (L.) Koch.	scentless mayweed	1
Carduus or *Cirsium* sp.	thistle	4
ALISMATACEAE		
Alisma sp.	water plantain	5
JUNCACEAE		
Juncus sp.	rush	80*
SPARGANIACEAE		
Sparganium erectum L.	bur-reed	5
CYPERACEAE		
Eleocharis sp.		1
Carex sp.	sedge	3
GRAMINEAE		
gen. et sp. indet.	grass	2
varia		51
Total		**597**

Table 28

MOLLUSCA	
GASTROPODA	
PROSOBRANCHIA	
HYDROBIIDAE	
Potamopyrgus jenkinsi (Sm.)	2
EUTHYNEURA	
ELLOBIIDAE	
Carychium sp.	1
LYMNAEIDAE	
Lymnaea truncatula (Müll.)	1
PLANORBIDAE	
Planorbis planorbis (L.)	1
P. carinatus Müll.	1
Anisus leucostoma (Milt.)	11
A. vortex (L.)	1
VALLONIIDAE	
Valonia pulchella (Müll.)	1
V. pulchella (Müll.) or *excentrica* Sterki	3
ENDODONTIDAE	
Discus rotundatus (Müll.)	1
Total	**23**

was virtually no mineral content. It was washed through a series of sieves to an aperture size of 0.2 mm and the residue sorted, a tenth subsample being examined for the finest sieve. The seeds and molluscs present are listed in Tables 27 and 28. It was not thought worthwhile to list the insects because there was not a very wide range of species and much better flood refuse lists have already been published. The cypress clippings resembled *Chamaecyparis lawsoniana* (Lawson's cyrpress).

From its contents the flood refuse is quite obviously a modern deposit. *C. lawsoniana* is a recent introduction from North America (Clapham *et al* 1962, 53) and *Potamopyrgus jenkinsi* was first recorded from freshwater in this country in 1893 (Boycott 1936, 140) but it is not without relevance to the interpretation of Iron Age samples from the floodplain at Farmoor.

This modern sample shows how the river is capable of making a deposit almost entirely of organic remains, many of which would have been preserved in a waterlogged archaeological feature. *P. jenkinsi* is an operculate snail of running water which would not come on land of its own volition (Boycott 1936, 146). Its presence helps to explain how *Bithynia tentaculata* occurred in some of the Iron Age samples. The results also serve as a warning. The mollusca are mostly aquatic species from the river yet the seeds are almost entirely from terrestrial or riverbank species. The origin of the seeds from the river is something that probably would not have been suspected had this been an ancient assemblage and the aquatic molluscs absent.

No doubt some of the seeds had been collected from Port Meadow as the floodwaters swept across it but the majority seem to have come from elsewhere. The most common species, *Lycopus europaeus* (gipsywort), is rare on the banks of Port Meadow but is very common on the steeper banks of the other side of the river. The large number of fruits of *Betula* sp. and *Alnus glutinosa* (alder) might suggest the presence of these trees yet Port Meadow is probably the largest treeless expanse in the area. The nearest alder trees up river are over half a mile (1 km) upstream on the other bank and the closest birch trees are perhaps in the gardens at Oxford or Wolvercote, even further away. The garden of The Trout at Godstow, three-quarters of a mile (1.3 km) up river, is the nearest source of cypress.

Although it is possible to argue that many of the seeds in the Iron Age samples from the floodplain at Farmoor were derived from plants growing locally (see p110), these results combined with the evidence for flooding show that a significant proportion of the seeds (and for that matter insects) could have been derived from sources a considerable distance up river, which would not be at all obvious.

Appendix V: Pollen enclosed by the bracts of hulled barley
by Mark Robinson

The presence of 60% cereal type pollen in a sample of peat from Pit 17 which was almost entirely composed of threshing debris suggested the posssibility that the pollen was introduced with the cereal remains (see p110). It was decided to analyse some modern hulled cereal grains to see if pollen was present. Full results of this experiment and its implications have been published elsewhere (Robinson and Hubbard 1977, 197-9) but a brief synopsis will be given here.

Twelve grains of hand-threshed six-row hulled barley (*Hordeum vulgare* L. emend. Lam.) were subjected to a modified form of a standard quantitative palynological sample process (Dimbleby 1961, 11). The results indicated that each hulled cereal grain had brought with it on average about 1,500 cereal pollen grains and 100 or so foreign pollen grains (175 pollen grains counted). Therefore it is quite possible that the cereal pollen in Layer 17/4 had been transported to it in the cereal remains.

Appendix VI: Radiocarbon dating
by R L Otlet

Four samples from Farmoor sent to the Carbon 14 Laboratory at Harwell were dated in the period 5 February 1976 to 29 September 1977. Sample details and results are given in Table 29. Evidence for supposing specific time differences between the associated phase.

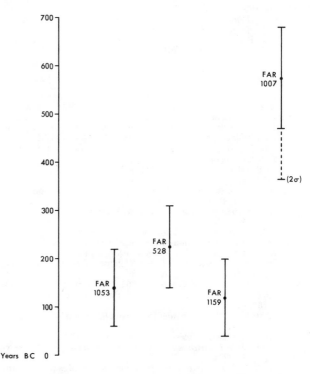

Fig 41 Calibrated radiocarbon dates with one standard deviation.

143

Table 29: Radiocarbon determinations

Feature sampled	Harwell reference	Sample type	δ13C (%/10)	benzene sample weight (g)	counting data and reference	Result (conventional radiocarbon years bc)*	Calibration correction (years to add)**	Calibrated result (calendar years BC)***
F1053	HAR-1910	Red deer antler	-21.3	6.3	1/8/77 (TCB 1)	120 ± 70	19 ± 30	140 ± 80
F528	HAR-1925	Bone	-23.1	2.0	29/9/77 (TCB 2)	180 ± 80	45 ± 30	225 ± 85
F1159	HAR-1926	Bone	-22.6	6.0	1/8/77 (TCB 1)	110 ± 70	10 ± 30	120 ± 80
F1007	HAR-1374	Charcoal	-26.0	2.6	5/2/76 (TCB 1)	460 ± 100	115 ± 30	575 ± 105

*Calculated in the usual way assuming a half-life of 5568y for 14C and the agreed modern level set by 0.95 x the NBS Oxalic standard. ** Corrections shown are the derived mean from five published calibration tables for this time period (R L Otlet, pers comm). Errors shown express the spread (1 σ, standard deviation) on the results from the different tables. ***Error terms given with the final results, all rounded to nearest ± 5y, incorporate the 1 σ shown for the calibration correction.

listed as Phase I and Phase II in the table, is inconclusive. The overlap at even the ±1σ range for the three bone samples (fig 41) makes these results statistically inseparable and the possibility of them all representing a single mean period of *c* 160 BC should not be ruled out. Statistically the charcoal date (calibrated) of 575 ± 105 BC is separated from this group but the species difference must also be considered. No identification was made of the charcoal type and the possibility should be considered that it may have come from the centre of a large tree or in some other way have been of a specific age earlier than the associated phase of occupation. Furthermore the sample was smaller than the ideal size required for dating and in consequence has a larger than normal error term. It is therefore acceptable that the date obtained from its measurement is earlier than the contemporary bone samples, but it is recommended that the interpretation should not be extended beyond this general conclusion.

Appendix VII: Bibliography

Abbreviations
ANHS Ashmolean Natural History Society of Oxfordshire Report
EMM Entomologists' Monthly Magazine
RES Royal Entomological Society of London Handbooks for the Identification of British Insects

Allen, A A, 1947 *Brachinus crepitans* (Col., Carabidae) away from chalk, *EMM*, **83**, 80
———1958 Notes on the larval feeding habits etc, of *Lebia* spp. (Col., Caribidae) especially *chlorocephala* Hoff., *ibid*, **94**, 95
———1965 *Stegobium paniceum* L. (Col. Anobiidae) becoming established in the open (?), *ibid*, **101**, 115
Angus, R B, 1964 *Dryops ernesti* Des. G. (Col. Dryopidae) associated with rotting vegetables, *ibid*, **101**, 117
———1970 A revision of the Genus Helophorus F. (Coleoptera: Hydrophilidae) Subgenera Orphelophorus D'orchymont, Gephelophorus Sharp and Meghelophorous Kurwent, *Acta Zoologica Fennica*, **129**, 1-62
———1973 Pleistocene Helophorus (Coleoptera, Hydrophilidae) from Borislav and Starunia in the Western Ukraine, with a reinterpretation of M Łomnickis' species, description of a new Siberian species, and comparison with British Weichselian faunas, *Phil Trans Roy Soc London*, **265**, 299-326
Angus, NS, Brown, G T, & Cleere, H, 1962 The iron nails from the Roman legionary fortress at Inchtuthil, Perthshire, *J Iron and Steel Instit*, **200**, 956-68
Anstee, J, 1967 Scythe blades from Roman Britain, *The Countryman*, **69**, 365-9
Applebaum, S, 1966 Peasant economy and types of agriculture, in *Rural Settlement in Roman Britain* (ed C Thomas), CBA Research Report **7**, 99-107
Atkinson, R J, 1942 Archaeological sites on Port Meadow, Oxford, *Oxoniensia*, **7**, 24-35
Aubrook, E W, 1939 Coleoptera, in *The Victoria County History of Oxfordshire*, **1**, 107-35

Avery, M, Sutton, J E G, & Banks, J W, 1967 Rainsborough, Northamptonshire, England: excavations 1961-1965, *Proc Prehist Soc*, **33**, 207-306
Baker, H, 1937 Alluvial meadows; a comparative study of grazed and mown meadows, *J Ecol*, **25**, 408-20
Balfour-Brown, F, 1940-58 *British Water Beetles*, 1-3, Royal Society
Benham, B R, 1975 Swarming of *Helophorus brevipalpis* Bedel (Col., Hydrophilidae) in north Devon, *EMM*, **111**, 127-8
Benson, D, & Miles, D, 1974 *The Upper Thames Valley: an archaeological survey of the river gravels*, Oxfordshire Archaeol Unit Survey 2
Beresford, MW, & Hurst, JG, 1962 Introduction to a first list of deserted medieval village sites in Berkshire, *Berkshire Archaeol J* **60**, 92-7
Berkshire Archaeol J, 1960 Archaeological notes from Reading Museum, *Berkshire Archaeol J*, **58**, 55-9
Biological flora of the British Isles, 1945-71 *J Ecol* **33, 36, 40, 45, 49-52, 56, 57, 59**
Boessneck, J, & Driesch, A von den, 1974 Kritische Anmerkingen zur Widerristhöhenberechnung aus Längenmassen vor und fruhgeschichtlicher Tierknochen, *Säugetierkdle Mitt*, **22** (4), 325-48
Boulton, B, & Collingwood, C A, 1975 *Hymenoptera: Formicidae* RES **6**, pt 3(c)
Bowen, H J M, 1968 *Flora of Berkshire*
Boycott, A E, 1934 The habitats of land mollusca in Britain, *J Ecol*, **22**, 1-38
———1936 The habitats of fresh-water mollusca in Britain, *J Animal Ecol*, **5**, 116-86
Bradford, J S P, 1942 An early Iron Age site at Blewburton Hill, Berks, *Berkshire Archaeol J*, **50**, 4-29
Bradford, J S P, & Goodchild, R G, 1939 Excavations at Frilford, Berks, 1937-38, *Oxoniensia*, **4**, 1-70
Brendell, M J D, 1975 *Coleoptera Tenebrionidae* RES **5**, pt 10
Britannia 1973 Roman Britain in 1972 (eds DR Wilson *et al*), *Britannia*, **4**, 271-337
Britannia 1974 Roman Britain in 1973, (eds DR Wilson *et al*), *Britannia*, **5**, 396-480
Britton, E B, 1956 *Coleoptera: Scarabaeoidea* RES **5**, pt 11
Brodribb, A C C, Hands, A R, & Walker, D R, 1968 *Excavations at Shakenoak* **1**, privately printed
———1971 *Ibid*, **3**
———1973 *Ibid*, **4**
Brown, G T, 1965 The iron the Romans made, *Steel Times*, Feb 5, 1965
———forthcoming Metallurgical report on one of the Roman scythe blades from Great Chesterford
Brown, P D C, 1973 A Roman pewter hoard from Appleford, Berks, *Oxoniensia*, **38**, 184-206
Brown, P D C, & Miles, D, forthcoming *Excavations at Wally Corner, Berinsfield, Oxon; Romano-British enclosures and a Saxon cemetery*, Oxfordshire Archaeol Unit Report **4**, Oxfordshire Archaeol Unit and CBA
Bulleid, A, 1968 *The Lake-Villages of Somerset*, 6 edn
Bushe-Fox, J P, 1947 *Excavations of the Roman Fort at Richborough, Kent*, **4**
Case, H, 1963 Notes on finds and ring-ditches in the Oxford region, *Oxoniensia*, **28**, 19-52
Case, H, Bayne N, Steel, S, Avery, G, & Sutermeister, H, 1964 Excavations at City Farm, Hanborough, *ibid*, **29/30**, 1-98
Chaplin, R E, 1971 *The study of animal bones from archaeological sites*
Church, A H, 1922 *Introduction to the plant life of the Oxford district. I. General review*, Oxford Botanical Memoirs **13**
———1925a *Introduction to the plant life of the Oxford district. II. The annual succession (Jan-June)*, ibid **14**
———1925b *Introduction to the plant life of the Oxford district. III. The annual succession (July-December)*, ibid **15**
Clapham, A R, Tutin, T G, & Warburg, E F, 1962 *Flora of the British Isles*

Clark, J J, 1966   The distribution of *Lucanus cervus* (L.) (Col., Lucanidae), *EMM*, **102**, 199-204

Clark, J G D, & Fell, C I, 1953   An early Iron Age site at Micklemoor Hill, West Harling, Norfolk, *Proc Prehist Soc*, **19**, 1-40

Clarke, G R, 1954   Soils, in *The Oxford Region* (eds A F Martin and R W Steel), 50-5

Collins, A E P, 1947   Excavations on Blewburton Hill, 1947, *Berkshire Archaeol J*, **50**, 4-29

——— 1953   Excavations on Blewburton Hill, 1948 and 1949, *ibid*, **53**, 21-64

Conway, E, & Stephens, R, 1957   Sporeling establishment in *Pteridium aquilinum:* effects of mineral nutrients, *J Ecol*, **45**, 389-99

Cook, C B K, 1962   *Sparganium erectum* L., *ibid*, **50** 247-55

Coope, G R, 1970   Interpretation of quaternary insect fossils, *Annual Review of Entomology*, **15**, 97-120

——— 1976   Assemblages of fossil Coleoptera from terraces of the Upper Thames near Oxford, in *Quaternary Research Association Field Guide to the Oxford Region* (ed D Roe), 20-2

Coope, G R, & Angus, R B, 1975   An ecological study of a temperate interlude in the middle of the last glaciation based on fossil Coleoptera from Isleworth, Middlesex, *J Animal Ecol*, **44**, 365-91

Cotton, M A, & Frere, S S, 1968   Ivinghoe Beacon excavations 1963-5, *Rec Buckinghamshire*, **18**, pt 3, 187-234

Crowson, R A, 1956   *Coleoptera: introduction and key to Families*, RES 4, pt 1

Cunliffe, B W, 1970   A Bronze Age settlement at Chalton, Hants *Antiq J*, **50**, 1-13

——— 1971   *Excavations at Fishbourne 1961-1969, Vol II, The finds*

——— 1974   *Iron Age Communities in Britain*

——— 1976   Danebury, Hampshire: second interim report on the excavations 1971-5, *Antiq J*. **56**, 198-216

Curle, J, 1911   *A Roman frontier post and its people*

Dimbleby, G W, 1961   Soil pollen analysis, *J Soil Sci*, **12**, 1-11

Dimbleby, G W, & Evans, J G, 1974   Pollen and land-snail analysis of calcareous soils, *J Archaeol Sci*, **1**, 117-33

Donisthorpe, H St J K, 1927   *British ants*

——— 1939   *A preliminary list of the Coleoptera of Windsor Forest*

Druce, G C, 1886   *The flora of Oxfordshire*

——— 1897   *The flora of Berkshire*

Drummond, D C, 1956   Food plants of *Chrysolina violacea* (Müll) *C. Haemopters* (L.), *C. crassicornis* (Hell.) and *C. polita* (L.) (Col., Chrysomelidae), *EMM* **92**, 368

Drury, P J, 1973   Little Waltham, *Curr Archaeol*, **36**, 10-13

Drury, P J, & Rodwell, W, 1973   Excavations at Gun Hill, West Tilbury, Essex, *Trans Essex Archaeol Soc*, **5**, 48-112

Durham, B G, 1977   Archaeological investigations in St Aldates, Oxford, *Oxoniensia*, **42**

Easton, A M, 1947   The Coleoptera of flood-refuse. A comparison of samples from Surrey and Oxfordshire, *EMM*, **83**, 113-5

——— 1966   The Coleoptera of a dead fox (*Vulpes vulpes* (L.)) including two species new to Britain, *ibid*, **102**, 205-10

Elton, C S, 1966   *The pattern of animal communities*

Emery, F, 1974   *The Oxfordshire landscape*

Erith, F H, & Holbert, P R, 1970   The Iron Age 'A' farmstead at Vince's Farm, Ardleigh, Essex, *Colchester Archaeol Group Quart Bull*, **13**, No 1, 1-26

Evans, J G, 1972   *Land snails in archaeology*

Finberg, H P R, (ed) 1972   *The agrarian history of England and Wales* **1**, pt 2.

Forsyth, A A, 1954   *British poisonous plants*, Ministry of Agriculture and Fisheries Bulletin No 161

Fowler, P J, 1960   Excavations at Madmarston Camp, Swalcliffe 1957-58, *Oxoniensia*, **35**, 3-48

Fowler, W, 1887-1913   *The Coleoptera of the British Isles*, **1-6**

——— 1891   *The Coleoptera of the British Isles*, **5**

Frere, S S, 1962   Excavations at Dorchester-on-Thames 1962, *Archaeol J*, **119**, 114-49

——— 1972   *Verulamium Excavations*, **1**

Freude, H, Harde, K W, & Lohse, G A, 1964-1974   *Die Käfer Miteleuropas*, **3, 4, 8, 9**, Krefeld

——— 1969   *ibid*, **8**

Gelling, M, 1973, 1974, 1976   *The place names of Berkshire* Pts 1-3, Eng Place-Name Soc, **49-51**

Gilbert, E W, 1954   The growth of the city of Oxford, in *The Oxford Region* (eds A F Martin and R W Steel), 165-73

Gillam, J P, 1970   *Types of Roman coarse pottery vessels in Northern Britain*, 2 edn

Gillham, M E, 1974   Seed dispersal by birds, in *The flora of a changing Britain* (ed F Perring)

Girling, M, 1976   Fossil Coleoptera from the Somerset Levels: The Abbots' Way, *Somerset Levels Pap* **2**, 28-33

Godwin, H, 1975   *The history of the British flora*

Gray, M, 1970   Excavations at Northfield Farm, Long Wittenham, Berks, *Oxonensia* **35**, 107-9

Green, H J M, 1975   Roman Godmanchester, in *Small towns of Roman Britain* (eds W Rodwell and R T Rowley), Brit Archaeol Rep **15**, 184-210

Green, J, 1952   The food of *Typhaea stercorea* (L.) (Col. Mycetophagidae), *EMM*, **88**, 62

Green, M, 1976   *Religions of Roman Britain*, Brit Archaeol Rep **24**

Greenslade, P J M, 1965   On the ecology of some British carabid beetles with special reference to life histories, *Trans Soc Brit Entomology*, **16**, 149-74

Greenslade, P J M, & Southwood, T R E, 1962   The relationship of flight and habitat in some Carabidae (Coleoptera), *The Entomologist*, **95**, 86-8

Greenstead, L W, 1939   Colonisation of new areas by water-beetles, *EMM*, **75**, 174-5

Greig-Smith, P, 1948   *Urtica* L., *J Ecol*, **36**, 339-55

Guilbert, G, 1973   Moel y Gaer, Rhose More: a progress report, *Curr Archaeol*, **37**, 38-44

Halstead, D G H, 1963   *Coleoptera: Histeroidea*, RES **4**, pt 10

Hamlin, A, 1966   Early Iron Age sites at Stanton Harcourt, *Oxoniensia*, **31**, 1-27

Harcourt, R A, 1974   The dog in prehistoric and early historic Britain, *J Archaeol Sci*, **1**, 151-75

Harding, D W, 1967   Blewburton, *Curr Archaeol*, **4**, 83-5

——— 1972   *The Iron Age in the Upper Thames Basin*

——— 1974   *The Iron Age in Lowland Britain*

Harris, E, & Young, C J, 1974   The Overdale kiln site at Boars Hill near Oxford, *Oxoniensia*, **39**, 12-25

Head, J F, & Piggott, C M, 1944   An Iron Age site at Bledlow, Bucks, *Rec Buckinghamshire*, **14**, 189-209

Helbaek, H, 1953   Early crops in southern Britain, *Proc Prehist Soc*, **18**, 194-233

Hewett, D G, 1964   *Menyanthes trifoliata* L., *J Ecol*, **52**, 723-35

Hickin, N E, 1963   *The woodworm problem*

——— 1975   *The insect factor in wood decay*

Higgs, E S, & White, J P, 1963   Autumn killing, *Antiquity*, **37**, 282-9

Hill, P V, Carson, R A G, & Kent, J P C, 1960   *Late Roman bronze coinage*

Hinchliffe, J, forthcoming   Report on excavations at Appleford, Oxfordshire (for *Oxoniensia*)

Hinton, H E, 1940-1941   The Ptinidae of economic importance, *Bull Entomological Res*, **31**, 331-81

——— 1945   *A monograph of the beetles associated with stored products*, 1

Hoffman, A, 1950   *Faune Fr. 52, Coléoptères Curculionides*, Paris

——— 1954   *ibid*, **59**

——— 1958   *ibid*, **62**

Hogg, A H A, 1960   Garn Boduan and Tre'r Ceiri, excavations at two Caernarvonshire hill forts, *Archaeol J*, **117**, 1-39

Horion, A D, 1941-1967   *Faunistik der Mitteleuropaischen Käfer* Uberlingen-Bodensee, Frankfurt am Main Krefeld, Munchen

——— 1958   *ibid*, **6**

——— 1961   *ibid*, **8**

——— 1965   *ibid*, **10**

Jackson, D A, 1975   An Iron Age site at Twywell, Northamptonshire, *Northamptonshire Archaeol*, **10**, 31-93

——— 1976   Two Iron Age sites north of Kettering, Northamptonshire, *ibid*, **11**, 71-88

Jarvis, M G, 1973   *Soils of the Wantage and Abingdon district*, Memoirs of the Soil Survey of Great Britain: England and Wales

Jennings, F B, 1915   On the food plants of various British weevils, *EMM*, **51**, 167-9

Jobey, G, 1959   Excavations at the native settlement at Huckhoe, Northumberland 1955-7, *Archaeol Aeliana* Ser 5, **37**, 217-78

Johnstone, A, 1962   *Chenopodium album* as a food in Blackfoot Indian prehistory, *Ecology*, **43**, 129-30

Jones, M U, 1974   Excavations at Mucking, Essex, a second Interim Report, *Antiq J* **54** pt 2, 183-99

Joy, N H, 1932   *A practical handbook of British beetles*

JRS 1969   Roman Britain in 1968 (eds D Wilson & R P Wright), *J Roman Stud*, **59**, 198-246

Kay, Q O N, 1971   *Anthemis cotula* L., *J Ecol*, **59**, 623-36

Kelly, M, & Osborne, P J, 1964   Two faunas and floras from the alluvium at Shustoke, Warwickshire, *Proc Linnean Soc London*, **176**, 37-65

Kenward, H K, 1974   Methods for palaeoentomology on site and in the laboratory, *Sci & Archaeol*, **13**, 16-24

——— 1975a   The biological and archaeological implications of the beetle *Aglenus brunneus* (Gyllenhall) in ancient faunas, *J Archaeol Sci*, **2**, 63-9

——— 1975b   Pitfalls in the environmental interpretation of insect death assemblages, *ibid*, **2**, 85-94

——— 1976a   Reconstructing ancient ecological conditions from insect remains; some problems and an experimental approach, *Ecological Entomology*, **1**, 7-17

——— 1976b   Further archaeological records of *Aglenus brunneus* (Gyll.) in Britain and Ireland including confirmation of its presence in the Roman period, *J Archaeol Sci*, **3**, 275-7

Kerney, M P, 1966   Snails and man in Britain, *J Conchology London*, **26**, 3-14

——— 1976a   A list of fresh and brackish-water Mollusca of the British Isles, *ibid*, **29**, 26-8

——— 1976b   *Atlas of the non-marine Mollusca of the British Isles*, Cambridge: Institute of Terrestrial Ecology

Kloet, G S, & Hincks, W D, 1945   *A check list of British insects*

Lambrick, G M, 1969   Some old roads of North Berkshire, *Oxoniensia*, **34**, 78-92

Lambrick, G H, & Woods, H, 1976   Excavations on the second site of the Dominican Priory, Oxford, *ibid*, **41**, 168-231

Landin, B, 1961   Ecological studies on dung-beetles, *Opuscula Entomologica* Supplementum **19**, 1-227

Leeds, E T, 1931   An Iron Age site near Radley, Berks, *Antiq J*, **11**, 399-404

Limbrey, S & Evans, J G 1978   *The effect of man on the landscape: the lowland zone*, CBA Res Rep **21**

Lindroth, C H, 1974   *Coleoptera: Caribidae*, RES **4**, pt 2

Luff, M L, 1965   A list of Coleoptera occurring in grass tussocks, *EMM*, **101**, 240-5

Mabey, R, 1975   *Food for free*

Mattingly, H, Sydenham, E A, *et al*, 1923-1967   *The Roman Imperial coinage*

McCormick, A G, 1975   Grendon, Northamptonshire, *CBA Group 9 Newsletter*, **5**, 12-14

McNaughton, I H, & Harper, J L, 1964   Papaver L, *J Ecol*, **52**, 767-93

Miles, D, 1977   Abingdon/Radley, Barton Court Farm, *CBA Group 9 Newsletter*, **6**, 11-13

——forthcoming   *Archaeology at Barton Court Farm, Abingdon, Oxfordshire*, Oxfordshire Archaeol Unit Report **3**, Oxfordshire Archaeol Unit and CBA

Moore, B P, 1955   Notes on carrion Coleoptera in the Oxford district, *EMM*, **91**, 292-5

——1957   The British Carabidae (Coleoptera) Part II. The county distribution of species, *Entomologists' Gazette*, **8**, 171-2

Morris, M G, 1965a   *Otiorrhynchus ligustici* (L.) (Col., Curculionidae) in Shropshire with notes on its recorded distribution in Britain, *EMM*, **101**, 169-71

——1965b   Weevils (Col., Curculionoidea) collected from some important ecological sites in Shropshire, *ibid*, **101**, 125-31

Munro, J W, 1926   *British bark beetles*, Forestry Commission Bulletin **8**

Myres, J N L, 1930   A prehistoric settlement on Hinksey Hill, near Oxford, *J Brit Archaeol Ass*, **36**, 360-90

——1937   A prehistoric and Roman site on Mount Farm, Dorchester, *Oxoniensia*, **2**, 12-40

Nash, D R, 1971   Some Coleoptera found inhabiting the same beech stump in the New Forest, Hants, *EMM*, **107**, 191

Neville, R C, 1856   Description of a remarkable deposit of Roman antiquities of iron, discovered at Great Chesterford, Essex, in 1854, *Archaeol J*, **13**, 1-13

New, J K, 1961   Spergula arvensis L, *J Ecol*, **49**, 205-15

Osborne, P J, 1955   *Lucanus cervus* (L.) (Col., Lucanidae) in North Berkshire breeding at Brightwell, *EMM*, **91**, 262

——1969   An insect fauna of late Bronze Age date from Wilsford, Wiltshire, *J Animal Ecol*, **38**, 555-66

——1971   An insect fauna from the Roman site at Alcester, Warwickshire, *Britannia*, **2**, 156-65

Osmaston, F C, 1959   *The revised working plan for the Wytham Woods or the Woods of Hazel for the period 1959/60 to 1968/69*, Imperial Forestry Institute, Oxford

Oswald, F, 1936-1937   *Index of figure-types on Terra Sigillata*

Oxoniensia 1946   Notes and News, *Oxoniensia*, **11-12**, 162-3

Parrington, M, 1976   Roman finds and animal bones from Kingston Hill Farm, Kingston Bagpuize, Oxon, *Oxoniensia*, **41**, 65-9

——1978   The excavation of an Iron Age settlement, Bronze Age ring-ditches and Roman features at Ashville Trading Estate, Abingdon, (Oxfordshire) 1974-76, Oxfordshire Archaeol Unit Report **1**, Oxfordshire Archaeol Unit and CBA

Paulian, R, 1959   *Faune Fr. 63 Coléoptères Scarabeides*, Paris

Payne, S, 1973   Kill-off patterns in sheep and goats: the mandibles from Asvan Kale, *J Anatolian Stud*, **11**, 281-303

Peacock, D P S, 1962   A Roman site at Tallington, Lincolnshire, *Lincolnshire Architectural and Archaeol Soc Report Pap* **9**, pt 2, 110-24

Peake, H J E, Coghlan, H H, Marshall, C F B, & Birbeck, J M, 1935   Excavations on the Berkshire Downs, *Trans Newbury and District Fld Club*, **7**, No 1, 90-108

Pearson, R G, 1959-1960   The ecology of the Coleoptera from some late-Quaternary deposits, *Proc Linnean Soc London*, **172**, 65-70

Percival, J, 1974   *The wheat plant*

Perring, F K, & Walters, S M, (eds) 1962   *Atlas of the British flora*

Piggot, C D, & Walters, S M, 1953   Is the box tree a native of England? in *The changing flora of Britain* (ed J E Lousley)

Piggott, S, 1962   Heads and hoofs, *Antiquity*, **36**, 110-18

Pliny   *Natural History* (trans H Rackham 1961)

RCHM 1975   *An inventory of the historical monuments in the county of Northampton 1*, HMSO

Raw, F, 1951-1952   The ecology of the garden chafer, *Phyllopertha horticola* (L.) with preliminary observations on control measures, *Bull Entomological Res*, **42**, 605-46

Rees, W J, 1965   The aerial dispersal of mollusca, *Proc Malacological Soc London*, **36**, 269-82

Reid, C, 1889-1894   On the natural history of isolated ponds, *Trans Norfolk and Norwich Nat Soc*, **5**, 272-86

——1903   in W H St J Hope, Excavations on the site of the Roman city of Silchester, Hants, in 1902, *Archaeologia*, **58**, pt 2, 413-28

——1909   in W H St J Hope, Excavations on the site of the Roman City of Silchester, Hants, in 1908, *Archaeologia*, **61**, pt 2, 473-86

Reitter, E, 1908-1916   *Fauna Germanica Die Käfer des Deutschen Reiches*, **1-5**

——1916   *ibid*, **5**

Renfrew, J M, Monk, M, & Murphy, M, 1976   *First aid for seeds*, Rescue Publication **6**,

Richardson, K M, & Young, A, 1951   An Iron Age 'A' site on the Chilterns, *Antiq J*, **31**, 132-48

Richmond, I A, 1968   *Hod Hill* **2**

Riley, D N, 1946   A late Bronze Age and Iron Age site on Standlake Downs, Oxon, *Oxoniensia*, **11-12**, 27-43

Robinson, M, 1975   The environment of the Roman defences at Alchester and its implications, in The defences of Roman Alchester, (C J Young), *Oxoniensia*, **40**, 161-70

Robinson, M, & Hubbard, R N L B, 1977   The transport of pollen in the bracts of hulled cereals, *J Archaeol Sci*, **4**, 197-9

Ross, A, 1967   *Pagan Celtic Britain*

Rowley, R T, 1973   An Iron Age settlement at Heath Farm, Milton Common, *Oxoniensia*, **38**, 23-40

Royal Entomological Society 1953-1975   *Handbooks for the identification of British insects* **4**, pts 2, 3, 8a, 10; **5**, pts 2c, 7, 9-12, 15

Salisbury, E, 1961   *Weeds and aliens*

Sanders, J E, 1973   *Late Roman shell-gritted ware*, unpublished BA thesis, Institute of Archaeology, London

Sandford, K S, 1924   The river gravels of the Oxford district, *Quart J Geol Soc*, **80**, 113-79

Shotton, F W, 1978   Archaeological inferences from the study of alluvium in the lower Severn-Avon Valleys, in *The effect of man on the landscape: the Lowland Zone* (eds S Limbrey & J G Evans), CBA Research Report **21**

Silver, I A, 1969   The ageing of domestic animals, in *Science in Archaeology* (eds D Brothwell & E S Higgs)

Simmonds, N W, 1945-1946   Polygonum L., *J Ecol*, **33**, 117-43

Simpson, W G, 1966   Romano-British settlement on the Welland gravels in *Rural Settlement in Roman Britain* (ed C Thomas), CBA Research Report **7**, 15-25

Sisson, S, 1953   *Anatomy of the domestic animals*

Southwood, T R E, & Leston, D, 1959   *Land and water bugs of the British Isles*

Sparks, B W, 1959-1960   The ecological interpretation of quaternary non-marine mollusca, *Proc Linnean Soc London*, **172**, 71-80

Stainton, H T, (ed) 1857   Coleoptera, *Entomologists Weekly Intelligencer*, **2**, 117-9

Sturdy, D, 1963   Traces of Saxon nomadic life near Oxford, *Oxoniensia*, **28**, 95-8

Tansley, A G, 1965   *The British Isles and their vegetation*

Taylor, E, 1941   Records of *Lucanus cervus* L. (Col.) in the Oxford University Museum, *EMM*, **77**, 199-200

Teichert, M, 1975   Osteometrische Untersuchungen zur Berechnung der Widerrsthöhe bei Schafen, in *Archaeological Studies* (A T Clason), Amsterdam

Thomas, K D, 1977   Preliminary study of molluscs from the lynchet section, Bishopstone, *Sussex Archaeol Collect*, **115**, 258-66

Tottenham, C E, 1954   *Coleoptera: Staphylinidae section (a), Piestinae to Euaesthetinae*, RES **4**, pt 8a

Varro   *De Re Rustica*

Walden, H W, 1976   A nomenclatural list of the land mollusca of the British Isles, *J Conchology London*, **29**, 21-5

Walker, J J, 1906   Preliminary list of Coleoptera observed in the neighbourhood of Oxford from 1819 to 1907, *ANHS*, **49-100**

——1907   *ibid*, first supplement, *ANHS*, **49-60**

——1909   *ibid*, second supplement, *ANHS*, **59-70**

——1911   *ibid*, third supplement, *ANHS*, **45-54**

——1914   *ibid*, fourth supplement, *ANHS*, **62-68**

——1920   *ibid*, fifth supplement, *ANHS*, **23-31**

——1929   *ibid*, sixth supplement, *ANHS*, **32-36**

——1908   Coleoptera in flood-refuse at Oxford, *EMM*, **44**, 135-6

——1916   Granary beetles at Cothill, Berks, *ibid*, **52**, 16-17

——1939   Coleoptera in a limited area at Oxford, *ibid*, **75**, 9-11

——1926   *The natural history of the Oxford district*

Walters, S M, 1949   Eleocharis L., *J Ecol*, **37**, 192-206

Webster, G, 1967   Excavations at the Romano-British villa in Barnsley Park, Cirencester, 1961-1966, *Trans Bristol and Gloucester Archaeol Soc*, **86**, 74-87

Wheeler, R E M, 1943   *Maiden Castle*

White, K D, 1967   *Agricultural implements of the Roman world*

——1970   *Roman farming*

Whitley, M, 1943   Excavations at Chalbury Camp, Dorset, *Antiq J*, **23**, 98-121

Willcox, G H, 1977   Exotic plants from Roman waterlogged sites in London, *J Archaeol Sci*, **4**, 269-82

Williams, A, 1946   Excavations at Langford Downs, Oxon (near Lechlade) in 1943, *Oxoniensia*, **11-12**, 44-63

——1951   Excavations at Beard Mill, Stanton Harcourt, Oxon, 1944, *Oxoniensia*, **16**, 5-22

Williams, J H, & Mynard, D C, 1974   *Two Iron Age sites at Moulton*

Park, Northampton Development Corporation Archaeol Monograph **1**
Williams, J T, 1969   Chenopodium rubrum L., *J Ecol*, **57**, 831-41
Woods, P J, 1972   *Brixworth excavations*, **1**, pt 1
Young, C J, 1977   *The Roman pottery industry of the Oxford region*, Brit Archaeol Rep **43**
Zeist, W van, 1974   Palaeobotanical studies of settlement sites on the coastal area of the Netherlands, *Palaeohistoria*, **6**, 223-371

Appendix VIII: Index of features and layers

The page numbers given below refer to the beginning of the subsections in which the main descriptions and interpretations of features occur. The references are first, the archaeological description of the feature; second, its place in the archaeological interpretation; and third, where applicable, its biological interpretation (a specific reference and a more general one).

The finds are covered by the various specialist reports and may be found by reference to the Table of Contents; the description of the biological material is covered by a subsection entitled 'The samples' (p78) and by the tables of results (Tables 4 - 26).

Area I

Context No	Pages			
2,3	17	75		
4	16	73		
5,7	13	73		
8,9	17	75		
10	16	74		
11,12	17	76		
15,16	13	73		
17	16	75	110,118ff	
18	13	68		
24	16	74		
27,28	17	75		
29	16	74		
30,31	17	75		
32,33	16	74		
34	16	74		
35	16	74		
37	16	74		
43	17	75	110,118ff	
44	16	74		
47	17	75		
51,53,55,56	13	73		
57	17	75		
58-60	13	73		
63	16	74		
67	17	75		
69	13	73		
74	13	73		
75-77	16	74		
83	13	73		
84,86,87	16	74		

Area II

501	9			
503	9	66		
504	9			
505,507	9	66		
510	13	76		
514,515,517	9	66		
527	12	66		
528-531	9	66	109,111ff	
532	13	76		
535,534,547	9	66		
550	13	76		
553,554	12	66		
557	13			
560,567,569	12	66		
574,575	13	76		
576,578	12	66		
579,581,583,584	12	66		
587	12	66		
590, 592	12	66	109,111ff	
600,609	12	66		

Area III

Context No	Pages			
1002	34	75	104,120	
1003	34	76		
1004,1005	25	72-74		
1007-1010,1012	21	69	109,111ff	
1013,1015	19	65	111	
1016	34			
1018	19	74		
1019	19	68		
1020	32	73		
1021,1022	19	68		
1023-1025	25	72		
1027	34	76		
1029-1031	29	73		
1032,1033	32	73		
1034	34	76		
1037,1039,1040	19	65		
1041	32	73		
1042,1044	19	65		
1045	19	68		
1046	32	75	110,118ff	
1047,1048	32	74,73		
1049	29	72		
1050	32	73		
1051,1052	32	73		
1053-1057	19	65		
1058	34	75		
1059	19	65		
1060,1061	33	73	110,118ff	
1062-1064	19	65		
1065	25	72		
1066	29	73		
1067,1068	19	65		
1070	32	73		
1071-1077,1079	27	72-74	110,118ff	
1083	32			
1084	34			
1085,1086	25			
1087	32			
1088-1093	34			
1096	32	74		
1097-1099	29	72		
1100-1105	23	70	109,111ff	
1106	23	70		
1107	23	70		
1108-1115	23	70		
1116	23	70		
1117	23	70		
1118-1121	23	70		
1122	23	70		
1123,1124	34			
1126	32	74		
1128-1132	34	73		
1134	19			
1135	29	72		
1136	34	76		
1139	34			
1140	34	76		
1143-1151,1153,1155	34			
1156,1157,1159,1164	25	70	109,111ff	
1169	32	74	110,118ff	
1170-1172,1174,1179,1182-1184	25	70	109,111ff	
1185	34			

Pl I ` Air photograph of cropmarks looking west towards Lower Whitley Farm

Pl II   Area II. The annexe containing the semicircular structure from the north

148

Pl IV Area II. The palisade slot (F560) at its junction with F528

Pl III Area II. Rubble in the top of F528 and F529

Pl V Area I: The penannular gully (F5) from the north

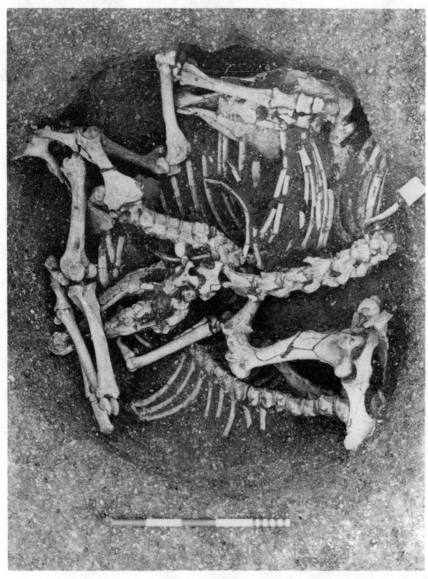

Pl VI Area I: The double horse burial (F37)

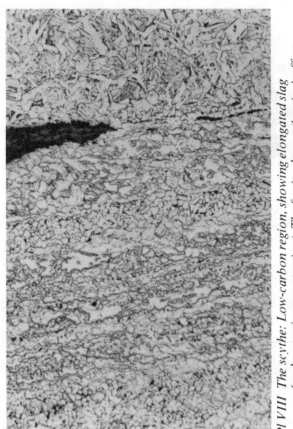

Pl VIII The scythe: Low-carbon region, showing elongated slag (and corrosion penetration). The ferrite shows a 'coring' effect (Etched; x60)

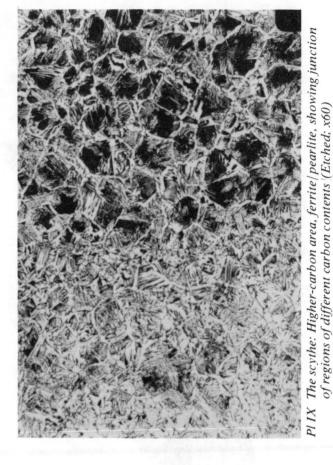

Pl IX The scythe: Higher-carbon area, ferrite/pearlite, showing junction of regions of different carbon contents (Etched; x60)

Pl VII Area III: Enclosure group 3: Section through enclosure ditch (F1179), gravel path (F1170) and post Iron Age alluvium (L1164)

151

*Pl X   Animal pathology:
Fracture on right distal humerus of
Iron Age dog from F1054*

Pl XI   Pathological maxillae teeth of horse I in F37

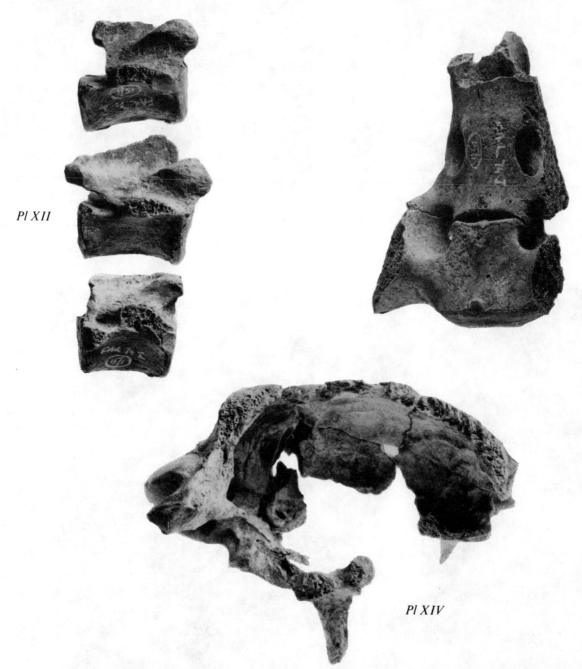

Pl XII

Pl XIII

Pl XIV

Pls XII - XIV Butchery: Evidence for the halving of a sheep carcass from F57